Online Store Made Easy

**Accelerated Internet Selling
Release 4.6B**

SAP Labs, Inc.

Palo Alto, California

Copyright

Disclaimer

Trademarks

R/3 Simplification Group
SAP Labs, Inc.
3475 Deer Creek Road
Palo Alto, CA 94304

www.saplabs.com/simple
simplify-r3@sap.com

Printed in the United States of America.
ISBN 1-893570-88-6

CONTENTS

Chapter 2: Creating the Product Catalog   43

Chapter 3: Prices in the Product Catalog

77

Chapter 6: Multiple Employees Making Purchases for One Corporation 165

Chapter 7: Credit Card Authorizations and Settlement 195

Chapter 8: Sales Order Status 207

Chapter 9: Available to Promise   **223**

Chapter 10: Customer Account Information   **241**

Chapter 15: The ITS User: Logging on to R/3   349

Chapter 16: Internet Users: Passwords for Customers   367

Part 4: Technical Infrastructure **379**

Chapter 19: Interfacing with Third-Party Components   411

Chapter 20: Outsourcing   425

Chapter 21: System Administration for Accelerated Internet Selling
431

Chapter 22: Performance
439

Part 5: Starting an E-commerce Project 449

Chapter 23: Project Planning   451

Chapter 24: Monitoring Project Costs   455

Chapter 25: The Value-Add Side   465

Chapter 27: Internet Selling Information   489

Part 6: Appendixes 493

Appendix A: SAPNet Frontend Notes   495

Appendix B: Technical SAP Enhancement: ATP in the Product Catalog   499

Appendix C: The Shopping Basket   511

Appendix D: Technical SAP Enhancement: Purchase Order Entry   523

Index

Acknowledgements

I wish to express appreciation to the following individuals who provided the time, material, expertise, and resources that helped make the Online Store Made Easy guidebook possible:

Customers and partners: Ted Dean (independent); Andrew Goldberg (TeaLeaf Technology); Joe Megibow (TeaLeaf Technology); Nicole Papa (TeaLeaf Technology); Manfred Schaeffer (Card America); Christian Zbinden (TeaLeaf Technology)

SAP AG: Ruediger Bolz, Clemens Daeschle, Joachim Hartmann

SAP America: Lorra Moyer, Thomas Ryan

SAP Labs: Jenny Alkema, Cathrin Barsch, Martin Botschek, Ingo Helbig, Marie-Laurence Poujois, Miklos Szorenyi, Udo Waibel

Contributing authors: Jaideep Adhvaryu, Nihad Al-Ftayeh, Ramon Balagot, Mark Finnern, Hanumachastry Rupakula, "Willie" Beng Giap Lim, Oliver Mainka, Gary Nakayama, Julie Sasaki, Irmgard Stenger

Documentation and production: Scott Bulloch, Kurt Wolf

Birgit Starmanns

SAP Labs, Inc., October 2000

Introduction

E-commerce and SAP's Online Store

As more and more consumers are using the Internet not only for communication and entertainment, but for conducting business, many companies are expanding their sales channels. It is not only the "dot.coms" that have no physical stores and offer products on the web. Established companies are also entering the arena, either as Internet pioneers in their industries, or in response to pressure from their competitors who already have running e-commerce sites.

A company web site in the past only contained corporate data, contact details, press releases, and similar types of information. To attract their customers by providing an additional sales channel, as well as other services, many of these companies now include e-commerce components. This trend does not mean that the traditional corporate information is no longer available on these sites. A web shop does not become the site; it is integrated as an important component of the site.

Other customer services in addition to shopping, such as checking the status of an order or maintaining customer data, are usually also integrated as part of the overall web site.

SAP has two solutions for companies who are selling on the Internet, the Online Store, and the Internet Sales scenarios within CRM (Customer Relationship Management). The Online Store is ideal for customers who already have an R/3 System up and running, and who would like to have an e-commerce component of their site running as quickly as possible. The Internet Sales product is integrated into the CRM solution, which is designed to strategically manage all aspects of customer interaction through all sales channels, including the Internet, personal meetings with a sales representative using mobile sales, and through the customer interaction center.

The Online Store solution has been available since Release 3.1. The Online Store is directly integrated into a backend R/3 System. It is an Internet-enabled transaction, called Internet Application Component (IAC), that contains the business logic for selling products on the Internet, and uses the master data and configuration settings available within the R/3 System. The IACs enable customers to integrate their Internet and Intranet processes with their core R/3 functionality. The Internet Transaction Server (ITS) technology facilitates this integration.

Accelerated Internet Selling: Online Store 4.6B

The Simplification Group has developed an implementation package, called the Accelerated Internet Selling solution, which allows customers to quickly implement sell-side Internet solutions. This product focuses on Release 4.6B of the Online Store. This package enables customers to be up and running with the Online Store and related functionality quickly, and provides additional functionality over what is offered in the standard R/3 Online Store IAC.

The *Online Store Made Easy* guidebook accompanies the Online Store preconfiguration available from our web site *www.saplabs.com/ecom*. The guidebook is a "cookbook" that describes all the steps necessary to implement the Online Store. The guide also indicates which steps are already included in the preconfiguration. The guide can therefore be used to manually configure the R/3 System, or as a supplement to the preconfiguration transports.

The preconfiguration includes:

- Installation Guide
- R/3 transports for configuration
- ITS templates with a new look and feel
- Add-on functionality

- Sample project plans

- Cost budget and collection template

The *Online Store Made Easy* guidebook is divided into six sections, each of which covers a particular aspect of an implementation.

Configuration in R/3. The configuration section covers the configuration within R/3 that allows the business functionality of the Online Store and the related sell-side functionality to be implemented. The configuration also addresses how the sales functions carried out through the Online Store integrate with order fulfillment processing in the R/3 System.

Reporting. The reporting section addresses how to analyze the business generated by the Online Store. Sales volume reporting is available within R/3, while reporting that captures user behavior is available outside of R/3.

Overview of the ITS. The ITS overview covers the basic concepts of how an Internet Application Component (IAC) functions, and how the Online Store on a web site communicates with the R/3 System.

Technical Infrastructure. The technical infrastructure covers the landscape, performance considerations, application hosting options, and security issues that need to be addressed in an implementation of the sell-side processes. This section focuses on the systems and parameters that need to be addressed on the SAP side.

Starting an E-commerce Project. The project management section addresses issues outside of the R/3 System. Chapters cover project planning, monitoring, and cost tracking, as well as a high-level overview of how an e-commerce project can be evaluated. The integration into the mySAP.com Marketplace is also discussed.

Appendixes. The first appendix collects all the technical information about the SAPNet R/3 Frontend Notes. The rest cover add-ons provided by the Accelerated Internet Selling solution, explained in detail. These appendixes supplement the functional information in the configuration section.

Scenarios in the Online Store AIS Solution

The AIS Solution includes four preconfigured scenarios for the Online Store. These scenarios encompass the decisions that need to be made as part of the implementation, such as the path that customers should take through the Online Store, the types of customers to be created, how customers should be allowed to pay for their purchases, and other issues.

Selling to Customers. A customer may browse the product catalog without logging on. The customer can then place items into a shopping basket. When the customer is ready to order, an existing customer can log in with an ID (e-mail address) and password. A new customer can register with an e-mail address. The only available payment option is by credit card.

Selling to Consumers. The business process is the same as in the selling to customers. However, a different type of customer master record, called a consumer, is created. Consumer master records contain personal data, but do not contain sales area data, to reduce the size of the master records in R/3.

Selling to Business Partners. A customer must already have a logon (e-mail) and password before being able to access the product catalog. The customer can then browse the catalog and place items into shopping baskets. Different portions of the catalog can be hidden or displayed, based on the customer who logged into the site. In addition, a customer hierarchy allows employees to make purchases, while still being linked to their corporation for discounts, payment, and delivery. Payment options include credit cards and invoices.

Selling to One-Time Customers. A customer may browse the catalog and place orders. However, customers are only rarely expected to return to the site. For this reason, a customer master is not created, and customer information is stored within the order. Customers must re-enter their information each time when visiting the site. Both credit cards and invoices are allowed in this preconfiguration.

Preconfigured Functionality

As part of an integrated web site, the e-commerce portion is not the only piece that must be considered. In addition to normal corporate data, other services may be offered to customers on a site. Some of these services are handled by IACs. For this reason, several IACs were preconfigured as part of the AIS solution.

Online Store. The Online Store is the central IAC that is most often implemented, and is the central topic of this guide. The Online Store allows customers to browse a product catalog, register as a customer, and place an order through the Internet.

Product Catalog. Some companies may not allow customers to place orders on the Internet. Instead, they may wish to present their products, attach multimedia files and specifications to the catalog, and then provide a number for customers to call to place an order.

Sales Order Status. After an order has been placed, customers like to track the status of their delivery. This IAC allows customers to do this on the web site. A link to freight carriers' tracking sites is also provided once the delivery has been processed.

Available to Promise. Certain business partners may be allowed to obtain availability information about the products in the catalog. Customers may enter a quantity and date, and then obtain the date on which the product(s) will be available.

Customer Account Information. Certain business partners may wish to see their customer master and banking information. In addition, accounts receivable information is available, such as open and cleared invoices.

Add-On Functionality

As part of the Accelerated Internet Selling solution, the Simplification Group has developed add-on functionality that the customers we surveyed found to be the most important to their implementations. This add-on functionality is transported into the R/3 System as user exit programs and function modules. No standard programs are transported. The *Installation Guide* explains, step by step, how the standard code of the Online Store must be modified to call the user exits and function modules. The add-ons that are delivered include:

Reporting. Three new SIS (Sales Information System) structures have been created to facilitate reporting within R/3. In addition, together with TeaLeaf Technology ™, we facilitate the implementation of business intelligence by capturing the customer experience on the web site.

Availability in the Product Catalog. This add-on provides the capability to display the availability of products in the product catalog. Either real-time ATP (available to promise) information, or only the unreserved stock level, can be displayed. A "traffic light" indicator or the actual quantity in stock can be displayed on the site.

Shopping Basket Enhancements. The ability to save and retrieve a shopping basket has been added. In addition, the ability to display the contents of the shopping basket while browsing is also included, which displays a running total of the items in the basket.

Choosing a Shipping Method. On most sites, a customer is allowed to choose the type of shipping desired, such as overnight or standard ground shipping. In addition, the choice of the shipping method drives the selection of different freight pricing in the R/3 System, using incoterms.

Entering Purchase Order Data. In a business partner scenario, many customers require the ability to enter a purchase order number and date to allow simpler reconciliation with their own systems.

Single Sign-On. Since several different IACs have been preconfigured, and the customer is required to log on to each IAC when it is first called, we have provided a single sign-on capability. This functionality is accomplished using a memory cookie that is deleted as soon as the browser session is closed.

"My Profile" Service. The "My Profile" service is a new IAC, written by the Simplification Group. It can be called directly, or from any of the existing services. It provides a central location to allow the customer to register, change address information, save default credit card information, save a default shipping type, change a password, and obtain a password reminder. To accompany this functionality, the default credit card and default shipping type is accessed from the Online Store.

Data Loads and Utilities. Data load programs are provided for the product catalog, and for Internet users (which store customer passwords). In addition, utilities are provided to change the text of buttons displayed on the site, and to FTP data.

About this Guide

Who Should Read this Book?

This guidebook is written for consultants and customers who have at least one to two years of experience with the R/3 System, preferably in the Sales and Distribution (SD) module.

The guidebook focuses on the Online Store and related sell-side applications. These Internet Application Components (IACs) provide a tight integration into the backend R/3 System processes in SD. The book is not intended to include a thorough discussion of basic SD functionality within R/3.

We assume the reader has experience in the SD configuration required for master data, sales order processing, deliveries, and billing, has used the condition technique in configuring pricing and output determination, and has a good base knowledge of Materials Management (MM) and the material master as it relates to SD.

How Is It Organized?

The guidebook describes the business issues surrounding an implementation of the Online Store and related sell-side applications, and explains the technical configuration settings and considerations that must be part of the implementation.

In the configuration section, each chapter begins with an overview of the topic to assist customers and consultants with little experience. This first portion can also be used during presales and by non-R/3 literate readers. Names of customers are used to illustrate the shopping experiences. However, these names only serve as an example and are not associated with particular roles. The bulk of these chapters assist consultants or customers who have one to two years experience with the R/3 System, but do not have knowledge of the IACs and ITS. This second portion of these chapters covers the master data and configuration required to implement the Online Store and related sell-side applications. An indication is made whether each step has already been preconfigured if the transports are used in conjunction with the guidebook

A similar format is followed for the discussion of most of the ITS overview section and most of the appendices. Some programming knowledge is required to follow the detail program specifications of the add-ons.

The technical infrastructure section illustrates the system landscape, and addresses the parameters that must be set within the SAP products. Since there are many vendors of related products, such as networking and security, individual solutions are not addressed. The project management section discusses the project and cost templates that are delivered with the AIS solution, and how they may be of help during an implementation of the Online Store and related sell-side functionality.

Conventions

In the table below you find some of the text conventions used throughout this guide.

Text Convention	Description
Sans-serif italic	Screen names or on-screen objects (buttons, fields, screen text, etc.)
`Monospace`	User input (text the user types verbatim)
Name1 → *Name2*	Menu selection *Name1* is the menu name, and *Name2* is the item on the menu
`Sans-serif`	Command syntax

Sample R/3 Release 4.6 Screen

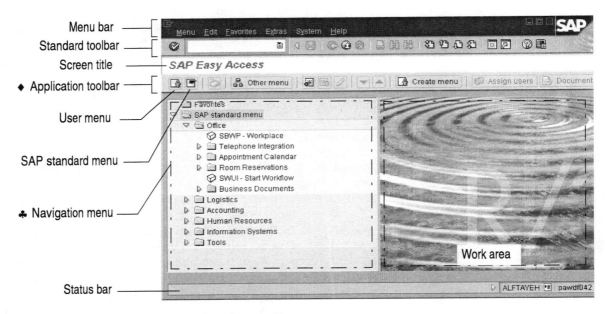

Menu bar

Standard toolbar

Screen title

◆ Application toolbar

User menu

SAP standard menu

♣ Navigation menu

Status bar

◆ **Application toolbar:**

The screenshots shown in this guide are based on full user authorization (SAP_ALL). Depending on your authorizations, some of the buttons on your application toolbar may not be available.

♣ **Navigation menu:**

Depending on your authorizations, your navigation menu may look different from screenshots in this guide that are based on SAP_ALL. The *User menu* and *SAP standard menu* buttons provide different views of the navigation menu.

To learn how to build user menus, see *Authorizations Made Easy* guidebook Release 4.6A/B.

Special Icons

Throughout this guide special icons indicate important messages. Below are brief explanations of each icon:

Exercise caution when performing this task or step. An explanation of why you should be careful is included.

Caution

This information helps you understand the topic in greater technical detail. It is not necessary to know this information to perform the task.

TechTalk

Tips & Tricks

These messages provide helpful hints and more detailed information to make your work faster and easier.

Note

This information clarifies a statement in the accompanying text.

PART ONE

Configuration in R/3

Section Overview

The sell-side Internet functions available with R/3 are referred to as Internet Application Components (IACs). These IACs are actually transactions coded within the R/3 System. However, these IAC transactions are intended for use only on the Internet. These sell-side IACs use existing Sales and Distribution (SD) configuration and processes.

The IACs illustrate an "inside-out" approach, meaning that the logic of the sales processes carried out on the Internet is inside R/3. All information resides within R/3, including the configuration of the sales processes and the master data. This approach has the following advantages:

- **The sales processes used on the Internet can use the same configuration used for existing SD processes within R/3**

  Using the same configuration allows for a more homogeneous process, in which order fulfillment takes place the same way, regardless of how the order was taken. Configuration is also faster, since much of the existing configuration of internal sales processes can be used.

- **No duplication of data**

  Not only is the configuration and process logic maintained in one system, the master data also resides in one place. This structure allows for faster updates to the available products and prices. Business users are also not required to know HTML in order to update a product catalog. The margin for error and inconsistencies is also reduced, since it is no longer necessary to update several data sources.

- **Faster order fulfillment**

  Since the data is updated in R/3 immediately, there is no need for complex, periodic interfaces to replicate the order into R/3 delivery and billing.

- **Real-time information.**

  Since the product availability information resides within R/3, a customer can immediately know whether a product is available. In checking on the order status, no additional updates on the web server are required to allow the customer to see the status of an order.

An example of how the product catalog is represented on the Internet is shown below.

The structure of the product catalog is maintained within R/3. If the text of a portion of the catalog should be changed, the change is immediately reflected on the Internet.

The following sell-side IACs are discussed:

- **Product catalog** – This IAC allows customers to browse the product catalog, determine the prices, and display images, sound files, and spec sheets.

- **Online Store** – A shopping basket is added to the product catalog that allows customers to place orders on the Internet. Different order, customer, and product profiles are used to determine the business processes available on the Internet.

- **Sales order status** – A customer can check on the status of any order placed, regardless of whether it was placed through the Internet. A link to freight carrier web sites allows real-time tracking of deliveries.

- **Available-to-promise** – A customer, usually a business partner, enters the quantity of items required. The ATP configuration within R/3 informs them when these items are available.

- **Customer account information** – A customer can verify that all account information is correct and display all financial transactions.

Creating the Online Store with the Catalog

Overview

The Online Store uses the product catalog and adds shopping capability. Customers can browse the product catalog, add items to their basket, and place an order. A registration process for new customers can be included as part of the Online Store. Once the order has been placed, an e-mail confirmation goes out to the customer who placed the order.

As an Internet Application Component (IAC), the Online Store is tightly integrated with the backend R/3 System, meaning that all transactions occur in real-time. The product catalog is maintained in R/3. If a new product is added to the catalog, the customers can immediately see the change. No duplication of data occurs between systems, reducing the chance for errors, such as a customer ordering a product that is no longer available.

When a customer registers in the Online Store, a customer master record is instantly created in the R/3 System. When an order is placed, the order is immediately available for fulfillment processing. Delays in the delivery processing of the order are avoided, allowing you to get your products to the customer more quickly. Once the order is created, normal delivery, invoicing, payment card processing, and clearing processes within the R/3 System apply to the order.

You must make several decisions while setting up your Online Store. These questions include:

- Will you allow customers to browse your product catalog before identifying themselves, or will you require an early logon?

- Will you allow customers to log on with an e-mail address or with a customer number?

- Do you have existing customers that will want to access your web site? If so, you need to collect e-mail addresses and create passwords for these customers.

- How much reporting do you wish to capture on your customers? Reporting needs determine the types of customers you create within R/3 when new customers register on the Internet.

- What types of payment options will you allow your customers to use?

- How will you capture the reporting of your Internet business? For example, do you wish to use additional distribution channels, additional sales document types, or additional customer account groups?

The answers to these questions determine to what extent you need to change the setup of your current Sales and Distribution (SD) functions, and how you choose to configure your Online Store.

What We Deliver

In the Online Store preconfiguration, we provide the following deliverables:

- Preconfiguration of Online Store and related profile settings
- Preconfiguration of SD settings to support the Online Store
- Preconfiguration of the ITS look and feel
- Documentation on Online Store functionality

The Customer Experience

The Online Store allows customers to browse the product catalog, place items into a shopping basket, and purchase the items from the Internet. The Online Store is often used as an integral part of the web site. The content of the web site should motivate customers to return.

1. In the Internet browser:

   a. Our customer, Desiree, enters the URL of your home page, which you configured as part of the ITS installation.

   b. Desiree chooses the *Online Store* from your home page.

Online store link

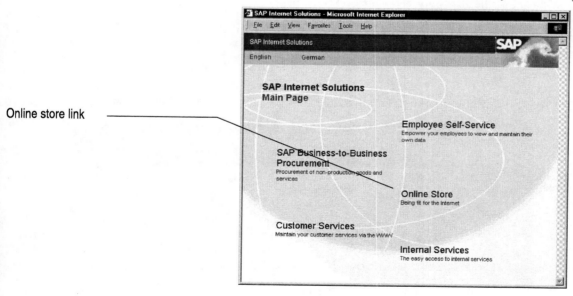

2. Desiree chooses *Online Store.*

Online Store ——————

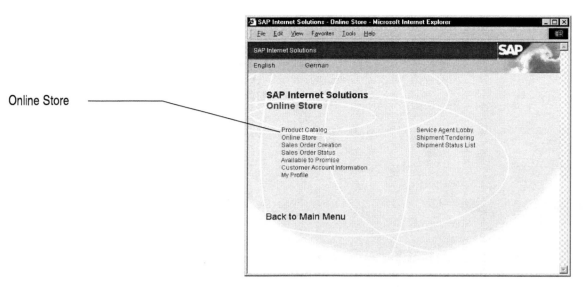

3. Desiree chooses the second option, *YGUIDES-C.*

A list of the different available stores is displayed. Normally, one of these will be called by default through your hyperlink.

Note

Once a catalog is chosen from this screen, it is not possible to switch to a different catalog, or Online Store, unless you start again from the first step to enter this store area.

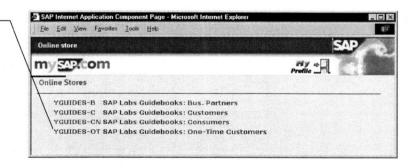

4. On the next screen, Desiree chooses the first shop, *Guidebooks.*

The shops, or different divisions within the catalog, are displayed. A small image represents each shop.

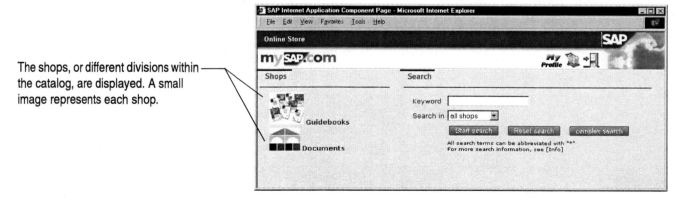

5. Desiree chooses the product group *Guidebooks 4.5x*.

The shop is displayed.

A list of product groups is displayed in the left frame.

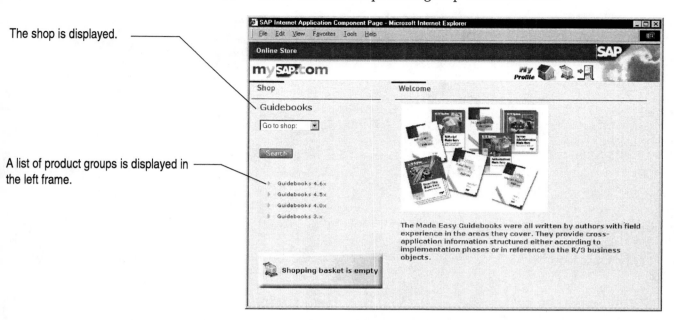

6. Desiree then adds the first product, *Accelerated Internet Selling 4.5B*, to the shopping basket.

All of the products linked to the selected product group are displayed in the right frame.

The availability of each item is shown. This is an add-on provided by the Online Store preconfiguration.

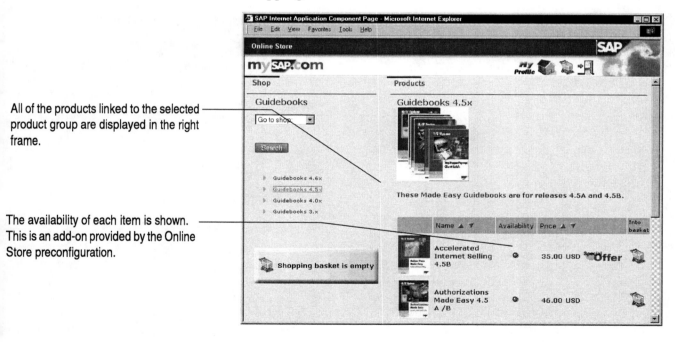

7. Desiree chooses the detail screen of the second product.

The message indicates that the product
has been added.

The shopping basket in the left frame
shows all items in the basket. This is an
add-on provided by the Online Store
preconfiguration.

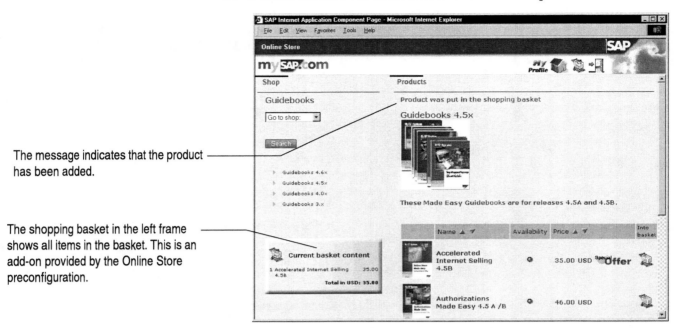

8. Desiree changes the quantity and adds this item to the basket as well.

The detail screen of the next product is
displayed.

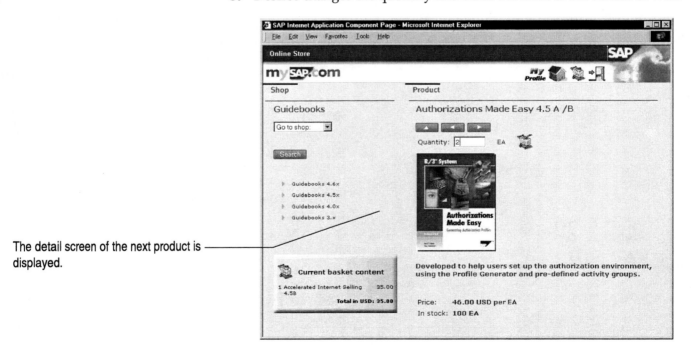

9. To initiate the order, Desiree chooses the shopping cart. She can do this from the top navigation screen or from the shopping basket display in the left frame.

The message indicates that the products have been added to the basket.

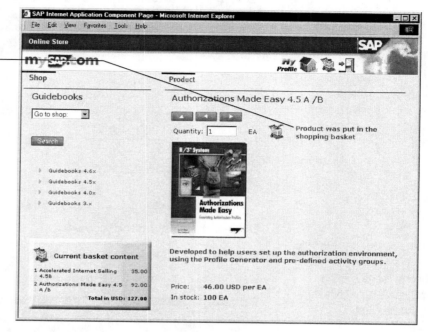

10. Desiree chooses *Quotation*.

The ability to save these items for a later session is provided on this screen, as well as the ability to load a previously saved basket. This functionality is an add-on provided by the Online Store preconfiguration.

The shipping method can be chosen from this screen. Standard shipping is the default choice. This functionality is an add-on provided by the Online Store preconfiguration.

A purchase order number and date can be entered. This functionality is an add-on provided by the Online Store preconfiguration.

A list of all ordered items is displayed. The quantities can be changed, or items can be deleted from this screen.

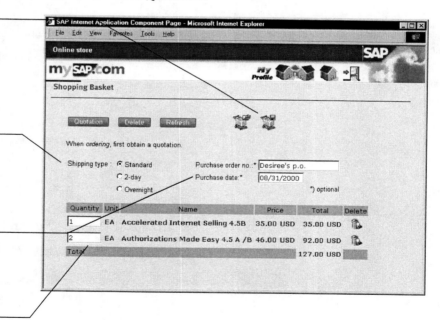

11. In this example, Desiree is visiting the site for the first time, and chooses *Register*.

If the customer has visited the web site before, an e-mail address and password may be used to log on.

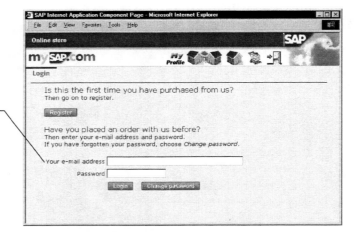

12. Desiree registers on the web site:

a. Desiree enters her address information.

b. At the bottom of the screen, Desiree chooses *Save*.

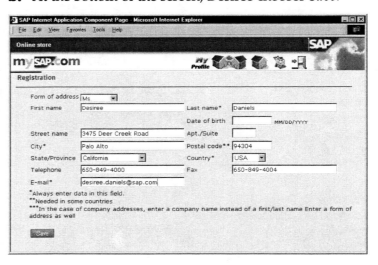

13. Desiree enters her password, and chooses *Change password*. The password is now stored in the Internet user in the backend R/3 System.

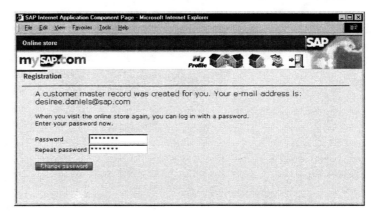

14. Desiree chooses *Cont.*

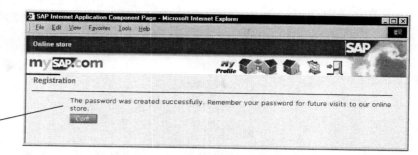

The password is confirmed.

15. Desiree has not stored her credit card number in her profile information, so she chooses *By credit card* to enter her information at this time.

All items in the shopping basket are again displayed. The appropriate freight and taxes are calculated. If a customer discount had been offered, it would have been displayed above the freight total line.

The customer can also change their shipping address by choosing *Goto Change deliv. address*, which will change the shipping address only within the order being created.

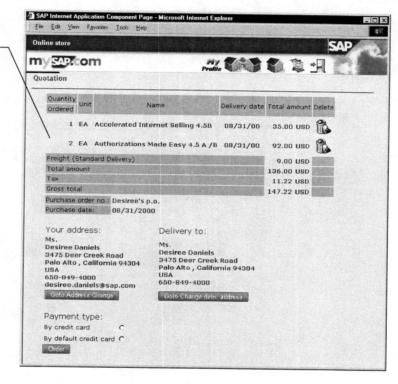

In the Online Store for the consumer, credit cards are the only payment method available.

16. Desiree enters her credit card information and chooses *Order*.

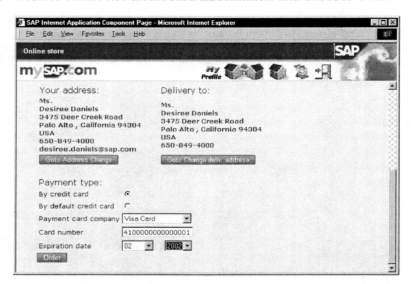

This order is now available for processing in the backend R/3 System.

The order number is displayed.

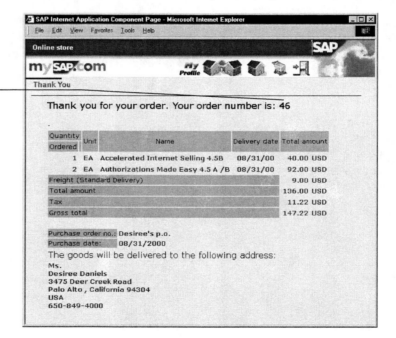

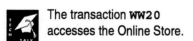 The transaction **WW20** accesses the Online Store.

For more detailed documentation on topics surrounding this user experience, please refer to the following chapters:

- Chapter 2 details the product catalog navigation.

- Chapter 3 explains pricing in the product catalog and orders created from the Online Store.

- Chapter 4 describes limiting a customer's authorization to display only portions of the product catalog.

- Chapter 5 explains customer creation during registration.

- Chapter 6 describes the scenario in which multiple customers from the same company shop at your store.

Making it Happen: The Online Store

The Online Store uses the product catalog master data and adds profiles that determine how the product catalog is processed during browsing and shopping.

The Online Store contains a link to the product catalog variant that should be displayed when the Online Store is accessed. The product catalog variant determines the stores's language and currency. The same product catalog and variant can be used in multiple stores.

The Online Store also contains a series of profiles that determine how the products, customers, and orders are handled. The following profiles determine how the Online Store is processed:

- The product presentation profile determines which product data is displayed, how many products can be displayed on one web page, and how searches take place.

- The customer administration profile determines the type of customer created during registration in the Online Store, and how that customer logs on in the future.

- The order and quotation profile determines the order type used for Internet orders and the payment types allowed.

Four scenarios are delivered with the Online Store preconfiguration:

- **Selling to Customers**
A customer may browse the product catalog without logging on. The customer can then place items into a shopping basket. When the customer is ready to order, an existing customer can log in with an ID (e-mail address) and password. A new customer can register with an e-mail address. The only available payment option is by credit card.

- **Selling to Consumers**
The business process is the same as in the selling to customers. However, a different type of customer master record, called a consumer, is created. Consumer master records contain personal data, but do not contain sales area data, to reduce the size of the records in R/3.

- **Selling to Business Partners**
A customer must already have a logon (e-mail) and password before being able to access the product catalog. The customer can then browse the catalog and place items into shopping baskets. Payment options include credit cards and invoices.

TIPS 'N' TRICKS

A series of add-on functionality has been developed as part of the Online Store preconfiguration. The screens in the previous section include these add-ons. This functionality is described in detail in the designated chapters.

- Availability information for products within the catalog (appendix B, "Technical SAP Enhancement: ATP in the Product Catalog" on page 499)

- Saving the shopping basket, and displaying the contents of the basket while shopping (appendix C, "The Shopping Basket" on page 511)

- A "my profile" service is accessible, which allows the maintenance of personal data, such as a default credit card (appendix F, "Modification: Changing the Customer Type for IKA1" on page 533)

- Entering a purchase order number (appendix D, "Technical SAP Enhancement: Purchase Order Entry" on page 523)

- Choosing a shipping option (chapter 3, "Prices in the Product Catalog" on page 90)

- **Selling to One-Time Customers**
  A customer may browse the catalog, and place orders. However, customers are only rarely expected to return to the site. For this reason, a customer master is not created, and customer information is stored within the order. Customers must re-enter their information each time when visiting the site. Both credit cards and invoices are allowed in this preconfiguration.

Accessing the Online Store

In *The Customer Experience* section earlier in this chapter, the Internet customer chose a link, which displayed a list of available Online Stores. Once the customer chooses one store, it is impossible to switch to another store, unless they start from the beginning.

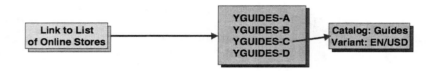

Hyperlink
http://<homeURL>scripts/wgate/ww20/!?~language=EN

It is likely that only one Online Store, or product catalog, will be active at a time. In that case, the link provided from the company web site to the store should link directly to the Online Store.

Hyperlink
http://<homeURL>scripts/wgate/ww20/!?~okcode=START&ostore=STORENAME&~language=EN

There may be cases in which an item from the catalog should be displayed directly, instead of forcing the customer to scroll through the catalog levels to find it. This option is especially useful if a press release or product review is promoted on the company web site. By providing a direct link to the item, the customer is encouraged to take a more detailed look and purchase the item.

Hyperlink
http://<homeURL>/scripts/wgate/ww20/!?~okcode=STARTITE&ostore=YGUIDES-C&selected_area=3&selected_item=1&~language=en

Master Data in R/3 to Support the Online Store

To set up master data in R/3 to support the Online Store, you need to perform the following steps as described in the next sections. You must:

- Create a product catalog

- Create the prices for your products

- Create a reference customer master record

- Create the output type master record

- Ensure that correct parameters are entered in the ITS user's profile

All of these topics are covered in detail in other chapters in this guide.

Create a Product Catalog

You must create a product catalog that includes products, prices, and documents with references to the images and data files displayed on the web. For details about creating a product catalog, please refer to chapter 2, "Creating the Product Catalog" on page 43.

In the *Command* field, enter transaction **WWM1** and choose *Enter* (or from the navigation menu, choose *Logistics → Materials Management → Product Catalog → Product Catalog → Create*).

Create the Prices for Your Products

For each product linked to the product catalog, you must create a price to be displayed on the web. The price may be the same as the prices that already exist in your R/3 System, or you may wish to create discounted prices for your Internet customers. For details about pricing the products in the catalog and in the orders created using the Online Store, please refer to chapter 3, "Prices in the Product Catalog" on page 77.

In the *Command* field, enter transaction **VK31** and choose *Enter* (or from the navigation menu, choose *Logistics → Sales and Distribution → Master Data → Conditions → Create*).

Create a Reference Customer Master Record

Since customer master records are created though the Online Store, you must create a reference customer, consumer, or one-time customer. The customer master records are then used to create the master records for customers who register on the Internet. For details about creating customers, please refer to chapter 5, "Customers in the Online Store" on page 133.

In the *Command* field, enter transaction **XD01** and choose *Enter* (or from the navigation menu, choose *Logistics → Sales and Distribution → Master Data → Business Partners → Customer → Create → Complete*).

Create the Output Type Master Record for Order Confirmations

When an order is created over the Internet, the condition records for the output type must be created so that an e-mail confirmation can be sent to the customer. The steps below illustrate how the condition record is created. This procedure has been preconfigured for you when you run CATT procedure *ZESHOP_OUTPUT_RECORDS*. These steps do not need to be performed unless you choose to create additional condition records. Please refer to appendix H, "Introduction to Computer-Aided Test Tools (CATTs)" on page 547 for details about the CATT procedure.

> **Task**
>
> Create output master record for the Internet sales order

1. In the *Command* field, enter transaction **VV11** and choose *Enter* (or from the navigation menu, choose *Logistics → Sales and Distribution → Master Data → Output → Sales Document → Create*).

2. On the *Create Output - Condition Records* screen:

   a. In *Output type*, enter **YEWO**. This output type has been preconfigured.

   b. Choose *Key combination*.

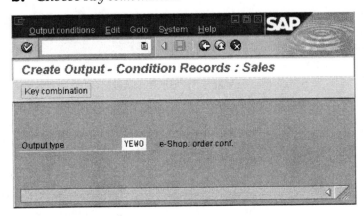

3. On the *Key Combination* dialog box, choose ✔️ .

Only one combination has been configured. *Sales Organization/Order Type* defaults as selected.

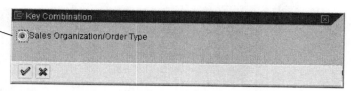

4. On the *Create Condition Records (e-Shop: order conf.): Fast Entry* screen:

   a. Under *Sal* (sales document type), enter **YWO**. This sales document type has been preconfigured.

   b. Under *PartF* (partner function), enter **SP**, which represents the sold-to party.

   c. Under *M* (medium), enter **5**, which means an external send.

   d. In *Time*, enter **4**, which means to send immediately upon saving the order.

   e. Choose *Communication*.

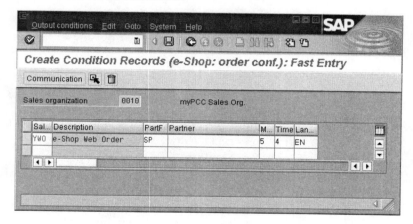

5. On the *Create Condition Records (e-Shop: order conf.): Communi...* screen:

   a. In *Comm. strategy* (communication strategy), enter **CS01** for *Internet/Letter*. **CS01** is delivered with the standard R/3 System.

   b. In *Output device*, enter a printer. This entry is required even though the output will be sent by e-mail.

c. Choose  .

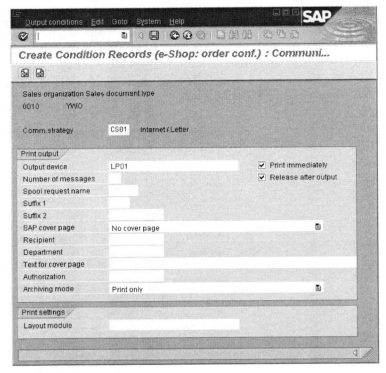

6. Repeat steps 1-5, using sales order type **YWB** instead of **YWO**.

Create the Output Type Master Record for Delivery Confirmations

When an order created over the Internet is delivered, the condition records for the output type must be created so that an e-mail confirmation can be sent to the customer when the order is shipped. The steps below illustrate how the condition record is created. This step has been preconfigured for you when you run CATT procedure *ZESHOP_OUTPUT_RECORDS*. These steps do not need to be performed unless you choose to create additional condition records. Please refer to appendix H, "Introduction to Computer-Aided Test Tools (CATTs)" on page 547 for details about the CATT procedure.

Task

Create output master record for the delivery confirmation

1. In the *Command* field, enter transaction **VV21** and choose *Enter* (or from the navigation menu, choose *Logistics → Sales and Distribution → Master Data → Output → Shipping → Create*).

2. On the *Create Output - Condition Records* screen:

   a. In *Output type*, enter **YEWD**. This output type has been preconfigured.

   b. Choose *Key combination*.

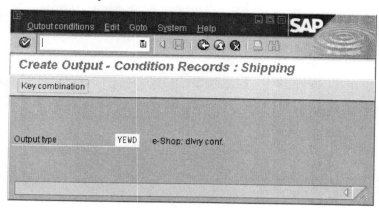

3. On the *Key Combination* dialog box, choose ✅ .

Only one combination has been configured. *Sales Organization/Delivery Type* defaults as selected.

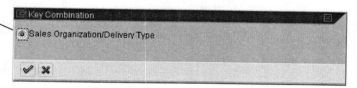

4. On the *Create Condition Records (e-Shop: dlvry conf.): Fast Entry* screen:

   a. Under *Del* (delivery type), enter **LF**. This delivery type is standard delivered with the R/3 System.

   b. Under *PartF* (partner function), enter **SP**, which represents the sold-to party.

   c. Under *M* (medium), enter **5**, which means an external send.

   d. In *Time*, enter **4**, which means to send immediately upon saving the order.

   e. Choose *Communication*.

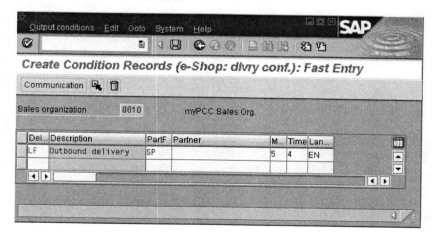

5. On the *Create Condition Records (e-Shop: dlvry conf.): Communication* screen:

a. In *Comm. strategy* (communication strategy), enter **CS01** for *Internet/Letter*. **CS01** is delivered with the standard R/3 System.

b. In *Output device*, enter a printer. This entry is required even though the output will be sent by e-mail.

c. Choose 💾.

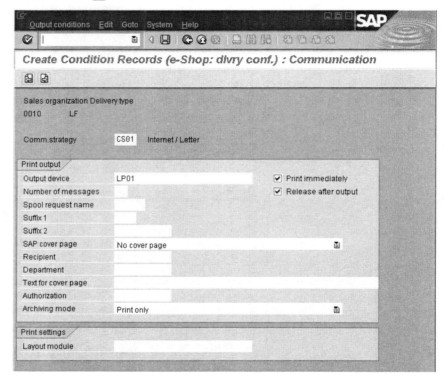

Create the Output Type Master Record for Billing Confirmations

When an order created over the Internet is billed, the condition records for the output type must be created so that an e-mail confirmation can be sent to the customer. If the customer is using a credit card, the e-mail will be an electronic receipt. If the customer is being billed, the e-mail will be an electronic invoice. The steps below illustrate how the condition record is created. A confirmation has also been preconfigured for credit memos. This step has been preconfigured for you when you run CATT procedure ZESHOP_OUTPUT_RECORDS. These steps do not need to be performed unless you choose to create additional condition records. Please refer to appendix H, "Introduction to Computer-Aided Test Tools (CATTs)" on page 547 for details about the CATT procedure.

> **Task**

Create output master record for billing confirmations

1. In the *Command* field, enter transaction **VV31** and choose *Enter* (or from the navigation menu, choose *Logistics → Sales and Distribution → Master Data → Output → Billing Document → Create*).

2. On the *Create Output - Condition Records* screen:

    a. In *Output type*, enter **YEWI**. This output type has been preconfigured.

    b. Choose *Key combination*.

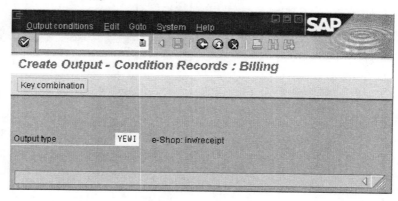

3. On the *Key Combination* dialog box, choose ✔ .

Only one combination has been configured. *Sales Organization/Billing Type* defaults as selected.

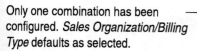

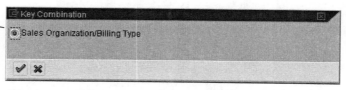

4. On the *Create Condition Records (e-Shop: inv/receipt): Fast Entry* screen:

    a. Under *Bill* (billing document type), enter **YWI**. This billing document type has been preconfigured.

    b. Under *PartF* (partner function), enter **SP**, which represents the sold-to party.

    c. Under *M* (medium), enter **5**, which means an external send.

    d. Under *Time*, enter **4**, which means to send immediately upon saving the order.

    e. In the next row, enter the same parameters for billing type **YWRE**. This billing document type has been configured for returns.

f. Select the first row (you will return to this step to select each of the following rows).

g. Choose *Communication.*

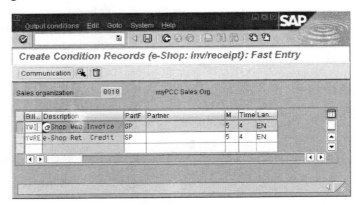

5. On the *Create Condition Records (e-Shop: inv/receipt): Communi...* screen:

a. In *Comm. strategy* (communication strategy), enter **CS01** for *Internet/Letter.* **CS01** is delivered with the standard R/3 System.

b. In *Output device*, enter a printer. This entry is required even though the output will be sent by e-mail.

c. Choose ⟲ to access the previous screen and enter the same parameters for the second entry.

d. Choose 🖫 .

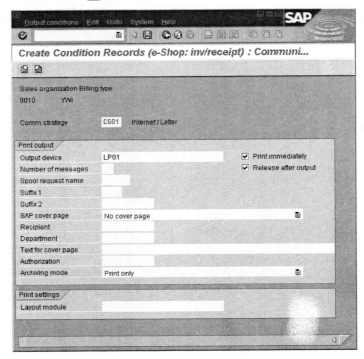

6. Return to step **4f**, select another row, and complete the rest of the steps. Repeat for all rows on the *Create Condition Records (e-Shop: inv/receipt): Fast Entry* screen.

Ensure Correct Parameters Are Entered in the ITS User's Profile

In order to access the Online Store from the Internet, the correct parameters must be entered in the ITS user's profile. The ITS user that logged into the R/3 System in the background during the *Online Store* transaction must have the correct sales area parameters in the user profile. Please refer to chapter 15, "The ITS User: Logging on to R/3" on page 349 for details on the ITS user.

To double-check the ITS user's profile parameters, enter transaction **SU01** in the *Command* field and choose *Enter* (or from the navigation menu, choose *Tools → Administration → User Maintenance → Users*).

Configuration to Support the Online Store

Note

For changes that we deliver for the look and feel of the Online Store functionality, and for instructions on how to make changes to the ITS Business HTML templates, please refer to chapter 14, "ITS Templates" on page 327.

The configuration steps listed below for supporting the Online Store are described in detail in the following sections. You must configure:

- The application types for images in the Online Store (standard delivery)
- The product presentation profile (preconfigured)
- The country selection profile (preconfigured)
- The customer administration profile (preconfigured)
- The quotation and order profile (preconfigured)
- The Online Store (preconfigured)
- Sales document types used for the Internet (preconfigured)
- An additional item category for the Internet (preconfigured)
- Billing types for the Internet (preconfigured)
- Pricing procedures for the Internet (preconfigured)
- Output determination for e-mail order confirmation (preconfigured)
- Output determination for e-mail delivery confirmation (preconfigured)
- Output determination for e-mail receipt/invoice confirmation (preconfigured)
- Output SAPscript form (preconfigured)

You should also check the SAPNet – R/3 Frontend notes.

Configure the Application Types for Images in the Online Store

To support the image and data files displayed in the Online Store, the types of files expected are defined in configuration. This step is standard-delivered in R/3.

> **Task**
>
> Define the application types for images in the Online Store

In the *Command* field, enter transaction **WCPC** and choose *Enter* (or in the IMG, choose *Logistics - General* → *IAC Product Catalog and Online Store* and choose 🔄 next to *Determine Pictures and Sound Files for Web Server*).

The table below shows the workstation applications expected in the Online Store. No changes have been made to the R/3 standard-delivered settings.

Usage	Application Type
WS carrier type	WS (Webserver)
WA large	LIM (Large Image)
WA small	SIM (Small Image)
WA sound file	SND (Sound)

Configure the Product Presentation Profile

The product presentation profile determines how the products in the catalog are displayed, how access to the catalog is controlled, and how searches of products are handled. Two profiles have been preconfigured for you. For the business partner scenario, material numbers and descriptions are displayed. For the business-to-consumer scenario, different (usually less technical) texts are available.

> **Task**
>
> Configure the product presentation profiles

In the IMG, to view the product presentation profiles, choose *Logistics - General* → *IAC Product Catalog and Online Store* and choose 🔄 next to *Profiles for Product Presentation*.

The table below shows the primary settings in the two preconfigured product presentation profiles. The profiles are:

- *YPCB* – Selling to business partners
- *YPCC* – Selling to consumers

Fields	YPCB	YPCC
Display product with catalog header	Off	On
Display product with material number	On	Off
Display product with material short text	On	Off
Lines per page	20	10
Product group hierarchy: expanded	Off	Off
Product group hierarchy: dynamic	On	On
Product group hierarchy: step-by-step	Off	Off
Limit for product search	100	100
Search catalog heading	Off	On
Search material number	On	Off
Search material short text	On	Off
Search price	Off	On
Search long text	Off	On
Search all shops	On	On
Display additional documents: list	Off	Off
Display additional documents: detail	On	On

In addition to the settings above, the filter criteria for both profiles is set to **CUSTOMER_FILTER_CHAR_READ** to allow a limit on customers' access to portions of a catalog. For additional details, please refer to chapter 4, "Limiting Access to Product Groups Within a Product Catalog" on page 109.

The function module **IAC_STANDARD_SEARCH** is entered. This is the standard search function module used by R/3, even when no entry is made. If different search logic is required, a different function module must be delivered. **IAC_SEARCH_ALTAVISTA** is also available. However, additional configuration is required to activate the Alta Vista search functionality. The Alta Vista search functionality has not been preconfigured.

All other fields are either blank or relevant only to IS-Retail installations.

Configure the Country Selection Profile

When a new customer is created within the Online Store, all countries available for selection are sorted alphabetically. A country schema has been preconfigured to limit the countries available for selection. You can limit the selection to the countries with which you expect to do business.

Task

Configure the country selection profile

To view the country selection profile, in the IMG choose *Logistics - General* → *IAC Product Catalog and Online Store* and choose ⊕ next to *Country Selection for Customer Address*.

The table below shows the countries included in the preconfigured country selection profile. The U.S. is the selected country that defaults into the address screen.

Country	With regions	Default
CA (Canada)	Yes	No
US (USA)	Yes	Yes

Configure the Customer Administration Profile

The customer administration profile determines how customers are created in the R/3 System when they register in the Online Store, and how logon is handled. For the business partner scenario, customers are required to log in before browsing the product catalog. New customers cannot register online. For the business-to-consumer scenario, customers can browse the catalog online, and only need to sign in immediately prior to obtaining a quote and ordering.

Task

Configure the customer administration profiles

To view the customer administration profile, in the IMG choose, *Logistics - General* → *IAC Product Catalog and Online Store* and choose ⊕ next to *Customer Administration Profiles*.

The table below shows the primary settings in the two preconfigured customer administration profiles. The profiles are:

- *YPCB* – Selling to business partners
- *YPCC* – Selling to consumers
- *YPCN* – Selling to consumers (consumer master)
- *YPOT* – Selling to consumers, OT customer

The configuration in the customer administration profile specifies that a customer will log on with an e-mail address, not a customer number. This configuration applies to the Online Store (WW20) and product catalog (WW10) Internet Application Components.

In order for a customer to log on with an e-mail address for checking the Sales Order Status (VW10), the configuration for customer logon is not within R/3. A parameter is set in the ITS service file to allow customers to log on with an e-mail address here as well. Please refer to chapter 8, "Sales Order Status" on page 207 for details.

E-mail logon is not available for the available to promise (CVAK) and customer account information (IKA1) IACs.

Field	YPCB	YPCC	YPCN	YPOT
Early registration (logon)	On	Off	Off	Off
No customer registration Customers cannot create a new customer number online	On	Off	Off	On
Allow SSL (off for our delivery, but should be turned on for live sites)	Off	Off	Off	Off
Allow one-time customers	Off	Off	Off	On
One-time customer reference	Blank	Blank	Blank	2000000
Customer logon	E-mail	E-mail	E-mail	E-mail
Country default	YUS1	YUS1	YUS1	YUS1
Customers are created as consumers	Off	Off	On	Off

Configure the Quotation and Order Profile

The order profile determines the screen progression for creating an order, whether delivery dates may be entered, and which payment methods are allowed. For the business partner scenario, payment by invoice and credit card is allowed, and a requested delivery date may be entered. For the business-to-consumer scenario, customers may only pay with credit cards. For the one-time customer, both credit cards and invoices are allowed, although you may wish to change this setting in your installation.

In all cases, a quotation is generated before a customer places the order. We recommend you not change this setting for doing business in the U.S., because the subtotals displayed, including discounts and freight, are only available using quotation processing.

Task

Configure the quotation and order profiles

To view the quotation and order profiles, in the IMG choose *Logistics - General → IAC Product Catalog and Online Store* and choose 👆 next to *Profiles for Quotation and Order Control*.

The table below shows the primary settings in the two preconfigured customer administration profiles. The profiles are:

- *YPCB* – Selling to business partners

- *YPCC* – Selling to consumers

- *YPOT* – Selling to one-time customers

The configuration in the quotation and order profile is set to display a quote for the customer before the order can be placed. This setting is necessary if the display of a price breakdown is desired (that is, a breakdown of discounts, freight, and tax). This breakdown is not available if the quotation is not generated first.

Field	YPCB	YPCC	YPOT
Order type	YWB	YWO	YWO
Creation quotation before order	On	On	On
Payment by credit card allowed	On	On	On
Payment by invoice allowed	On	Off	On
Payment by cash-on-delivery allowed	Off	Off	Off
Credit card with SET (Secure Electronic Transaction)	Off	Off	Off
Requested delivery date entry allowed	On	Off	Off
Maximum requested delivery time	30 days	Blank	Blank

Configure the Online Store

The Online Store contains links to the product catalog master data and to configuration that determine handling procedures for products, customers, and sales orders. Four different Online Stores are delivered. Each of these stores uses the same product catalog as master data. The Online Store also contains the configuration profiles previously described.

This step has been preconfigured for you. However, if you are not using the Online Store preconfiguration in conjunction with the Preconfigured Client, the sample product catalog is not delivered and you must create a catalog manually. For details on creating product catalogs, please refer to chapter 2, "Creating the Product Catalog" on page 43.

Two stores supports a "selling to the consumer" scenario. In this scenario, a customer can browse the product catalog, but is not required to log on until ready to place an order. The only type of payment allowed is credit card payment. One store is configured to create a complete customer master record. The other store is configured to create a "minimal" customer master record, or consumer master record. Please refer to chapter 5, "Customers in the Online Store" on page 133 for details.

A third store supports the "selling to a business partner" scenario. A customer is assumed to be a close business partner who must log on before being allowed to browse the product catalog. In this scenario, both invoices and credit cards are allowed as payment options. A full customer master record is created in this scenario.

The fourth store supports one-time customers. No customer master record is created. All customer information is stored in the order. Customers are allowed to browse the catalog, and may pay by invoice or with credit card. In terms of subsequent services available on the Internet, one-time customers cannot check their order status, since no customer master record is created.

Task

Configure the Online Stores

To view the configuration of the Online Stores, in the IMG choose *Logistics - General → IAC Product Catalog and Online Store* and choose 🔧 next to *Online Stores*.

The table below shows the primary settings in the two preconfigured customer administration profiles. The Online Stores are:

- *YGUIDES-B: SAP Labs Guidebooks: Bus. Partners*

- *YGUIDES-C: SAP Labs Guidebooks: Customers*

- *YGUIDES-CN: SAP Labs Guidebooks: Consumers*

- *YGUIDES-OT: SAP Labs Guidebooks: One-Time Customers*

Field	YESHOP-B	YESHOP-C	YESHOP-CN	YESHOP-OT
Use as prod cat only (no shopping basket functionality)	Off	Off	Off	Off
Product catalog	YESHOP-B2C	YESHOP-B2C	YESHOP-B2C	YESHOP-B2C
Variant	001	001	001	001
Product profile	YPCB	YPCC	YPCB	YPCC
Order profile	YPCB	YPCC	YPCB	YPOT
Sales office	0010	0010	0010	0010
Customer profile	YPCB	YPCC	YPCN	YPOT
Reference customer (overrides the customer in the product catalog basic data)	Blank	Blank	Blank	Blank

All other fields are blank.

If the Online Store descriptions should be maintained in multiple languages, choose *Utilities → Choose languages*, and select an additional language in which the texts should be maintained. Then choose *Edit → Translation* to enter the text.

Configure Sales Document Types Used for the Internet

The new sales order types *YWO*, *YWB*, and *YWRE* have been preconfigured for Online Store orders and returns. These new order types have been created according to requirements for a different pricing procedure and credit handling. Additionally, the new order types facilitate reporting of Internet orders.

Order types *YWO* and *YWB* are the same, with the exception of the partner determination procedure. *YWB* is configured to use the customer hierarchy delivered with the Online Store preconfiguration. Please refer to chapter 8, "Sales Order Status" on page 207 for details.

Task

Configure the sales document types

In the *Command* field, enter transaction **VOV8** and choose *Enter* (or in the IMG, choose *Sales and Distribution → Sales → Sales Documents → Sales Document Header* and choose 🕐 next to *Define Sales Document Types*).

The table below shows the primary settings in the two preconfigured sales document types. *YWO* and *YWB* are copied from order type *OR* and *YWRE* is copied from order type *RE*.

Field	YWO	YWB	YWRE
SD document category	C (order)	C (order)	H (returns)
Internal number range	01	01	01
External number range	02	02	02
Item increment	10	10	10
Sub-item increment	10	10	10
Check division	2 (error)	2 (error)	Blank
Item division	On	On	Off
Read info record	On	On	On
Check credit limit	Off	Off	Off
Credit group	Blank	Blank	Blank
Enter PO number	Off	Off	Off
Probability	100	100	100
Output application	V1	V1	V1
Screen sequence group	AU (sales order)	AU (sales order)	RE (returns)
Incompletion procedure	11 (standard order)	11 (standard order)	14 (credit memo)
Transaction group	0 (sales order)	0 (sales order)	0 (sales order)
Document pricing procedure	X	X	X
Display criteria	UALL	UALL	UALL
Function code: overview screen	UER1	UER1	UER1
Product attribute messages	A (dialog)	A (dialog)	Off
Delivery type	LF	LF	LR
Delivery-relevant billing type	YWI	YWI	YWRE
Order-relevant billing type	YWI	YWI	YWRE
Intercompany billing type	IV	IV	IG

Field	YWO	YWB	YWRE
Billing block	Off	Off	08
Costing cond. type for line items	EK02	EK02	Blank
Payment guarantee proc.	01 (standard)	01 (standard)	01 (standard)
Payment card plan type	03 (payment card)	03 (payment card)	03 (payment card)
Checking group	01 (standard)	01 (standard)	01 (standard)
Propose delivery date	On	On	Blank

All other entries are blank. Note that the copy rules have been adjusted as necessary to reflect the new document types.

Configure an Additional Item Category for the Internet

The new item category *YREN* is preconfigured for Online Store orders and returns. The new item category handles delivery-based returns, since the standard-delivered *REN* handles only order-based returns.

Task

Configure the item category

In the IMG, choose *Sales and Distribution → Sales → Sales Documents → Sales Document Item* and choose ⊕ next to *Define Item Categories*.

The table below shows the primary settings in the preconfigured item category *YREN*. Item category *YREN* was copied from item category *REN*.

Field	Value
Relevant for billing	A (delivery-related)
Schedule line allowed	On
Returns	On
Weight/volume relevant	On
Determine cost	On
Pricing	X (standard)
Incompletion procedure	20
Partner determination procedure	N
Text determination procedure	01
Item category statistics group	2
Screen sequence group	N

All other fields are left blank.

Task

Assign the item category to the returns sales document type

In the *Command* field, enter transaction **VOV4** (or in the IMG, choose *Sales and Distribution → Sales → Sales Documents → Sales Document Item* and choose ⏣ next to *Assign Item Categories*).

The table below shows the assignment made for the item category.

Sales Document Type	Item Category Group	Usage	Higher-level Item Category Group	Default Item Category
YWRE	NORM	Blank	Blank	YREN

Configure Billing Types Used for the Internet

The new billing types *YWI* and *YWRE* are preconfigured for Online Store orders and returns. The new billing types have been created according to requirements for a different pricing procedure in the originating order.

Task

Configure the billing types

In the *Command* field, enter transaction **VOFA** (or in the IMG, choose *Sales and Distribution → Billing → Billing Documents* and choose ⏣ next to *Define Billing Types*. Then on the *Choose Activity* dialog box, select *Define Billing Types* and choose 🔲 *Choose*).

The table below shows the primary settings in the two preconfigured sales document types. *YWI* is copied from billing types *F2*, and *YWRE* is copied from order type *RE*.

Field	YWI	YWRE
Internal number range	19	19
SD document category	M (invoice)	O (credit memo)
Transaction group	7 (billing documents)	7 (billing documents)
Statistics	On	On
Invoice list type	LR	LG
Relevant for rebate	On	On
Cancellation billing type	S1	S2
Account determination procedure	KOFI00	KOFI00
Document pricing procedure	X	X

Field	YWI	YWRE
Account determination for payment cards	A00001	A00001
Output determination procedure	V10000	V10000
Application	V3	V3
Output type	RD00	RD00
Header partners	FK	FK
Item partners	FP	FP
Text determination procedure	03	03
Text determination proc. (item)	04	04

All other entries are blank. Note that the copy rules are adjusted as necessary to reflect the new billing types.

Configure Pricing Procedures Used for the Internet

If the majority of customers who will do business on the Internet with your company do not have established business relationships with you, a simple pricing procedure is appropriate. If you plan to sell to business partners on the web, you may choose to use your existing pricing procedures for selling on the Internet. For details about pricing in the Online Store and the delivered preconfiguration, please refer to chapter 3, "Prices in the Product Catalog" on page 77.

Task

Configure the pricing procedures used for the product catalog and Internet sales orders

In the *Command* field, enter transaction **V/08** (or in the IMG, choose *Sales and Distribution → Basic Functions → Pricing → Pricing Control* and choose ⊕ next to *Define and Assign Pricing Procedures*. Then on the *Choose Activity* dialog box, select *Maintain Pricing Procedures* and choose ▨ *Choose*).

Configure the Output Determination for E-mail Order Confirmation

The new output type *YEWO* is preconfigured for e-mail order confirmation. When the order created on the Internet is saved, the e-mail is sent to the customer with details about the items ordered, the cost, and the order number. For details on configuring the technical e-mail integration, please refer to chapter 19, "E-mail and Fax" on page 416.

Task

Configure the output type for order confirmation

The output type determines when and by which method output is generated for the order. For the Internet order, output is generated through e-mail as the order is saved.

In the *Command* field, enter transaction **V/30** and choose *Enter* (or in the IMG, choose *Sales and Distribution* → *Basic Functions* → *Output Control* → *Output Determination* → *Output Determination Using the Condition Technique* → *Maintain Output Determination for Sales Documents* and choose ⏚ next to *Maintain Output Types*).

The table below shows the primary settings in the preconfigured output type.

Field	Setting
Access sequence	0004 (sales organization/sales order type)
Access to conditions	On
Dispatch time	Send immediately (when saving the application)
Transmission medium	External send
Partner function	SP (sold-to party)
Communication strategy	CS01 (Internet/letter)
Archiving mode	Print only
Document type	SDORDER
Print parameter	Sales organization

All other fields are left blank.

Task

Include the output type in the output determination procedure

The output type must be assigned to an output determination procedure. This step has been preconfigured for you.

In the *Command* field, enter transaction **V/32** and choose *Enter* (or in the IMG, choose *Sales and Distribution* → *Basic Functions* → *Output Control* → *Output Determination*→ *Output Determination Using the Condition Technique* → *Maintain Output Determination for Sales Documents* and choose ⏚ next to *Maintain Output Determination Procedure*).

The standard-delivered output determination procedure *V10000* is used. The new output type is added as the last step in the procedure.

Step	Counter	Condition Type	Requirement	Manual only
99	0	YEWO (e-Shop: order conf.)	2 (order confirmation)	Off

Task

Assign the output determination procedure to the sales order type

The output determination procedure is now assigned to the sales order type used for the Internet. This step has been preconfigured for you.

In the *Command* field, enter transaction **V/43** and choose *Enter* (or in the IMG, choose *Sales and Distribution* → *Basic Functions* → *Output Control* → *Output Determination* → *Output Determination Using the Condition Technique* → *Maintain Output Determination for Sales Documents* and choose ⊕ next to *Assign Output Determination Procedures*. Then on the *Choose Activity* dialog box, select *Allocate sales document header* and choose ▣ *Choose*).

Sales document type	Output procedure	Output Type
YWO	V10000	YEWO

Task

Assign the SAPscript form to the output medium

The correct SAPscript form must be assigned to the output type to ensure that the correct information is sent to the customer. This step has been preconfigured for you.

In the *Command* field, enter transaction **V/G7** and choose *Enter*. In the pop-up window, enter *Output type* **YWEO** and *Application* **V1**. The settings for assigning the form to the transmission medium are documented below.

Field	Setting
Output type	YEWO (e-Shop: order conf.)
Application	V1 (sales)
Transmission medium	5 (external send)
Program	RVADOR01
FORM routine	ENTRY
Form	YPCC_ORDCONF_WEB

Configure the Output Determination for E-mail Delivery Confirmation

The new output type *YEWD* is preconfigured for e-mail delivery confirmations. When the delivery of an Internet order is created, the e-mail is sent to the customer with details about the items shipped and the order number. For details on configuring the technical e-mail integration, please refer to chapter 19, "E-mail and Fax" on page 416.

Task

Configure the output type for delivery confirmation

The output type determines when and by which method output is generated for the delivery. For the delivery of an Internet order, output is generated through e-mail as the delivery with goods issue is saved.

In the *Command* field, enter transaction **V/34** and choose *Enter* (or in the IMG, choose *Logistics Execution → Shipping → Basic Shipping Functions → Output Control → Output Determination → Maintain Output Determination for Sales Activities* and choose 🕹 next to *Maintain Output Types*).

The table below shows the primary settings in the preconfigured output type.

Field	Setting
Access sequence	0004 (sales organization/delivery type)
Access to conditions	On
Dispatch time	Send immediately (when saving the application)
Transmission medium	External send
Partner function	SP (sold-to party)
Communication strategy	CS01 (Internet/letter)
Archiving mode	Print only
Document type	SDODELNOTE
Print parameter	Shipping point

All other fields are left blank.

Task

Include the output type in the output determination procedure

The output type must be assigned to an output determination procedure. This step has been preconfigured for you.

In the IMG, choose *Logistics Execution → Shipping → Basic Shipping Functions → Output Control → Output Determination → Maintain Output Determination for Sales Activities* and choose 🕹 next to *Maintain Output Determination Procedure*).

The standard-delivered output determination procedure *V10000* is used. The new output type is added as the last step in the procedure.

Step	Counter	Condition Type	Requirement	Manual only
99	1	YEWD (e-Shop: order conf.)	1 (delivery GI posted)	Off

Task

Assign the SAPscript form to the output medium

The correct SAPscript form must be assigned to the output type to ensure that the correct information is sent to the customer. This step has been preconfigured for you.

In the *Command* field, enter transaction **V/G7** and choose *Enter*. In the *Determine Work Area: Entry* dialog box, in *Output type* enter **YWED** and in *Application* enter **V2**. Then choose ✔ . The settings for assigning the form to the transmission medium are documented below.

Field	Setting
Output type	YEWD (e-Shop: dlvry conf.)
Application	V2 (shipping)
Transmission medium	5 (external send)
Program	RVADDN01
FORM routine	ENTRY
Form	YPCC_PACKLST_WEB

Configure the Output Determination for E-mail Billing Confirmation

The new output type *YEWI* is preconfigured for e-mail billing confirmation. When the invoice created for the Internet order is saved, the e-mail is sent to the customer, with details about the items ordered, the cost, and the order number. For details on configuring the technical e-mail integration, please refer to chapter 19, "E-mail and Fax" on page 416.

Task

Configure the output type for billing confirmation

The output type determines when and by which method output is generated for the billing document. For the billing document created for an Internet order, output is generated through e-mail as the order is saved.

In the *Command* field, enter transaction **V/40** and choose *Enter* (or in the IMG, choose *Sales and Distribution → Basic Functions → Output Control → Output Determination→ Output Determination Using the Condition Technique → Maintain Output Determination for Billing Documents* and choose 🕭 next to *Maintain Output Types*).

The table below shows the primary settings in the preconfigured output type.

Field	Setting
Access sequence	0002 (sales organization/billing type)
Access to conditions	On
Dispatch time	Send immediately (when saving the application)
Transmission medium	External send
Partner function	SP (sold-to party)
Communication strategy	CS01 (Internet/letter)
Archiving mode	Print only
Document type	SDOINVOICE
Print parameter	Sales organization

All other fields are left blank.

Task

Include the output type in the output determination procedure

The output type must be assigned to an output determination procedure. This step has been preconfigured for you.

In the IMG, choose *Sales and Distribution → Basic Functions → Output Control → Output Determination→ Output Determination Using the Condition Technique → Maintain Output Determination for Sales Documents* and choose 🖑 next to *Maintain Output Determination Procedure*).

The standard-delivered output determination procedure *V10000* is used. The new output type is added as the last step in the procedure.

Step	Counter	Condition Type	Requirement	Manual only
199	1	YEWI (e-Shop: inv/receipt)	62 (BillDoc: ReleasePost.)	Off

Task

Assign the output determination procedure to the billing type

The output determination procedure is now assigned to the billing type used for the Internet. This step has been preconfigured for you.

In the *Command* field, enter transaction **V/25** and choose *Enter* (or in the IMG, choose *Sales and Distribution → Basic Functions → Output Control → Output Determination→ Output Determination Using the Condition Technique → Maintain Output Determination for Sales Documents* and choose 🖑 next to *Assign Output Determination Procedures*).

Sales document type	Output procedure	Output Type
YWI	V10000	YEWI
YWRE	V10000	YEWI

Task

Assign the SAPscript form to the output medium

The correct SAPscript form must be assigned to the output type to ensure that the correct information is sent to the customer. This step has been preconfigured for you.

In the *Command* field, enter transaction **V/G7** and choose *Enter*. In the *Determine Work Area: Entry* dialog box, in *Output type* enter **YWEI** and in *Application* enter **V3**. Then choose ✔ . The settings for assigning the form to the transmission medium are documented below.

Field	Setting
Output type	YEWI (e-Shop: inv/receipt)
Application	V3 (billing)
Transmission medium	5 (external send)
Program	RVADIN01
FORM routine	ENTRY
Form	YPCC_INVOICE_WEB<

Configure the Output SAPscript Form

Three SAPscript forms are included in the Online Store preconfiguration:

- *YPCC_ORDCONF_WEB* is used for the e-mail confirmation sent to the customer when the order is saved.

- *YPCC_PACKLST_WEB* is used for the e-mail confirmation sent to the customer when the delivery is shipped.

- *YPCC_INVOICE_WEB* is used for receipts, invoices, and credit memos mailed to the customer. For initial invoice processing, if a credit card is used, a receipt instead of an invoice is printed.

For details and documentation about the preconfigured SAPscript forms in general, please visit our web site at *www.saplabs.com/forms*, or the Preconfigured Client (PCC) at *www.saplabs.com/pcc*.

Task

Configure the SAPscript forms

In the *Command* field, enter transaction **SE71** and choose *Enter* (or in the IMG, choose *Sales and Distribution* → *Basic Functions* → *Output Control* → *Output Determination*→ *Process Output and Forms* and choose ⊕ next to *Define Forms*).

Check the SAPNet – R/3 Frontend Notes

Information from SAPNet – R/3 Frontend notes (formerly OSS) is also essential to the configuration of the Online Store.

TechTalk

For the Online Store transaction to function as described in this chapter, the following SAPNet – R/3 Frontend notes must be applied:

- *135661* defines the correct customizing required for the Euro. This configuration is required for multiple currencies to be displayed in the product catalog.

- *169091* allows subtotals from the pricing procedure to be passed to the Internet. This note is required for the detailed price breakdown delivered with the Online Store preconfiguration.

- *196608* and *213898* allow the state (region) field to be displayed in the Online Store.

For additional informational notes, please refer to appendix A, "SAPNet Frontend Notes" on page 495.

Creating the Product Catalog

Overview

The product catalog presents your products to your existing and potential customers on the Internet. Customers can browse the catalog, either purchasing products directly from the Internet or calling your customer service department to place an order.

In collecting the data you wish to present, maintaining this information, and operating your web site, there are several decisions that must be made. For example:

- Should customers have the ability to purchase products directly from your web site, or should the catalog only be used for product presentation?

- What is the short description of each product that you want to display on the web?

- How detailed should the descriptions and specifications of each product be presented to your customers?

- Which images and graphics will you use to illustrate your products?

- Will you allow customers to download additional data, such as detailed product specs, from your web site?

- Do you wish to offer different prices and price breaks to your Internet customers?

- In how many languages will you need to maintain your product catalog?

The most critical and time-consuming effort in creating your product catalog is to determine the data you want your customers to see on the web. If you have never done business on the web, it is unlikely that you will have all of the appropriate images and descriptions ready for use. If you have a print catalog, you may have a starting point. However, since the Internet is a different medium, requiring a different layout to keep the interest of customers who are "just browsing," it is unlikely that you will be able to convert all of your existing data without making modifications. The earlier you begin the process of collecting data for your product catalog, the more accurately you can present your products and use the store on your web site as a true marketing tool.

What We Deliver

In the Online Store preconfiguration, we provide the following deliverables:

- Preconfiguration of product catalog and document management system settings

- ITS "look and feel" preconfiguration

- Data load program for the product catalog

- Documentation on the functionality of the product catalog

- Documentation of the BAPI programs available for the data load of the product catalog

The Customer Experience

While browsing the catalog, customers may see your products for the first time. The images, descriptions, and prices are critical to keeping the interest of the customers, and motivating them to purchase your products. The product catalog is likely only a portion of your web site. You may wish to use other parts of your web site, such as press releases, to draw your customers' attention to your products, and provide links to individual products in the catalog.

1. In the Internet browser, our customer, Alan, enters the URL of your home page, which you configured as part of the ITS installation.

2. Alan chooses the *Online Store* from your home page.

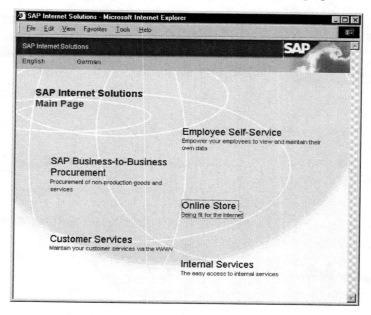

3. Alan chooses *Product Catalog*.

Product catalog ————

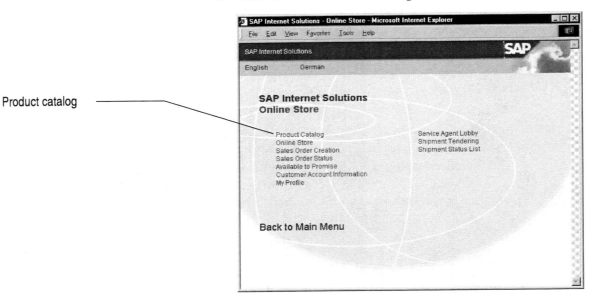

Since this IAC is a product catalog display, a shopping basket is not available. If a company wishes to only display their products on the Internet, a means of contacting the company via a phone number or mailing address should be available on the web.

 Once a catalog is chosen from this screen, it is not possible to switch to a different catalog, or Online Store, unless you start again from the first step to enter the store area. It may be desirable to only have one product catalog, and call it up directly from the home page to bypass this selection screen.

4. From the list of different available catalogs, Alan chooses *YGUIDES-C*.

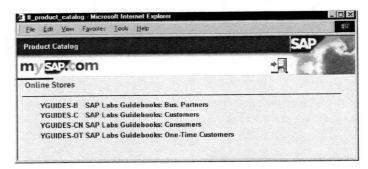

5. Alan chooses the first shop, *Guidebooks*.

The shops, or different divisions within the catalog, are displayed. A small image is displayed for each shop.

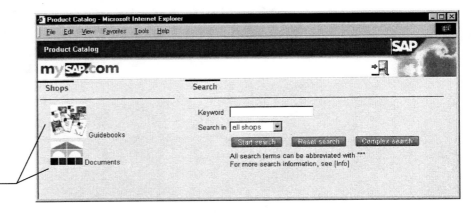

6. The shop is displayed. Alan chooses the product group *Guidebooks 4.5x.*

The *Go to shop* list box arrow provides the customer with the option of visiting another shop within the catalog.

A large image of the *Guidebook* shop is now displayed in the right frame. It is also possible to play a sound file or data file at this point.

A list of product groups is displayed in the left frame. If lower-level groups existed, they could either be displayed immediately, or be dynamically opened with folder icons, depending on the configuration within R/3.

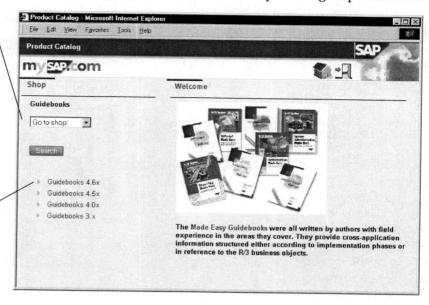

 A large image and text linked to the product group is displayed in the right frame. Other types of documents, such as sound files or PDF files, can also be displayed at this time.

Any text formatting for the product group, such as highlighted text or line breaks, is stored in the product catalog text in R/3 using HTML tags.

All of the products linked to the selected product group are displayed in the right frame. A small image and description are displayed. The short description could be read from the material master record or from the product catalog. It is also possible to display the material number, but this option has not been configured for this catalog.

The prices are displayed. If a sale price exists, the *Special Offer* icon is displayed, and only the sale price is shown in this product list.

7. Alan chooses the first product, *Accelerated Internet Selling 4.5B.*

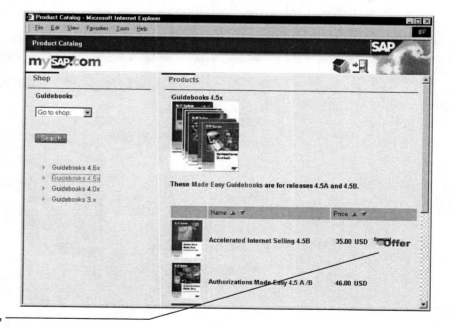

8. Alan scrolls forward to display the next guidebook within this product group.

The icons above the large image allow you to scroll up to the product group list, or backward and forward within this product group.

The original price is displayed in addition to the sale price.

A large image is displayed in the right frame, as well as detailed text from the product catalog. The text formatting is also controlled by the data in the R/3 product catalog, and can be formatted by placing HTML tags into the product catalog descriptions within R/3.

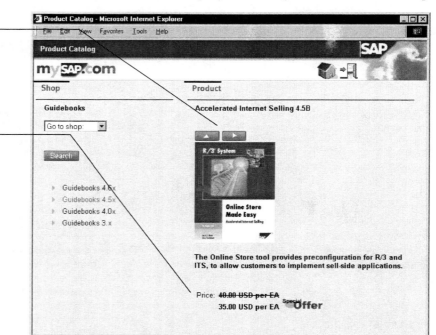

9. Alan now chooses the product group *Guidebook 4.6x* from the list of product groups in the left frame.

The icons above the large image allow you to scroll up to the product group list, or backward and forward within this product group. The customer scrolls forward to the next product.

The detail screen of the product is displayed.

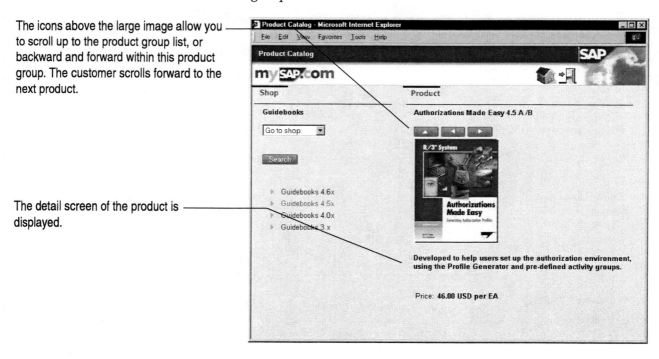

10. Alan chooses the first product, *Accelerated Internet Selling 4.6B.*

A list of all products within this product group is displayed. The same graphic used for the 4.5 product group is associated with the 4.6 product group. You can use a different graphic if you prefer.

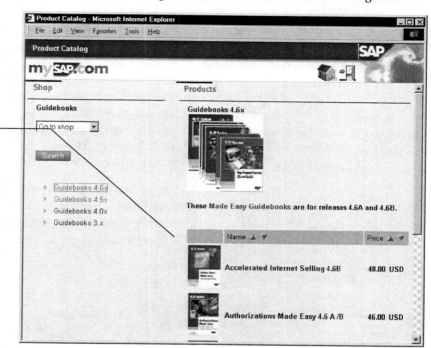

11. To display the PDF file, Alan chooses the PDF hyperlink.

Additional files related to the product, such as PDF files, can be displayed or downloaded.

The transaction that supports the browsing of the product catalog, without allowing shopping basket functionality, is `WW10`. Before the product catalog can be displayed on the web, it must be linked to an Online Store profile in configuration, even if online shopping is not allowed.

PDF hyperlink

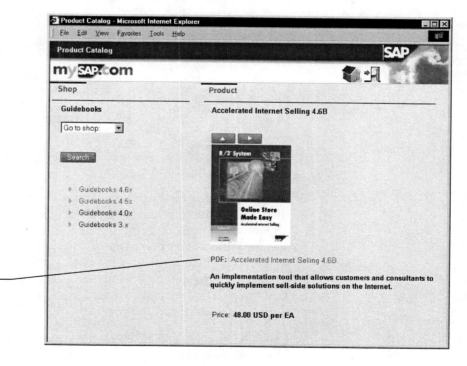

Making it Work: The Product Catalog

Product Catalogs in R/3

The product catalog allows customers to browse a company's product offerings on the web. The catalog is organized into several categories, similar to store departments, which make it simpler to find particular products. For each product, descriptions, graphics, sound files, and other types of multimedia files can be accessed on the web.

The product catalog resides within R/3. The advantage of this is that data does not need to be maintained in multiple locations (R/3 and the web server). Additionally, since the master data is taken from the R/3 System, there is no HTML work involved in adding a new product to the catalog.

Product Catalog Structure

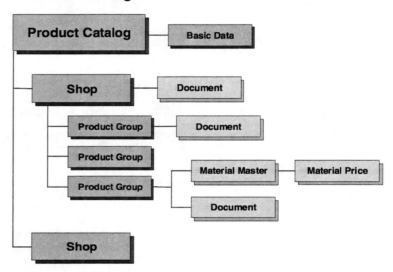

The **basic data** of the product catalog describes the data used when displaying products and when placing orders from within the Online Store. One or more variants is maintained within the basic data. A variant is the combination of language and currency in which the products can be displayed. The product catalog basic data also contains the sales area, a pricing schema determination procedure, and a reference customer. The reference customer master record is copied when a new customer registers on the Internet.

Once the basic data is in place, the structure, or layout, is built. On the first level, the product catalog is divided into **shops**. A document from the Document Management System (DMS) can be linked to a shop in the product catalog layout. The **document** contains information that references images to be displayed, sound files to be played, and other data files to be accessed from the web. Products should not be linked to the catalog at this level, because they cannot be displayed on the web.

The shops are further divided by **product groups**, which may themselves have subordinate product groups. Documents can also be linked to the product groups, but small images are not displayed at this level.

At the lowest level of the catalog structure, **material master records** are linked to the product groups. Once a material has been linked to a product group, subordinate product groups can no longer be created. The materials linked to the product group use the prices already maintained in the R/3 System. Documents are again used to reference the images and other files on the web server that should be displayed for each material master record.

Assigning Products to the Catalog

The product catalog structure is most often created manually. It is also possible to copy the catalog structure, together with products, from the classification system.

Once the catalog structure has been created, material master records can be manually assigned to the product catalog. It is possible to automate this process by copying materials into the catalog from a class in the classification system or from a material group.

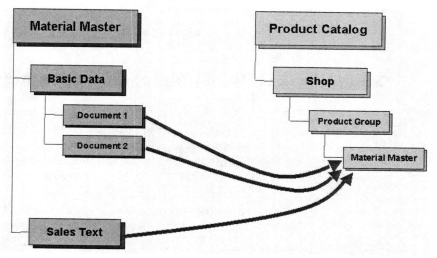

When a material is assigned to a product group, data from the master record may be copied into the product catalog. The rules that determine the data copied are defined by the product catalog type. The data that can be copied includes any text in the material master and any documents linked to the master record.

The data is copied to the product catalog at the time the material master record is assigned to a product group. Once the data has been copied, manual changes can be made in the product catalog. The copy procedure is a one-time occurrence. Any changes made to the material master after the data has been copied are not automatically reflected in the product catalog, or vice versa.

Accessing the Product Catalog

When the product catalog is ready for use, it is linked to an Online Store in configuration. Multiple Online Stores may be displayed on the web. Selecting an Online Store displays the product catalog structure and its materials. It is possible to use the same product catalog as the base master data for several different Online Stores. Please refer to chapter 1, "Creating the Online Store with the Catalog" on page 5 for details about the links between the product catalog and the Online Store profiles.

Master Data in R/3 to Support the Product Catalog

To set up master data in R/3 to support the product catalog, you need to perform the steps as described in the next sections. You must:

- Create documents in R/3 that reference image and data files

- Add data to the material master that can be copied automatically into the product catalog

- Create the product catalog master data within R/3

Create Documents in R/3 that Reference Image and Data Files

Documents from the Document Management System (DMS) within R/3 are needed to display image and other files on the web in the product catalog. A document is used to reference the location and filename of the graphics, sound, and data files related to the products in the catalog. These files do not reside within R/3, but are stored on the web server. The steps below describe how to create a document in the Document Management System, using the document type delivered with the Online Store preconfiguration. This example demonstrates how the location of these files is identified.

Task

Create documents for files to display a product or product catalog structure

1. In the *Command* field, enter transaction **CV01N** and choose *Enter* (or from the navigation menu, choose *Logistics → Materials Management → Product Catalog → Environment → Document Management → Document → Create*).

2. On the *Create Document: Initial Screen*:

    a. In *Document*, you may enter a document ID. If you leave this field blank, the system assigns a number.

    b. In *Document type*, enter **Y01**.

    c. In the *Document part,* enter **000**.

    d. In *Document version,* enter **00**.

    e. Choose 🗸 .

> **Note**
>
> Zeros are used in steps **c** and **d** because this document type does not use status and version functionality.

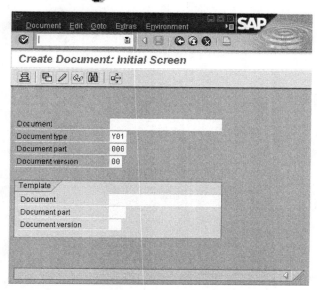

3. On the *Create Document: Basic Data e-Shop Prod Catalog (Y01)* screen:

    a. In *Description*, describe the document.

    b. Near the bottom of the screen, under the *Originals* section, choose 📄 .

Enter a description to later help you locate the document. This description will not be displayed on the Internet.

The create icon used to reach the next screen is located under the *Originals* section.

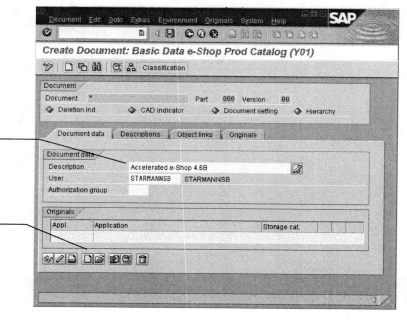

4. On the *Create Document* dialog box:

    a. In *Applic.*, enter the application of the file (for example, **LIM** references a GIF or JPG graphic).

    b. In *Data carrier*, enter **YESHOP**. This data carrier points to the ITS WGate directory on the web server. The data carrier is case-sensitive.

    c. In *Original,* enter the filename that you wish to reference on the web. The entire filename, including the file extension, must be entered.

    d. Choose ✅ .

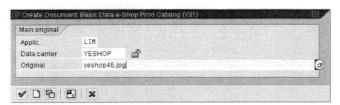

5. Returning to the *Create Document: Basic Data e-Shop Prod Catalog (Y01)* screen, at the bottom of the screen choose 🗋 .

If you need to change the entry, select it and choose 🔳 .

Note that the actual image may be displayed, provided the **PC** carrier type has been configured, by selecting the line and choosing 👓 .

The new entry is displayed. ————

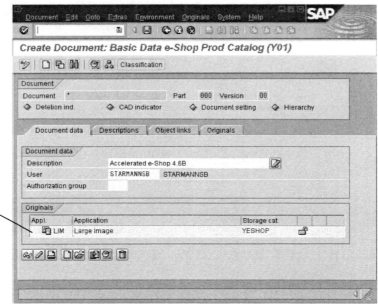

6. On the *Create Document* dialog box:

    a. Follow the instructions in step **4** to complete the data.

    b. Choose ✅ .

Note

Only two documents can be assigned to this document type.

If additional files need to be linked to the same product or product group in the product catalog, an additional document needs to be created to store the file links.

7. Returning to the *Create Document: Basic Data e-Shop Prod Catalog (Y01)* screen, choose 💾 .

Another file is linked to the document, this time a small graphic. Small images are displayed in the product list, while large images and other data files are displayed on the detail screen on the web.

8. The document ID number appears in the status bar.

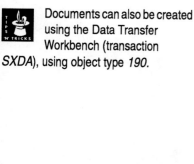

Documents can also be created using the Data Transfer Workbench (transaction *SXDA*), using object type *190*.

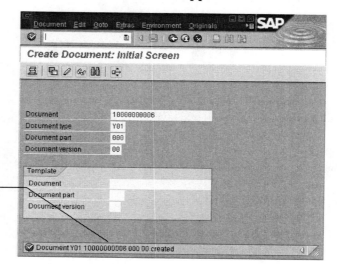

Since no document ID was specified at the beginning of this transaction, the system uses the internal number range to assign the document number.

Add Data to Material Master for Automatic Copying into Product Catalog

 This is an optional step. If the appropriate data is maintained in the material master, a one-time copy occurs to the product catalog when the material master is assigned. If this data is not maintained, it must be manually added directly in the product catalog.

To allow for an easier product catalog setup, data can be copied from the material master records into the catalog, a process that occurs when the product is linked to a product group in the catalog. The material master records need to be updated to include the information that should be copied into the catalog. If the Online Store preconfiguration is implemented together with the Preconfigured Client in a fresh install, the appropriate master data settings are delivered in the sample products created by the CATT procedure *ZESHOP_PROD_CATALOG*. Please refer to appendix H, "Introduction to Computer-Aided Test Tools (CATTs)" on page 547 for details about the CATT procedure.

Only the data in the material master record that can be automatically copied into the product catalog is discussed.

Task

Change the material master to include all data

1. In the *Command* field, enter transaction **MM02** and choose *Enter* (or from the navigation menu, choose *Logistics → Materials Management → Material Master → Material → Change → Immediately*).

2. On the *Change Material (Initial Screen)*:

    a. In *Material*, enter the material number you wish to link to a product group in the product catalog.

    b. Choose *Select view(s)*.

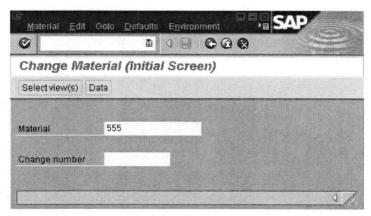

3. On the *Select View(s)* screen:

    a. Select the *Basic Data 1* and *Sales Text* views.

    b. Choose ✅.

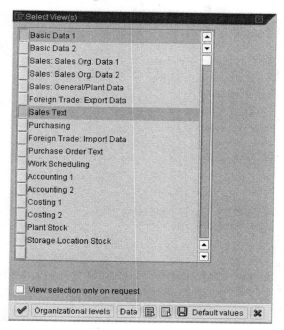

4. On the *Organizational Levels* dialog box:

    a. In *Plant,* enter the primary delivery plant of the material for Internet orders.

    b. In *Sales org.,* enter the sales organization you are using for Internet orders.

    c. In *Distr. Channel,* enter the distribution channel you are using for Internet orders.

    d. Choose ✅.

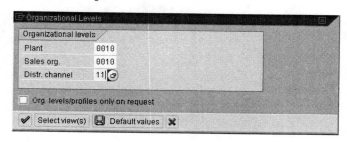

5. On the *Change Material xxx (Semifinished products)* screen:

   a. Choose ➡ *Additional data*.

   b. On the revised screen, choose the *Documents data* tab.

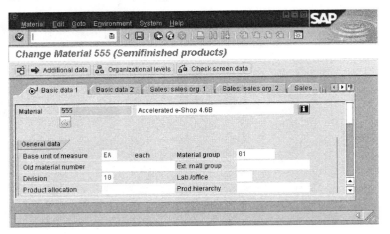

6. On the *Document data* tab:

   a. Enter the documents that reference the image and data files on the web server. The complete document data, including the type, number, version, and status, must be entered.

   b. Choose ⬅ *Main data*.

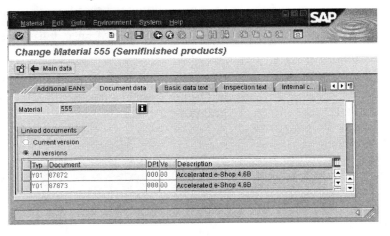

7. Choose ✅ on the *Change Material <XXX>(Semifinished products)* screen.

8. On the *Sales text* tab:

   a. Enter the sales text in the box on the lower portion of the screen.

   b. Choose 🖫 .

The sales text should be automatically copied into the product catalog when this product is linked to the catalog structure. The product catalog type determines whether this copying function occurs and for which long text. Some product catalog types may be configured to copy the basic data or purchase order text.

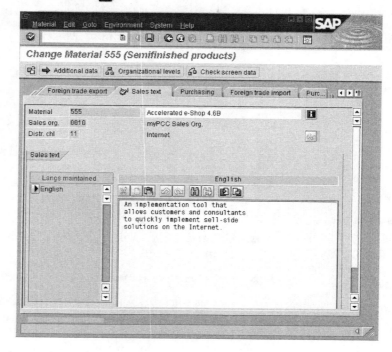

Create the Product Catalog Master Data Within R/3

The product catalog master data needs to be created within R/3 before it can be displayed on the Internet. If you implement the Online Store preconfiguration together with the Preconfigured Client in a fresh install, a sample product catalog is delivered by running the CATT procedure *ZESHOP_PROD_CATALOG*. Please refer to appendix H, "Introduction to Computer-Aided Test Tools (CATTs)" on page 547 for details about the CATT procedure.

> **Task**

Create the product catalog master within R/3

1. In the *Command* field, enter transaction **WWM1** and choose *Enter* (or from the navigation menu, choose *Logistics → Materials Management → Product Catalog → Product Catalog → Create*).

2. On the *Create Product Catalog: Initial Screen*:

   a. In *Catalog*, enter the catalog you wish to create.

Note

The catalog type determines which texts and documents are copied from the material master record when products are linked to the catalog structure.

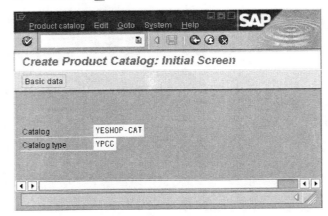

b. In *Catalog type*, enter the product catalog type.

c. Choose ✅ .

Note

In step **3a**, the schema is treated as the document procedure for determining the pricing procedure. The pricing procedure is used to find the prices displayed on the web while browsing the catalog.

Note

In step **3b**, when a new Internet customer registers, the data from this customer is copied to create the new customer. Only the data entered by the customer on the Internet is replaced, such as address data. In configuration, you can determine whether this customer, or one in the Online Store configuration, is used as a base for creating the new customer.

Note

In step **3f**, the variant defines the combination of language and currency of the product catalog for display on the Internet. The same catalog can have multiple variants, in which case the text must be maintained in all languages available here.

3. On the *Product Catalog: Create Basic Data* screen:

a. Under *Data relevant to prices*, in *Document schema*, enter the document schema.

b. In *Ref. customer*, enter the reference customer.

c. Under *Sales area*, enter the appropriate information for *Sales org. Distr.chl.*, and *Division* that you will use for your Internet business. All customers, products, and prices need to be created for this sales area. All sales orders created from the product catalog will be created using this sales area. Usually a new distribution channel is used only to differentiate Internet orders.

d. Select *Display prices*. This checkbox allows you to see the prices for the products as you maintain the product catalog links within R/3. This selection does not affect whether prices are displayed on the Internet.

e. In *Display currency*, enter the currency in which you wish to display prices during product catalog maintenance within R/3. This selection does not affect the currency displayed on the Internet.

f. Under *Var.* (variant), enter the variant number.

g. Under *L* (language), enter the language for the variant.

h. In *Curr.*, enter the currency for the variant.

i. Choose *Layout*.

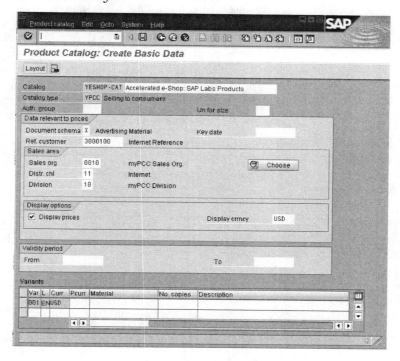

4. On the *Exit basic data processing* dialog box, choose *Yes* to save the product catalog before continuing.

5. On the *Product Catalog: Maintain Layout* screen:

    a. The highest layout level is automatically created. Select it with your cursor.

    b. Choose 📄 .

The 📠 *Hier. Suggestion* button may be used to manually copy a class from the classification system, with associated materials, into the product catalog.

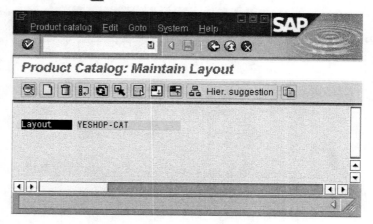

6. On the *Product Catalog: Maintain Base Layout Area* screen:

    a. In *Area,* enter a description. This description will not be displayed on the Internet.

    b. If an image, sound, or data file should be accessible from the web for this shop, place your cursor on the description and choose *Documents,* or double-click on the *Documents* checkbox.

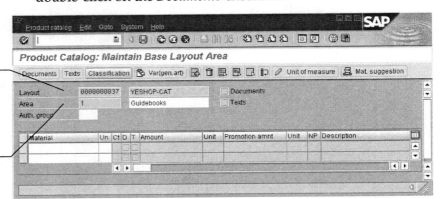

A new layout is created that is subordinate to the prior layout. The *Layout* number is unique to the entire product catalog. At this level, the layout is referred to as a "shop."

The *Area* specifies the shops and product groups within the catalog layout. In the standard system, each area is numbered sequentially in the order it is created, within the layout.

7. On the *Layout area - Link to Documents* screen:

    a. In the *Typ* (type), column, enter document type **Y01**.

    b. Under *Document,* enter the document number(s) that you wish to link to the shop.

    c. Choose ✓ .

Note

In the Online Store preconfiguration, the document part (DPt) and document version (Vs) funtionality is not used and should contain zeros.

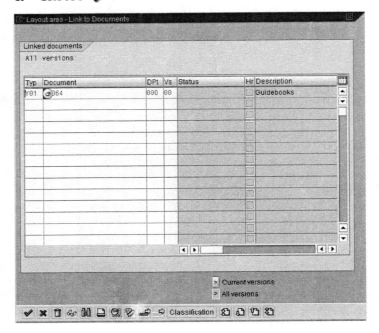

8. On the *Product Catalog: Maintain Base Layout Area* screen, to maintain the text displayed on the web for this shop, double-click on the *Texts* checkbox.

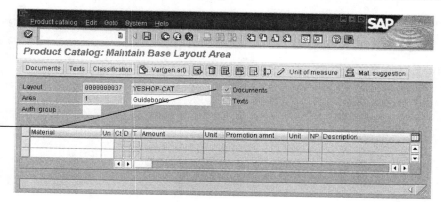

The *Documents* checkbox is now automatically selected, indicating that a document has been linked.

9. On the *Product Catalog: Maintain Texts* screen, choose ↩.

The short text, or *Title*, appears on the web as the short description.

The *Long txt* will appear on the shop's overview screen on the web.

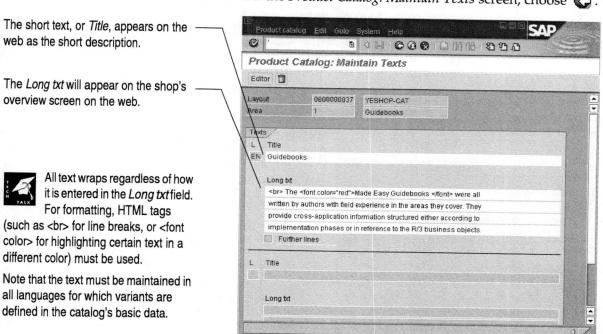

All text wraps regardless of how it is entered in the *Long txt* field. For formatting, HTML tags (such as <br> for line breaks, or <font color> for highlighting certain text in a different color) must be used.

Note that the text must be maintained in all languages for which variants are defined in the catalog's basic data.

10. On the *Product Catalog: Maintain Base Layout Area* screen, choose 💾.

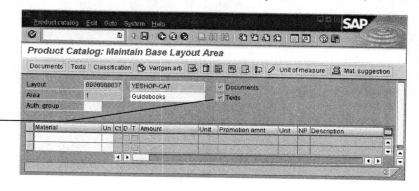

Note that the *Texts* checkbox is now selected, indicating that text has been maintained.

11. On the *Product Catalog: Maintain Layout* screen:

   a. Select the newly created shop.

   b. Choose 🗋 .

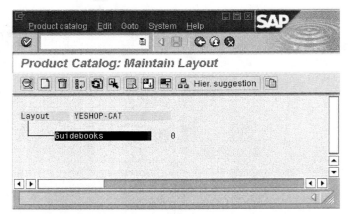

12. On the *Create Layout Area* dialog box:

   a. Choose whether to create a new:

     • Shop – Select *same place, below*

     • Product group – Select *lower level, first place*

   b. Choose ✔ .

13. On the *Product Catalog: Maintain Base Layout Area* screen, the same steps should be taken to create text and link documents for this layout area:

   a. In the *Material* column, enter the material numbers of the products that should be linked to this product group.

The SD prices of the material are determined based on the pricing procedure found through the document schema of the basic data, and are displayed in the currency from the *Basic data* screen.

b. Choose 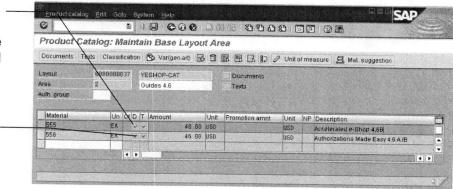 . The prices of the materials are found, and any existing documents and texts are copied from the material master at this time.

c. To display the document, select the product with your cursor and choose *Documents*, or double-click on the checkbox in column *D*.

To display the text displayed on the web for this product, place your cursor on the product and choose *Texts*, or double-click on the checkbox in column *T*.

The checkbox in column *D* (Document) is automatically selected, indicating that one or more documents are already linked to the product. These are copied from the material master, based on the configuration of the product catalog type.

The checkbox in column *T* (Text) is automatically selected, indicating that text is already maintained for the product. The text is copied from the material master, based on the configuration of the product catalog type.

14. On the *Layout area items - Link to Documents* screen, choose 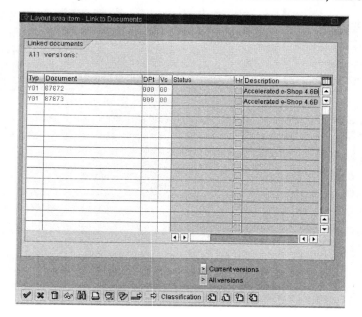 .

The documents from the material master record have been copied. The assignment can now be manually changed within the product catalog.

Note that these changes do not affect the material master. Also, future changes to the material master are not automatically reflected in the product catalog.

15. On the *Product Catalog: Maintain Texts* screen, choose 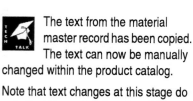.

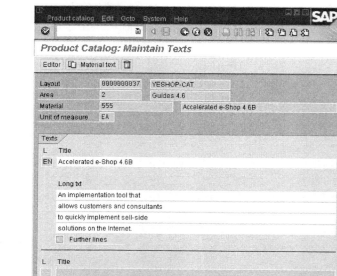

 The text from the material master record has been copied. The text can now be manually changed within the product catalog.

Note that text changes at this stage do not affect the material master. Also, future changes to the material master are not automatically reflected in the product catalog.

16. From the *Product Catalog: Maintain Base Layout Area* screen, choose 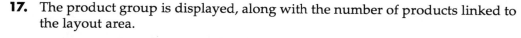 .

17. The product group is displayed, along with the number of products linked to the layout area.

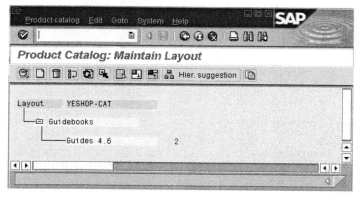

It is possible to create the product catalog in one of the following ways:

- Using a manual process, as described in the previous section
- Using the product catalog data load provided with the Online Store preconfiguration
- Using the standard-delivered BAPIs for your data load (please refer to the end of this chapter for details about data loads)
- Copying from the classification system for the product catalog structure and material assignments
- Copying from material groups for material assignments
- Copying from layout modules for material assignments
- Note that copying from promotions is only possible in an IS-Retail installation.

Configuration to Support the Product Catalog

Note

For changes that we deliver for the look and feel of the product catalog functionality, and instructions on how to make changes to the ITS Business HTML templates, please refer to chapter 14, "ITS Templates" on page 327.

The configuration steps listed below for supporting the product catalog are described in detail in the following sections. You must configure the:

- Number ranges for the document type (standard-delivered)
- Document type used for the product catalog (preconfigured)
- Data carrier that locates the files on the web server (preconfigured)
- Workstation applications (preconfigured)
- Product catalog type (preconfigured)
- Link the product catalog master data to an Online Store
- Check the SAPNet - R/3 Frontend Notes

Configure the Number Ranges for the Document Type

The number ranges for the documents in the DMS (document management system) allow both internal and external ranges. If you enter a number, the system checks to see whether it is in the correct number range. If you do not enter a document number, an internal sequential number is assigned.

In the *Command* field, enter transaction **OD00** and choose *Enter* (or in the IMG, choose *Cross-Application Components* → *Document Management System* → *Control Data* and choose ⊕ next to *Define document types*). The table below shows the number ranges to which the document type is assigned. No changes have been made to the R/3 standard-delivered number ranges.

Number Range	From Number	To Number	External Indicator
01	00000000000000000001	00000000000000999999	X (external)
02	00000000010000000000	00009999999999999999	Blank (internal)

Configure the Document Type Used for the Product Catalog

To support the product catalog, the document type used for the product catalog needs to be configured. This step is preconfigured for you.

Task

Configure the document type used for the product catalog

1. In the IMG, choose *Cross-Application Components* → *Document Management System* → *Control Data* and choose ⊕ next to *Define document types*.

2. On the *Change View "Define document types": Overview* screen, choose 🖳 .

3. On the *Change View "Define document types": Details* screen:

a. With the deselection of the *Status change* checkbox, status management is turned off.

b. With the deselection of the *Version assign.* checkbox, version management is turned off.

c. An internal and external number range is assigned. If the user does not enter a document number, the system assigns one automatically.

The document type delivered with the Online Store preconfiguration is shown on this screen. The most critical configuration settings are described.

For the field selection, class data is displayed. The user creating the document, the authorization group, and the two workstation (WS) applications are optional. All other fields are suppressed.

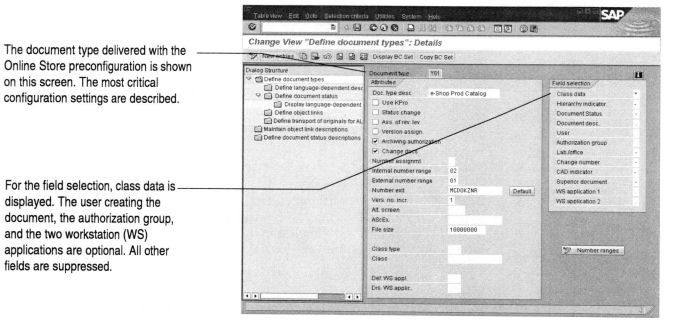

d. In the navigation menu, choose *Define language-dependent descriptions*. For document type *Y01*, the following descriptions were defined:

Language	Description
DE	e-Shop Layoutdoku
EN	e-Shop Prod Catalog

e. In the navigation menu, choose *Define object links*. For document type *Y01*, the following links are allowed:

Object	Object Description	Screen Number
MARA	Material master	201
TWGLV	Layout area	229
TWML	Layout module	230
WLBM	Layout area item	228

All other options for the object links are blank, or not activated.

Configure the Data Carrier that Locates Files on the Web Server

To support the product catalog, the data carrier that locates the files on the web server must be configured. This step is preconfigured for you. Two data carriers have been preconfigured:

- *WS* – Defines the web server directory on which the image and data files are located

- *PC* – Allows the image and data files from the web server to be accessed from within the R/3 document in the Document Management System (DMS)

Task

Configure the data carrier to locate files on the web server

1. Use the following path in the IMG: *Cross-Application Components – Document Management System → General Data* and choose ⊕ next to *Define data carrier.*

2. On the *Information* dialog box, choose ✔ .

3. Double-click the node *Define data carrier type "server, front end."*

Carrier Type	Description	Path
PC	PC workstation	c:\
WS	Webserver	

4. Select carrier type *WS,* and double-click on the node *Define servers and files or folders.* The data carrier is case-sensitive.

Data Carrier	Carrier Type	Description
YESHOP	WS	Data carrier for e-commerce

5. Choose ⟵ .

6. Select carrier type *PC,* and double-click on the node *Identify frontend computers.*

Field	Value
Frontend Computer	Default
Data carrier type	PC
Network address	DEFAULT
Description	Default for local PC

7. Choose ⟵ .

8. Double-click on the node *Define mount points/logical drive*. The settings under this option define the directory of the location of the ITS WGate on the web server.

Data Carrier	Carrier Type	Path
YESHOP	PC	j:/y_images/
YESHOP	WS	/sap/its/y_images/

The path for data carrier *WS* is found automatically through the ITS configuration, since it is designed as the appropriate data carrier in the Online Store configuration (please refer to chapter 1, "Creating the Online Store with the Catalog" on page 5).

The path for data carrier *PC* only locates the files on the web server if a mapping has been made to the web server using the local Windows® or Windows NT® Explorer. This configuration is not required for the appropriate files to be accessed on the web server. It allows for the multimedia files to be displayed during the creation of a document in R/3.

Configure the Workstation Applications

To support the product catalog, the workstation applications must be configured. This step is preconfigured for you. Linking the workstation applications to the *PC* data carrier allows you to display the graphics you plan to use in the product catalog while creating each document, provided a network link to the web server exists. This configuration is not required for the appropriate files to be accessed on the web server.

Task

Configure workstation applications

1. In the IMG, choose *Cross-Application Components – Document Management System → General Data* and choose 🕒 next to *Define workstation application*.

2. Select *LIM, PDF, SIM,* and *SND,* and double-click on the node *Define workstation application in network*.

Data Carrier Type	Application	Description	Application Type	Application Path
PC	LIM	Large Image	1 (display)	%auto%
PC	LIM	Large Image	2 (change)	%auto%
PC	LIM	Large Image	3 (print)	%auto%
PC	SIM	Small Image	1 (display)	%auto%
PC	SIM	Small Image	2 (change)	%auto%
PC	SIM	Small Image	3 (print)	%auto%
PC	PDF	Acrobat Reader	1 (display)	%auto%

Data Carrier Type	Application	Description	Application Type	Application Path
PC	PDF	Acrobat Reader	2 (change)	%auto%
PC	PDF	Acrobat Reader	3 (print)	%auto%
PC	SND	Sound	1 (display)	%auto%
PC	SND	Sound	2 (change)	%auto%
PC	SND	Sound	3 (print)	%auto%

The image files are defined for *JPG* and *GIF* images only.

Note that *LIM*, *SIM*, and *SND* have been translated in the Online Store preconfiguration. Other than the link to the *PC* data carrier, no other changes have been made to the standard-delivered workstation applications.

Configure the Product Catalog Type

To support the product catalog, the product catalog type must be configured. This step is preconfigured for you. The product catalog type determines which fields are populated automatically in the catalog at the time the products are linked to the catalog layout. Two product catalog types are preconfigured for the following scenarios:

- *YPCB* – Selling to business partners

- *YPCC* – Selling to consumers

Task

Configure the product catalog type

1. In the IMG, choose *Logistics – General* → *Product Catalog Basic Data* and choose 🕹 next to *Maintain Product Catalog Type.*

2. Configure the basic parameters for the node *Maintain Product Catalog.* For each product catalog type, additional settings can be configured by double-clicking on *Adoption of Document Links at Creation.*

Field	YPCB	YPCC
Copy heading	On	On
Copy long text	4 (copy PO text)	2 (copy SD text)
Adoption of document links at creation	Document type Y01	Document type Y01

The other settings in this table are only relevant to IS-Retail installations, and are therefore not discussed here. These fields include the P.O. number determination, promotions, and generic articles.

Link the Product Catalog Master Data to an Online Store

The product catalog must be linked to an Online Store in configuration in order to be visible on the Internet. This is true, even if shopping basket functionality will not be used on the Internet.

Use the following path in the IMG to view the configuration of the Online Stores: *Logistics - General → IAC Product Catalog and Online Store* and choose ⊕ next to *Online Stores*. Please refer to chapter 1, "Creating the Online Store with the Catalog" on page 5 for details about this configuration.

Check the SAPNet – R/3 Frontend Notes

Information from SAPNet – R/3 Frontend notes (formerly OSS) is also essential to the configuration of sales order status. Please refer to appendix A, "SAPNet Frontend Notes" on page 495 for informational notes related to the product catalog.

Data Load for the Product Catalog

Prerequisites

The product catalog data load assumes that all necessary master data has already been created.

If you have not yet implemented the SAP R/3 System, you need to consider data load in the following areas, all of which are handled in the Data Transfer Workbench:

- Material master
- Customer master
- Material prices
- Document Management System

If you are already live with your system using Financial Accounting (FI), Materials Management (MM), and SD, and are using the Online Store preconfiguration as an add-on, you need to consider a data load for document management before the product catalog can be created. If you choose a different organizational area within SD, such as a new distribution channel, you also need to extend your customer and material master data, as well as your prices.

The data load can be accomplished in two ways, with either:

- A data load program provided by the Online Store preconfiguration package. This program should be used as a one-time load of the catalog.

- BAPIs in the standard delivery of the R/3 System. This should be used if ALE and IDoc scenarios will be implemented.

Data Load Program

The product catalog load program has been integrated in the Data Transfer Workbench, as object number *0320*. This load program directly updates the product catalog tables and is therefore much faster than other techniques. However, it performs minimal validations and expects that the data input file provided is accurate.The program documentation describes the technical details, such as the structure of the input file.

Task

Use the data load program to directly create the product catalog tables

1. In the *Command* field, enter transaction **SXDA_OLD** and choose *Enter* to start the Data Transfer Workbench.

2. On the next screen:

   a. In *Data transfer object*, enter **0320**, the product catalog number.

   b. Choose ✅ .

3. On the main *Data Transfer Workbench* screen:

   a. Under *Application server*, in *Phys file name*, enter a filename.

   b. Choose 🗋 .

   c. Choose 🐎

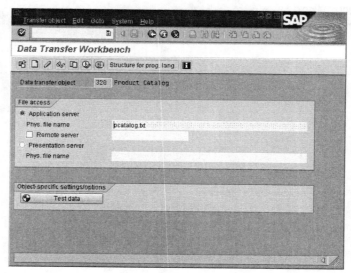

4. On the *File: _Transactions* screen, choose 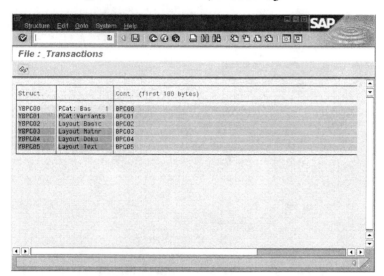.

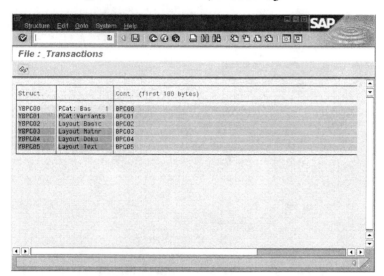

 The details of the structures and format of the data to be provided is documented in program documentation of ABAP report *YPCC_PRODCAT_DILOAD*.

5. After reviewing the structures on the *Generic structure editor* screen, in which the product catalog data has to be provided, choose 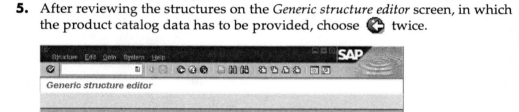 twice.

 Use either third-party tools or the LSMW workbench, downloadable from the SAPNet, to convert your product catalog into the input file format required by the load program.

6. On the *Data Transfer Workbench* screen:

a. Once the input file is created, enter that name in *Phys file name* under *Application server*.

b. Choose ⊕ .

 Please note that the product catalog load program supports "create mode" only. If the target system has a product catalog with the same name as the input file, the product catalog in the target system is first deleted and then the new product catalog—based on the input file—is created.

7. On the *ProdCat: Load program using Direct Input* screen, the system asks you to confirm the filename. Reenter and choose ⊕ to load.

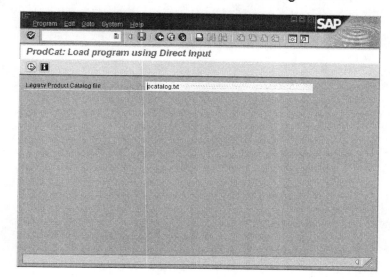

BAPIs for Data Load

 If you need to create the product catalog only once, we recommend that you use the load program. It is much easier to complete in fewer steps. However, there could be a need to look at ALE scenarios if you need to exchange the product catalog with other systems or if you want to integrate third-party search engines such as Alta Vista.

As of R/3 Release 4.6x, BAPIs and ALE scenarios have been provided that can also be used for data load of the product catalog. The two provided BAPIs create the product catalog:

- **Header information** – *SaveHeadReplica* creates the basic data and structure of the product catalog. The corresponding IDoc is *PCHEAD*.

- **Items information** – *SaveItemsReplica* creates the items in the product catalog with the long text. The corresponding IDoc is *PCITEMS*. Please note that the documents are linked with this BAPI and therefore have to be a separate task. Look up the methods supported by the "DRAW" object.

To make use of BAPIs directly or through ALE scenarios, you need to convert the legacy data in the IDoc formats. The whole process takes two steps—first for the basic data and the structure and second for the items.

For details about the Data Transfer Workbench, please refer to the *Data Transfer Made Easy Guidebook*. You can find out more information at *www.saplabs.com/dx*.

Prices in the Product Catalog

Overview

While browsing the product catalog on the web, the customer can look at descriptions of the features and the currently valid prices for each product. The price of each product displayed in the catalog may be a standard price or a current sale price.

The prices displayed on the Internet use the normal pricing functionality within the R/3 System. Each company has the choice of using either the same pricing valid for all orders, or special discounted prices for Internet sales. It may be advantageous to offer discounts on products if customers purchase them through the web, since this method of advertising and selling a product frees up customer service representatives and reduces the transactional cost of placing orders.

What We Deliver

In the Online Store preconfiguration, we provide the following deliverables:

- Preconfiguration of pricing procedures that work with the Internet

- Instructions on how to change your pricing procedures (for existing installations)

- Incoterms and sample rates for the freight calculation

- Preconfiguration of the ITS look and feel and the service file parameter to incorporate pricing breakouts

- Modifications to the R/3 System and ITS templates to support the selection of a shipping method in the Online Store

- Documentation on the pricing functionality of the product catalog

The Customer Experience

In browsing the product catalog, the prices are displayed, including sales prices. During checkout, the complete price breakdown, including freight and taxes, is displayed. These values are the same ones calculated for the sales order created in R/3.

1. In the Internet browser, our customer, Desiree, enters the URL of the home page you configured as part of the ITS installation.

2. She chooses the *Online Store* from your home page.

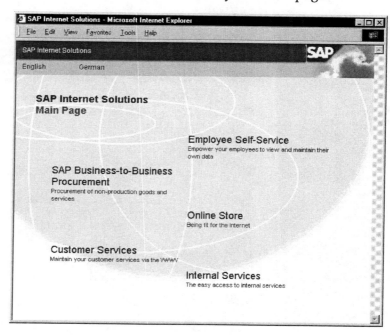

3. Desiree chooses *Online Store*.

Online Store —————————

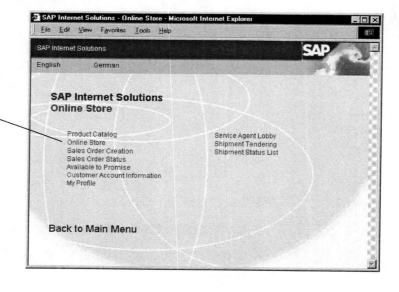

4. Desiree chooses the first store, *YGUIDES-B*, *SAP Labs Guidebooks for Bus. Partners*.

A list of the different available stores is displayed.

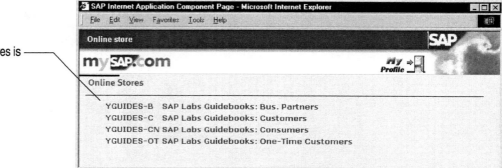

5. A logon is required before the catalog can be browsed.

a. Desiree enters her e-mail address.

b. She enters her password to log on to the Online Store.

c. She chooses *Login*.

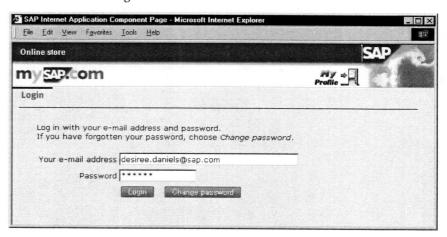

6. Desiree chooses the *Guidebooks* shop.

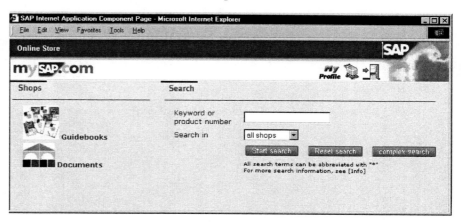

7. She chooses the *Guidebooks 4.5* product group.

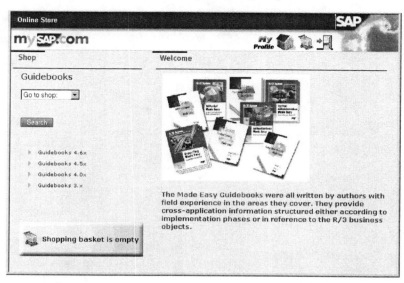

8. The list of guidebooks is displayed. Desiree chooses the first product, *Accelerated Internet Selling 4.5B*, to obtain more details.

A list of the *4.5x Made Easy Guidebooks* product group is displayed.

Note that the prices displayed are not specific to the customer who has logged on.

The first product is currently on sale, as indicated by the *Special Offer* icon.

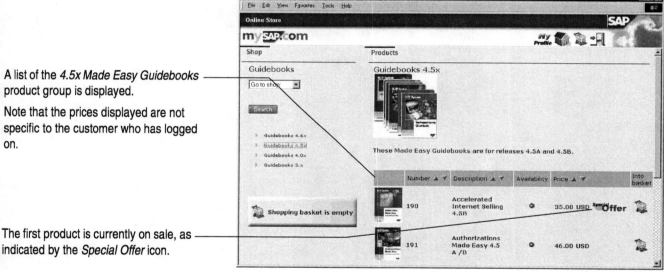

9.   Desiree places the product into the shopping basket.

The original price, as well as the sale price, are displayed. The *Special Offer* icon also remains on the screen.

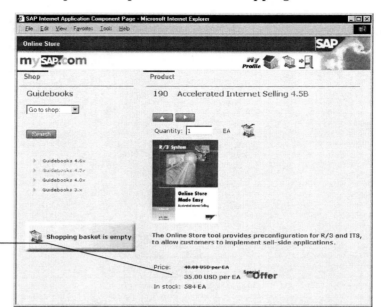

10.   Desiree chooses the shopping cart.

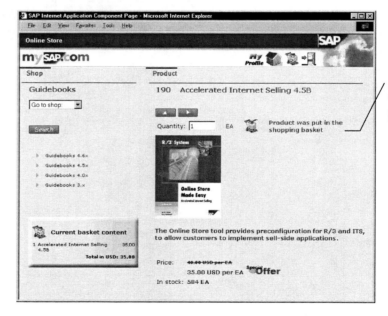

A message confirms the product was placed into the basket

11. To obtain a more accurate price breakdown:

    a. Desiree chooses overnight delivery instead of the defaulted standard shipping.

    b. To begin the ordering process, she chooses *Quotation*.

Quotation button

The purchase order is not displayed on the subsequent screen if none is entered here.

A list of the products and the quantity ordered is displayed. The sale price of the second item is the final price.

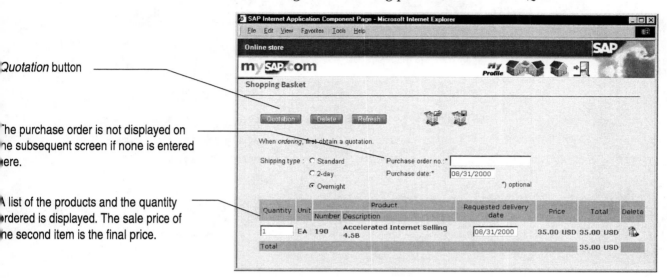

12. She places the order by choosing *Order*.

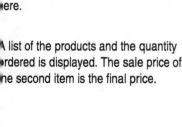

The price of the ordered products is displayed. An additional discount being applied to the order is also displayed.

The price reduction is not a customer-specific price or a sale price; it is a discount specific to the customer or to all customers as a special promotion. This discount is not displayed while scrolling the product catalog.

Freight is calculated based on the chosen shipping method (Incoterms) and the weight of the products.

The taxes may be calculated using R/3 or an external tax package.

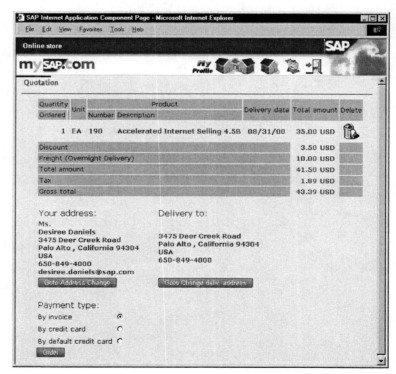

13. The order number created in R/3 is displayed. The price breakdown is again
displayed.

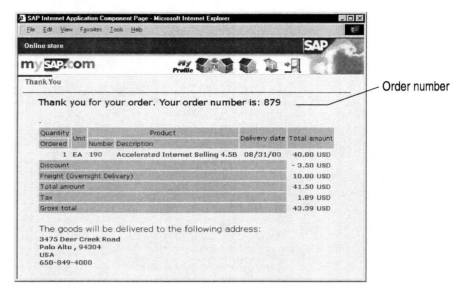

Order number

The View from Inside your Company

The order created over the Internet is now available from inside your
company.

Task

View the order inside the company

1. In the *Command* field, enter transaction **VA03** and choose *Enter* (or from the
navigation menu, choose *Logistics → Sales and Distribution → Sales → Order*
→ Display).

2. On the *Display Sales Order: Initial Screen*:

a. In *Order*, enter the number of the order created from the Internet.

b. Choose ✅ .

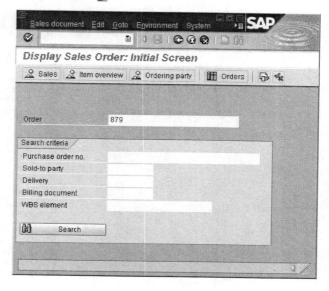

3. On the *Display e-Shop Web Order xxx: Overview* screen, choose *Goto → Header → Conditions* from the menu bar.

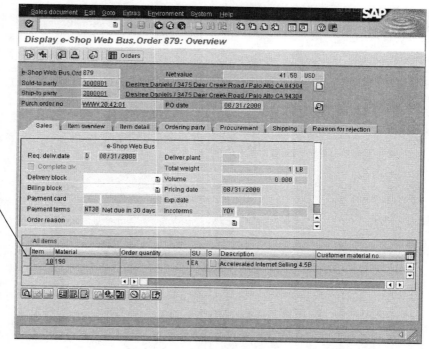

The item purchased on the Internet is displayed.

4. On the *Display e-Shop Web Order <XXX>: Header Data* screen:

a. Review the information on screen.

b. Choose 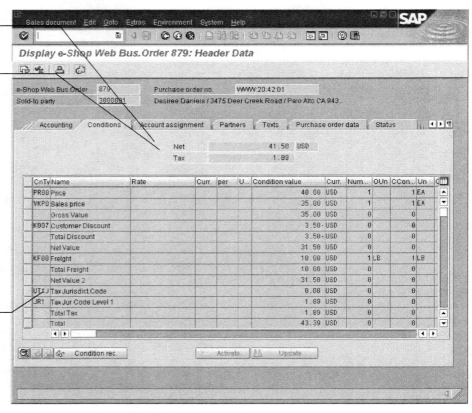.

The *Net* value corresponds to the *Total without tax* line on the Internet.

The *Tax* value corresponds to the *Tax* line on the Internet.

At the header level, all price conditions for the items are summarized.

The discount, freight, and tax values are displayed for the entire order, not by line item. These values from the web are added together based on the value of the line items. In the pricing procedure, subtotal **3** is configured to display the discounts on the Internet. Subtotal **4** is configured to display the freight.

The *Total Tax* (subtotal **5**) and *Total* (subtotal **6**) are calculated to be the same as the values on the Internet, so that these values can be captured by SIS in the preconfiguration. The total displayed on the Internet is calculated by adding the *Net* and *Tax* values.

5. On the *Display e-Shop Web Order <XXX>: Overview* screen:

a. Select the first item purchased.

b. At the bottom of the screen, choose 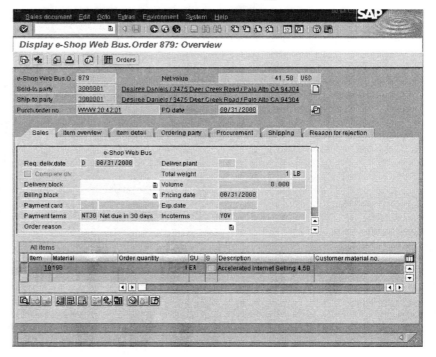.

6. On the *Display e-Shop Web Order <XXX>: Item Data* screen:

   a. Review the information on the *Conditions* tab. See below.

   b. Choose the *Billing* tab.

The normal price, represented by condition type *PR00*, is displayed. This price is designated as the normal price because. In the pricing procedure, subtotal **1** is entered for this condition type.

The sales price, represented by condition type *VKP0*, is the price used for further calculations. It overrides the normal price. This price is designated as the sales price. In the pricing procedure, subtotal **2** is entered for this condition type.

The freight is calculated based on the Incoterms copied from the header to each line item. The rate created for each Incoterm is per unit of weight of the product.

7. On the *Billings* tab, the *Incoterms* copied from the header level are displayed.

The Incoterms of the sales order that are copied from the customer master may be overwritten by choosing the shipping method from the Online Store. These Incoterms are used to calculate the freight charges. They are copied from the header level to each item of the sales order.

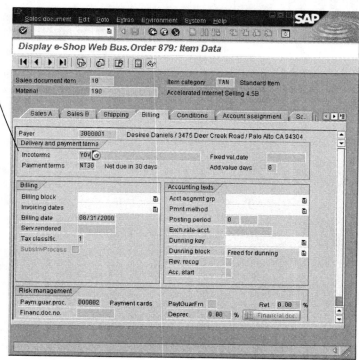

Making It Happen: Pricing in the Product Catalog

Implementation of the Online Store preconfiguration depends upon either prior installation of the Preconfigured Client (PCC) U.S., or previous implementation of a working Sales and Distribution (SD) configuration. The same pricing logic used for sales orders input manually into R/3 is also used for pricing on the web. This chapter is not intended to be a thorough discussion of how SD pricing should be configured in your system. The following sections provide a high-level overview of changes you should make to allow for effective use of these prices in your business on the Internet.

Determining the Pricing Procedure

While in the Online Store, the pricing procedure is determined in the following situations:

- When a customer browses the product catalog and prices are displayed. This option includes all browsing and the display of the final list of products before the customer begins the quotation process (up to step 11 in the previous "Customer Experience" section).

- When an order is simulated and later saved during checkout (after step 11 in the previous demonstration).

The first pricing procedure is based on the document schema in the product catalog. The second pricing procedure is based on the document schema in the sales order type. The two options in configuring this scenario are as follows:

- Both the product catalog and the sales order type used for the orders determine the same pricing procedure

- Different document schemas are used. The pricing procedure in the product catalog is leaner, containing only prices and sales prices, and no discounts, freight, or tax calculations for performance reasons. This information is only displayed during quotation and ordering during checkout.

Before the simulation and creation of the order, the pricing procedure that displays the product prices while browsing the product catalog, should be as lean as possible for performance reasons.

In the basic data of the product catalog, a document schema is entered that determines the pricing procedure for the product catalog. This pricing procedure determines the prices displayed for a customer on the Internet.

The product catalog is linked to an Online Store in configuration, so the catalog can be displayed on the web. Within the Online Store, the quotation and order profile contains the order type used to create any order a customer wishes to place. The order type, in turn, contains its own document schema for pricing. The document type's schema determines the pricing procedure used to calculate the prices for the sales order.

If the schema used in the product catalog is not the same one used to create the sales order, the prices could be different in the order than those displayed in the product catalog. Such inconsistencies could cause customers to avoid placing orders in the future. If a different pricing procedure is used, it is imperative that the resulting prices and sales prices are the same during browsing and checkout.

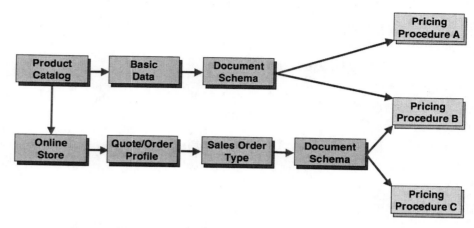

Based on the document schemas used in the product catalog and sales order type, either the same pricing procedure may be determined or a different one.

Customer-Specific Discounts

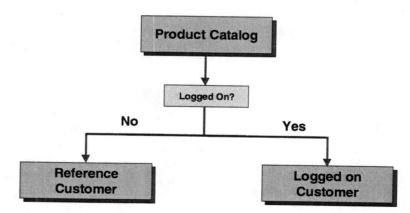

Some pricing conditions rely on the use of a customer master record, such as customer-specific prices. These are the base prices created for an individual customer. If a product catalog is set up for a late logon, a customer may browse the products before logging in. In this case, the reference customer is used for all price determinations. This reference customer is the customer entered in the Online Store in configuration. If no customer is maintained there, the reference customer in the product catalog is used.

Note

In the next release (4.6C) of the Online Store, it will be possible to display customer-specific base prices if an early logon is configured.

In the standard system, even if the product catalog is set up for an early logon, the reference customer is used for all price determination, until the order quotation is reached. Once the customer chooses to display the quotation, the detailed price breakdown displayed includes all customer-specific pricing. In this case, the customer about to place the order is used for the price determination.

Additional discounts applied to the order, such as customer-specific discounts, are also only displayed once the quotation is requested on the web. These discounts are typically valid for a shorter term than a customer-specific price. Also, the additional discount may be based on the total value of the order so that it does not apply to a specific product.

Freight Calculation

Freight is calculated when the sales order is created. The exact freight carrier charge may not be available at that time. However, since the Internet customer expects that the same amount displayed on the Internet will be charged to the credit card used for the purchase, adjustments to this value should not be made once the customer has agreed to the prices by placing the order.

Essentially, the freight must be estimated as accurately as possible. By estimation, a customer occasionally may pay a little more than the actual freight cost, but may also pay a little less the next time an order is placed. Customer confidence increases if the freight charges are close to what the perceived actual freight value is. The difference between the freight charged on a sales order and the actual payment made to the freight carrier is usually written off. If the freight is estimated accurately, the value of write-offs will be reduced. A company must make several decisions in determining the freight pricing, such as:

- Should the freight calculation be based on the value of the product ordered or on the weight? Most freight carriers charge by weight. However, if there is little difference in the weight of the different items available in the product catalog, a value-based method could be achieved. This option may not be possible if the weight difference between the products, in relation to their prices, cover too large a spread.

- Should the base prices of the products be raised, and do not charge extra for shipping. "Free" shipping has been used in advertising in many Internet stores. However, if a customer is shopping for a commodity item, and is searching for the lowest price without taking the freight into account, the sale may still be lost.

For the accurate estimation of freight to take place, the following data must be correctly maintained, especially if a weight-based method is chosen:

- Material master records must contain the accurate weight of the product. The standard pricing condition used for the Incoterms is based on the weight of the material. If the gross and net weights of the material are not maintained accurately, the freight charged to the customer will not be accurate. This inaccuracy may result in a company paying more than expected on freight, especially if the type of packaging necessary to deliver the product safely is not taken into account.

- Condition records must be maintained with the most current rates. Keep in mind that rates change regularly. You need the most up-to-date prices to calculate the freight correctly in the sales order. It may be possible to write an interface with the freight carrier's system to facilitate this integration.

Tax Calculation

 If an external tax package is used, the customer master record should always be set to taxable. The rules about which customers are truly taxable, based on the ship-to information of the order, is configured within these packages, not within R/3.

The taxes may be calculated with the logic within R/3, or by an external tax package such as Vertex or Taxware. The pricing procedure is configured differently, based on which software is used for tax calculations. A product being purchased is taxed if both the customer and product are taxable, as indicated in the customer master and material master records.

If the internal R/3 calculation is used, keep in mind that the master record of the reference customer is copied to all Internet customers who register on the web. If taxes are to be collected appropriately, a user exit must determine which customers registering on the web are truly taxable. The logic behind this process is unique to each company and their tax status.

Master Data Setup for Pricing

The following steps describe the master data that must exist in your system to support the pricing described in the initial scenario in this chapter. You must:

- Create all appropriate prices and discounts for your products (preconfigured with the PCC, or assumed to exist within your current implementation)

- Create the basic data in the product catalog with the correct document pricing schema

- Create the rates for the Incoterms for the freight calculation (preconfigured)

- Enter the default Incoterms for the reference customer in the product catalog

Create All Appropriate Prices and Discounts for Your Products

A prerequisite of the Online Store preconfiguration is either the Preconfigured Client (PCC) U.S. is being implemented at the same time, or a working SD configuration has already been implemented. The prices for the products must be created as master data in the system.

Keep in mind that customers may not log on to the Online Store until the end of the ordering process, and that some product catalogs on your web site may not have ordering capability and would not require a customer to log on.

Unless you configure an early logon in the Online Store, your prices should be based on the materials linked to the product catalog, not on customer-specific prices. Even if you do configure an early logon, customer-specific prices and customer-specific discounts are only displayed on the quotation and order confirmation screens in the Online Store in 4.6B.

Task

Create a price for the product

1. In the *Command* field, enter transaction **VK31** and choose *Enter* (or from the navigation menu, choose *Logistics → Sales and Distribution → Master Data → Conditions → Create*).

2. On the *Create Condition Records* screen:

    a. Click the *Prices* node.

    b. Double-click on 🕀 *Material Price*.

3. On the *Create Condition Records: Overview* screen, choose 🗋 next to *CnTy SORg. DChl Material*.

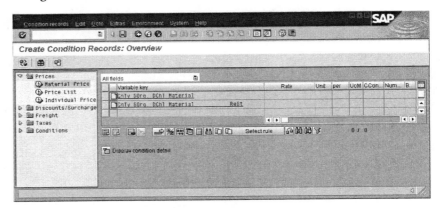

4. On the *Create Condition Records: Fast Entry* screen:

    a. Under *Co.* (condition type), enter the condition used for the price.

    b. Under *Material*, enter the product number.

    c. Under *Rate*, enter the price.

    d. Under *Unit*, the unit of measurement defaults from the material master.

    e. The *Valid on* date defaults to the current date. The *Valid to* date defaults to 12/31/9999.

 If a price should be used that is specific to a product catalog, a new condition type may be created using the product catalog code as one of the keys. This option allows each product catalog to have its own price for the products assigned to it.

f. Choose 💾 .

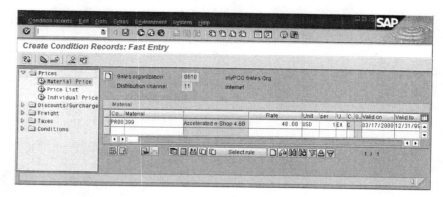

Create Basic Data in Product Catalog with Correct Document Pricing Schema

The document schema is entered into the product catalog basic data, as shown. If you use the Online Store preconfiguration in conjunction with the PCC, the CATT procedure *ZESHOP_PROD_CATALOG* creates a sample product catalog that contains the settings shown below. If you use the Online Store preconfiguration as an add-on, you need to create your product catalog manually. Please refer to chapter 2, "Creating the Product Catalog" on page 43 for details on the product catalog.

Task

Verify that the correct pricing schema and sales area are maintained in the product catalog basic data

1. To change the basic data settings in an existing product catalog, enter transaction **WWM2** in the *Command* field and choose *Enter* (or from the navigation menu, choose *Logistics → Material Management → Product Catalog → Product Catalog → Change*).

2. On the *Change Product Catalog: Initial Screen*:

a. In *Catalog*, enter the product catalog code.

b. Choose *Basic data*.

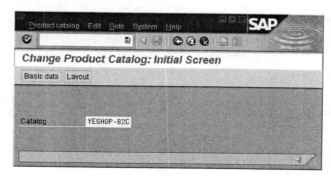

3. On the *Product Catalog: Change Basic Data* screen:

  a. The *Document schema* used in the Online Store preconfiguration is **X**.

  b. .In *Sales org.*, the sales organization used in the Online Store preconfiguration is **0010**.

  c. In *Distr. chl*, the distribution channel used in the Online Store preconfiguration is **11**.

  d. In *Division*, the division used in the Online Store preconfiguration is **10**.

The *Display prices* indicator determines whether prices are displayed in R/3 while maintaining the product catalog. Turning this indicator off would increase performance of product catalog maintenance. This indicator does not affect whether prices are displayed on the Internet.

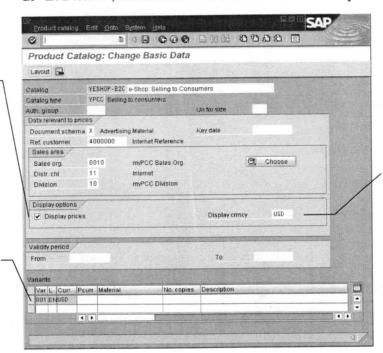

The *Display crrncy* (currency) determines the currency in which prices are displayed while maintaining the product catalog. It does not determine the currency displayed on the Internet.

The *Var* (variant) contains the language and currency combination in which prices are displayed on the Internet. The variant linked to an Online Store in configuration determines the currency displayed on the web.

Create the Rates for the Incoterms for the Freight Calculation

The steps below illustrate how the rates for the Incoterms are created. This step has been preconfigured for you when you run the CATT procedure *ZESHOP_ INCOTERMS* during installation. These steps do not need to be performed unless you choose to create additional Incoterm rates or change the existing rates. Please refer to appendix H, "Introduction to Computer-Aided Test Tools (CATTs)" on page 547 for details about the CATT procedure.

Task

Create a price for freight deliveries

1. In the *Command* field, enter transaction **VK31** and choose *Enter* (or from the navigation menu, choose *Logistics → Sales and Distribution → Master Data – Conditions → Create*).

2. On the *Create Condition Records* screen:

    a. Click the *Freight* node.

    b. Double-click on ⊕ *Freight Incoterms 1+2.*

3. On the *Create Condition Records: Overview* screen, choose ⬜ next to *CnTy SOrg. DChl Dv IncoT.*

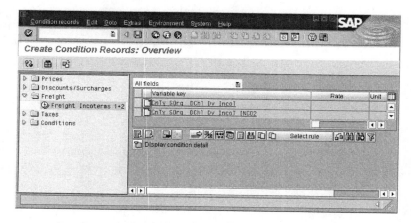

4. On the *Create Condition Records: Fast Entry* screen:

    a. Under *Condition type*, enter **KF00** .

    b. Under *In.* (Incoterms), enter the Incoterm that represents a type of shipping.

    c. Under *Rate*, enter the charge for freight.

    d. Under *U.* (unit of measure), enter the unit of measure to which the rate applies. The default is tons, which may result in an erroneous calculation.

    e. Choose 💾 .

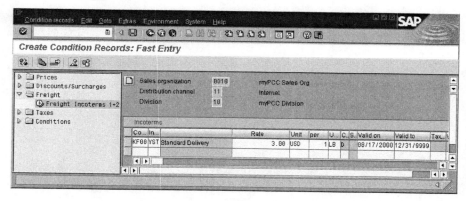

Enter Default Incoterms for the Product Catalog's Reference Customer

The default Incoterms that most customers choose should be maintained in the reference customer copied when a new customer registers on the Internet. The Incoterms are then copied into each newly registered customer master record. This step is carried out during the creation of the reference customer in the CATT procedure *ZESHOP_PROD_CATALOG*, which creates a sample product catalog. However, this catalog is only sample data created with the Online Store preconfiguration and used in conjunction with the PCC.

Task

Verify that the correct Incoterms and taxable indicator are maintained in the customer master

1. In the *Command* field, enter transaction **XD02** and choose *Enter* (or from the navigation menu, choose *Logistics → Sales and Distribution → Master Data → Business partners → Customer → Change → Complete*).

2. On the *Change Customer: Initial Screen*:

   a. In *Customer*, enter the number of the customer used as the reference for newly registered Internet customers.

   b. In *Company code*, enter your company code.

   c. In *Sales organization*, enter the sales organization used for Internet business.

   d. In *Distribution channel*, enter the distribution channel used for Internet business.

   e. In *Division*, enter the division used for Internet business.

   f. Choose ✔ .

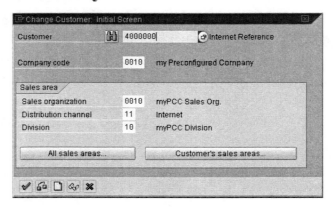

3. On the *Change Customer: General data* screen, choose *Sales area data.*

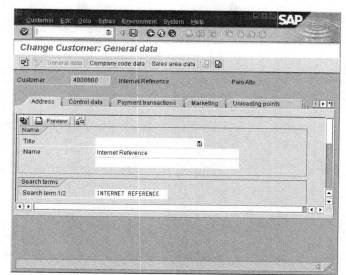

Note

The *Tax...* column is set to *1*, or taxable. The corresponding tax indicator in the material master is found on the *Sales: Sales Org. 1 Data* view.

4. On the *Change Customer: Sales area data* screen:

a. Choose the *Billing document* tab.

b. Under *Delivery and payment terms*, enter the default freight used for most customers in *Incoterms*. Only the first part of the Incoterms is taken into consideration for pricing.

c. Choose 🖫 .

Since the reference customer is copied each time a customer from the Internet registers, the Incoterms corresponding to the customer's most commonly required shipping method should be defaulted into this customer master record. The Incoterms with the Online Store preconfiguration do not reflect different freight carriers, since many companies have individual agreements with the freight carriers they choose for the majority of their business.

All Internet customers, therefore, also contain these Incoterms. These Incoterms are copied into the sales order created on the Internet, unless the customer chooses a different shipping method. This choice is an add-on provided by the Online Store preconfiguration. Please refer to the configuration section below for details

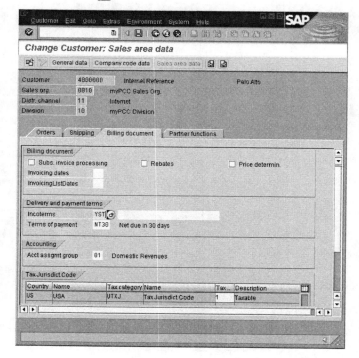

Pricing Configuration

The steps involved in setting up pricing for the product catalog and the orders created using the Online Store are described below in detail. You must:

- Define the subtotals in the pricing procedures to work with the Internet preconfiguration (preconfigured)

- Create supporting configuration for the pricing procedures (preconfigured)

- Define the pricing procedure determination for the product catalog and Internet order type (preconfigured)

- Create the Incoterms to be used for freight (preconfigured)

- Verify that the ITS templates contain the code to support the pricing breakout (preconfigured)

- Modify the code to allow Incoterms to be chosen from the Internet (Online Store preconfiguration add-on)

- Verify that the ITS templates contain the code to support the Incoterm's modification

- Check the SAPNet – R/3 Frontend Notes

Define Subtotals in Pricing Procedures to Work with Internet Preconfiguration

A prerequisite of the Online Store preconfiguration is either the Preconfigured Client U.S. (PCC) is being implemented at the same time, or a working SD module has already been implemented.

If the PCC is being used, three pricing procedures are delivered that already contain the appropriate subtotals for pricing and the SAPscript forms used to print the receipt and e-mail confirmation messages.

The following three pricing procedures are delivered with the PCC:

Pricing Procedure	Description
ZWAJUS	e-Shop www US w/ Jurisdiction
ZWAXUS	e-Shop www US w/extern.Jurisd.
ZWAXUD	e-Shop www USextern.Jurisd.NEW

Within the Online Store preconfiguration, when used in conjunction with the PCC, these pricing procedures are used with document pricing procedure *X* and sales area *0010-11-10*.

If you are not using the PCC, the subtotals below must be used in order to display the correct prices within the product catalog and price breakdowns during the quotation and order confirmation processes. These subtotals may be entered for individual condition types or for subtotal lines

Subtotal	Use
1	Display of gross price in the product catalog
	Display of gross price in the order quotation for a line item, if no sale price exists
2	Display of sale price in the product catalog
	Display of sale price in the order quotation for a line item
3	Display of customer discounts in the order quotation
	(These discounts are offered to customers in addition to any customer-specific prices and sale prices)
4	Display of freight based on the weight of the product in the order quotation
5	Total taxes
6	Total value

Note

In the order quotation and price breakdown on the Internet, the logic now allows the discounts and freight to be broken out separately from the item totals. Subtotals *3* and *4* are configured for the Online Store preconfiguration for this purpose; if these subtotals are changed, the ITS templates must also be changed.

Subtotals *1* and *2* are required by the Online Store transaction logic for browsing the product catalog and allow the *Special Offers* icon to be displayed.

All subtotals are used to update the preconfigured Sales Information System (SIS) structures. Please refer to chapter 11, "Sales Activity Reports" on page 263 for details on reporting.

To configure the pricing procedures, enter transaction **V/08** in the *Command* field and choose *Enter* (or in the IMG, choose *Sales and Distribution* → *Basic Functions* → *Pricing* → *Pricing Control* and choose 🕒 next to *Define And Assign Pricing Procedures*. On the *Choose Activity* dialog box, select *Maintain Pricing Procedures* and choose 🔲 *Choose*). The following three pricing procedures are delivered with the Online Store preconfiguration.

Pricing Procedure	Description
ZWAJUS	e-Shop www US w/ Jurisdiction
ZWAXUS	e-Shop www US w/extern.Jurisd.
ZWASUD	e-Shop www USextern.Jurisd.NEW

Pricing Procedure ZWAJUS. This pricing procedure is applied when R/3 is used for the tax calculation.

Step Number	Counter	Condition Type	Description	From	To	Manual	Mandatory	Statistical	Print	Subtotal	Requirements	Alt. calc. type	Alt. CondBase Val	Account Key	Accruals
11	0	PR00	Price	0	0		X		X	1	2	0	0	ERL	
12	0	VKP0	Sales Price	0	0				X	2	0	0	0		
100	0		Gross Value	0	0				X		0	0	0		
101	0	KA00	Sales deal	0	0				X		2	0	0	ERS	
102	0	K032	Price Group/Material	0	0				X		2	0	0	ERS	
104	0	K007	Customer Discount	0	0				X		2	0	0	ERS	
105	0	K004	Material Discount	0	0				X		2	0	0	ERS	
106	0	ZDP1	Mat. price grp. in %	0	0				X		2	0	0	ERS	
108	0	K030	Customer/Mat.Pr.Grp.	0	0				X		2	0	0	ERS	
111	0	HI01	Hierarchy	0	0				X		2	0	0	ERS	
112	0	HI02	Hierarchy/Material	0	0				X		2	0	0	ERS	
300	0		Total Discount	101	299				S	3	0	0	0		
320	0	PMIN	Minimum Price	0	0				X		2	15	0	ERL	
800	0		Net Value	0	0				S		0	0	0		
815	0	KF00	Freight	0	0						0	0	0	ERF	
880	0		Total Freight	812	816				S	4	0	0	0		
890	0	SKTV	Cash Discount	0	0			X			14	0	0		
900	0		Net Value 2	800	812						0	0	0		
910	0	UTXJ	Tax Jurisdict. Code	900	0						0	0	0		
911	0	JR1	Tax Jur Code Level 1	900	0	X					0	301	16		
912	0	JR2	Tax Jur Code Level 2	900	0	X					0	302	16		
913	0	JR3	Tax Jur Code Level 3	900	0	X					0	303	16		
914	0	JR4	Tax Jur Code Level 4	900	0	X					0	304	16		
915	0	DIFF	Rounding Off	0	0	X					13	16	4	ERS	
919	0		Total Tax	910	916				S	5	0	0	0		
920	0		Total	0	0					6	0	4	0		
921	0		Total	0	0					A	0	4	0		
940	0	VPRS	Cost	0	0			X		B	4	0	0		
950	0		Profit Margin (Net minus cost	0	0						0	11	0		

Pricing Procedure ZWAXUS. This pricing procedure is applied when an external tax package is used for the tax calculation. This procedure is used with an older calculation method.

Step Number	Counter	Condition Type	Description	From	To	Manual	Mandatory	Statistical	Print	Subtotal	Requirements	Alt. calc. type	Alt. CondBase Val	Account Key	Accruals
11	0	PR00	Price	0	0		X		X	1	2	0	0	ERL	
12	0	VKP0	Sales Price	0	0				X	2	0	0	0		
100	0		Gross Value	0	0				X		0	0	0		

Step Number	Counter	Condition Type	Description	From	To	Manual	Mandatory	Statistical	Print	Subtotal	Requirements	Alt. calc. type	Alt. CondBase Val	Account Key	Accruals
101	0	KA00	Sales deal	0	0				X		2	0	0	ERS	
102	0	K032	Price Group/Material	0	0				X		2	0	0	ERS	
104	0	K007	Customer Discount	0	0				X		2	0	0	ERS	
105	0	K004	Material Discount	0	0				X		2	0	0	ERS	
106	0	ZDP1	Mat. price grp. in %	0	0				X		2	0	0	ERS	
108	0	K030	Customer/Mat.Pr.Grp.	0	0				X		2	0	0	ERS	
111	0	HI01	Hierarchy	0	0				X		2	0	0	ERS	
112	0	HI02	Hierarchy/Material	0	0				X		2	0	0	ERS	
300	0		Total Discount	101	299				S	3	0	0	0		
320	0	PMIN	Minimum Price	0	0				X		2	15	0	ERL	
800	0		Net Value	0	0				S		0	0	0		
815	0	KF00	Freight	0	0						0	0	0	ERF	
880	0		Total Freight	812	816				S	4	0	0	0		
890	0	SKTV	Cash Discount	0	0			X			14	0	0		
900	0		Net Value 2	800	812						0	0	0		
910	0	UTXJ	Tax Jurisdict. Code	900	0						0	0	0		
911	0	XR1	Tax Jur Code Level 1	900	0	X					0	301	16		
912	0	XR2	Tax Jur Code Level 2	900	0	X					0	302	16		
913	0	XR3	Tax Jur Code Level 3	900	0	X					0	303	16		
914	0	XR4	Tax Jur Code Level 4	900	0	X					0	304	16		
915	0	XR5	Tax Jur Code Level 5	900	0	X						305	16		
916	0	XR6	Tax Jur Code Level 6	900	0	X						306	16		
917	0	DIFF	Rounding Off	0	0	X					13	16	4	ERS	
919	0		Total Tax	910	916				S	5	0	0	0		
920	0		Total	0	0						6	0	4	0	
921	0		Total	0	0						A	0	4	0	
940	0	VPRS	Cost	0	0			X			B	4	0	0	

The taxes can be configured using either the R/3 logic or an external tax package, such as Vertex or Taxware. The tax condition types need to be configured appropriately. Please refer to the PCC U.S. at *www.saplabs.com/pcc* for details on available preconfiguration for these tax packages.

Pricing Procedure ZWAXUD. This pricing procedure is applied when an external tax package is used for the tax calculation. This procedure is used with the newest calculation method.

Step Number	Counter	Condition Type	Description	From	To	Manual	Mandatory	Statistical	Print	Subtotal	Requirements	Alt. calc. type	Alt. CondBase Val	Account Key	Accruals
11	0	PR00	Price	0	0	X			X	1	2	0	0	ERL	
12	0	VKP0	Sales Price	0	0				X	2	0	0	0		
100	0		Gross Value	0	0				X		0	0	0		
101	0	KA00	Sales deal	0	0				X		2	0	0	ERS	
102	0	K032	Price Group/Material	0	0				X		2	0	0	ERS	
104	0	K007	Customer Discount	0	0				X		2	0	0	ERS	
105	0	K004	Material Discount	0	0				X		2	0	0	ERS	

Step Number	Counter	Condition Type	Description	From	To	Manual	Mandatory	Statistical	Print	Subtotal	Requirements	Alt. calc. type	Alt. CondBase Val	Account Key	Accruals
106	0	ZDP1	Mat. price grp. in %	0	0				X		2	0	0	ERS	
108	0	K030	Customer/Mat.Pr.Grp.	0	0				X		2	0	0	ERS	
111	0	HI01	Hierarchy	0	0				X		2	0	0	ERS	
112	0	HI02	Hierarchy/Material	0	0				X		2	0	0	ERS	
300	0		Total Discount	101	299				S	3	0	0	0		
320	0	PMIN	Minimum Price	0	0				X		2	15	0	ERL	
800	0		Net Value	0	0				S		0	0	0		
815	0	KF00	Freight	0	0						0	0	0	ERF	
880	0		Total Freight	812	816				S	4	0	0	0		
890	0	SKTV	Cash Discount	0	0			X			14	0	0		
900	0		Net Value 2	800	812						0	0	0		
910	0	UTXD	US Tax per document	0	0			X			0	500	0		
911	0	UTXE	US Tax per document	0	0			X			0	510	0		
912	0	XR1	Tax Jur Code Level 1	900	0	X					0	301	16		
913	0	XR2	Tax Jur Code Level 2	900	0	X					0	302	16		
914	0	XR3	Tax Jur Code Level 3	900	0	X					0	303	16		
915	0	XR4	Tax Jur Code Level 4	900	0	X					0	304	16		
916	0	XR5	Tax Jur Code Level 5	900	0	X						305	16		
917	0	XR6	Tax Jur Code Level 6	900	0	X						306	16		
918	0	DIFF	Rounding Off	0	0		X				13	16	4	ERS	
920	0		Total Tax	910	916				S	5	0	0	0		
921	0		Total	0	0					6	0	4	0		
922	0		Total	0	0					A	0	4	0		
940	0	VPRS	Cost	0	0			X		B	4	0	0		
950	0		Profit margin (Net minus cost)	0	0						0	11	0		

Create Supporting Configuration for Pricing Procedure

To support the pricing procedures delivered with the Online Store preconfiguration, a new condition type has been created that supports a percentage discount on products, based on the material pricing group in the material master record. These steps have been preconfigured for you.

The material pricing group allows a discount to be created for a group of materials. These materials are grouped using the material pricing group field that is maintained in the *Sales: Sales org. 2* view of the material master record. To create the material pricing group, enter transaction **ovsj** in the *Command* field and choose *Enter* (or in the IMG, choose *Sales and Distribution → Basic Functions → Pricing* and choose ⟳ next to *Maintain Price-Relevant Master*

Data Fields. On the *Choose Activity* dialog box, select *Define Material Groups* and choose ▧ *Choose*).

Material Pricing Group	Description
10	e-Shop materials

A condition type has been created using the material pricing group that allows you to enter a percentage discount. To create the condition type, enter transaction **V/06** in the *Command* field and choose *Enter* (or in the IMG, choose *Sales and Distribution → Basic Functions → Pricing → Pricing Control* and choose ⤵ next to *Define condition types*. On the *Choose Activity* dialog box, select *Maintain Condition Types* and choose ▧ *Choose*). The configuration of condition type *ZDP1* is documented below.

Field	Setting
Condition class	A (discount or surcharge)
Calculation type	A (percentage)
Plus/minus	X (negative)
Scale basis	B (value scale)
Header condition	Off
Item condition	On
Delete	On
Amount/percent	On
Value	Off
Quantity relation	Off
Calculation type	Off

Define Pricing Procedure Determination for Product Catalog and Internet Order Type

Both the product catalog and the order type used for the Internet contain a document schema for the pricing procedure determination. The product catalog is master data that is linked in configuration to an Online Store. The Online Store is accessible from the Internet. During the configuration of the Online Store, the quotation and order profile contains the order type. The order type, in turn, contains the document schema for pricing determination. This document schema should be the same schema used for the basic data of the product catalog.

CATT procedure *ZESHOP_PRICE_DET* can be used to assign the pricing procedure, or this step may be performed manually. The document procedure for determining the pricing procedure used for both the Online Store and Internet order type is *X*.

To assign the pricing procedure you wish to use for the Internet, enter transaction **OVKK** in the *Command* field and choose *Enter* (or in the IMG, choose *Sales and Distribution* → *Basic Functions* → *Pricing* → *Pricing Control* and choose 🔁 next to *Define and Assign Pricing Procedures*. On the *Choose Activity* dialog box, select *Define Pricing Procedure Determination* and choose 📇 *Choose*).

Sales Organization	Distribution Channel	Division	Document Procedure	Customer Procedure	Pricing Procedure
0010	11	10	X	1	ZWAJUS or ZWAXUS or ZWAXUD

The proposed condition type column is blank.

Create the Incoterms to be Used for Freight

To set up the pricing configuration for the freight calculation, the Incoterms to be used for freight must be created. This step has been preconfigured for you.

To view the Incoterms created for freight, enter transaction **OVSG** in the *Command* field and choose *Enter* (or use the in the IMG, choose *Sales and Distribution* → *Master Data* → *Business Partners* → *Customers* → *Billing Document* and choose 🔁 next to *Define Incoterms*).

Incoterms	Descriptions	Location Mandatory
Y2D	2-Day Delivery	
YOV	Overnight Delivery	
YST	Standard Delivery	

Location Mandatory means that the second part of the Incoterms is required when these Incoterms are used. The second part is a free-form text field. The condition records are currently only based on the first part of the Incoterms listed above. These Incoterms are used as a key when creating freight rates for the condition type *KF00*. The second portion of the Incoterms is not filled while ordering from the Internet.

Verify the ITS Templates Can Support the Pricing Breakout

Note

For more information about ITS templates, see chapter 14, "ITS Templates" on page 327.

For discounts and freight price breakouts to be visible on the Internet, changes need to be made in the ITS templates. Your ITS templates must contain the code to support pricing breakout. This step has been preconfigured for you.

The template files in the AGate directory structure of the ITS have been modified to allow customers to display a price breakout. The template files are located in the ITS AGate directory under the directory structure

<its_root>\templates\ww20\sg, where the *<its_root>* is your virtual ITS installation and *sg* is the theme delivered with the Online Store preconfiguration. In addition, the language-resource file has been changed so variables can be added for the new pricing descriptions.

The following files are modified to support the display of price breakouts:

Template	Change
SAPMWWMJ_4230.HTML	Display the discounts and freight totals
SAPMWWMJ_4235.HTML	Display the discounts and freight totals
WW20_EN.HTRC	Variables for descriptions of the new prices

The following changes have been made in templates *SAPMWWMJ_4230.HTML* and *SAPMWWMJ_4230.HTML* as the line items and total of the items in the basket are built.

- Change the price displayed for each product from the net price to the gross price.

- Add a line that contains discounts applied during ordering, which is only displayed when the value is not zero.

- Add a line that contains the freight calculated during ordering, which includes a description (from R/3) of the shipping method (Incoterms) chosen previously, which is only displayed when the value is not zero.

WW20_EN.HTRC

The file *ww20_en.htrc* (located under the directory structure *<its_root>\templates\ww20\sg*) is the language-resource file that contains values for the language-specific variables used for the IACs. The following variables have been added to support the price breakouts:

Parameter	Value
_z_4230_freight	Freight
_z_4230_discounts	Discount

Modify Code to Allow Incoterms to be Chosen from the Internet

The Incoterms are used to calculate the freight charged to the customer. In the standard functionality of the Online Store, it is not possible to choose different Incoterms and thereby estimate a different freight cost. This modification allows Internet customers to choose the freight they prefer for their orders.

Five programs must be changed. In the *Command* field, enter transaction **SE38** and choose *Enter* (or from the navigation menu, choose *Tools → ABAP Workbench → Development → ABAP Editor*).

The following programs must be changed to incorporate the Incoterms functionality into your Online Store. The detailed code is documented in the Installation Guide delivered with the preconfiguration transports.

After saving your modifications, you must activate and generate the programs.

- MWWMJF03_ORDER_CREATE

- MWWMJF03_QUOTATION_CREATE

- MWWMJF03_TRANSPORT_ITEMS_OUT

- MWWMJTOP

- MWWMJF03_USER_COMMAND_4000

Note that these changes to the function modules are not configuration changes; they are modifications to the R/3 System. Please thoroughly document and test these changes if you choose to apply them.

Verify the ITS Templates Contain Code to Support Incoterm Modification

For Incoterm modification to be usable on the Internet, changes need to be made in the ITS templates. This step has been preconfigured for you. If you choose not to use this modification, you need to remove this code.

The template files in the AGate directory structure of the ITS have been modified to allow customers to choose a shipping method. The shipping methods reflect the Incoterms in the R/3 System. The template files are located in the ITS AGate directory under the directory structure *<its_root>\templates\ww20\sg*, where the *<its_root>* is your virtual ITS installation and *sg* is the theme delivered with the Online Store preconfiguration.

Note

For more information about ITS templates, see chapter 14, "ITS Templates" on page 327.

The following templates are modified to support the Incoterms logic:

Template	Change
SAPMWWMJ_4220.HTML	Logic to choose the shipping method
SAPMWWMJ_4230.HTML	Display the description of the shipping method
SAPMWWMJ_4235.HTML	Display the description of the shipping method
WW20_EN.HTRC	Text for the new freight selection function

The following changes have been made in the template *SAPMWWMJ_4220.HTML*:

- Selection radio buttons so the customer can select the shipping method

- Logic to pass the selected value to R/3

WW20_EN.HTRC

The file *ww20_en.htrc* is the language-resource file that contains values for the language-specific variables used for the IACs. The following variables are added to support the selection of Incoterms:

Parameter	Value
_4220_shipping	Shipping type:
_standard	Standard
_twodays	2 days
_overnight	Over night
_colon	:

Check the SAPNet – R/3 Frontend Notes

To properly complete your customer account information configuration, you should check for applicable SAPNet – R/3 Frontend notes (formerly OSS). For details on SAPNet – R/3 Frontend notes, please refer to appendix A, "SAPNet Frontend Notes" on page 495.

CHAPTER

4

Limiting Access to Product Groups Within a Product Catalog

Overview

Authorization groups are available to determine which users can manage the content of the catalog within R/3. These authorization groups are available for the catalog as a whole, and for the product groups in the catalog layout. For additional information about authorizations, please refer to the *Authorizations Made Easy* guidebook at *www.saplabs.com/auths.*

When doing business on the web, it may be beneficial to limit customer access to different portions of a product catalog. A distributor may have several different product lines. Some of these products are common to all customers of the distributor, while others are special brands only sold to particular customers.

It may not be desirable to create several different product catalogs, especially if they contain many common products. Instead, you might prefer that all customers have access to several of the product groups, while only specific customers have access to their own product group. This situation requires that the customer logs on before the product catalog can be browsed.

When a customer browses a product catalog on the Internet, a customer number or an e-mail address is used for identification. However, this customer identification is not an R/3 user that can log on to the system directly. Since authorizations within R/3 use an R/3 user ID, these authorizations cannot be used to limit what a customer can see while browsing the catalog on the Internet.

Instead, a classification system provides the functionality for these authorizations to limit access to product groups. The classification system allows a company to create characteristics that describe their customers and their product groups. If the customer's characteristic values match a product group's characteristic values, the customer can see the products in that group. If no values are assigned to a particular product group within the catalog, all customers may display these products.

What We Deliver

In the Online Store preconfiguration, we provide the following deliverables:

- Preconfiguration of customer and product catalog classes, with a corresponding characteristic for limiting access to portions of a product catalog
- Documentation on how to limit access to portions of the product catalog

The Customer Experience

In the scenario below, two different customers (Peter and Robert) log on to the Online Store, and browse the product catalog. Peter has the ability to see the entire catalog, while Robert cannot see one of the product groups within the catalog.

1. In the Internet browser, Peter enters the URL of your home page, which you configured as part of the ITS installation.

2. Peter chooses the *Online Store* from your home page.

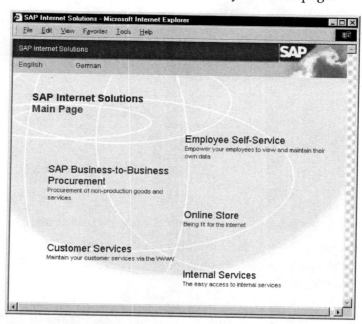

3. Peter chooses *Online Store*.

Online Store —————————————

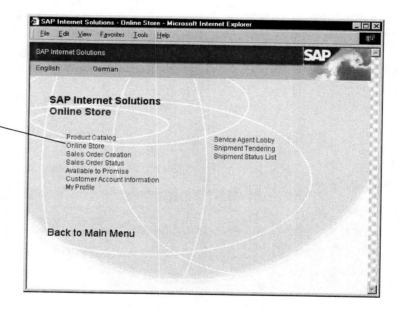

4. To access the store in which he wishes to shop, Peter chooses *YGUIDES-B.*

A list of the different available stores is displayed.

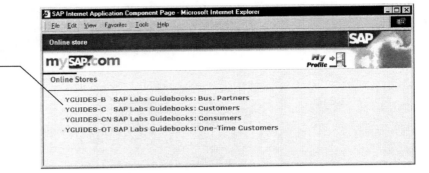

5. Peter must log in before browsing the product catalog.

a. Peter enters his e-mail address.

b. He enters his password.

c. Peter chooses *Login.*

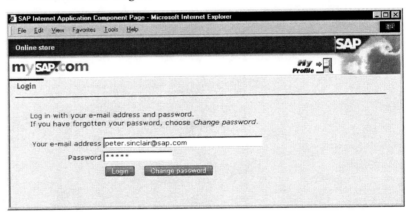

6. Peter chooses the first shop, *Guidebooks.*

The shops, or different product categories within the catalog, are displayed.

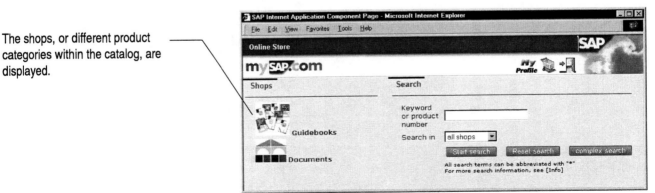

7. Four product groups within the *Guidebooks* shop are displayed.

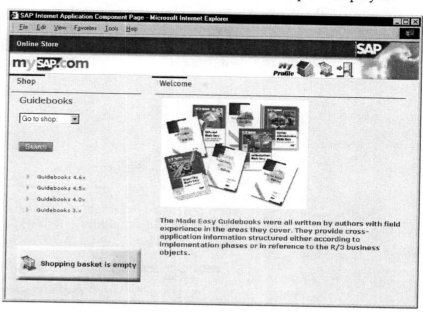

8. Meanwhile, the other customer, Robert, logs on to the Online Store. He also follows steps **1–4**.

    a. Robert enters his e-mail address.

    b. He enters his password.

    c. He chooses *Login*.

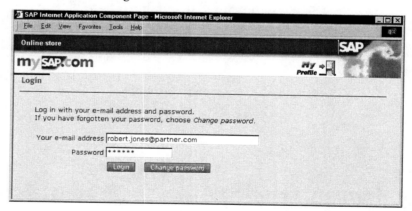

9. Robert also chooses the first shop, *Guidebooks*.

The shops, or different product categories within the catalog, are displayed.

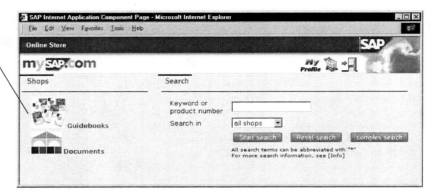

10. Although this is the same product catalog as Peter displayed, Robert does not have access to the *Guidebooks 4.6x* product group. This time, only three product groups within the *Guidebooks* shop are displayed.

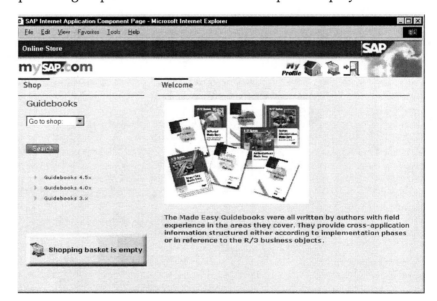

Making it Happen: Limiting Access to Product Groups Within the Catalog

The classification system in R/3 limits the access to product groups within the catalog. Maintaining only one catalog requires less effort than maintaining multiple product catalogs.

What Is the Classification System?

The classification system allows you to define **characteristics** that describe master data. In essence, user-defined fields can be added to master data records. A **class** is an umbrella used to group together similar types of characteristics. For example, a class called *CARS* may include characteristics that define a car, such as *COLOR, ENGINE_SIZE,* and *TRANSMISSION*. Each characteristic contains a list of valid **values** that can be assigned to each master record. For example, valid values for the characteristic *COLOR* may be red, blue, silver, green, white, and black.

In our example, we created a characteristic called **customer type** that describes the customer's relationship to the company. This customer type limits access to documents that should not be publicly accessible. The characteristic *CUSTOMER_TYPE* contains values that define the customer. Sample values for customer type include internal, partner, and public.

Using Classification to Filter Portions of the Product Catalog

Classification values between the product catalog and the customer master record are compared using a filter mechanism. A class containing the characteristic *CUSTOMER_TYPE* is linked to a shop or to any product group level. This class cannot be linked to the product catalog as a whole, or to individual material master records. The values of the customer type characteristic determine which customers can see the product group and the materials (or lower-level product groups) within it. If no class is linked, or if the characteristic value is blank, all customers can see the product group.

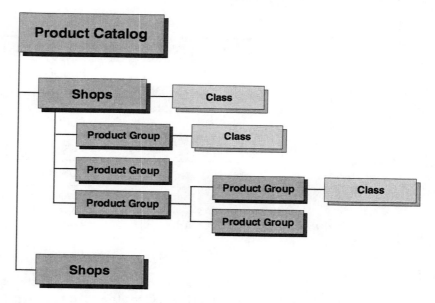

A class containing the customer type is linked to a customer master record. The values of the customer type characteristic determine which product groups the customer can see within the catalog.

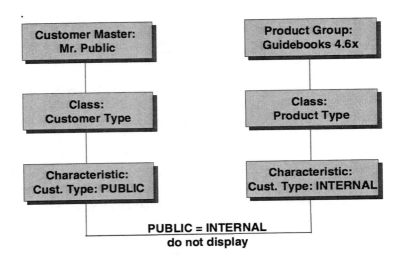

If the customer type in the product group and the customer master match, the product group is displayed. If these values do not match, the product group is not displayed. In the standard R/3 System, the comparison occurs between all characteristic values of all classes linked to the customer and the product catalog layout. The function module *CUSTOMER_FILTER_CHAR_READ* activates the logic. The table below documents the result of different combinations of customer types.

Customer Master	Product Group	Displayed on Web?
PUBLIC	PUBLIC	YES
PUBLIC	INTERNAL	NO
INTERNAL	PUBLIC	NO
PUBLIC	BLANK	YES
BLANK	PUBLIC	YES
BLANK	BLANK	YES
PUBLIC PARTNER	PARTNER	NO
PARTNER	PUBLIC PARTNER	NO

For this scenario to function correctly, early logon to the product catalog must be configured. Once the customer logs on, the system can recognize the identity of the customer. If you allow the customer to browse the catalog before logging in, this validation does not take place. Please refer to chapter 1 "Creating the Online Store with the Catalog" on page 5 for information about configuring early logons.

Master Data Required to Limit Access to the Catalog

The classes and characteristics are master data records within the R/3 System. The steps involved in setting up this scenario are described below in detail. You must:

- Create a characteristic that contains the customer types (preconfigured)

- Create a class (type *011*) for customer master records (preconfigured)

- Link the customer class to the customer master records

- Create a class (type 060) for the product catalog (preconfigured)

- Link the layout class to the layout areas (shops or product groups) in the catalog

Create a Characteristic that Contains the Customer Types

In order to limit access to product groups within a catalog, a characteristic containing the customer types must be created. The steps below illustrate how the characteristic is created. This step is preconfigured for you when you run CATT procedure *ZESHOP_CLASSES*. These steps do not need to be performed unless you choose to create another characteristic. Please refer to appendix H, "Introduction to Computer-Aided Test Tools (CATTs)" on page 547 for details about the CATT procedure.

Task

Create a characteristic with customer types

1. In the *Command* field, enter transaction **CT04** and choose *Enter* (or from the navigation menu, choose *Logistics → Central Functions → Classification → Master Data → Characteristics*).

2. On the *Characteristics* screen:

   a. In *Characteristic*, enter the name or code of the characteristic.

   b. Choose ▯ .

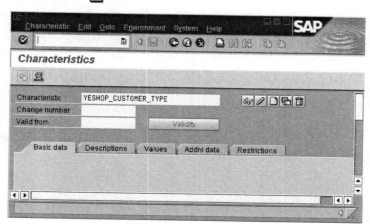

3. On the *Create Characteristic* screen:

a. In *Description,* enter a short text for the characteristic.

b. In *Status,* choose the status of the characteristic. The class can only be used once the status is set to **Released**.

c. In *Data type,* choose the data format (for example, *Character format* so text will be entered as the characteristic values).

4. On the revised *Basic data* tab:

a. In *Number of chars.,* enter the number of characters allowed for the characteristic codes.

b. Under *Value assignment,* select *Multiple values.*

c. Choose the *Values* tab.

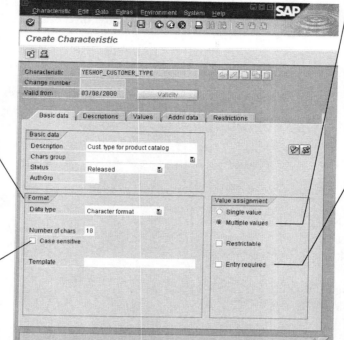

Additional fields are displayed in the *Format* section once the data type has been chosen.

The *Case sensitive* checkbox is not selected by default. It should only be selected if the characteristic codes should be case-sensitive.

In the *Value assignment* section, the *Multiple values* radio button is selected, which allows a customer to be assigned more than one characteristic value. The default value in the characteristic is *Single values*.

The *Entry required* checkbox is not selected by default. Selecting this checkbox would require an entry for all assignments to customers and the product catalog. The option of not assigning any characteristic values, which allows all access, would no longer be available if this checkbox were activated.

5. On the *Values* tab:

a. Enter the codes, or values, of the characteristic in the *Char. value* column.

b. In the *Description* column, enter the corresponding description of each value.

c. Choose the *Addnl data* tab.

The *Additional values* checkbox defaults to deactivated. This setting means that characteristic values must be chosen from this list. Selecting this checkbox would allow ad-hoc entry of values for customers and product groups, making the coordination between customers and the product catalog difficult.

Existing text can be changed. New values can be added to the list of allowed values at any time. A value can be deleted, but only if it has not been assigned, for example to a customer or to a product catalog.

6. On the *Addnl data* tab:

   a. If a table containing the values to be used for customer types already exists, this table can be referenced by entering the table and field into the *Table name* and *Field name* fields. This option is available in place of manually entering the list of values on the previous screen.

   b. Choose 💾 .

Table name and Field name fields

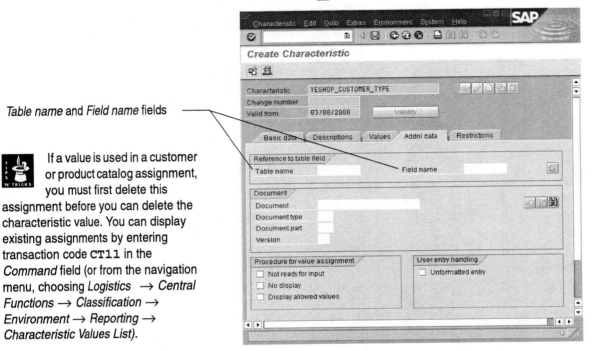

If a value is used in a customer or product catalog assignment, you must first delete this assignment before you can delete the characteristic value. You can display existing assignments by entering transaction code **CT11** in the *Command* field (or from the navigation menu, choosing *Logistics → Central Functions → Classification → Environment → Reporting → Characteristic Values List*).

Create a Class (Type 011) for Customer Master Records

To limit access to product groups within a catalog, a class (type 011) must be created and later linked to customer master records. The steps below illustrate how the class is created. This step has been preconfigured for you when you run CATT procedure *ZESHOP_CLASSES*. These steps do not need to be performed unless you choose to create another class. Please refer to appendix H, "Introduction to Computer-Aided Test Tools (CATTs)" on page 547 for details about the CATT procedure.

Task

Create a class for customer master records

1. In the *Command* field, enter transaction **CL02** and choose *Enter* (or from the navigation menu, choose *Logistics → Central Functions → Classification → Master Data → Classes*).

2. On the *Change Class* screen:

   a. In *Class*, enter the name or code of the class.

b. In *Class type*, enter **011**, which is a class that can be assigned to customer master records.

c. Choose ▢ .

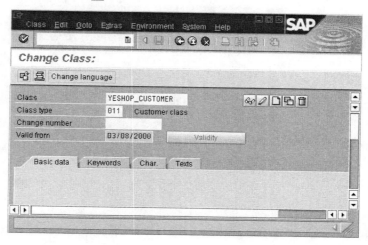

3. On the *Create Class* screen:

a. In *Description*, enter a short text for the class.

b. In *Status*, choose the status of the class. The class can only be used once the status is set to *Released.*

c. Choose the *Char.* tab.

The validity date for the class defaults to the current date.

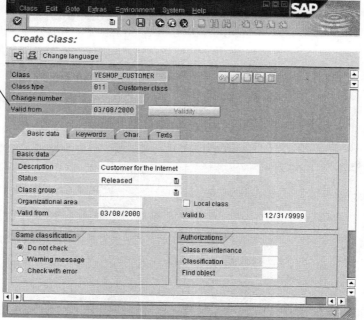

4. On the *Char.* tab:

a. In the *Characteristic* column, enter the characteristic created previously.

b. Choose 💾.

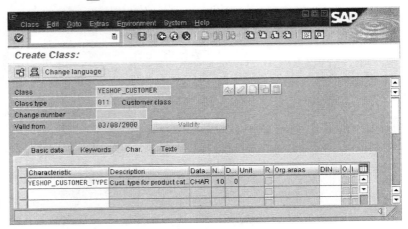

Link the Customer Class to the Customer Master Records

The next step to limiting access to product groups within a catalog is to link the customer class to the customer records. You need to perform this step manually for your customer master records.

Task

Link the customer class to customer master records

1. In the *Command* field, enter transaction **XD02** and choose *Enter* (or from the navigation menu, choose *Logistics → Sales and Distribution → Master Data → Business Partners → Customer → Change → Complete*).

2. On the *Change Customer: Initial Screen*:

   a. In *Customer*, enter the customer number.

   b. Choose ✔.

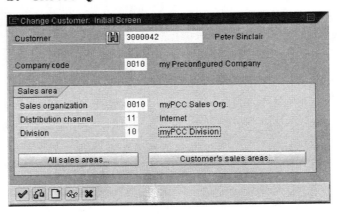

> **Note**
>
> The values for the company code and sales area are not required for entering classification data. The class is linked to the customer master at the basic data level, which goes across companies and sales areas.

3. On the *Change Customer: General data* screen, choose *Extras → Classification*.

4. On the *Change Customer: Classification* screen:

   a. In the *Class* column, enter the class created for customers.

   b. Choose 🖱.

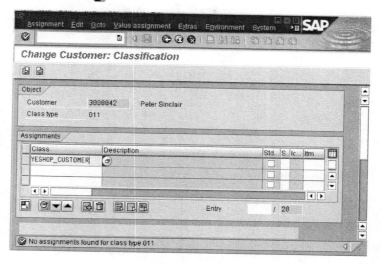

5. On the *General* tab, in the *Value* column, use *possible entries* to select the characteristic value.

Possible entries button

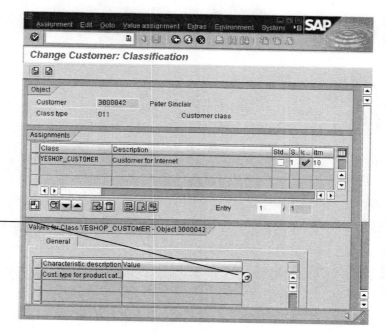

6. On the *Cust. type for product catalog* dialog box:

   a. Select the checkboxes for one or more values that apply to this customer (for example, *INTERNAL*).

b. Choose ✅.

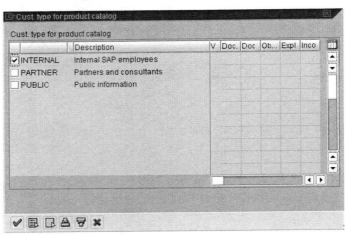

The Data Transfer Workbench (object 130, Classification) can be used to link a class to customer master records. For additional information about the Data Transfer Workbench, please refer to the web site *www.saplabs.com/dx*.

7. Back on the *Change Customer: Classification* screen:

a. Choose 🗹.

b. Choose ⬅.

c. Choose 💾 from the initial customer screen.

The ID (for example, *INTERNAL*) is displayed in the Value column until you choose 🗹 in step **7a**.

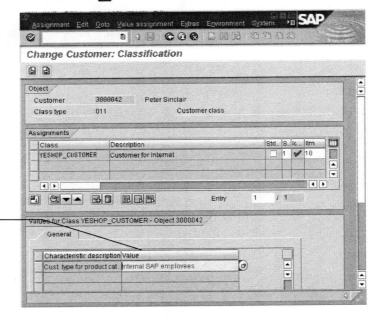

Create a Class (Type 060) for the Product Catalog

Limiting access to product groups within a catalog also requires that a class (type *060*) be created and linked to product groups. The steps below illustrate how the class is created. This step has been preconfigured for you when you run CATT procedure *ZESHOP_CLASSES*. These steps do not need to be performed unless you choose to create another class. Please refer to appendix H, "Introduction to Computer-Aided Test Tools (CATTs)" on page 547 for details about the CATT procedure.

Task

Create a class for the product catalog (shop or product group level)

1. In the *Command* field, enter transaction **CL02** and choose *Enter* (or from the navigation menu, choose *Logistics* → *Central Functions* → *Classification* → *Master Data* → *Classes*).

2. On the *Change Class* screen:

   a. In *Class*, enter the name or code of the class.

   b. In *Class type*, enter **060**, which is a class that can be assigned to layout records in the product catalog.

   c. Choose ⬜.

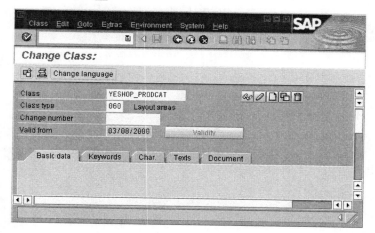

3. On the *Create Class* screen:

   a. In *Description*, enter a short text for the class.

   b. In *Status*, choose the status of the class. The class can only be used once the status is set to *Released*.

c. Choose the *Char.* tab.

The validity date for the class defaults to the current date.

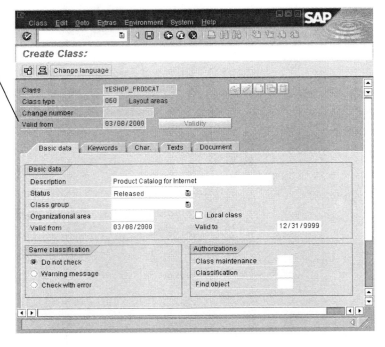

4. On the *Char.* tab:

a. In the *Characteristic* column, enter the characteristic created previously.

b. Choose 💾 .

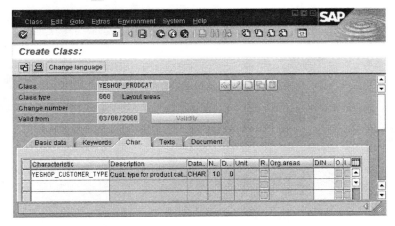

Link the Layout Class to the Layout Areas in the Catalog

To limit access to product groups within a catalog, you must link the layout class to the layout areas (shops or product groups) in the catalog. You need to perform this step for the product groups in your product catalogs.

Task

Link the layout class to layout areas

1. In the *Command* field, enter transaction **WWM2** and choose *Enter* (or from the navigation menu, choose *Logistics → Materials Management → Product Catalog → Product Catalog → Change*).

2. On the *Change Product Catalog: Initial Screen*:

   a. In *Catalog*, enter the product catalog.

   b. Choose *Layout*.

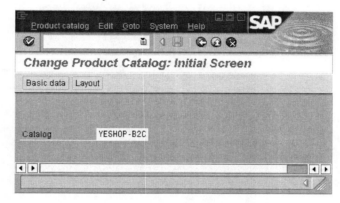

3. On the *Product Catalog: Maintain Layout* screen:

   a. Select the shop for which you would like to add an authorization check.

   b. Choose 🔲 .

Note

You can place the authorization check at any layout level (shop or product group) within the product catalog.

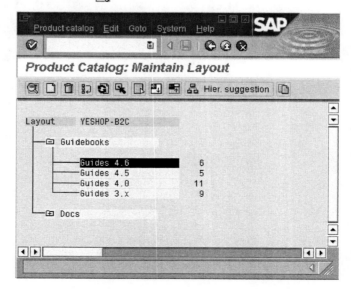

4. On the *Product Catalog: Maintain Base Layout Area* screen, choose *Classification*

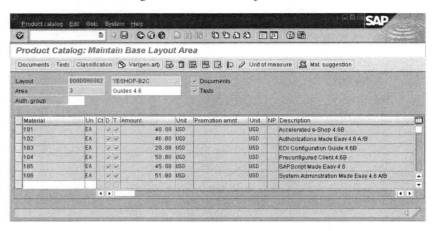

5. On the *Product Catalog: Classification* screen:

a. In the *Class* column, enter the class created for layout areas (product catalogs).

b. Choose .

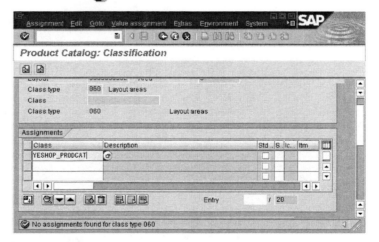

6. On the *General* tab, in the *Value* column, use *possible entries* to select the characteristic value.

Possible entries button ——————

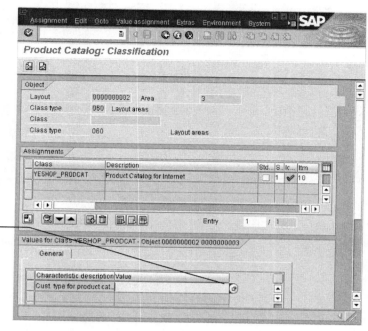

7. On the *Cust. type for product catalog* dialog box:

a. Select the one or more customer types allowed to see the products in this product group (for example, *INTERNAL*).

b. Choose ✔ .

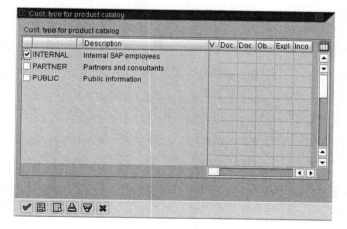

The Data Transfer Workbench (object 130, Classification) can be used to link a class to layout records in the product catalog. For additional information about the Data Transfer Workbench, please refer to the web site *www.saplabs.com/dx*.

8. Back on the *Product Catalog: Classification* screen:

a. Choose ✅ .

b. Choose ⬅ .

c. Choose 🖫 from the initial product catalog layout screen.

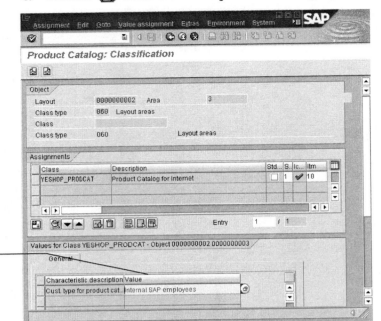

The ID (for example, *INTERNAL*) is displayed in the Value column until you choose 🔵 in step **7a**.

Configuration to Limit Access to Product Groups Within the Catalog

The steps involved to ensure that characteristic values are taken into account are described in the following section. You must:

- Define an early logon in the Online Store (preconfigured)
- Define the filter criteria in the product presentation profile (preconfigured)
- Determine whether to modify the filtering logic to select customer characteristics
- Determine whether to modify the filtering comparison logic

Define an Early Logon in the Online Store

The filtering functionality can only be supported if the Online Store requires an early logon. This step has been preconfigured for you.

To view the product presentation profiles, in the IMG choose *Logistics - General → IAC Product Catalog and Online Store* and choose ⊕ next to *Profiles for Product Presentation*. Please refer to chapter 1, "Creating the Online Store with the Catalog" on page 5 for a detailed description.

Define the Filter Criteria in the Product Presentation Profile

To support limited access to product groups within the catalog, the filter criteria must be defined in the product presentation profile. This step has been preconfigured for you.

To access the product presentation profile, in the IMG choose *Logistics – General → IAC Product Catalog and Online Store* and choose 🔄 next to *Profiles for Product Presentation*.

The *FM filter criteria* specifies the function module used for authorizations to the product catalog. The function module used in the Online Store preconfiguration is standard-delivered with the R/3 System, and is included in the preconfigured product presentation profiles.

Profile for Product Presentation	FM Filter Criteria
YPCB (Selling to business partners)	CUSTOMER_FILTER_CHAR_READ
YPCC (Selling to consumers)	CUSTOMER_FILTER_CHAR_READ

Determine Whether to Modify the Filtering Logic to Select Customer Characteristics

In the standard-delivered *CUSTOMER_FILTER_CHAR_READ* function module, all characteristic values associated with the customer (for all characteristics and classes) are selected for comparison to all characteristic values associated with the product group in the catalog.

If you wish to use a different mechanism to filter the characteristic values in the customer master, you need to copy the standard-delivered function module *CUSTOMER_FILTER_CHAR_READ*. You can then code your own filtering mechanism. For your own function module, make sure you do not change the interface structure. To copy and change your own function module, enter transaction **SE37** in the *Command* field and choose *Enter* (or from the navigation menu, choose *Tools → ABAP Workbench → Development → Function Builder*).

After programming your own filtering mechanism, you need to enter your function module into the presentation product presentation profile as previously described.

Determine Whether to Modify the Filtering Logic

In the current functionality, all values in the customer class are compared with all values in the product catalog class. If all values are equal, or if the customer or product catalog class is not maintained, then that portion of the product catalog is displayed.

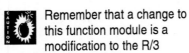 Remember that a change to this function module is a modification to the R/3 System. Modifications can be overwritten during an upgrade. Make sure to thoroughly test and document any changes you make, so that those changes can be made again, if necessary.

It may be more desirable to create characteristic values in a way that a modification is not necessary.

If a different comparison between the customer and product catalog characteristics is required, a modification must be made to the function module *IST_AREA_FILTER*. This function is called using the following function:

```
FUNCTION 'IST_AREA_FILTER'
    EXPORTING
    LAYVR = PI_LAYOUT
    SORTF = PI_AREA
    MPORTING
    DISPLAY = DISPLAY
    TABLES
    CHARACT_VALUES = PI_T_CHAR.
```

The function returns the values *1* (display) or *0* (do not display). If only one mismatch occurs between the customer and product catalog characteristic values, the area is not displayed. Any change in this logic needs to be made in this function module. To access the function module, enter transaction **SE37** in the *Command* field and choose *Enter* (or from the navigation menu, choose *Tools* → *ABAP Workbench* → *Development* → *Function Builder*).

C H A P T E R

5

Customers in the Online Store

Overview

When Internet customers visit your web site, they must register before placing an order. The customers must be identified so that customer information can be created in the system, making order processing possible. Additionally, once the customer has been identified, taxes can be calculated based on the shipping address, and credit card data can be verified.

When a customer registers on the Internet, a customer master record is either created within R/3, or the address information is stored directly in the sales order created in R/3. Having all the information available immediately facilitates the order fulfillment process. Whether a customer master record is created depends on how much data should be available for reporting, and how often customers are expected to repeat their visits to the site. You may want to consider the following points:

- If each customer that visits the site creates a master record, detailed reporting of these customers will be available and trends can be analyzed

- If many repeat customers are expected, they may not have the patience to enter their address information each time they order.

- If each customer visiting the site creates a master record, this must be considered when sizing the R/3 database. If it is not expected that many repeat customers will visit the site, it may be more desirable to use one-time customers.

What We Deliver

In the Online Store preconfiguration, we provide the following deliverables:

- Preconfiguration of the customer account group

- Preconfiguration of a user exit to correctly determine the customer's tax jurisdiction code

- Documentation on the options for creating the customer master record

The Customer Experience

In the Online Store scenario, the customer is created before an order is processed. The following screens show Oliver's customer experience while registering on the Internet. The customer record created in the R/3 System may be either a normal customer, consumer, or one-time customer.

1. If the customer has visited the web site before, an e-mail address and password may be used to log on. Please refer to chapter 1, "Creating the Online Store with the Catalog" on page 5 about entering the store and placing products into the shopping basket.

2. In this example, Oliver is visiting the site and chooses *Register*.

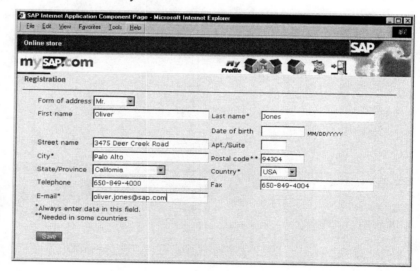

3. Oliver registers in the store:

a. Oliver enters his address information.

b. Oliver chooses *Save*. A customer master record is now created in the backend R/3 System.

4. To complete the registration process:

  a. Oliver enters a password for the new account twice.

  b. He chooses *Change password*. His password is stored in the Internet user in the backend R/3 System.

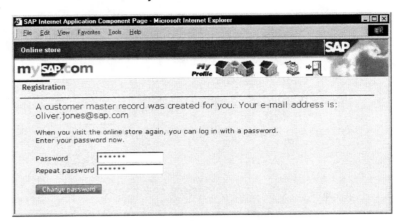

5. Oliver chooses *Cont.*

The password is confirmed. ————

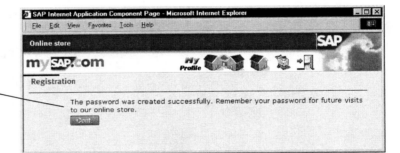

6. To change his shipping address, Oliver chooses *Goto Change deliv. address.*

The customer can change their address by choosing *Goto Address Change*. The change is reflected immediately in the customer master record.

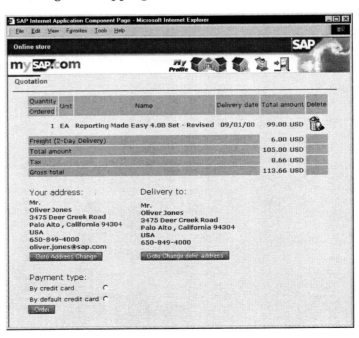

7. On the address screen:

    a. Oliver enters an alternate name, and the shipping address information.

    b. He chooses *Change dlvy address*.

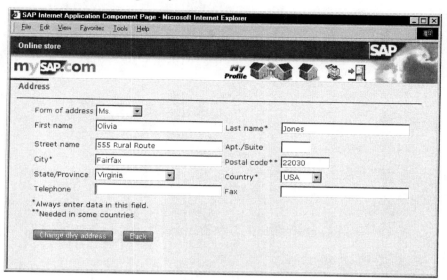

8. Oliver selects *By credit card* to use a new credit, since he did not store one using the "My Profile" service.

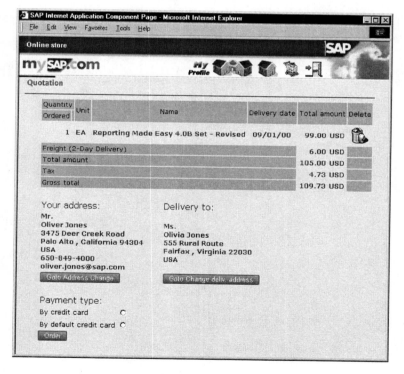

9. Oliver enters his credit card information, and places the order.

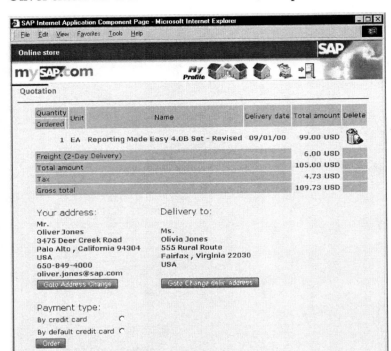

10. The confirmation screen confirms the delivery address.

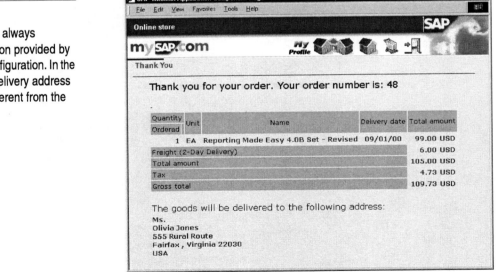

The View from Inside your Company

When a customer registers on the Internet, a customer master record is immediately created in R/3. All data is copied from a reference customer, with the exception of the customer-specific address and contact data. The customer master record that was created from the Internet can be displayed.

Task

Verify the customer who registered on the Internet is created correctly in R/3

1. In the *Command* field, enter transaction **XD03** and choose *Enter* (or from the navigation menu, choose *Logistics → Sales and Distribution → Master Data → Business Partners → Customer → Display → Complete*).

2. On the *Display Customer: Initial Screen*:

   a. In *Customer*, enter the customer number.

   b. In *Sales organization*, enter the sales organization you use to do business on the Internet.

   c. In *Distribution channel*, enter the distribution channel you use to do business on the Internet.

   d. In *Division*, enter the division you use to do business on the Internet.

   e. Choose ✔ .

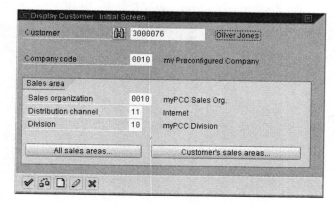

3. On the *Display Customer: General data* screen:

   a. On the *Address* tab, all address information entered by the Internet customer is displayed. The tax jurisdiction code is determined based on the customer address.

   b. Scroll to the bottom of the address tab.

Note

Since the customer number is not displayed on the web (e-mail addresses are used), the customer number must be found using the matchcode (the *Search term* is the customer's last name).

c. The e-mail address entered on the web is stored in the *E-mail* field.

d. Choose the *Contact persons* tab.

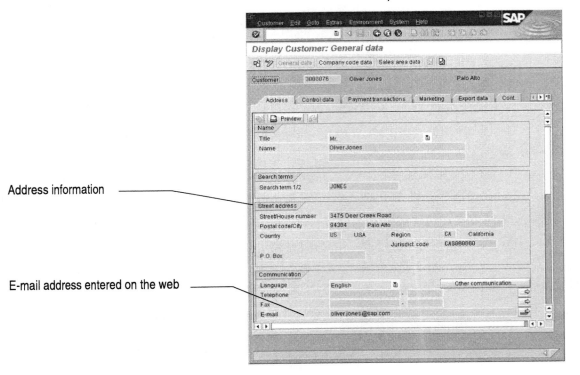

Address information

E-mail address entered on the web

4. On the *Contact persons* tab, double-click on the contact name.

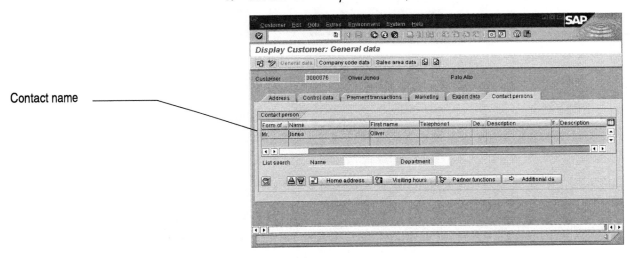

Contact name

5. On the *Display Customer: Contact person details* screen:

a. The birth date, as entered on the web, is stored in the *Date of birth* field.

b. At the bottom of the screen, the address information displayed on the *Display Customer: General data* screen is also stored in the *Contact person details* information (not shown).

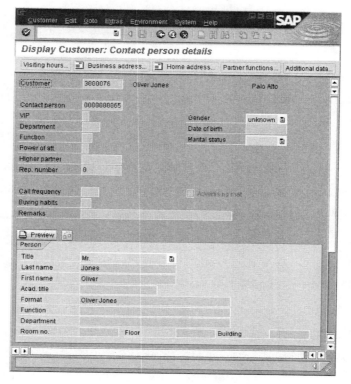

Task

Verify the delivery address is correctly entered in the sales order

The sales order that was created from the Internet can be displayed. The delivery address is stored within this sales order, not as a ship-to party in the customer master record.

1. In the *Command* field, enter transaction **VA03** and choose *Enter* (or from the navigation menu, choose *Logistics* → *Sales and Distribution* → *Sales* → *Order* → *Display*).

2. On the *Display Sales Order: Initial Screen*:

   a. In *Order*, enter the number of the order created from the Internet.

   b. Choose 🅥 .

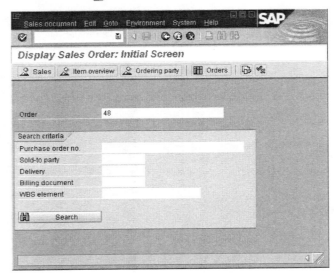

3. On the *Display e-Shop Web Order <XXX>: Overview* screen, choose *Goto* →
   Header → *Partner* from the menu bar.

4. On the *Display e-Shop Web Order <XXX>: Header Data* screen, double-click on
   the ship-to party.

Ship-to party ————

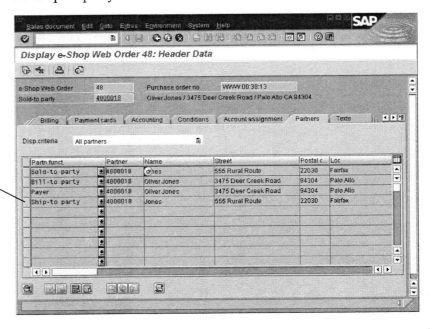

5. The customer data is displayed within the order.

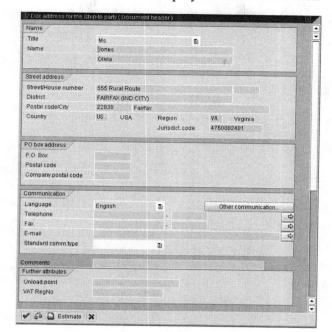

Another Possibility: Consumers

If a consumer master record had been created instead of a normal customer master record, the customer master would display differently.

Task

Display a consumer master created from the Internet

1. In the *Command* field, enter transaction **XD03** and choose *Enter* (or from the navigation menu, choose *Logistics → Sales and Distribution → Master Data → Business Partners → Customer → Display → Complete*).

2. On the *Display Customer: Initial Screen*:

a. In *Customer*, enter the customer number.

b. In *Sales organization*, enter the sales organization you use to do business on the Internet.

c. In *Distribution channel*, enter the distribution channel you use to do business on the Internet.

d. In *Division*, enter the division you use to do business on the Internet.

e. Choose ✔ .

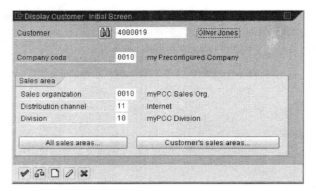

3. On the *Information* dialog box, choose ✔ .

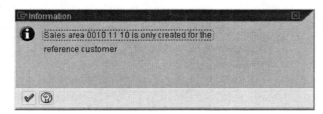

4. On the *Display Customer: General data* screen:

a. Under *Personal data*, the personal data is only created for the consumer master record.

b. The address data can be displayed by scrolling down.

Another Possibility: One-Time Customers

Note

The order displayed in this section is only an example. It is not the order created in the customer experience section.

If one-time customers are used instead of customer master records, all customer information would be contained in the order.

Task

Display an order with the one-time customer data created from the Internet

1. In the *Command* field, enter transaction **VA03** and choose *Enter* (or from the navigation menu, choose *Logistics* → *Sales and Distribution* → *Sales* → *Order* → *Display*).

2. On the *Display Sales Order: Initial Screen*:

   a. In *Order*, enter the number of the order created from the Internet.

   b. Choose 🗸.

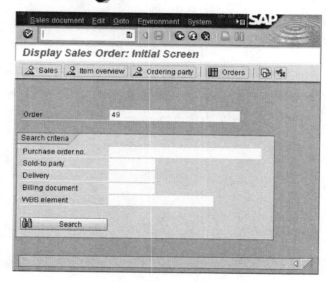

3. On the *Display e-Shop Web Order <XXX>: Overview* screen, choose *Goto* → *Header* → *Partner* from the menu bar.

4. On the *Display e-Shop Web Order <XXX>: Header Data* screen, double-click on the bill-to party.

Bill-to party ────────

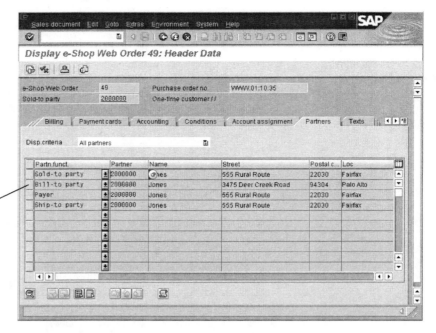

5. The customer data is displayed within the order.

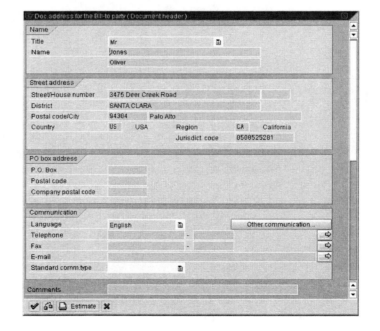

Making it Happen: Customers in the Online Store

As a prerequisite to implementing the Online Store preconfiguration, either the Preconfigured Client (PCC) U.S. is being implemented at the same time, or a working Sales and Distribution (SD) configuration has already been implemented. This prerequisite means that the configuration that supports the customer master record creation is already complete. If an existing SD configuration has already been implemented, any customer master records that have been created can also be used on the Internet for processing. This chapter is not intended to be a thorough discussion of customer master records, and how customers and partner functions should be configured. This section provides guidelines related to how customers are used within the Online Store.

The different types of customers that can be created through the Online Store are:

- Full sold-to customer master

- Consumer, which is a minimal customer master with personal and company code data

- One-time customer, in which the customer data is stored only in the sales order and not as a separate master record

The first option, in which a full customer master record is created, was the only option available until Release 4.6. To create the new master record for each newly registered Internet customer, a reference customer is copied. Only the address and contact data is replaced with the customer-specific data. The reference customer can be stored in the Online Store or the product catalog. The R/3 System first checks the Online Store customer. If a reference customer is not maintained there, the customer in the product catalog is used. The customer in the basic data of the product catalog is a mandatory entry. It may be desirable to create a different customer account group to identify these customers in reporting.

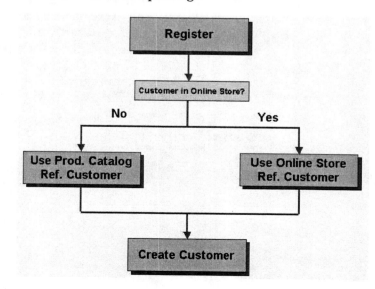

In the second option, a reference customer is designated for all consumers. When the Internet customer registers, a consumer record is created. The address is updated in the personal data of the consumer. The consumer is a customer master record with limited data. When used in the Online Store, the company code data, such as accounting and payment information, is copied to the consumer master record. The sales area data is taken from the reference customer during order processing, but is not copied directly into the consumer master record. Therefore, the amount of data that needs to be stored for the consumer is very limited. In the "My Profile" add-on provided by the Online Store preconfiguration package, a default shipping type cannot be maintained for consumers, since it is stored in the sales area data of a customer master record, and this view is not created for consumers.

In addition, any partners (other than sold-to, ship-to, bill-to, and payer) are also copied from the reference customer during order processing, which makes it possible to store the forwarding carrier for deliveries in the reference customer. The carrier is then copied to all sales orders placed by the consumer. The carrier used should be the primary carrier you use for the majority of your Internet business, thus reducing the amount of data entry required for order fulfillment.

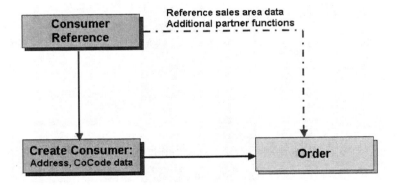

Finally, a one-time customer can be used. The one-time reference customer is stored in the customer administration profile of the Online Store. This one-time customer is used to create the sales order. All information entered by the Internet customer is stored directly in the order. Storing customer information in an order makes it more difficult for reporting, and customers will need to reenter their address data each time they order. However, the amount of data stored in the R/3 System is greatly reduced.

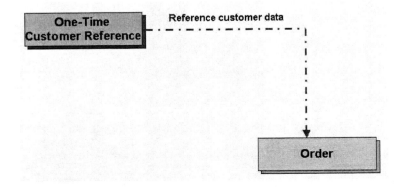

In addition to creating the customer master record, an Internet user is created for customers and consumers that store the password for the customer master record. Please refer to chapter 15, "The ITS User: Logging on to R/3" on page 349 for details on the Internet user created for customers. No password is created if the one-time customer option is chosen.

If the delivery address is changed for full customers and for consumers, it is not stored in the partner data of the customer master. The alternate delivery address is stored only within the order created from the Online Store.

TechTalk

If you wish to convert all of your customers into consumers, you must perform the following steps:

1. Execute program *RINTCON_P*, which creates personal addresses from existing Internet customer master records.

2. Execute program *RINTCON_C*, which converts customers to consumers.

Master Data Required for Creating Customers in the Online Store

To allow customers on the Internet to register, reference customer data must already exist. Depending on your configuration of the Online Store, you may be using normal customer master records, consumer records, or one-time customers. For each of these scenarios, a different reference customer must be created. The views of the customer master record are not shown below.

The following customers may need to be created:

- A reference customer

    Link the reference customer to the:

    - Product catalog

    - Online Store (see the *Configuration* section)

    - Consumer default

- A one-time customer

    Link the one-time customer to the customer administration profile. For more information, see "Configuration to Support Customer Master Creation in the Online Store" on page 153.

Create a Reference Customer Master Record

Since customer master records are created though the Online Store, you must create a reference customer that can be used as a base for creating records for customers who register on the Internet. Either a normal sold-to customer or a consumer is created that uses this reference customer's data. The customer master record is not discussed here in detail.

Remember that the customer master record must be created using the sales area used on the Internet. A sold-to party should be used as the reference customer. The following data is critical to this customer master:

- The accounting information, taxation indicator, and sales area data, will be used for all Internet customers that register on the Internet.

- The Incoterms used will be the default shipping type copied into all master records for customers that register on the Internet.

- If the customer should be used as a reference for consumers, a forwarding agent (freight carrier) should be entered into the *Partner functions* view. The freight carrier will be copied into all consumers' sales documents created using this reference customer.

In the *Command* field, enter transaction **XD01** and choose *Enter* (or from the navigation menu, choose *Logistics → Sales and Distribution → Master Data → Business Partners → Customer → Create → Complete*).

Link the Reference Customer to the Product Catalog

Once the reference customer is created, it can be linked to the product catalog. This reference customer is used if no customer is specified in the Online Store configuration. The reference customer is a required field within the product catalog. Please refer to chapter 2, "Creating the Product Catalog" on page 43 for details about the product catalog.

Task

Link the reference customer to the product catalog

1. In the *Command* field, enter transaction **WWM2** and choose *Enter* (or from the navigation menu, choose *Logistics → Materials Management → Product Catalog → Product Catalog → Change*).

2. On the *Change Product Catalog: Initial Screen*:

   a. In *Catalog*, enter the product catalog code used in the Online Store.

   b. Choose *Basic data*.

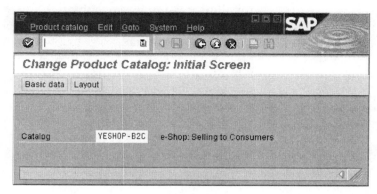

3. On the *Product Catalog: Change Basic Data* screen:

   a. In *Ref. customer*, enter the reference customer.

   b. Under *Sales area*, enter the appropriate information for *Sales org., Distr.chl.,* and *Division* that you will use for your Internet business. All customers, products, and prices need to be created for this sales area.

   c. Choose 💾 .

Note

In configuration, you can determine whether the reference customer is used as a base for creating the new Internet customers during registration. All fields are copied from this reference customer. However, the data entered by the customer on the Internet, such as address and contact data, replaces the reference data.

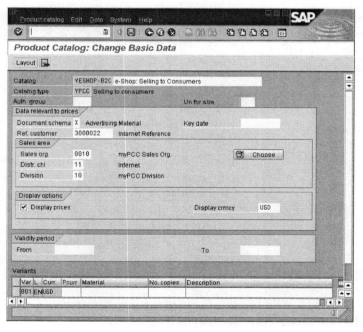

Link the Reference Customer to the Online Store

For more information, see "Configuration to Support Customer Master Creation in the Online Store" on page 153.

Link the Reference Customer to the Consumer Default

Once the reference customer is created, it can be designated as the reference customer for all consumers. The sales area of this reference customer is used for all processing for consumers. Only one reference customer can be designated as the consumer reference for the client.

Task

Designate the customer as the reference for all consumer master records

1. In the *Command* field, enter transaction **VD07** and choose *Enter* (or from the navigation menu, choose *Logistics → Sales and Distribution → Master Data → Business partners → Customer → Assign consumer – ref. customer*).

2. On the *Maintain Reference Customer for Consumer* screen:

   a. In *Ref. customer*, enter the customer to be used as the reference for all consumer data.

   b. Choose ✅.

   c. Choose 💾.

The sales areas and company codes for which the reference customer is maintained are displayed. Since only one reference customer can be created for the R/3 client, additional sales areas and company codes may need to be maintained if the reference customer should be used for consumers in other organizational areas.

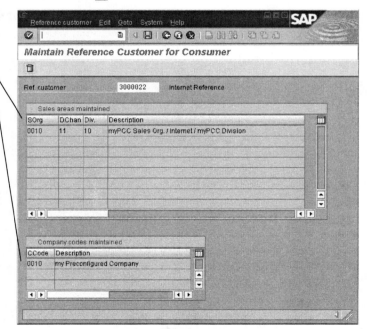

Create a One-Time Customer

Since customer master records are created though the Online Store, you must create a one-time customer if you choose not to store customer information. The one-time customer master record is then used as the base for creating orders, and customer-specific information is updated only in the sales order. The standard account group *CPD* is used for one-time customers.

In the *Command* field, enter transaction **XD01** and choose *Enter* (or from the navigation menu, choose *Logistics → Sales and Distribution → Master Data → Business Partners → Customer → Create → Complete*).

Link the One-Time Customer to the Customer Administration Profile

Please refer to the next section.

Configuration to Support Customer Master Creation in the Online Store

To ensure the customers are correctly created for your Internet business, you must:

- Verify the settings in the Online Store (preconfigured)
- Verify the settings in the customer administration profile (preconfigured)
- Create a number range for the Internet customers (preconfigured)
- Create a customer account group for Internet customers (preconfigured)
- Verify that all account groups for customers use internal number assignment (preconfigured)
- Create the user exit that allows the correct determination of the tax jurisdiction code of the customer (preconfigured)
- Check the SAPNet – R/3 Frontend Notes

Verify Settings in the Online Store

The Online Store contains links to the product catalog master data and to configuration that determines product, customer, and sales orders handling. Four different Online Stores are delivered with the Online Store preconfiguration. None of these stores contains a reference customer. For details about Online Store customization, please refer to chapter 1, "Creating the Online Store with the Catalog" on page 5.

Task

Verify the configuration of the Online Store

In the IMG, choose *Logistics - General → IAC Product Catalog and Online Store* and choose ⊕ next to *Online Stores*. You must choose whether you wish to enter a reference customer in the Online Store directly.

Verify the Settings in the Customer Administration Profile

The customer administration profile determines how customers are created in the R/3 System when they register in the Online Store, and how logon is handled. For the business partner scenario, new customers cannot register online; normal customer master records are expected for customers who log on. For the first business-to-consumer scenario, customers register online, and a normal customer master record is created. For the second business-to-consumer scenario, a consumer is created as the customer master record. For the one-time customer scenario, a reference CPD customer is used, and no customer master record is created. For details about the customer administration profiles, please refer to chapter 1, "Creating the Online Store with the Catalog" on page 5.

Task

Verify the configuration of the customer administration profiles

In the IMG, choose *Logistics - General → IAC Product Catalog and Online Store* and choose ⏰ next to *Customer Administration Profiles.*

In the customer administration profile, the following settings must be made for the creation of particular customer master records:

Customer Created	No Registration	Allow OTA	OTA Customer	Consumer
Normal customer	Either on or off	Off	Off	Off
Consumer	Either on or off	Off	Off	On
One-time customer	On	On	Customer #	Off

Create a Number Range for the Internet Customers

Customers are created from the Online Store during registration, where the customer is not given the opportunity to enter a customer number. For this reason, the customer number range for customers created from the Internet must be internal. A new number range has been created to support the new customer account group created in the next step.

Task

Create an internal number range for customer account groups

In the *Command* field, enter transaction **OVZC** and choose *Enter* (or in the IMG, choose *Logistics - General → Business Partner → Customer → Control* and choose ⏰ next to *Define and Assign Customer Number Ranges.* Then on the *Choose Activity* dialog box, select *Define Number Ranges for Customer Master* and choose ▣ *Choose).*

Number Range	Number From	Number To	External Indicator
YE	0004000000	0004999999	Off

Create a Customer Account Group for Internet Customers

A new customer account group may be created for the Internet customers. This account group allows fields not populated during the customer creation process to be turned off. Account group *YWEB* has been preconfigured.

Task

Configure the customer account group for Internet usage

In the *Command* field, enter transaction **OVT0** and choose *Enter* (or in the IMG, choose *Logistics - General* → *Business Partner* → *Customer* → *Control* and choose 🖑 next to *Define Account Groups and Field Selection for Customers*).

The primary settings in the account group table are documented below.

Field	Value
Number range	YE
One-time account	Off
Central text determination procedure	01
Text determination procedure SD	01
Customer pricing procedure	1 (standard)
Partner determination procedure	AG (sold-to party)

All other entries are blank. The field status settings are documented below.

YWEB – myPCC Internet Sold-to

Note

The table indicates, for each field, whether it is suppressed, required, optional, or display only.

YWEB – myPCC Internet Sold-to Party	Suppressed	Required	Optional	Display Only
General Data – Address Data				
Name 1/last name		X		
Form of address			X	
Search term A		X		
Name 2/first name			X	
Name 3, name 4	X			
Postal code, city		X		
Street			X	
Location			X	
Region			X	
P.O. box			X	

Note

The table indicates, for each field, whether it is suppressed, required, optional, or display only.

YWEB – myPCC Internet Sold-to Party	Suppressed	Required	Optional	Display Only
General Data – Address Data				
P.O. box postal code	X			
Transportation zone			X	
Tax jurisdiction			X	
P.O. Box city	X			
Search term B	X			
c/o name	X			
Street 2			X	
Street 3	X			
Street 5	X			
Buildings	X			
Floor	X			
Room number	X			
Company postal code	X			
Comments	X			
Time zone	X			
Delivery district			X	
Street 4	X			
Regional structure group			X	
Sex	X			
Date of birth			X	
Marital status	X			
Academic title	X			
Name prefix	X			
2. academic title	X			
2nd prefix	X			
Name at birth	X			
Nickname	X			
Name affix	X			
Initials			X	
Country for format			X	
Format name			X	

YWEB – myPCC Internet Sold-to Party	Suppressed	Required	Optional	Display Only
General Data – Address Data				
Alternative place of re			X	
P.O. box without number			X	
PO box country			X	
PO Box Region			X	

YWEB – my PCC Internet Sold-to Party	Suppressed	Required	Optional	Display Only
General Data – Communication				
Telex, fax, tel.			X	
Teletex	X			
Telebox	X			
Data line	X			
Internet address			X	
Standard comm. Type	X			
Internet mail address			X	

YWEB – my PCC Internet Sold-to Party	Suppressed	Required	Optional	Display Only
General Data – Control				
Vendor			X	
Corporate group			X	
Tax code 1			X	
Sales equalization tax			X	
International location number			X	
Fiscal address			X	
Industry			X	
Location code			X	
Train station/express train station			X	
Authorization			X	
VAT registration number			X	
Trading partner			X	
County Code, City Code			X	
Tax code 2			X	

YWEB – my PCC Internet Sold-to Party	Suppressed	Required	Optional	Display Only
General Data – Control				
Taxes on sales/purchases			X	
Natural person	X			
Reference account group (OTA)	X			
Business place	X			
Tax type	X			
CFOP category	X			
Tax number 3	X			
Tax number 4	X			
Brazilian taxes: ICMS,I	X			
Tax categories	X			

YWEB – my PCC Internet Sold-to Party	Suppressed	Required	Optional	Display Only
General Data – Marketing				
Nielsen ID			X	
Regional market			X	
Customer class			X	
Industry sectors			X	
Sales			X	
Employees			X	
Business form			X	
Fiscal year			X	
Hierarchy allocation	X			

YWEB – my PCC Internet Sold-to Party	Suppressed	Required	Optional	Display Only
General Data – Payment Transactions				
Bank details			X	
Alternative payer account			X	
Alternative payer in doc			X	
DME details	X			

YWEB – my PCC Internet Sold-to Party	Suppressed	Required	Optional	Display Only
General Data – Unloading Points				
Unloading Points			X	

YWEB – my PCC Internet Sold-to Party	Suppressed	Required	Optional	Display Only
General Data – Contact Person				
Contact Person			X	

YWEB – my PCC Internet Sold-to Party	Suppressed	Required	Optional	Display Only
General Data – Foreign Trade				
Foreign Trade			X	

YWEB – my PCC Internet Sold-to Party	Suppressed	Required	Optional	Display Only
Company Code Data – Account Management				
Reconciliation account		X		
Cash management group			X	
Previous account number	X			
Sort key			X	
Head office			X	
Authorization			X	
Preference indicator			X	
Interest calculation			X	
Buying group			X	
Personnel number			X	
Release approval group	X			
Gross income tax	X			
Value adjustment key			X	

YWEB – my PCC Internet Sold-to Party	Suppressed	Required	Optional	Display Only
Company Code Data – Payment Transactions				
Terms of payment			X	
Bill of exch. Charges term			X	
Payment block			X	
Payment methods			X	

YWEB – my PCC Internet Sold-to Party	Suppressed	Required	Optional	Display Only
Company Code Data – Payment Transactions				
Alternative payer account			X	
Clearing with vendor			X	
Bill of exchange limit			X	
Next payee			X	
Indicate payment history			X	
Tolerance group			X	
House bank			X	
Known/negotiated leave			X	
Lockbox			X	
Payment advice via EDI			X	
Payment advice notes			X	
Single payment, group key, PM s			X	
Credit memo terms of payment	X			
Diff. payer in document	X			
Accounts receivable factoring indicator			X	

YWEB – my PCC Internet Sold-to Party	Suppressed	Required	Optional	Display Only
Company Code Data – Correspondence				
Payment notices			X	
Accounting clerk's communication			X	
Dunning data	X			
Account statement			X	
Local processing			X	
Collective invoice variant			X	
Account at customer			X	
Accounting clerks			X	
Users at customer			X	
Account memo			X	

YWEB – my PCC Internet Sold-to Party	Suppressed	Required	Optional	Display Only
Company Code Data – Insurance				
Export credit insurance			X	

YWEB – my PCC Internet Sold-to Party	Suppressed	Required	Optional	Display Only
Company Code Data – Withholding tax data				
W/hold.tax deduction, w/h t			X	
Withholding tax code (2)			X	
Withholding tax number			X	
Withholding tax types			X	

YWEB – my PCC Internet Sold-to Party	Suppressed	Required	Optional	Display Only
Sales and Distribution Data – Sales				
Sales group			X	
Statistics group		X		
Customer group			X	
Sales district			X	
Pricing procedure		X		
Price group			X	
Price list type			X	
Units of measure group			X	
Currency		X		
Our account with customer			X	
Order probability			X	
Cust. scheme product proposal			X	
Default product proposal			X	
Sales office			X	
Authorization			X	
Exchange rate type			X	
Switch off rounding for cu			X	
ABC class			X	
Agency business			X	

YWEB – my PCC Internet Sold-to Party	Suppressed	Required	Optional	Display Only
Sales and Distribution Data – Shipping				
Shipping cond. /POD relevant		X		
Default plant			X	
Partial deliveries/tolerance			X	
Order combination			X	
Delivery priority			X	

YWEB – my PCC Internet Sold-to Party	Suppressed	Required	Optional	Display Only
Sales and Distribution Data – Billing				
Account assignment group			X	
Terms of payment			X	
Incoterms			X	
Subsequent invoice process			X	
Billing period			X	
Hedging and credit contr.			X	
Taxes and licenses		X		
Rebate/pricing			X	

YWEB – my PCC Internet Sold-to Party	Suppressed	Required	Optional	Display Only
Sales and Distribution Data – Partner Usage				
Business Partner Assignment			X	

YWEB – my PCC Internet Sold-to Party	Suppressed	Required	Optional	Display Only
Sales and Distribution Data – Documents				
Documents			X	

Verify All Customer Account Groups Use Internal Number Assignment

Customers are created from the Online Store during registration, where the customer is not given the opportunity to enter a customer number. For this reason, the customer number range for customers created from the Internet must be internal. The standard-delivered number range for consumers is external, so this account group is reassigned to the newly created internal number range.

Task

Verify the customer account group's number ranges

In the *Command* field, enter transaction **OVT0** and choose *Enter* (or in the IMG, choose *Logistics - General* → *Business Partner* → *Customer* → *Control* and choose ⬦ next to *Define Account Groups and Field Selection for Customers*).

Customer account group	Number range assignment
YWEB (e-Shop Internet sold-to party)	YE
0170 (consumer)	YE

Create User Exit for Correct Determination of Customer's Tax Jurisdiction Code

Using SAP enhancement functionality, a user exit allows the correct determination of the tax jurisdiction code for Internet customers to take place.

If internal taxes are active, the user exit determines a tax jurisdiction code based on the user's state of residence. The level of detail in the tax jurisdiction code determination corresponds to the same level of detail as the taxes delivered with the Preconfigured Client (PCC). If tax processing within R/3 is used, and a more detailed tax jurisdiction code determination is necessary, changes need to be made to the user exit.

If external taxes are active, the tax jurisdiction code and district (county) are determined. A standard R/3 function module is called to populate these fields. We tested the external tax functionality with Vertex and Taxware. In addition, error handling is coded in the user exit, again using a standard R/3 function module. The error handling sends a warning message to the web notifying the customer to correct their address information when the tax jurisdiction code cannot be determined due to inconsistent address fields, while still leaving the entry fields open to changes.

The changes made to implement the user exit are described below. To deactivate the user exit, simply deactivate the enhancement project.

Task

Create the user exit

In the *Command* field, enter transaction **CMOD** and choose *Enter* (or from the navigation menu, choose *Tools → ABAP Workbench → Utilities → Enhancements → Project Management*). The project is active in the Online Store preconfiguration.

Project	Enhancement	Function Exit	Include
YE_TAX	WWCC1001 (function exit for WWW component customer)	EXIT_SAPLWWCC1_001	ZXWC1U01

Check the SAPNet – R/3 Frontend Notes

Information from SAPNet – R/3 Frontend notes (formerly OSS) is also essential to the configuration of sales order status. Please refer to appendix A, "SAPNet Frontend Notes" on page 495 for information about these notes.

TechTalk

For the consumers to function as described in this chapter, the following SAPNet – R/3 Frontend notes must be applied:

- *212783* corrects a problem with the tax calculation when a different delivery address is entered, or when one-time customers are used. The user exit delivered with the Online Store preconfiguration, which determines the tax jurisdiction code, is required for the tax calculation to take place.

- *197511* corrects a problem with the personal data of consumers.

- *187143* solves a problem with the address management of one-time customers.

- *315142* corrects a problem with the partner determination of consumers.

CHAPTER

6

Multiple Employees Making Purchases for One Corporation

Overview

In larger corporations, many employees may be authorized to make purchases. These corporations are often hesitant to provide the same customer number and password to all of their employees, since it is then no longer possible to track who made a particular purchase. In the Online Store scenario, it is not possible to maintain multiple passwords for the same customer account and provide tracking. At the same time, many corporations do not wish to have multiple customer numbers for each employee of a business partner without a way to tie them together, as this would make tracking the total number of purchases difficult.

To solve this problem, a customer hierarchy is used. Each employee of the corporation has a separate customer number and password, which allows the tracking of the person who actually placed an order. The customer hierarchy then links these employees to a higher-level customer, which is the corporation. A business process must be put in place in which the employee master record is created in the R/3 System and linked to the corporation. At the same time, it must be verified that this employee is authorized to make purchases on behalf of the corporation. Through the customer hierarchy, it is then possible to consolidate, in reporting, the total purchases of the corporation, which includes the orders placed by all customers (individuals).

It is also likely that the corporation, not the individual employee, should be billed for the purchase, and that the ordered items be shipped to the corporation. Partner determination can be configured to send the bills directly to the company, instead of the individual purchaser. Since the corporation remains the bill-to and payer for these orders, billing and accounts receivable (A/R) processes are consolidated as well.

What We Deliver

In the Online Store preconfiguration, we provide the following deliverables:

- Preconfiguration of a new customer hierarchy type and associated partner determination, is executed through CATT procedure *ZESHOP_CUSTOMER_HIERARCHY*. This configuration is delivered using a CATT since it is optional, and will likely be used only by customers who have this requirement.

- Sample master data is delivered through CATT procedure *ZESHOP_MULT_PASSWORDS* (to be used only with the PCC). Do not run this CATT in a production environment.

- Documentation covers the use of the customer hierarchy for creating multiple passwords for one customer (corporate) account.

For information about executing CATT procedures in general, and these CATTs in particular, please refer to appendix H, "Introduction to Computer-Aided Test Tools (CATTs)" on page 547.

The Customer Experience

An employee, Peter, logs on to the Online Store to make a purchase. He scrolls through the catalog and selects the appropriate item. Prior to placing the order, he verifies that he is receiving the corporate discount. The corporation will be billed for his purchase once it is shipped.

1. In the Internet browser, Peter enters the URL of your home page, which you configured as part of the ITS installation.

2. On the initial screen, Peter chooses the *Online Store* from your home page.

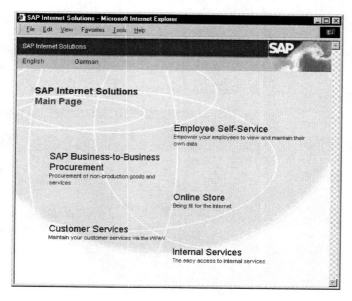

3. Peter chooses *Online Store*.

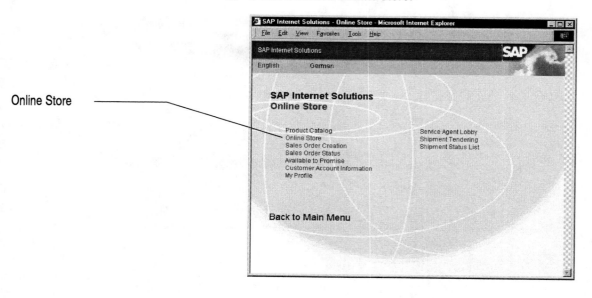

Online Store

4. Peter chooses the first store, *YGUIDES-B, SAP Labs Guidebooks for Bus. Partners.*

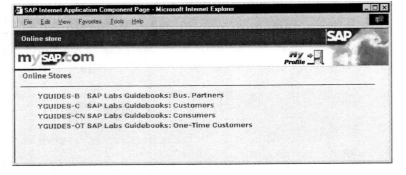

5. To identify himself to the site:

a. Peter enters his e-mail address and password.

b. He chooses *Logon.*

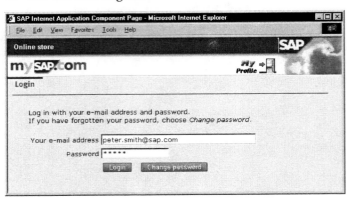

6. Peter chooses the first shop, *Guidebooks.*

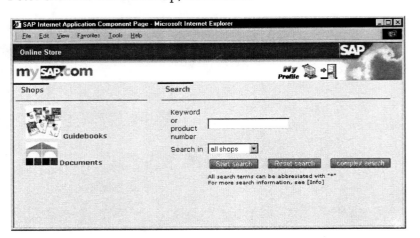

7. He then chooses the first product group, *Guidebooks 4.6x*.

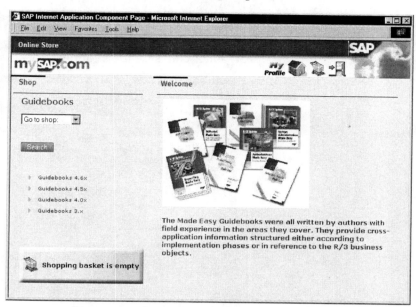

8. Peter places the first product into the shopping basket.

The product numbers are shown in the business partner store.

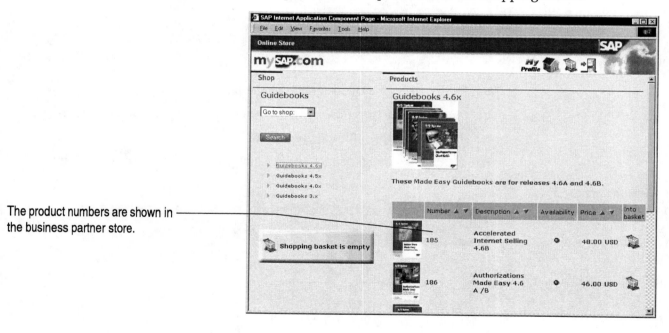

9. After placing the product into the basket:

  a. A confirmation message is displayed, verifying that the product is now in the basket.

  b. Peter clicks on the shopping basket icon to display his shopping basket.

Confirmation message

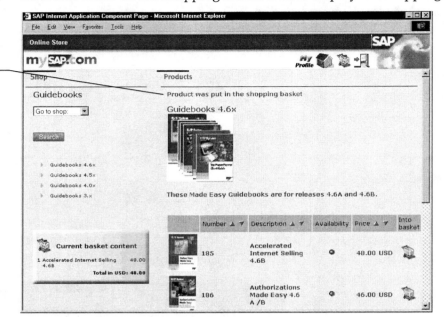

10. A list of the items in the shopping cart is displayed.

  a. Peter selects the overnight shipping option.

  b. He enters the purchase order number and date provided by his company.

  c. He accepts the default delivery date.

  d. He chooses *Quotation* to obtain a complete price breakdown of his purchase.

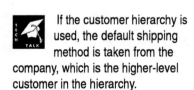 If the customer hierarchy is used, the default shipping method is taken from the company, which is the higher-level customer in the hierarchy.

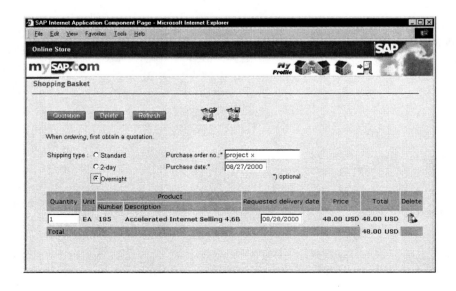

11. A complete breakdown of all prices is displayed.

    a. Peter verifies his address information.

    b. He chooses the *By invoice* payment option, since his company will be billed for this purchase.

    c. Peter chooses *Order*.

The company discount is included in the final price breakdown.

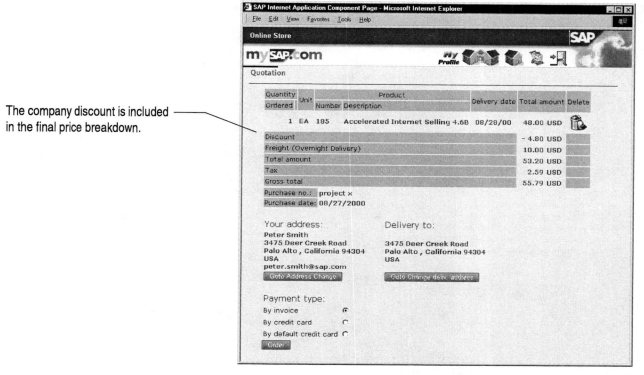

12. The order number created in R/3 is displayed. This number is also Peter's reference number.

Order number

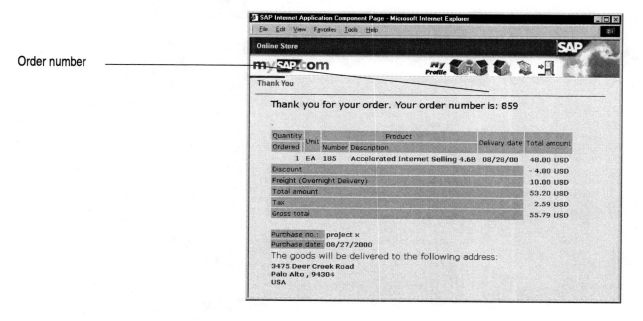

The View from Inside Your Company

The order created over the Internet can now be displayed.

1. In the *Command* field, enter transaction **VA03** and choose *Enter* (or from the navigation menu, choose *Logistics → Sales and Distribution → Sales → Order → Display*).

2. On the *Display Sales Order: Initial Screen*:

   a. In *Order*, enter the order number

   b. Choose 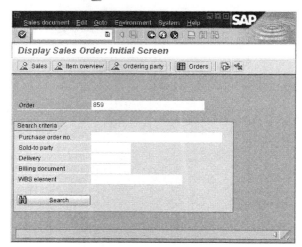.

3. On the *Display e-Shop Web Bus. Order <XX>: Overview* screen, choose *Goto → Header → Partner*.

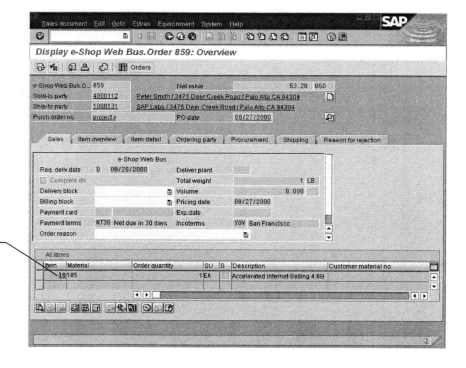

The item purchased on the Internet is displayed.

4. On the *Display e-Shop Web Bus. Order <XX>: Header Data* screen, choose 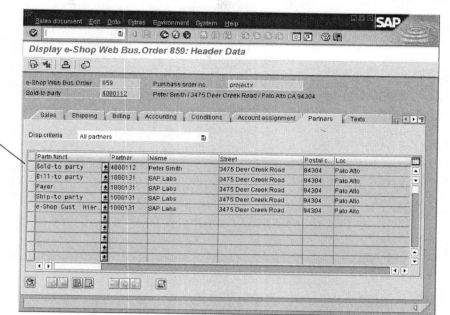.

The sold-to party is the employee who made the purchase.

All other partner functions point to the corporation, based on the partner determination configuration.

5. Back on the *Display e-Shop Web Bus. Order <XX>: Overview* screen:

   a. Select the item purchased.

   b. From the menu bar, choose *Goto → Item → Conditions.*

Item purchased

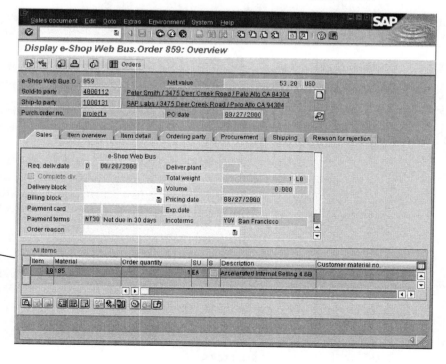

6. The discount—assigned to the corporation and not to the individual employee—is still valid for the employee. This discount is also due to the customer hierarchy.

Discount

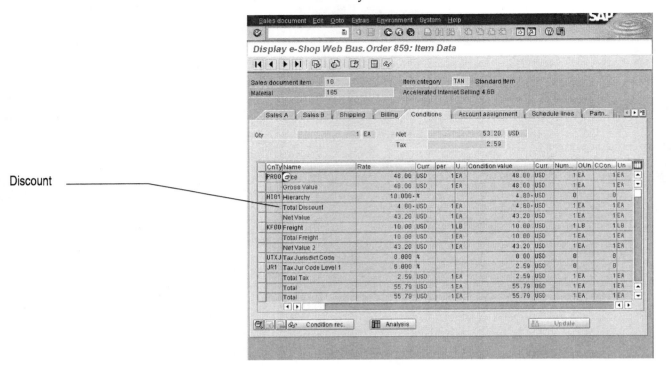

Making It Happen: Multiple Passwords for One Customer

If multiple employees of a corporation need to make purchases on behalf of their corporation, configuration within the R/3 System must first be carried out. The customer hierarchy needs to be configured before any purchases should be allowed through the Online Store. Customers who are purchasing on behalf of a corporation should not be allowed to register as a new customer online, since this action would create a new customer number. Additionally, a verification that they have purchasing authorization from their employer should take place before master data is created, which is a manual process. For this reason, the Online Store customer profile used in this scenario should be configured to require an early logon, without the option of creating a customer master record online. Please refer to chapter 5, "Customers in the Online Store" on page 133 for details about the customer profile in the Online Store.

Structure of the Hierarchy

The preconfiguration-delivered partner functions (*YA*, *YB*, *YC*, and *YD*) for the Online Store are displayed below. The system determines the customer hierarchy by starting with the customer who placed the order, then working its way upward in the customer hierarchy. The system then determines each higher level above the customer master records. The delivered hierarchy type *Y* points to customer hierarchy level *YD*, which is the lowest hierarchy level configured with the delivered partner functions. If additional levels are required, they must be configured during the implementation. An example of how the levels may be implemented is shown in the right portion of the figure below.

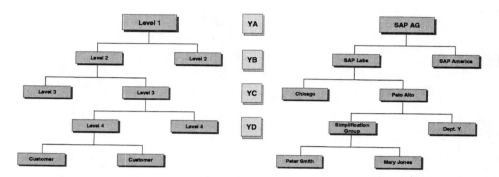

In the delivered configuration, three customer account groups may be mapped to each other in the delivered hierarchy. The account groups in the hierarchy levels are defined as a sold-to party (the corporation), an Internet sold-to party (an employee), and a hierarchy node (grouping levels). In the Online Store preconfiguration, an Internet Sold-to party (account group *YWEB*) can only be linked to a higher-level "regular" sold-to party (account group *0001*). The sold-to party can only be linked to a higher level hierarchy node (account group *0012*). Hierarchy nodes can only be linked to higher level hierarchy nodes. The partial hierarchy displayed below illustrates this linking order.

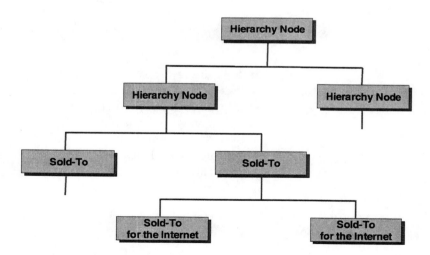

Online Store Scenario

The customer the employee represents creates the order on the Internet. In each sales order, the higher-level customer—or the corporate customer—is determined based on the customer hierarchy. This determination allows reports to be generated that provide consolidated information for the corporate customer, and tracks the employees that made the purchases. Please refer to chapter 11, "Sales Activity Reports" on page 263 for information on these reports.

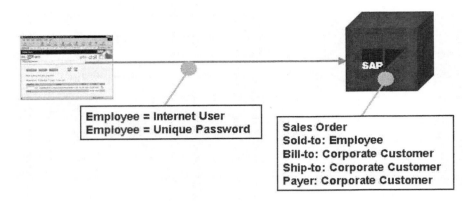

In our delivered scenario, a one-level hierarchy is used. The employee of the business partner who is purchasing products is at the lowest hierarchy level. These are the Internet sold-to customers who purchase products (account group *YWEB*). Only one level of hierarchy node is created above these customer master records. This customer represents the corporation, a higher level sold-to party, to which bills and shipments are sent (account group *0001*). We do not use the hierarchy node (account group *0012*) in our example.

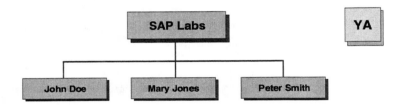

If there are fewer than the four preconfigured hierarchy levels, the system works its way up from the bottom of the partner functions shown previously, starting with *YD*. However, as the system uses the logic in configuration to work its way up to the highest level of the hierarchy, and only one level exists above the customer, the last code (highest) to be checked, or *YA*, is used. Therefore, *YA* will always be the highest level of the hierarchy, *YB* the second-highest, and so on.

Pricing

Discount pricing can be associated with the customer hierarchy, not just with individual customers. In the scenario above, it is possible to create a discount for the company (for example, SAP Labs), which is only valid if an "SAP Labs" user purchases a product. If the employees of SAP Labs should also receive this discount, then it should be created as a discount for the customer in the higher level of the hierarchy. The following condition types are standard-delivered with R/3 for customer hierarchy pricing:

Condition Type	Description
HI01	Percentage discount based on the customer hierarchy node
HI02	Quantity discount based on the material and customer hierarchy node

For the customer hierarchy to function consistently in partner determination and pricing, the customer hierarchy must have the same structure for price determination and for determining partner functions, such as the bill-to, payer, and ship-to parties.

In processing the customer hierarchy, the system works its way from the bottom up, to find the first valid discount on the hierarchy level. Once a valid hierarchy discount is found, the price is accepted, based on the access sequence delivered with R/3. If a different logic is required, the access sequence must be changed in configuration.

In the scenario and associated configuration delivered with the Online Store preconfiguration, only one hierarchy level exists above the employee's customer master record. The employees in this scenario should not be configured for pricing relevance for the customer hierarchy. In this way, only the corporate discounts are taken into account in pricing determination.

In processing the customer hierarchy for pricing, the customer hierarchy for pricing must be the same hierarchy used for partner determination. In this way, the corporate customer is designated as the bill-to, payer, and ship-to party. Additionally, the hierarchy should be balanced.

Master Data Setup for the Customer Hierarchy

The steps involved in setting up this scenario are described below in detail. You must create:

- The corporation as a sold-to party
- The employees as Internet sold-to parties
- An Internet user for each employee
- The customer hierarchy
- A discount for the corporation

CATT procedure *ZESHOP_MULT_PASSWORDS* is used to create sample master data, only if you are using the Online Store in conjunction with the Preconfigured Client (PCC) in a fresh installation. Please refer to appendix H, "Introduction to Computer-Aided Test Tools (CATTs)" on page 547 for details on running CATT procedures.

Create the Corporation as a Sold-to Party

The customer master can be created as usual. The parameters relevant to pricing are discussed.

Create the corporation as a sold-to party

1. In the *Command* field, enter transaction **XD01** and choose *Enter* (or from the navigation menu, choose *Logistics* → *Sales and Distribution* → *Master Data* → *Business partners* → *Customer* → *Create* → *Complete*).

2. On the *Create Customer: Initial Screen:*

   a. In *Account group*, enter the account group of the customer (for example, **0001** delivered with the PCC).

   b. In *Company code*, enter the company code.

   c. Under *Sales area*, enter the sales area information.

   d. Choose ✔ .

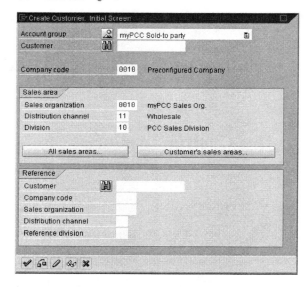

3. On the *Create Customer: General data* screen:

   a. In *Name*, enter the name of the corporation.

   b. Enter the remaining customer information, in all screens that are normally completed for a customer in your company.

   c. Choose *Sales area data*.

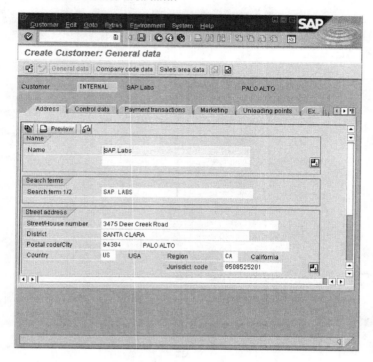

4. On the *Create Customer: Sales area data* screen:

   a. Choose the *Billing document* tab.

   b. If rebates are relevant to this customer, the *Rebates* checkbox should be selected.

   c. The *Price determin.* checkbox should be selected if discounts are to be given at the corporation level in the customer hierarchy.

d. Choose 💾 when you finish entering all relevant information for the customer.

Sales area data button ⎯⎯⎯⎯⎯⎯

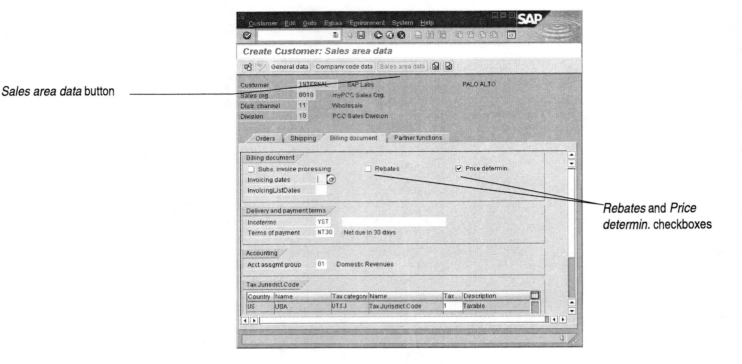

Rebates and Price determin. checkboxes

Create the Employees as Internet Sold-to Parties

The customer master can be created normally. The parameters that are relevant to pricing are discussed.

Task

Create employees as Internet sold-to parties

1. In the *Command* field, enter transaction **XD01** and choose *Enter* (or from the navigation menu, choose *Logistics → Sales and Distribution → Master Data → Business partners → Customer → Create → Complete*).

2. On the *Create Customer: Initial Screen*:

    a. In *Account group*, enter the account group of the customer (for example, **YWEB** delivered with the Online Store preconfiguration).

    b. In *Company code*, enter your company code

    c. Under *Sales area*, enter your sales area information.

    d. Choose ✔ .

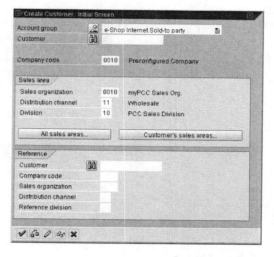

3. On the *Create Customer: General data* screen:

    a. In *Name*, enter the name of the employee to be linked to the corporation.

    b. Scroll down to display additional information.

    c. In *E-mail*, enter the employees e-mail address.

    d. Enter the remaining customer information in all screens usually completed for a customer in your company.

    e. Choose *Sales area data*.

> **Note**
>
> For the employee to be able to log on with an e-mail ID, and to receive e-mail confirmations of the order and its associated delivery, the e-mail address must be maintained.

4. On the *Create Customer: Sales area data* screen:

a. Choose the *Billing document* tab.

b. Deselect the *Rebates* checkbox. Rebates should not be relevant to an individual employee, but instead to the corporate customer.

c. Deselect the *Price determin.* checkbox. Discounts should be given at the corporation level in the customer hierarchy, not for an individual employee.

d. When you have completed entering all relevant information for the customer, choose 💾 .

Sales area data button ——————

Create an Internet User for Each Employee

An Internet user that stores the password for a customer number should be created for the employee, not for the corporation. Please refer to chapter 15, "The ITS User: Logging on to R/3" on page 349 for details on creating an Internet user.

In the *Command* field, enter transaction **SU05** and choose *Enter* (or from the navigation menu, choose *Tools → Administration → User Maintenance → Internet User*).

Create the Customer Hierarchy

The two types of customers should now be linked within the customer hierarchy.

Task

Create the customer hierarchy

1. In the *Command* field, enter transaction **VDH1N** and choose *Enter* (or from the navigation menu, choose *Logistics → Sales and Distribution → Master Data → Business partners → Customer hierarchy → Edit*).

2. On the *Process Customer Hierarchy* screen:

   a. If you have not changed the hierarchy type code in the CATT procedure *ZESHOP_CUSTOMER_HIERARCHY*, enter **Y** in the *Customer hierarchy type* field. If you changed the hierarchy type code, enter your hierarchy type.

   b. The *Validity date* defaults to the current date.

   c. In *Customer*, enter the number of the corporation.

   d. In the *Sales organization*, *Distribution channel*, and *Division* fields, enter your sales area information.

   e. Choose ⊕ .

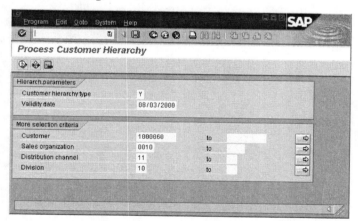

3. On the *Maintain Customer Hierarchy, e-Shop Cust. Hier., Date: <XX/XX/XXXX>*:

   a. Choose 📄 .

   b. In the *Higher-level customer* section, enter the corporation in the *Cust.* field.

   c. In the *Higher-level customer* section, enter your sales area in the *Sales organization*, *DistrChannel*, and *Divis.* fields.

   d. In the *Customer* section, enter the employee in the *Cust.* field.

   e. Choose ✅ *Transfer*.

   f. The top level of the hierarchy appears in the left frame.

g. Open the folder of the customer hierarchy in the left frame. The employee assignment to the higher-level customer (company) has been made.

h. Repeat the substeps for step **4** for any additional employees you wish to add to the customer hierarchy.

i. Choose 💾 .

Higher-level customer section

Customer section

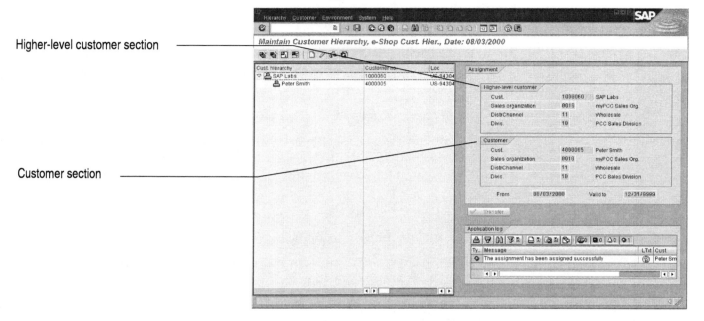

4. In order to display and edit the information on each employee in the right frame, double-click on the folder of the employee in the left frame.

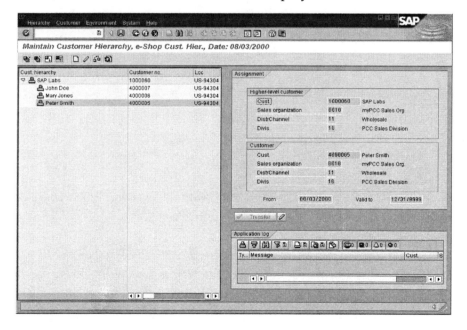

Create a Discount for the Corporation

The discount for the corporation is created using a hierarchy condition type. This configuration allows the employees to receive this discount as well.

> **Task**
>
> Create a discount for the corporation

1. In the *Command* field, enter transaction **VK31** and choose Enter (or from the navigation menu, choose *Logistics* → *Sales and Distribution* → *Master Data* → *Conditions* → *Create*. Then choose *Conditions* → *By Customer Hierarchy*).

2. On the *Create Condition Records: Overview* screen, choose 🗋 next to the first line, *CnTy Sorg DChl Dv Customer*.

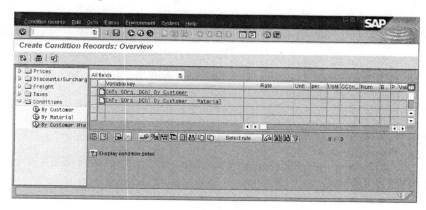

3. On the *Create Condition Records: Fast Entry* screen:

    a. Under *Co.*, enter condition type **HI01**.

    b. Under *Customer*, enter the corporation.

    c. Under *Rate*, enter the percentage discount.

    d. Choose ✅ . The *Valid on* and *Valid to* dates fill in automatically.

    e. Choose 💾 .

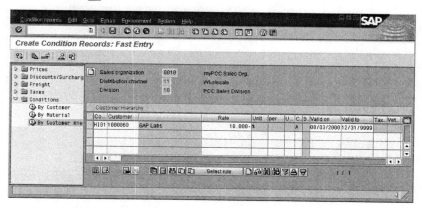

Customer Hierarchy Configuration

The steps involved in setting up the customer hierarchy for this scenario are described below. Although it is possible to use the standard-delivered customer hierarchy type in R/3, we configured a new hierarchy type so that existing customer hierarchies would not be affected. Therefore you must:

- Create a customer hierarchy type (preconfigured)

- Create new partner functions for the customer hierarchy (preconfigured)

- Assign the new partner functions to customer account groups (preconfigured)

- Create new partner determination procedures for sales documents (preconfigured)

- Assign the partner determination procedure to the Internet order type (preconfigured)

- Add the new partner functions to the delivery partner determination (preconfigured)

- Add the new partner functions to the billing header partner determination (preconfigured)

- Determine the account groups to be used (preconfigured with the PCC)

- Specify the account groups allowed in the new hierarchy type (preconfigured)

- Specify the sales areas allowed in the customer hierarchy type (preconfigured)

- Assign hierarchy type to the Internet sales order type for pricing (preconfigured)

- Check the SAPNet - R/3 Frontend Notes

CATT procedure *ZESHOP_CUSTOMER_HIERARCHY* delivers the preconfiguration for this scenario, for several reasons:

- Not all customers will require this scenario.

- The CATTs allow the keys, such as sales area and the sales order type, to be changed, allowing this configuration to fit with existing SD configuration more easily.

Create a Customer Hierarchy Type

This step has been preconfigured for you. During installation, the CATT procedure *ZESHOP_CUSTOMER_HIERARCHY* creates the correct entries. The hierarchy type code can be changed during the execution of the CATT.

In the *Command* field, enter transaction **OVH1** and choose *Enter* (or in the IMG, choose *Sales and Distribution → Master Data → Business Partners → Customers → Customer Hierarchy* and choose 🕮 next to *Define Hierarchy Types*).

Hierarchy Type	Partner Function
Y (e-Shop Cust. Hier.)	YD (e-Shop Cust. Hier. 4)

YD is the lowest level of the hierarchy, or the level immediately above the customer.

Create New Partner Functions for the Customer Hierarchy

This step has been preconfigured for you. During installation, the CATT procedure *ZESHOP_CUSTOMER_HIERARCHY* creates the correct entries. The partner function codes can be changed during the execution of the CATT.

In the *Command* field, enter transaction **VOPA** and choose *Enter* (or in the IMG: *Sales and Distribution → Master Data → Business Partners → Customers → Customer Hierarchy* and choose 🕮 next to *Set Partner Determination for Hierarchy Categories*). On the *Maintain Partner Determin.* screen, choose *Partner functions*.

The partner functions *YA, YB, YC,* and *YD* were created with the following settings:

Function	Description	Higher-Level Function	CustHTyp (Customer Hierarchy Type)
YA	e-Shop Cust. Hier. 1		Y
YB	e-Shop Cust. Hier. 2	YA	Y
YC	e-Shop Cust. Hier. 3	YB	Y
YD	e-Shop Cust. Hier. 4	YC	Y

Additionally, the following settings are the same for each partner function:

- The *Partner Typ* is **KU**, or customer.

- The *Error Group* is **07**, or customer.

- The *Unique In cust.mast* checkbox is deselected.

This configuration allows for four levels in the customer hierarchy above the actual customer who is placing the order. The lowest level is *YD*, the next subsequent higher level is *YC*, and so on. In this way, the entire customer hierarchy is stored in the sales order document. The highest level of the hierarchy, according to this configuration, will always be *YA*, regardless of the number of levels used.

Assign New Partner Functions to Customer Account Groups

This step has been preconfigured for you. During installation, the CATT procedure *ZESHOP_CUSTOMER_HIERARCHY* creates the correct entries. These account groups can be changed during the execution of the CATT.

In the *Command* field, enter transaction **VOPA** and choose *Enter* (or in the IMG, choose *Sales and Distribution → Master Data → Business Partners → Customers → Customer Hierarchy* and choose 🐝 next to *Set Partner Determination for Hierarchy Categories*). On the *Maintain: Partner Determin.* screen, choose *Partner functions*. Then choose *Environment → Acct grp assignment*.

The following assignments were made for all four delivered partner functions, *YA, YB, YC,* and *YD*.

Partner Function	Account Group
Entry for each hierarchy level *(YA, YB, YC, YD)*	0001 (sold-to party)
Entry for each hierarchy level *(YA, YB, YC, YD)*	0012 (hierarchy node)
Entry for each hierarchy level *(YA, YB, YC, YD)*	YWEB (sold-to used for the Internet)

The *YWEB* account group is delivered with the Online Store preconfiguration. Account groups *0001* and *0012* are available in the standard R/3 System. Your own account groups may be used instead.

Create New Partner Determination Procedures for Sales Documents

This step has been preconfigured for you. During installation, the CATT procedure *ZESHOP_CUSTOMER_HIERARCHY* creates the correct entries. The partner determination type can be changed during the execution of the CATT.

In the *Command* field, enter transaction **VOPA** and choose *Enter* (or in the IMG, choose *Sales and Distribution → Master Data → Business Partners → Customers → Customer Hierarchy* and choose 🐝 next to *Set Partner Determination for Hierarchy Categories*). On the *Maintain: Partner Determin.* screen, select *Sales document header* and choose *Partner procedures*. Entry *YWO* has been created, and the details are included by choosing *Procedure details*.

Partner determination procedure *YWB* has been created. The following partner functions have been assigned:

Function	Description	Not Changeable	Mandatory	Source	Sequ.
SP	Sold-to Party	X	X		
BP	Bill-to Party		X	YA (highest level)	1
PY	Payer		X	YA (highest level)	1
CR	Forwarding Agent				
SH	Ship-to Party		X	YA (highest level)	1
YA	e-Shop Cust.Hier. 1	X		B (customer hierarchy)	
YB	e-Shop Cust.Hier. 2	X		B (customer hierarchy)	
YC	e-Shop Cust.Hier. 3	X		B (customer hierarchy)	
YD	e-Shop Cust.Hier. 4	X		B (customer hierarchy)	

If a customer hierarchy exists, the system determines the bill-to party, payer, and ship-to party from the customer hierarchy. If no customer hierarchy exists, the sold-to party is determined as the bill-to party, payer, and ship-to party.

You may add these partner determination functions to your own sales document partner procedure instead.

Assign Partner Determination Procedure to Internet Order Type

This step has been preconfigured for you. During installation, the CATT procedure *ZESHOP_CUSTOMER_HIERARCHY* creates the correct entries. The sales document type can be changed during the execution of the CATT.

In the *Command* field, enter transaction **VOPA** and choose *Enter* (or in the IMG, choose *Sales and Distribution → Master Data → Business Partners → Customers → Customer Hierarchy* and choose ⊕ next to *Set Partner Determination for Hierarchy Categories*). On the *Maintain: Partner Determin.* screen, select *Sales document header*, and choose *Partner procedures*. On the next screen, choose *Procedure assignment*.

Sales Document Partner Determination Procedure	Sales Document Type
YWB (e-Shop Web Bus.Order)	YWB (e-Shop Web Bus.Order)

Add New Partner Functions to Delivery Partner Determination Type

This step has been preconfigured for you. During installation, the CATT procedure *ZESHOP_CUSTOMER_HIERARCHY* creates the correct entries. The billing determination type can be changed during the execution of the CATT.

In the *Command* field, enter transaction **VOPA** and choose *Enter* (or in the IMG, choose *Sales and Distribution* → *Master Data* → *Business Partners* → *Customers* → *Customer Hierarchy* and choose 🕹 next to *Set Partner Determination for Hierarchy Categories*). On the *Maintain: Partner Determin.* screen, select *Delivery*, and choose *Partner procedures*. Place your cursor on entry *LF*, and the choose *Procedure details*).

The partner functions were added to the billing partner determination procedure *LF*.

Partner Function	Not Changeable	Mandatory
YA (e-Shop Cust.Hier. 1)	X	
YB (e-Shop Cust.Hier. 2)	X	
YC (e-Shop Cust.Hier. 3)	X	
YD (e-Shop Cust.Hier. 4)	X	

You may add these to your own delivery partner determination procedure instead.

Add New Partner Functions to Billing Header Partner Determination Type

This step has been preconfigured for you. During installation, the CATT procedure *ZESHOP_CUSTOMER_HIERARCHY* creates the correct entries. The billing determination type can be changed during the execution of the CATT.

In the *Command* field, enter transaction **VOPA** and choose *Enter* (or in the IMG, choose *Sales and Distribution* → *Master Data* → *Business Partners* → *Customers* → *Customer Hierarchy* and choose 🕹 next to *Set Partner Determination for Hierarchy Categories*). On the *Maintain: Partner Determin.* screen, select *Billing header*, and choose *Partner procedures*. Place your cursor on entry *FW*, and the choose *Procedure details*).

The partner functions were added to the billing partner determination procedure *FW*.

Partner Function	Not Changeable	Mandatory
YA (e-Shop Cust.Hier. 1)	X	
YB (e-Shop Cust.Hier. 2)	X	
YC (e-Shop Cust.Hier. 3)	X	
YD (e-Shop Cust.Hier. 4)	X	

You may add these to your own billing partner determination procedure instead.

Determine Account Groups To Be Used for Customers

This step has been preconfigured for you. Account group *YWEB* is delivered with the Online Store preconfiguration. Account groups *0001* and *0012* are available in the standard R/3 System. You may wish to use your own account groups instead.

In the *Command* field, enter transaction **OBD2** and choose *Enter* (or in the IMG, choose *Financial Accounting → Accounts Receivable and Accounts Payable → Customer Accounts → Master Records → Preparations for Creating Customer Master Records* and choose 🕓 next to *Define Account Groups with Screen Layout [Customers]*).

The following account groups are used for customer hierarchy processing in the Online Store.

Group	Name	Purpose
0001	Sold-to party	Used for the corporation for which purchases will take place. Standard-delivery was modified in the PCC.
0012	Hierarchy node	May be used for hierarchy nodes. Standard-delivery with R/3.
YWEB	Sold-to party	Used for customers who register through the web, and for the employees who purchase on behalf of a corporation. Delivered with the PCC.

Additional configuration of account groups is not documented in this guide. Your own account groups may be assigned instead.

Specify Account Groups Allowed in the Customer Hierarchy Type

This step has been preconfigured for you. During installation, the CATT procedure *ZESHOP_CUSTOMER_HIERARCHY* creates the correct entries. The account groups used can be changed during the execution of the CATT.

In the *Command* field, enter transaction **OVH2** and choose *Enter* (or in the IMG, choose *Sales and Distribution* → *Master Data* → *Business Partners* → *Customers* → *Customer Hierarchy* and choose 🕭 next to *Assign Account Groups*).

Customer Hierarchy Type CustHType	Account Group (lower level) Acct group	Account Group (higher level) HgLvAcctGr
Y (e-Shop Business)	0001 (Sold-to Party)	0012 (Hierarchy Node)
Y (e-Shop Business)	012 (Hierarchy Node)	0012 (Hierarchy Node)
Y (e-Shop Business)	YWEB (Internet Sold-to Party)	0001 (Sold-to Party)

These account groups were also assigned to the partner procedures in a prior step. Additional configuration of account groups is not documented in this guide. Your own account groups may be assigned instead.

Specify Sales Areas Allowed in the Customer Hierarchy Type

This step has been preconfigured for you. During installation, the CATT procedure *ZESHOP_CUSTOMER_HIERARCHY* creates the correct entries. The sales areas used can be changed during the execution of the CATT.

In the *Command* field, enter transaction **OVH3** and choose *Enter* (or in the IMG, choose *Sales and Distribution* → *Master Data* → *Business Partners* → *Customers* → *Customer Hierarchy* and choose 🕭 next to *Assign Sales Areas*).

These settings determine the sales areas that can be used in the customer hierarchy for the lower and higher level customer.

Hierarchy Types	Sales Organizations	Distribution Channel	Division	Higher Level Sales Organization	Higher Level Distribution Channel	Higher Level Division
Y	0010	11	10	0010	11	10

This sales area is delivered with the PCC. Your own sales areas may be assigned instead.

Assign Hierarchy Type to the Internet Sales Order Type for Pricing

This step has been preconfigured for you. During installation, the CATT procedure *ZESHOP_CUSTOMER_HIERARCHY* creates the correct entries. The sales document type used can be changed during the execution of the CATT.

Note

The order type configured with the customer hierarchy partner determination is linked to the Online Store through the profile for quotation and order control. Please refer to chapter 1, "Creating the Online Store with the Catalog" on page 5 for details of the profile and of the sales order type.

In the *Command* field, enter transaction **OVH4** and choose *Enter* (or in the IMG, choose *Sales and Distribution* → *Master Data* → *Business Partners* → *Customers* → *Customer Hierarchy* and choose 🖑 next to *Assign Hierarchy Type for Pricing By Sales Document Type*).

Hierarchy Type	Sales Order Type
Y (e-Shop Cust. Hier.)	YWB (e-Shop Web Bus.Order)

Sales order type *YWB* is delivered with the Online Store. Your own sales order type may be assigned instead.

Check the SAPNet – R/3 Frontend Notes

Information from SAPNet – R/3 Frontend notes (formerly OSS) is also essential to the configuration of sales order status.

TechTalk

For the customer hierarchy to function as described in this chapter, the following SAPNet – R/3 Frontend notes must be applied:

- *197819* addresses the underlying SD functionality, allowing partner determination based on the customer hierarchy functions.

- *210298* allows the partner determination based on the customer hierarchy functions to occur in BAPIs, for example in the Online Store.

- *314819* allows the partner determination based on the customer hierarchy functions to occur in BAPIs, for example in the Online Store.

Credit Card Authorizations and Settlement

Overview

Credit card authorizations and settlement provide an efficient and convenient way to process payments in an online store. For the online merchant, payments are received more quickly than by sending and processing invoices, greatly increasing the likelihood of payment.

With a verification and authorization component, the web customer's credit card and payment information can be forwarded to a clearinghouse for authorization while the customer is online. If any authorization problems occur, the information can be immediately passed to the customer before the sales process is complete. The customer can then use a different card. This immediate verification reduces manual authorization handling, and prevents the shipment of a product if the bank will not honor the charge.

When the billing document is released to the Financial Accounting (FI) module, the credit card information, billing amount, and authorization information are copied into the resulting financial accounting document. On the basis of this information, the FI module requests settlement of the transaction from the merchant bank through the service provider. A settlement program creates a financial document that clears the open items and creates open items on a cash clearing account. The cash clearing account is then cleared once the money has been credited to your account.

SAP provides a flexible and secure Payment Card Interface program that works together with the software of selected partners that provide merchant processing or clearinghouse services.

What We Deliver

Note

Configuration of the settings to establish communications between R/3 and external credit card service providers is not provided in the Online Store preconfiguration. However, guidelines for configuring this area are documented.

In the Online Store preconfiguration, we provide the following deliverables:

- Preconfiguration of the payment card functionality in Sales and Distribution (SD)

- Documentation covering the credit card authorization and settlement processes

- Documentation covering the R/3 communication settings required to work with Cybercash WebAuthorize

Making It Happen

Credit Card Authorization

The credit card authorization process is integrated with standard Sales and Distribution (SD) sales order processing. When a customer pays for goods and services with a credit card, the sales order provides the following information to the clearinghouse for authorization:

- Credit card number
- Cardholder address
- Amount to be authorized
- Card expiration date
- Card type

When the customer places the order from the Internet, the order request is sent to the R/3 System. R/3 then communicates with the clearing house, which either approves or denies the amount. If the authorization is denied, R/3 sends a message to the customer on the Internet informing the customer of the denial. If the authorization is approved, an order is created in R/3 and the order number is sent to the web.

When a sales order delivery is created with a credit card payment, the system checks whether a valid authorization exists. When a goods issue is posted for the delivery, the system again checks for a valid authorization. When the billing document is forwarded to FI, the following information is copied from the sales order to the financial accounting document:

- Payer
- Card number
- Amount
- Transaction number
- Authorization number

Settlement

The financial documents created during the billing process result in debit entries to an accounts receivable account from the merchant bank. General Ledger (G/L) account *125300* (Accounts Receivable – Payment Card) has been established for this purpose. The customer accounts receivables are automatically cleared in the same accounting documents.

The settlement process is initiated by a request for payment through the clearinghouse, using settlement transaction **FCC1** (or from the navigation menu, choose *Accounting → Financial Accounting → Accounts Receivable →*

Periodic Processing → Payment Cards → Settle). This transaction creates settlement packages (batches) per company code, G/L account, and transaction currency. The batches are transmitted to the clearinghouse for settlement. The clearinghouse software subsequently "calls back" R/3 to log a response. For each package, a settlement document is created, clearing the open items in the receivables account (*125300*), and posting a credit entry in a cash clearing account (*113034*). G/L account *113034* has been established as a subledger account under the merchant bank account. The item is cleared from the clearing account when payment is made to the merchant's bank account.

Detail logs of the settlement batches can be viewed using transaction **FCC4** (or from the navigation menu, choose *Accounting → Financial Accounting → Accounts Receivable → Periodic Processing → Payment Cards → Display logs*). A report can be run that shows all of the accounting documents included in a settlement batch (In the *Command* field, enter transaction **FCCR** and choose *Enter* (or from the navigation menu, choose *Accounting → Financial Accounting → Accounts Receivable → Periodic Processing → Payment Cards → Standard reports*).

Payment Card Interface

The authorization and settlement functions described above are integrated processes with an external (non-R/3) system. The Payment Card Interface is application software that acts as a bridge between SAP's R/3 System and a third-party credit card processing vendor. It provides Remote Function Call (RFC) communication between R/3 and external financial institutions such as banks, credit services, or merchant services to support the authorization and settlement of credit card payments.

The interface program performs the following functions:

- Receives output data from R/3

- Converts R/3 data to the requested format of the financial institution

- Sends data to the service provider

- Obtains a response from the service provider

- Maps the response message back to R/3

The credit card processing vendor is responsible for:

- Correct interpretation of R/3 data

- Conversion to and from the financial institution's data structure

- Communication protocols between application software and financial institutions

- Transfer of data back to R/3

- Technical communication between computer systems

The Payment Card Interface is described in detail in a document entitled "Payment Card Interface to R/3 – Integration Scenarios." This document can be found in SAPNet.

Payment Card Configuration

Much of what is necessary for credit card processing to work with Visa, MasterCard, and American Express payment cards is included in R/3. Procurement cards (P-cards) are not configured. This section only describes those tables that required configuration additions or changes for credit card processing.

For all credit card configurations, refer to the IMG, and choose *Sales and Distribution → Billing → Payment Cards*.

Determine Card Categories

From the IMG, choose *Sales and Distribution → Billing → Payment Cards* and choose 🔧 next to *Maintain Card Categories*. On the *Choose activity* dialog box, select *Determine card categories* and choose 🔲 *Choose*.

Note

Although there is a function for Diner's Club, the Diner's Club card is not a standard-delivered card type, so it is not included in the preconfiguration at this time.

Card types Visa, MasterCard, and American Express use a checking algorithm to validate the card numbers. You can specify a range of acceptable numbers for each credit card. This table is more important for those cards that do not have these checking functions, such as P-cards. For consistency, we set a range of numbers acceptable to standard card types.

Type	Seq Ops	Payment Cards from	Payment Cards to	Card Cat	Description
VISA	1 BT	40000000000000000	49999999999999999	01	Credit Card
MC	1 BT	50000000000000000	59999999999999999	01	Credit Card
AMEX	1 BT	30000000000000000	39999999999999999	01	Credit Card

Assign Accounts

In the *Command* field, enter transaction **OV87** and choose *Enter* (or from the IMG, choose *Sales and Distribution → Billing → Payment Cards → Authorization and Settlement → Maintain Clearing House → Account Determination* and choose 🔧 next to *Assign G/L Accounts*).

A receivables account must be defined and linked to each of the payment card types available. In this scenario, all standard-delivered cards are linked to a single G/L account.

Application	Condition Type	Chart of Accounts	Sales Organization	Card Type	G/L Account
VD	A001	0010	0010	Visa	125300
VD	A001	0010	0010	MC	125300
VD	A001	0010	0010	Amex	125300

Set Authorizations and Settlement Accounts

Note

SAP delivers the function modules *CCARD_AUTH_SIMULATION* and *CCARD_SETTLEMENT_SIMULATION* so you can test the authorization process without integration to your clearinghouse's software. After receiving the software from your clearinghouse, you will replace the simulated function names with ones that match the external RFC server program names. Since the simulated authorization and settlement functions in the preconfigured system do not actually perform a remote function call, the RFC destinations in the authorization and settlement controls have not been entered.

For credit card transactions, a receivables account and clearing account are assigned for each chart of accounts. In addition, the names of the functions called for credit card authorizations, and for credit card settlement are specified. SAP delivers simulation functions in R/3 that must be replaced with functions in RFC destinations.

The Accelerated Internet Selling preconfiguration uses the delivered functions to simulate credit card authorizations. When a sales order is saved in the Online Store, it simulates a call to an RFC server that effectively returns an acceptance of the authorization.

From the IMG, choose *Sales and Distribution → Billing → Payment Cards → Authorization and Settlement → Maintain Clearing House* and choose ⊕ next to *Set Authorization/Settlement Control Per Account*.

Chart Of Accounts	Receivable	Clearing
0010	125300	113034

Authorization Function/Destination	Settlement Function
CCARD_AUTH_SIMULATION	CCARD_SETTLEMENT_SIMULATION

The function modules *CCARD_AUTH_SIMULATION* and *CCARD_SETTLEMENT_SIMULATION* simulate remote function calls to a third-party vendor's RFC server ID. These simulations can be done without having to configure the communication between R/3 and the third-party service provider.

The following section describes how you would change these settings when integrating R/3 with Cybercash's WebAuthorize software product.

Configuring the Communication

This section describes the communication settings that must be configured in R/3 to work with Cybercash WebAuthorize. The steps outlined here can also be followed when integrating with other certified credit card payment processing software products.

Cybercash WebAuthorize is a third-party software product that, when integrated with R/3, manages credit card payments and takes care of all connections to the consumer banks and merchant banks involved in credit card transactions. SAP does not deliver the Cybercash software. To download a demonstration version of the software, go to *www.cybercash.com/webauthorize*, or contact Gray McDowell, National Accounts Manager, at (510) 263-4381.

WebAuthorize runs on an NT computer that communicates with your R/3 System. The SAP RFC Gateway must also be installed on the same NT computer. Cybercash provides instructions on how to install WebAuthorize on the NT system when you obtain the software.

Define a Physical Destination

Communications between R/3 and Cybercash WebAuthorize are established using SAP Remote Function Calls (RFC). You must create an RFC destination that specifies the communication type and installation directory path for the authorization service executable. You must set up the RFC destination as a TCP/IP communication protocol. The destination name is user-defined.

Task

Define a physical destination

1. In the *Command* field, enter **SM59** and choose *Enter* (or in the IMG, choose *Basis Components → System Administration → Management of External Security Systems → Secure Network Communications → Communication → RFC Remote Function Call* and choose 🕹 next to *Define RFC destination*).

2. On the *Display and maintain RFC destinations* screen:

   a. Select *TCP/IP connections.*

   b. Choose *Create.*

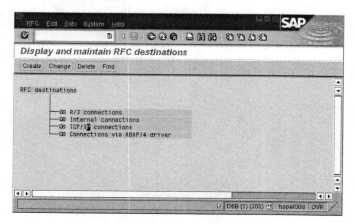

3. On the *RFC Destination* screen:

   a. In *RFC destination*, enter a user-defined name.

   b. In *Connection type*, enter **T.**

   c. Under *Description*, enter a short description text.

d. Choose 🗸.

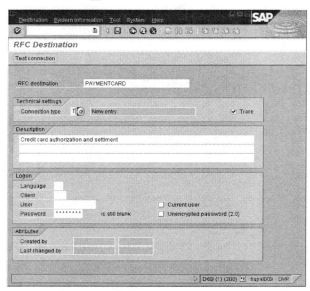

4. On the *RFC Destination PAYMENTCARD* screen, select *Registration*.

Registration button ————

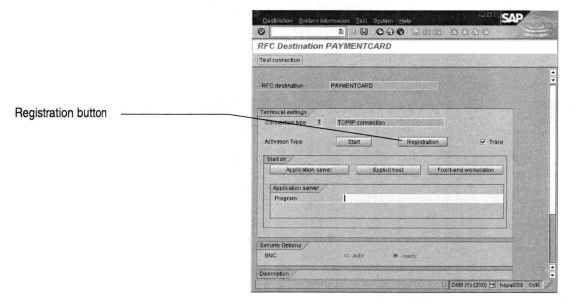

5. On the *RFC Destination PAYMENTCARD* screen:

   a. In *Program ID*, enter the appropriate program ID for the authorization service provider. The Cybercash program that handles authorization and settlement requests is called **PAYCARD**.

   b. From the menu bar, select *Destination → Gateway options*.

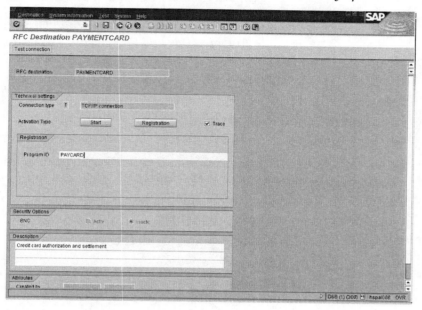

6. On the *RFC Destination PAYMENTCARD* dialog box:

   a. In *Gateway host*, enter the IP address of the RFC gateway computer.

   b. In *Gateway service*, enter the Gateway service name. The name should be in the format **SAPGW<instance>**, where instance is the system number of your R/3 System (in this example, the R/3 System is **00**).

   c. Choose *O.K.*

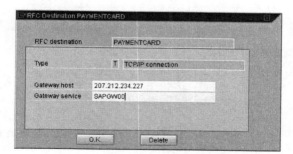

Specify Authorization and Settlement Functions

You should replace the standard-delivered functions with the external RFC function modules appropriate for your service provider, and enter the RFC destination created in the previous section. The following function modules are used by Cybercash:

- CC_AUTHORIZATION

- CC_SETTLEMENT

Task

Specify authorization and settlement functions

1. From the IMG, choose *Sales and Distribution → Billing → Payment Cards → Authorization and Settlement → Maintain Clearing House* and choose ⊕ next to *Set Authorization / Settlement Control Per Account*.

2. From the *Change View "Clearing account/external functions": Details* screen:

   a. In *Authorization function*, enter **CC_AUTHORIZATION**.

   b. In *Settlement function*, enter **CC_SETTLEMENT**.

   c. A *Destination* field resides under both *Authorization control* and *Settlement control*. Enter the appropriate RFC destination in both fields (for example, **PAYMENTCARD**).

   d. Choose 🖫 .

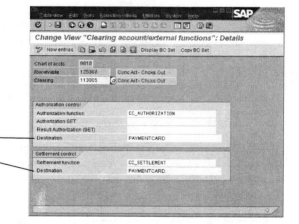

Destination fields

Maintain Merchant IDs

A merchant ID is a unique number assigned by the merchant bank to ensure that payment is credited to the appropriate merchant during settlement. The ID number must be defined in R/3 and assigned to an A/R account. The number defined in R/3 must match the merchant ID number configured in the WebAuthorize server.

From the IMG, choose *Sales and Distribution → Billing → Payment Cards → Authorization and Settlement → Maintain Clearing House* and choose ⊕ next to *Maintain Merchant IDs*.

Create a User ID

After a settlement request is made through WebAuthorize, a response is sent back to R/3. WebAuthorize must establish a connection to R/3 through an SAP user ID before communicating the settlement results. Therefore, you must create a user ID. The ID and password are specified as parameters in a configuration file required for defining the RFC server.

From the navigation menu, choose *Tools → Administration → User Maintenance→ Users.*

Sales Order Status

Overview

After placing an order, customers may wish to track the order's status. They will need to know whether the order has been shipped and when they can expect to receive it. By providing this data on the Internet, customer service representatives can spend less time researching information that customers can access electronically, twenty-four hours a day.

The sales order status check is an Internet Application Component (IAC) that allows customers to see the status of all of their orders in the delivery process. They can track all their orders, or limit the display by date, order number, product number, and/or purchase order number. Customers can track any of their orders, including orders not generated through the Internet.

The sales order status check is carried out using the information in the delivery document within R/3. The freight carrier and tracking number are entered at the header level of the delivery document. The sales order status check then reads the delivery document and displays the order and delivery information. If freight carrier information is maintained in the delivery document, a hyperlink to the freight carrier's web site is also available.

Only one delivery can be tracked for a sales order, since the tracking information is entered at header level. If partial deliveries of an order are permitted, and multiple packages are sent, only the first of these deliveries is accessible from the sales order status check.

What We Deliver

In the Online Store preconfiguration, we provide the following deliverables:

- Preconfiguration of the URLs of the most common freight carriers

- Preconfiguration of the ITS look and feel

- Sample master data for freight carriers (if the Online Store preconfiguration is implemented in conjunction with the PCC)

- Documentation on the functionality of the freight carrier tracking integration

The Customer Experience

The following procedure shows what our customer, Mary, sees while tracking the status of her order. This example assumes that she has previously registered her e-mail address on the web site, and placed an order. The tracking information is available once the delivery has been processed within the R/3 System. The data shown is sample data, and is not delivered with the Online Store preconfiguration.

Task

Customer Order Tracking

1. In the Internet browser, Mary enters the URL of your home page, which you configured as part of the ITS installation.

2. She chooses the *Online Store* from your home page.

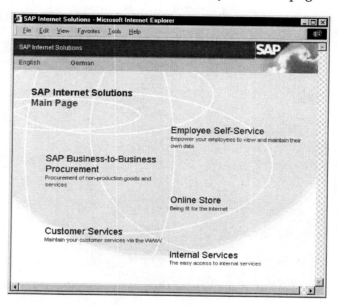

3. Mary chooses *Sales Order Status*.

Sales Order Status

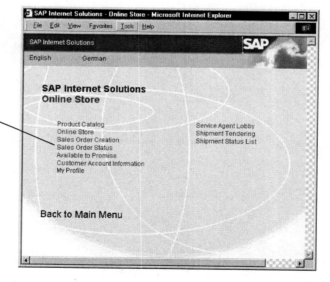

4. To access delivery information on her orders:

   a. Mary enters her e-mail address.

   b. She enters her password.

   c. She chooses *Log on*.

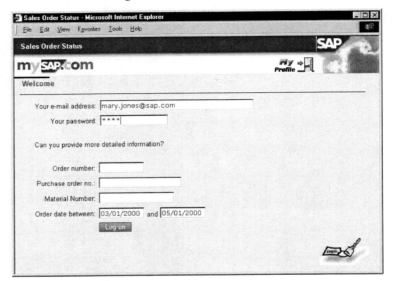

Additional information may be entered, that will help customers find a specific order. In this example, the default order date range is the only limiting characteristic used. The default is one month, ending on the current date.

5. Mary chooses her most recent order, which is order *227* in this example.

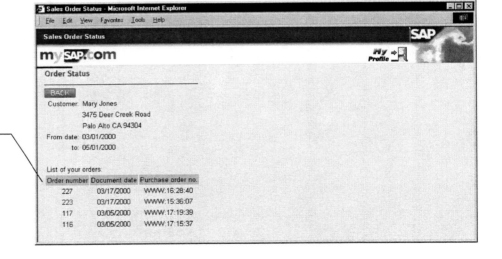

The orders that meet the criteria appear in the left frame of the browser.

6. If the *First delivery/tracking* column contains a hyperlink, the freight carrier web site can be directly accessed. If Mary wishes to see this tracking information, she chooses the hyperlink in the *First delivery/tracking* column.

The details of the selected order are displayed in the right frame of the browser.

First delivery/tracking column.

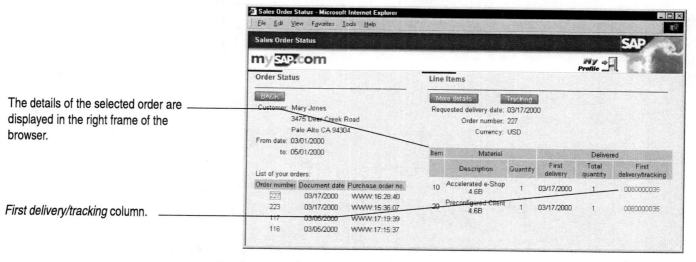

7. In a new browser window, the tracking information appears. (The actual tracking number is hidden in this example.)

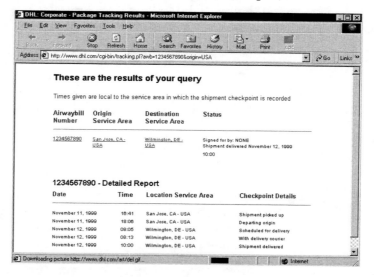

8. The order information is still available in the original browser window. On that window, Mary chooses *More details*.

9. Additional delivery confirmation details are displayed:

   a. If the *Number/tracking* information contains a hyperlink, the freight carrier site can be directly accessed. If no hyperlink exists, no further tracking is possible.

b. The confirmation information for each item is available here.

c. Mary chooses *BACK*.

Additional information about the order is displayed.

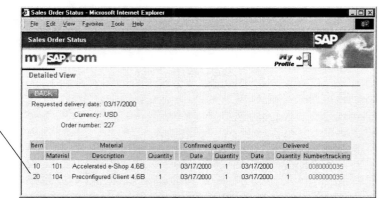

10. The original order information is again displayed in the right frame. Mary chooses *Tracking*.

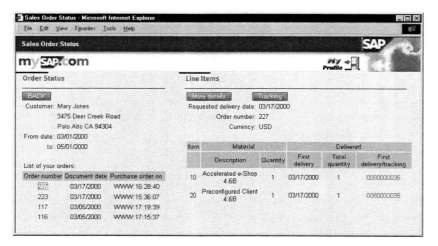

The R/3 transaction **VW10** supports the sales order status procedure.

11. Detailed information about the document flow of the delivery is displayed. Mary can find out whether the product has been picked in the warehouse, issued out of the warehouse, or whether a billing document has been processed.

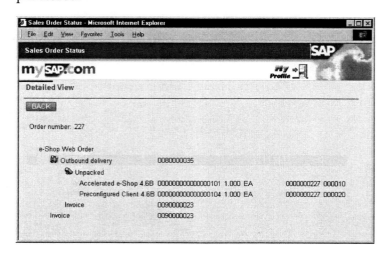

Making It Happen: Sales Order Status Procedures

Delivery Processing to Support Order Tracking

For an order to reach the R/3 System, the order may be entered:

- Directly into R/3 using transaction *VA01*.

- On the web through the Online Store, which uses transaction *WW20*.

- On the web through Sales Order Entry, which uses transaction *VW01*.

Normal sales order processing takes place once the information reaches R/3. A delivery is typically created from the sales order. The following information must be entered into the delivery document if a link to the freight carrier web site is to be activated:

- The freight carrier as a partner in the header

- The tracking number in the *Bill of lading* field of the delivery header

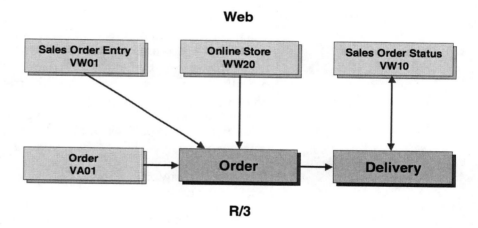

The sales order status process selects the delivery documents associated with the selected customer order. If the appropriate information is contained in the delivery document, a URL must be built by the R/3 System to allow access to the freight carrier's web site.

Defining the URL of the Freight Carrier

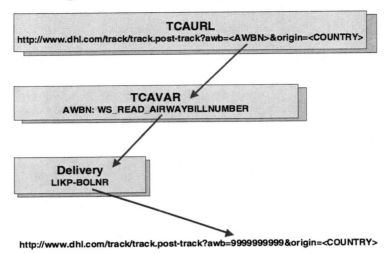

R/3 table *TCAURL* contains the URL for each freight carrier. Portions of the URL are specific to each delivery, such as an individual tracking number. These portions of the URL are stored as variables in table *TCAURL*. When a customer accesses their sales order status, these variables must be filled with details from the delivery document.

Each variable defined in table *TCAVAR* is linked to a function module. As the URL is built, the function module for the first variable reads the specific information from the delivery document. For example, the first variable is usually the tracking number. Once the tracking number is read from the delivery document, it is inserted into the URL, replacing the variable. Then the second variable, such as the country, must then be read from the delivery document. This continues until all variables in the URL have been replaced, and the entire hyperlink to the freight carrier has been built.

The following information needs to be read from the delivery document for each of the carriers:

- Federal Express: tracking number, destination country, and shipping date

- UPS: tracking number

- DHL: tracking number and destination country

- U.S. Postal Service: tracking number

- Airborne Express: tracking number

- Emery Worldwide: type of tracking number (hard-coded in our delivery as shipping number) and tracking number

Data in R/3 to Support Sales Order Status Tracking

The steps involved in setting up sales order tracking are described in the following sections. You must:

- Create a vendor master for each freight carrier (preconfigured if using the Online Store preconfiguration with the PCC)

- Ensure that all data is correctly entered into each delivery document

- Ensure that the correct parameters are entered in the ITS user's profile

- Ensure that the customer exists in the R/3 System and has been assigned a password

Create a Vendor Master for each Freight Carrier

CATT procedure *ZESHOP_FREIGHT_CARRIERS* creates sample master data, but only if you use the Online Store preconfiguration in conjunction with the Preconfigured Client (PCC) in a fresh installation. Otherwise, you need to create a vendor master record for each freight carrier manually, as described below. You should only create a vendor master for those freight carriers with whom you do business.

Task

Create a vendor master record for each freight carrier

1. In the *Command* field, enter transaction **XK01** and choose *Enter* (or from the navigation menu, choose *Logistics → Materials Management → Purchasing → Master Data → Vendor → Central → Create*).

2. On the *Create Vendor: Initial Screen*:

    a. In *Company code,* enter the company code for which you wish to create the vendor.

    b. In *Purch. organization,* enter the purchase organization of the vendor.

    c. In *Account group,* enter the account group of the vendor.

Note

The field values shown are only available if you are using the Online Store preconfiguration with the PCC. If you are not using the PCC, please substitute the values of your own organizational elements in these fields.

d. Choose 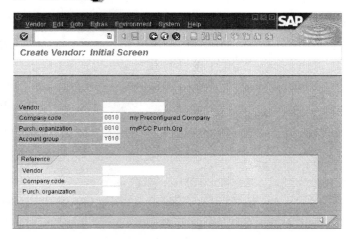.

3. On the *Create Vendor: Address* screen:

a. In *Name*, enter the freight carrier. This name should correspond to the object ID entered into table *TCAURL* in configuration.

b. Enter all other information as it pertains to the freight carrier for your company, on this and all other screens in the vendor master record.

c. When you are done, choose 💾 .

The technical name for the *Name* field is LFA1-NAME1.

Ensure Correct Data Is Entered into the Delivery Document

The next step to support sales order tracking is to ensure that the correct data is entered into the delivery document. This transactional data must be entered on all delivery documents for the freight carrier tracking integration to function correctly.

> **Task**
>
> **Verify the data in the delivery document**

1. In the *Command* field, enter transaction **VL03N** and choose *Enter* (or from the navigation menu, choose *Logistics → Sales and Distribution → Shipping and Transportation → Outbound Delivery → Display*).

2. On the *Display Outbound Delivery* screen:

   a. In *Outbound delivery*, enter the delivery document number displayed on the Internet.

   b. Choose 🗸.

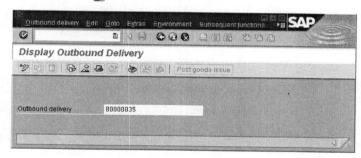

3. On the *Outbound delivery <XXXXXXX> Display: Overview* screen:

   a. Review the items included in the delivery.

   b. Choose the menu path *Goto → Header → Shipment*.

The items included in this delivery are displayed.

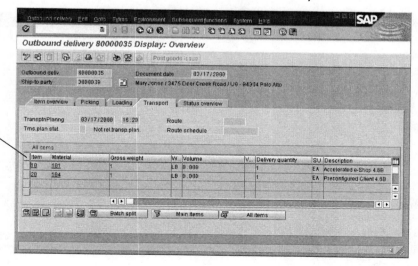

4. On the *Outbound delivery <XXXXXXX> Display: Header Details* screen:

   a. Review the information.

   b. Choose 🔙.

The *Incoterms* default from the sales order created on the web.

The *BillOfLad* (bill of lading) field contains the tracking number assigned by the carrier (the number is disguised here).

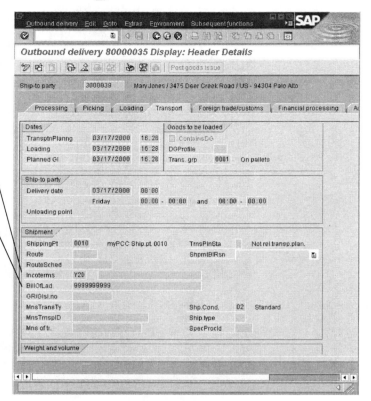

Note

Since the bill of lading is a header-level field, only one delivery can be displayed in the Sales Order Status tracking on the web.

5. Back on the *Outbound delivery <XXXXXXX> Display: Overview* screen, choose *Goto → Header → Partners*.

6. On the *Outbound delivery <XXXXXXX> Display: Header Details* screen, review the information.

In the *Partner* column, the vendor number specifies the freight carrier used for the delivery.

In the *Partn. funct.* (partner function) column, the *CR* partner type designates the forwarding agent, or freight carrier.

Note

The freight carrier may be entered manually, or default from the reference for consumer master records. Please refer to chapter 5, "Customers in the Online Store" on page 133 for details on consumer master records.

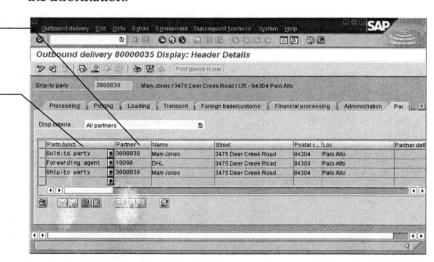

Ensure Correct Parameters Are Entered in the ITS User's Profile

The third step to supporting sales order status requires that the correct parameters are entered in the Internet Transaction Server (ITS) user's profile. The ITS user that is logged into the R/3 System in the background during the sales order status transaction must have the correct sales area parameters in the user profile. Please refer to chapter 15, "The ITS User: Logging on to R/3" on page 349 for details on the ITS user.

To double-check the ITS user's profile parameters, enter transaction **SU01** in the *Command* field and choose *Enter* (or from the navigation menu, choose *Tools → Administration → User Maintenance → Users*).

Ensure the Customer Exists in R/3 and Has Been Assigned a Password

New customers may not register using the sales order status IAC. The customer must already have a customer number with a valid e-mail address and password.

The customer master record must already exist for the sales area used for the Internet. To create the customer master record, enter transaction **XD01** in the *Command* field and choose *Enter* (or from the navigation menu, choose *Logistics → Sales and Distribution → Master Data → Business partners → Customer → Create → Complete*). Please refer to chapter 5, "Customers in the Online Store" on page 133 for details about customers in IACs.

The Internet user must be created using object type *KNA1*. To create the Internet user, enter transaction **SU05** in the *Command* field and choose *Enter* (or from the navigation menu, choose *Tools → Administration → User Maintenance → Internet User*). Please refer to chapter 15, "The ITS User: Logging on to R/3" on page 349 for details about the Internet user.

Sales Order Status Configuration

Note

For the changes we deliver to the look and feel of the sales order status functionality and instructions on how to make changes to the ITS HTML ^Business^ templates, please refer to chapter 14, "ITS Templates" on page 327.

The steps involved in setting up the sales order status configuration are described in the following sections. You must:

- Verify that delivery type partner procedure contains partner type *CR* (standard-delivery)

- Enter all URLs for the freight carriers in table *TCAURL* (preconfigured)

- Ensure that all variables in the URLs are read from the delivery document using a function module, as defined in table *TCAVAR* (standard-delivery)

- Determine the logon method for the sales order status (preconfigured)

- Check the SAPNet – R/3 Frontend notes

Verify Delivery Type Partner Procedure Contains Partner Type CR

To configure sales order status, the first step is to verify that the delivery type partner procedure contains partner type *CR*. This step is preconfigured for you only if you are using the partner determination for delivery documents *LF* (standard-delivered) or *ZLF* (PCC-delivered) in your delivery types. If you have changed the settings for this delivery partner determination, or have created your own, you must make sure the following settings are configured in your system.

To check for partner type *CR*, enter transaction **VOPA** in the *Command* field and choose *Enter* (or in the IMG, choose *Sales and Distribution → Basic Functions → Partner Determination* and choose 🔧 next to *Define Partner Functions*). Choose partner object *Delivery*, and choose the *Partner procedures* button. Select the partner determination procedure you use in your system, and choose the *Procedure details* button.

The following entry should be configured as part of your partner determination procedure.

Partner Function	Not Changeable	Mandatory Functions
CR (forwarding agent)	(blank)	(blank)

Enter all URLs for the Freight Carriers in Table TCAURL

The second step in configuring sales order status is to enter freight carrier URLs in the table *TCAURL*. This step has been preconfigured for you.

To display these settings, enter transaction **SM30** in the *Command* field and choose *Enter* (or from the navigation menu, choose *System → Services → Table maintenance → Extended table maintenance*). In *Table/view* enter **TCAURL** and choose *Display*.

The table entries are listed below. *DHL* and *FEDEX* are standard-delivered entries. The entry for *UPS* has been changed in the Online Store preconfiguration. All other freight carriers are added by the preconfiguration.

Object Type	Object ID	URL
TRACK_URL	AIRBORNE	http://www.airborne.com/cgi-bin/AirbillTrace?ShipmentNumber=<AWBN>
TRACK_URL	DHL	http://www.dhl.com/track/track.post-track?awb=<AWBN>&origin=<COUNTRY>
TRACK_URL	FEDEX	http://www.fedex.com/cgi-bin/track_it?trk_num=<AWBN>&dest_cntry=<DES_CTRY>&ship_date=<SHIPDATE>

Object Type	Object ID	URL
TRACK_URL	UPS	http://wwwapps.ups.com/tracking/tracking.cgi?tracknum=<AWBN>
TRACK_URL	USPS	http://www.usps.gov/cgi-bin/cttgate/ontrack.cgi?submit&tracknbr=<AWBN>
TRACK_URL	EMERY	http://www1.emeryworld.com/cgi-bin/track.cgi?TYPE=SHIPNUM&PRO1=<AWBN>

The *Object ID* must be used as the vendor name for the forwarding agents.

Ensure all Variables in URLs Are Read from Delivery Document

To configure the sales order status, you must also ensure that all variables in the URLs are read from the delivery document. The standard-delivered functions are used in this table.

To display these settings, enter transaction **SM30** in the *Command* field and choose *Enter* (or from the navigation menu, choose *System → Services → Table maintenance → Extended table maintenance*). In *Table/view* enter **TCAVAR** and choose *Display*.

Object Type - OBJTYPE	Object ID - OBJID	Function Name - FUNCNAME
URL	<AWBN>	WS_READ_AIRWAYBILLNUMBER
URL	<COUNTRY>	WS_READ_COUNTRY_OF_ORIGIN
URL	<DES_CITY>	WS_READ_DEST_COUNTRY
URL	<SHIPDATE>	WS_READ_SHIPDATE

The *Object ID* corresponds to the variables in the URL of table *TCAURL*. The *Function Name* field specifies the function module to which each variable is linked. These function modules read data from the delivery document. The data is then used to build the URL that accesses the freight carrier's web site.

Determine Logon Method for the Sales Order Status

Another step in sales order status configuration is determining the logon method. This step has been preconfigured for you.

The service file in the AGate directory structure of the ITS has been modified to allow a customer to log on with an e-mail address instead of with a customer number. This change makes the processing consistent for all sell-side applications. The service files are located in the ITS AGate directory under the directory structure *<its_root>\services*, where the *<its_root>* is your virtual ITS installation.

In the service file *vw10.srvc*, the following parameter has been added to allow customers to log on using their e-mail addresses:

Parameter Name	Value
~customeridentification	email

If you prefer customers to log on using a customer number, delete this parameter from the service file.

Check the SAPNet – R/3 Frontend Notes

Information from SAPNet – R/3 Frontend notes (formerly OSS) is also essential to the configuration of sales order status.

TechTalk

For the sales order status transaction to function as described in this chapter, the following SAPNet – R/3 Frontend notes must be applied:

- *179338* allows the state field to be displayed in the address on the Internet.

- *182633* ensures that customers can only display their own orders in the sales order status IAC.

- *206887* corrects problems in the order display when two customers have the same e-mail address and a different password.

For additional informational notes, please refer to appendix A, "SAPNet Frontend Notes" on page 495

Available to Promise

Overview

Customers may wish to know whether the product they are interested in buying is in stock. If it is not, they may want to wait if they know when the product will be available again. For this type of availability information to be accessible on the Internet, a separate IAC (Internet Application Component) is provided. A customer can log in, search a text-based product catalog, and enter the desired quantity and delivery date of the product. The information returned is the quantity currently available, and the date on which the remainder of the requested quantity of the product will be available.

The available-to-promise (ATP) information, which is already configured as part of the sales and distribution functionality within R/3, is accessible from the Internet. The real-time data from R/3 lets the customer know whether the product is available. ATP can be configured to include or exclude anticipated events that influence inventory levels, such as other order commitments, or anticipated receipts through purchases and production schedules. Although accessing this information requires a separate task outside the Online Store, customers can still determine when a regularly ordered product will be available.

What We Deliver

In the Online Store preconfiguration, we provide the following deliverables:

- Preconfiguration of the ITS look and feel
- Documentation on the functionality of the ATP functionality

TechTalk

In the standard R/3 System, the product catalog only provides a very high-level availability check at the time the order is submitted on the web. While scrolling the catalog, there is no indication about whether a product is in stock.

As part of the Online Store preconfiguration, we provide an add-on that allows you to display item availability within the product catalog, based on either the unreserved stock of a product or the ATP rules. This availability check within the product catalog is different from the IAC discussed in this chapter. For additional details, please refer to appendix B, "Technical SAP Enhancement: ATP in the Product Catalog" on page 499.

The Customer Experience

When the customer seeks material availability information, we assume that your company's product catalog information has been generated in a text version and is located on the web server. The data shown is sample data and is not delivered. If the Online Store preconfiguration is used in conjunction with the Preconfigured Client (PCC) in a fresh install, a sample product catalog is delivered. To use this product catalog, the steps in the master data section must still be processed manually during installation.

Determining Product Availability

Task

Determining the availability of a product

1. In the Internet browser, your customer Alan enters the URL of your home page, which you configured as part of the ITS installation.

2. He chooses the *Online Store* from your home page.

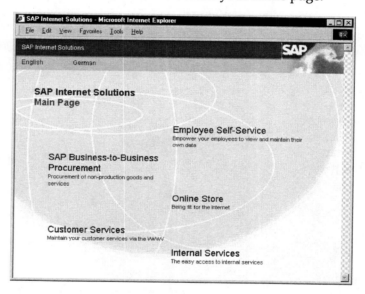

3. Alan chooses *Available to Promise.*

Available to promise

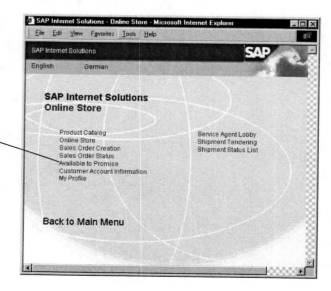

4. In order to access the availability information:

a. In *Customer number* and *Password*, Alan enters his number and password.

b. Alan chooses *Login*.

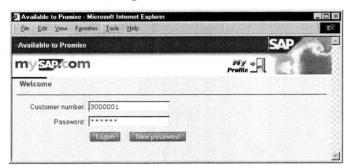

5. Alan opens the folder for the first shop, *Guidebooks*.

The shops, or top-most hierarchical levels of the product catalog, are displayed in the left frame. A Java applet is used for all processing that occurs while the customer scrolls the text-based catalog and selects the product for which ATP information is desired.

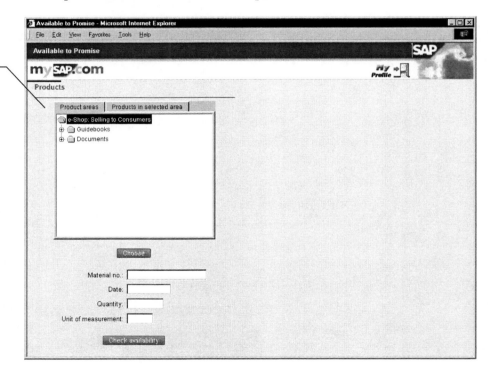

6. After opening the *Guidebooks* shop:

  a. Alan chooses the release level desired by highlighting it with the cursor.

  b. He chooses the *Products in selected area* tab.

The product groups within the *Guidebooks* shop appear. In this example, each product group represents guidebooks for a different release.

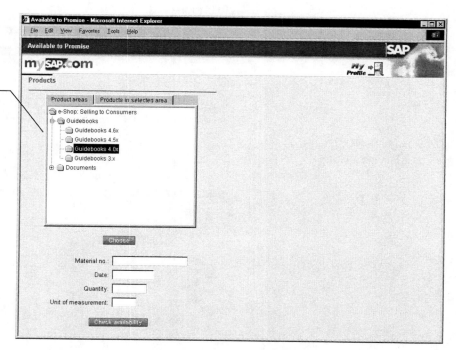

7. To find a particular book within this product group:

  a. Alan may now search for a particular text. In this example, the wildcard indicates that all products should be displayed.

  b. He chooses *New Search*.

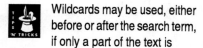
Wildcards may be used, either before or after the search term, if only a part of the text is known. For example, `Product*` would display all guidebooks beginning with this word, such as `Product Costing Scenarios Made Easy`. If only the term `Product` was entered without the wildcard, the guidebook would not be displayed.

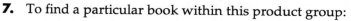
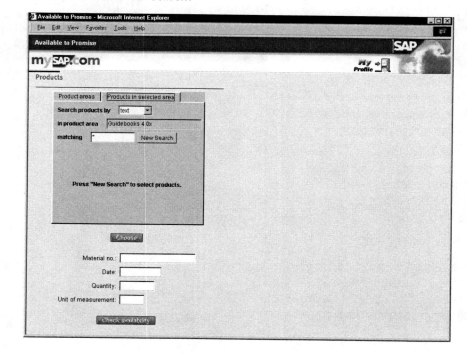

8. Once the search results are displayed:

   a. Alan chooses the guidebook *Product Costing Scenarios Made Easy* by placing his cursor on the line.

   b. He chooses *Choose*.

All guidebooks within the product group are displayed, based on the wildcard search.

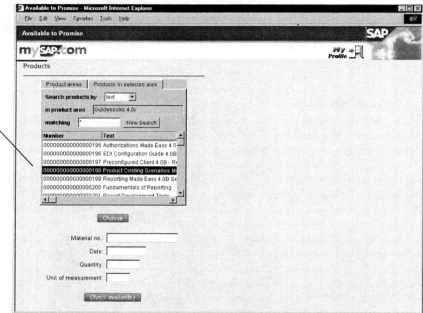

9. Once Alan has selected the guidebook in which he is interested:

   a. In *Date* and *Quantity*, Alan enters the date by which he wishes the guidebook to be delivered, and the quantity desired. If no date is specified, the current date is used as a default.

   b. He chooses *Availability information*.

The *Material no.* and the base *Unit of measurement* information is transferred into the selection criteria at the bottom of the screen.

If the customer already knew the product number, it could have been entered manually without conducting a search through the product catalog.

If no quantity is specified, the total quantity of the product available is displayed. If a quantity is specified, only the information related to the required quantity is displayed.

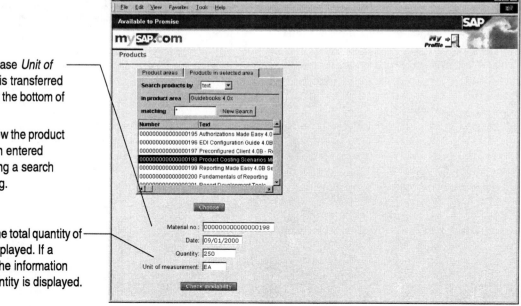

10. The right frame now displays the availability information.

Note

It is not possible to place an order from this IAC service.

The availability information indicates that a quantity of 97 is available on September 1, which is the date entered by the customer. The remaining 153 products will be not be available until September 15.

The R/3 transaction **CKAV** runs the available-to-promise function.

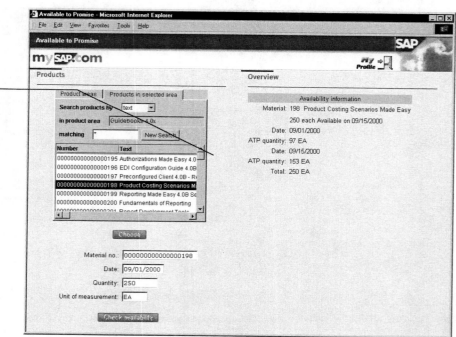

The View from Inside your Company

Display the Corresponding Stock Requirements List in R/3

The stock requirements data in R/3 contains the same quantities displayed on the Internet, provided that the ATP configuration for the web includes all stock that is also included in this MRP list. The customer does not see the R/3 screen. Within the company, however, you can verify that the data shown on the Internet matches what is in the R/3 System.

Task

Display R/3's corresponding stock requirements list

1. In the *Command* field, enter transaction **MD04** and choose *Enter* (or from the navigation menu, choose *Logistics → Production → MRP → Evaluations → Stock/Requmts List*).

2. On the *Stock/Requirements List: Initial Screen:*

    a. In *Material,* enter the product number for which you wish to see the available stock based on the current status of commitments and planned receipts.

b. Choose ✅ .

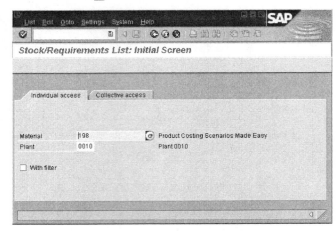

3. On the *Stock/Requirements List as of <XX:XX> Hrs* screen, the current stock level is displayed.

The quantity of product already committed to a sales order is subtracted from available stock.

The product quantity expected to be placed into inventory, based on purchases and production orders, is added to available stock.

Dates associated with the events relating to product availability are included on this screen. The ATP IAC uses this information to determine the planned availability date of the product required by the Internet customer, provided that ATP is configured to include this information.

Current stock level

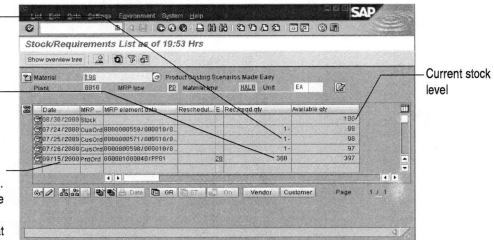

Making It Happen: Available-to-Promise Procedures

In the following sections, we demonstrate how to take existing ATP information and make it available on the web. This chapter is not intended to be a thorough discussion of how ATP should be configured in your system. This section provides a high-level overview of what information is included in an ATP check, and how the Internet accesses the ATP rules.

ATP: How Much Inventory Is Available?

The ATP check within the Sales and Distribution (SD) module verifies whether a product is available to be sold. If it is not available, the date on which it is expected to be available is confirmed. The ATP check in the example below is configured to determine how much stock is available, how much has already been committed to another customer, and how much stock is expected to be received or produced in the future. This data allows for a more accurate estimate of the delivery date than if only the unrestricted stock in inventory and material lead-time were checked.

Date	Material	Inventory	Description
07/31	233	100	Opening stock balance
07/31	233	-50	Committed: customer order
08/10	233	+200	Planned: production order
		250	ATP quantity

In the example above, if a customer ordered 100 items on 08/01, this quantity could not be confirmed until 08/10, due to the current customer commitments and the receipt into inventory that is planned based on the scheduled production order completion date.

ATP: Which Configuration Is Used on the Internet?

In the configuration of the Internet Application Component (IAC) for available-to-promise, the same ATP logic used within R/3 is also used for the Internet.

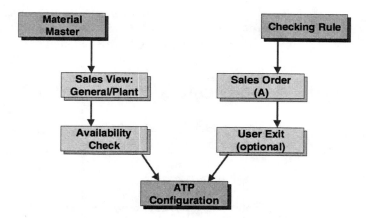

The material master record contains a checking rule for the availability check in the *Sales: General/Plant* view. The second checking rule used by the IAC is the checking rule for sales orders (value *A*). This checking rule can only be changed with a user exit. The ATP configuration occurs for the combination of the availability check and checking rule. The configuration indicates which types of inventory, commitments, and receipts are included in the ATP calculation.

Master Data in R/3 to Support ATP

The following sections describe the steps involved in setting up data in R/3 to support ATP. You must:

- Create the product catalog in R/3 (preconfigured if the Online Store preconfiguration is used in conjunction with the PCC; please refer to chapter 1, "Creating the Online Store with the Catalog" on page 5 for details)

- Generate the product catalog data for the web server

- Place the product catalog files on the web server

- Ensure that the correct parameters are entered in the ITS user's profile (preconfigured)

- Ensure that the customer exists in the R/3 System and has been assigned a password

Create the Product Catalog in R/3

If you are using the Online Store preconfiguration in conjunction with the PCC in a fresh installation, the CATT procedure *ZESHOP_PROD_CATALOG* creates sample master data. Otherwise, you need to manually create the product catalog.

Chapter 2 discusses the creation of the product catalog. Chapter 1 discusses the Online Store and contains references to other chapters that discuss additional business issues surrounding the product catalog, including pricing and creating customers.

To create the product catalog, enter transaction **WWM1** in the *Command* field and choose *Enter* (or from the navigation menu, choose *Logistics → Product Catalog → Product Catalog → Create*).

Generate the Product Catalog Data for the Web Server

To support the ATP configuration, you must generate the product catalog data for the web server manually.

Task

Generating product catalog data for the web server

1. In the *Command* field, enter transaction **SA38** and choose *Enter* (or from the menu bar choose, *System → Services → Reporting*).

2. On the *ABAP: Execute Program* screen:

   a. In *Program*, enter **PCATALOG**. This step generates the information from your product catalog into a usable format for the Java applet used on the web.

   b. Choose ⊕.

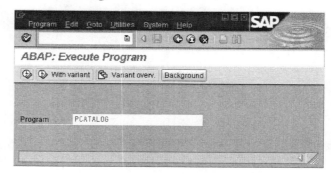

3. On the *Input Files for the Jav Applet from the IAC Availability Information* screen:

   a. In *Product catalog*, enter the product catalog for which you wish to provide ATP data to your customers.

   b. In *Variant*, enter the appropriate variant that represents the combination of language and currency of the product catalog.

   c. In *Language,* enter the language in which the product catalog texts should be extracted.

   d. To generate the correct descriptions for your products, select either the material *Short texts* or the *Headers from catalog*.

   e. Choose ⊕.

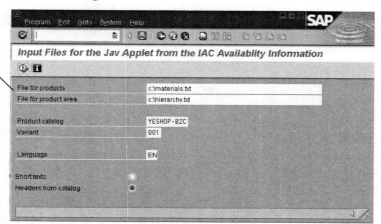

Note

In step **3d**, for consistency you should select the same option you used in the Online Store product presentation profile for this catalog. Please refer to chapter 1, "Creating the Online Store with the Catalog" on page 5 for additional information about this profile.

The filenames for the products and product area appear by default.

Note that if this filename is changed on this screen, then it must also be changed in the HTML Business templates for the ATP service.

4. A confirmation message is displayed, indicating that the files have been
successfully created.

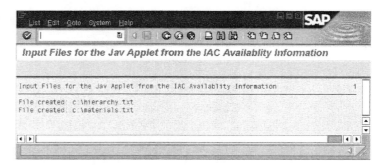

Place the Product Catalog Files on the Web Server

For the ATP configuration, you must manually place the product catalog files
generated in the previous step on the web server. The Java applet reads only
this text-based version of the catalog.

The data files in the WGate directory structure of the ITS must be updated
with the newly generated product catalog information. The data service files
are located in the ITS directory on the web server. In our example, we used
Microsoft's Internet Information Server (IIS). The directory structure into
which you must place the files is indicated in the table below.

WGate Directory Structure (using the default installation of IIS)
<wwwroot>\sap\its\mimes\ckav\<theme>\<language>\data

The two files specified in the table below must be placed into the WGate
directory structure on your web server.

File Name	Description
hierarchy.txt	Contains the product catalog layout
materials.txt	Contains the products within each layout area

Ensure the Correct Parameters Are Entered in the ITS User's Profile

The ITS user that is logged into the R/3 System in the background during the
available-to-promise IAC must have the correct plant parameter in the user
profile. Please refer to chapter 15, "The ITS User: Logging on to R/3" on
page 349 for details on the ITS user.

To double-check the ITS user's profile parameters, enter transaction **SU01** in
the *Command* field and choose *Enter* (or from the navigation menu, choose
Tools → Administration → User Maintenance → Users).

If the ITS user parameter for the plant should not be used, logic to determine the plant must be coded into the user exit *EXIT_SAPLW61V_001*, which must be linked to an enhancement project using enhancement component *W61V0001*.

Ensure the Customer Exists in R/3 and Has a Password

New customers may not register using the ATP IAC. The customer must already have a customer number and a password.

The customer master record must already exist for the sales area being used for the Internet. To create the customer master record, enter transaction **XD01** in the *Command* field and choose *Enter* (or from the navigation menu, choose *Logistics → Sales and Distribution → Master Data → Business partners → Customer → Create → Complete*). Please refer to chapter 5, "Customers in the Online Store" on page 133 for details about customers in IACs.

The Internet user must be created using object type **KNA1**. To create the Internet user, enter transaction **SU05** in the *Command* field and choose *Enter* (or from the navigation menu, choose *Tools → Administration → User Maintenance → Internet User*). Please refer to chapter 15, "The ITS User: Logging on to R/3" on page 349 for details about the Internet user.

ATP Configuration

The steps involved in setting up ATP configuration are described in the following sections. You must:

- Verify the availability checking rule for your products
- Check the default checking rule for the IAC
- Check the default ATP settings used by the IAC for insufficient stock
- Modify the Java applet configuration, if desired
- Check the SAPNet – R/3 Frontend notes

Note

For changes that we deliver for the look and feel of the ATP functionality, and instructions on how to make changes to the ITS HTML ^Business^ templates, please refer to chapter 14, "ITS Templates" on page 327.

Verify the Availability Checking Rule for your Products

For ATP configuration, you must verify the availability checking rule used for your products. The default rule delivered with the standard R/3 System may have been changed in your implementation. In our example, the availability checking rule *02* is used, which stipulates that individual requirements are generated during sales and delivery processing. This value must be populated in the *Sales: general/plant* view of the material master.

To maintain the correct value in the material master record, enter transaction **MM02** in the *Command* field and choose *Enter* (or from the navigation menu, choose *Logistics → Materials Management → Material Master → Material → Change → Immediately*). The *Sales: General/Plant* view must be maintained with your plant, sales organization, and distribution channel.

To verify the availability checking rule, enter transaction **OVZ2** in the *Command* field and choose *Enter* (or in the IMG, choose *Sales and Distribution → Basic Functions → Availability Check and Transfer of Requirements → Availability Check → Availability Check with ATP Logic or Against Planning* and choose ⊕ next to *Define Checking Groups*).

The example used in our sample product catalog uses checking group *02*.

Availability Checking Rule	Total Sales	Total Delivery
02 (Individual requirements)	A (single records)	A (single records)

All other columns are blank.

Check the Default Checking Rule Used by the IAC

As you configure for ATP, you must check the default checking rule used by the IAC. The default rule delivered with the standard R/3 System may have been changed in your implementation. The ATP service uses the checking rule *A* for sales and distribution. It is only possible to change the checking rule used for the ATP IAC with the user exit *EXIT_SAPLW61V_001*, which must be linked to an enhancement project using enhancement component *W61V0001*.

Task

Checking the IAC's default checking rule

1. In the *Command* field, enter transaction **OVZ9** and choose *Enter* (or in the IMG, choose *Sales and Distribution → Basic Functions → Availability Check and Transfer of Requirements → Availability Check → Availability Check with ATP Logic or Against Planning* and choose ⊕ next to *Carry Out Control For Availability Check*). This configuration is performed for the combination of the material checking rule (*02*) and the sales order checking rule (*A*).

2. The *Change View "Availability Check Control": Details* screen below shows an example of settings that may be used for the ATP check.

In the *Stocks* section, only unrestricted stock is included in the available quantity. Blocked and reserved stock is excluded.

The *Replenishment lead time* is not taken into account. If it were taken into account, the lead time would need to be maintained in one of the following views in the material master:

- Purchasing
- MRP 1
- MRP 2

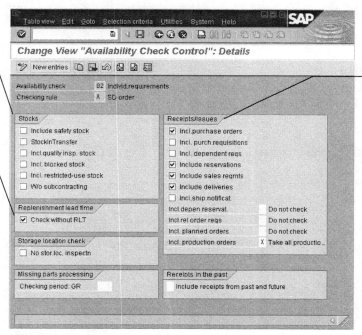

The *Receipts/Issues* section determines which types of documents are included in the ATP check. If purchase orders and production orders are included, the expected date of the goods receipt is used by ATP. If sales requirements are taken into account, the reserved stock for orders is subtracted from the available stock.

Note

The inclusion of production orders in the availability checking rule above is not turned on in the standard-delivered R/3 System. Additionally, for certain planning data to be included in ATP—such as requirements generated by sales order—MRP must be configured and requirements must be passed to MRP from the sales order item.

Check the Default ATP Settings Used by the IAC for Insufficient Stock

For ATP configuration, you must check the default ATP settings used by the IAC for insufficient stock. This setting, delivered with the standard R/3 System, determines how the system reacts when insufficient stock exists for a requirement entered by a customer. Since dialog boxes are not supported by the IAC, the system automatically substitutes full delivery for these settings.

To check the IAC's default settings for insufficient stock, enter transaction **OVZJ** in the *Command* field and choose *Enter* (or in the IMG, choose *Sales and Distribution* → *Basic Functions* → *Availability Check and Transfer of Requirements* → *Availability Check* → *Availability Check with ATP Logic or Against Planning* and choose 🕭 next to *Define Default Settings*).

The configuration of the availability checking rule not only affects the ATP IAC, but also the confirmation of available items when products in an Online Store order are confirmed. The setting *E* ensures that even if only a partial quantity is available, that quantity is already confirmed in the sales order.

We use setting *E* in our examples, which indicates the delivery proposal is used in case of shortages. Since a unique distribution channel *11* is used only for Internet orders in our preconfiguration, there is no conflict with normal order entry within R/3.

Sales Organization	Distribution Channel	Division	Fixed date and quantity	Availability Checking Rule
0010	11	10		E

Modify the Java Applet Configuration

A Java applet is used for executing the ATP functionality. The applet parameters are stored in the HTML [Business] template *SAPMAVCK_1200.HTML*.

The code that calls the Java applet is displayed below. The changeable parameters are shown in the next table.

```
<APPLET name=catalogApplet archive="catalog.zip"
codebase=`mimeURL(~name="classes",~language="")`
    code=catalogApplet.class width=320 height=285 mayscript>
    <PARAM name=cabbase value=catalog.cab>  <!-- Tells Internet
Explorer to download the cab file -->
    <PARAM name=products
value=`mimeURL(~name="data/materials.txt")`>
    <PARAM name=hierarchy
value=`mimeURL(~name="data/hierarchy.txt")`>
    <PARAM name=bgColor value=C0C0C0>
```

The following parameters can be modified if desired:

Parameter	Description	Value
Product value	Location and name of the file that contains the materials in each product group of the catalog	<wwwroot>/sap/its/mimes/ckav/<theme>/<language>/data/materials.txt
Hierarchy value	Location and name of the file that contains the product catalog layout	<wwwroot>/sap/its/mimes/ckav/<theme>/<language>/data/hierarchy.txt
BgColor	Background color of the tab in the window that displays the product catalog hierarchy and products	C0C0C0 (grey)

For the following example, the background color was changed to *FF0000*, or red.

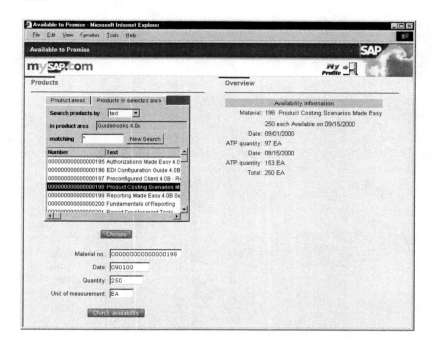

Check the SAPNet – R/3 Frontend Notes

To properly complete your ATP configuration, you should check for applicable SAPNet – R/3 Frontend notes (formerly OSS). For details on SAPNet – R/3 Frontend notes, please refer to appendix A, "SAPNet Frontend Notes" on page 495.

Customer Account Information

Overview

Customers may wish to see their account information on the Internet. Limited reviewing functionality allows the customer to verify that your internal company records contain the correct information, such as address and bank account information. Sensitive internal data, such as a payment block, is not available to your customer on the Internet.

Additionally, the customer may wish to determine whether they have been invoiced for their orders, and subsequently whether the payment has cleared. By providing this data on the Internet, accounting clerks can spend less time looking up information that customers can access electronically, twenty-four hours a day. This is an advantage especially for business partners that do not pay with credit cards.

It is not possible, however, for the customer to change this data online. If the customer wishes to make a change, feedback can be sent to you by e-mail directly from the customer account information function. You may also wish to provide a telephone number on your web site that your customers can use to contact you.

In general, once your accounts receivable A/R function has been configured, very little additional configuration is required to make this information available to your customers on the Internet.

What We Deliver

In the Online Store preconfiguration, we provide the following deliverables:

- Preconfiguration of the ITS look and feel

- Documentation on the functionality of the customer account information Internet Application Component (IAC)

The Customer Experience

The following procedure shows what our customer, Desiree, sees while displaying her customer account and A/R information. This example assumes that the customer has an existing customer record with your company and has been assigned a password. The A/R line item information is available after invoices and clearing transactions have been processed within the R/3 System. The data shown is sample data and is not delivered with the Online Store preconfiguration.

Task

Display Customer Account Information

1. In the Internet browser, Desiree enters the URL of your home page, which you configured as part of the ITS installation.

2. She chooses the *Online Store* from your home page.

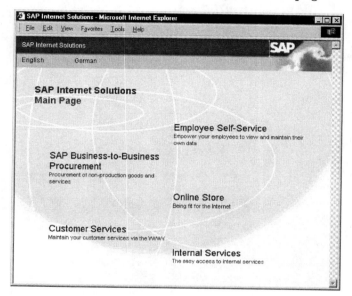

3. Desiree chooses *Customer Account Information*.

Customer account information ———

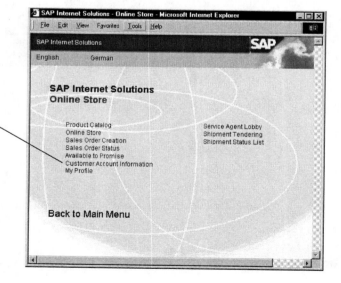

Note

It is not possible to use an e-mail address to log on for obtaining customer account information. This data is often only made available to business partners of a company who already have an established business relationship with you. Internally, this means you already have customer numbers for these business partners.

Note that if e-mail addresses are used for other functions on the Internet, a process needs to be put in place to inform customers of their customer numbers.

A list of all legal entities in which the customer does business with you is displayed.

4. In order to access the customer account information:

   a. Desiree enters her customer account number and password.

   b. She chooses *Logon*.

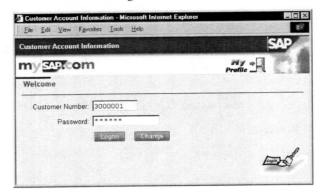

5. Desiree chooses a company code from the list.

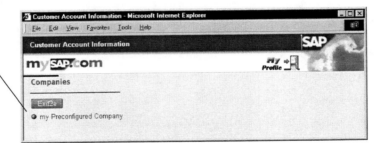

6. A list of the information available to Desiree is displayed in the left frame.

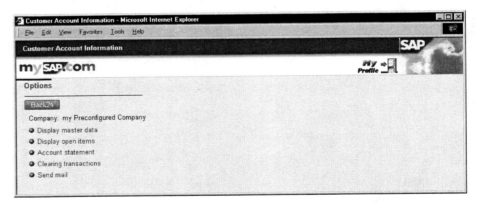

7. Desiree chooses *Display master data*.

The customer data is displayed in the top half of the right frame. This data is taken from the customer master record.

The bank data for the customer is displayed in the bottom half of the right frame. This data is also taken from the customer master record.

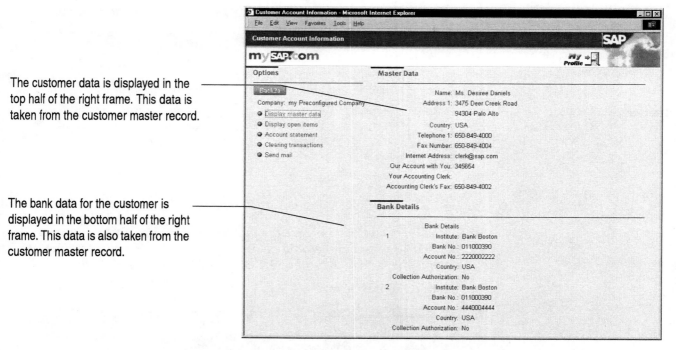

8. To view a list of all invoiced items that have not yet been paid:

a. Desiree chooses *Display open items*.

b. In *Date through*, a date through which the open items should be displayed may be entered. Desiree accepts the system default of the current date.

c. She chooses *Select*.

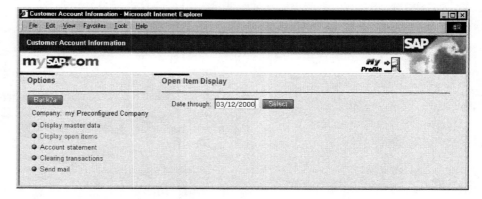

9. After reviewing her open items, Desiree chooses *Account statement*.

A list of all open items through the date entered is displayed. These are invoices that have been released to accounting, but have not yet been cleared.

Account statement

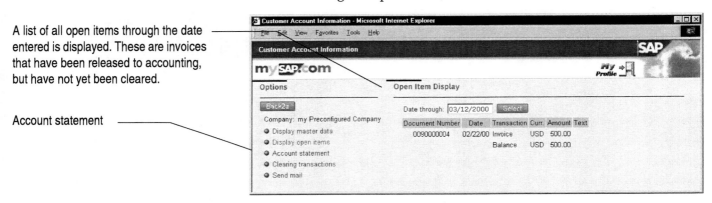

10. To view a consolidated list of her A/R balance:

a. In the *From* and *End* fields, a date range for which all the customer's financial transactions should be displayed may be entered. Desiree accepts the system default of the current date as the end date.

b. Desiree chooses *Select*.

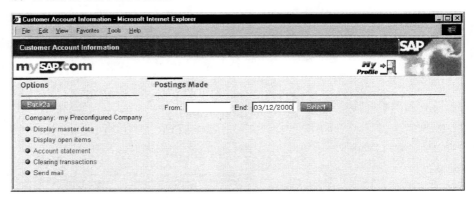

11. After reviewing the list of her transactions, Desiree chooses *Clearing transactions*.

A list of all transactions for the date range is displayed. These transactions include open and cleared items.

Clearing transactions

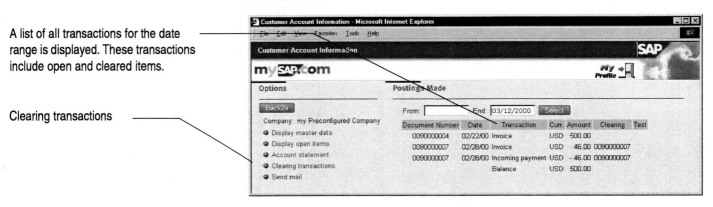

12. To view a list of all items that Desiree has paid and which have cleared:

a. In *From* and *End*, a date range for which the cleared items should be displayed may be entered. Desiree again accepts the system default of the current date as the end date.

b. Desiree chooses *Select*.

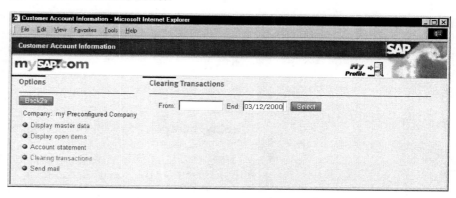

13. After reviewing the cleared items for the date range, Desiree decides to send a message to your company. She chooses *Send mail*.

A list of all cleared items for the date range is displayed. These are invoices that have been cleared by A/R.

Send mail

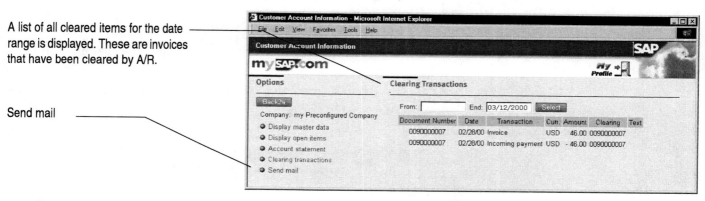

Note

This function has not been preconfigured.

The R/3 transaction **IKA1** supports the customer account information procedure.

14. A form in which the customer may enter correspondence with your company is displayed. Desiree can now enter her text and send her message.

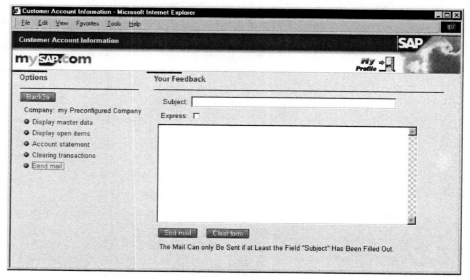

The View from Inside Your Company

Display the Corresponding Open Items in R/3

The open item data in R/3 contains the same information displayed on the Internet. The customer does not see the R/3 screen. Within the company, however, you can verify that the data shown on the Internet matches what is in the R/3 System.

Task

Display the open items for the customer

1. In the *Command* field, enter transaction **FBL5N** and choose *Enter* (or from the navigation menu, choose *Accounting → Financial Accounting → Accounts Receivable → Account → Display/change line items*).

2. On the *Customer Line Item Display* screen:

   a. In *Customer account*, enter the customer number of the customer that logged in on the Internet in the previous section.

   b. In *Company code*, enter the company code chosen by the customer on the Internet.

   c. Select *Open at key date*, and enter the date on which the A/R line items are open.

   d. Choose 🕒 .

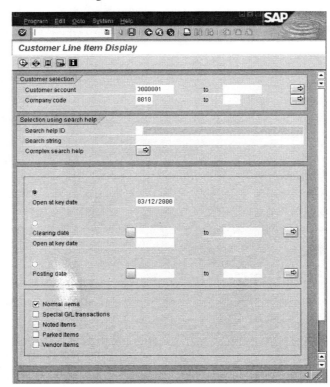

3. The list of open items is displayed. The information on this list should match the information displayed on the web.

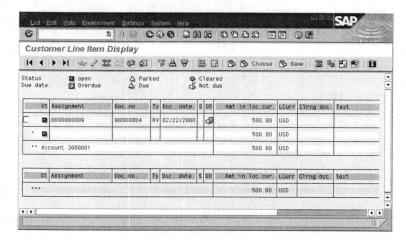

Display the Corresponding Cleared Items in R/3

The cleared item data in R/3 contains the same information displayed on the Internet. The customer does not see the R/3 screen. Within the company, however, you can verify that the data shown on the Internet matches what is in the R/3 System.

Task

Display the cleared items for the customer

1. In the *Command* field, enter transaction **FBL5N** and choose *Enter* (or from the navigation menu, choose *Accounting* → *Financial Accounting* → *Accounts Receivable* → *Account* → *Display/change line items*).

2. On the *Customer Line Item Display* screen:

    a. In *Customer account*, enter the customer number of the customer logged into the Internet in the previous section.

    b. In *Company code*, enter the company code chosen by the customer on the Internet.

    c. Select *Clearing date*.

    d. In the *to* field, enter the date through which the A/R line items have been cleared.

e. Choose 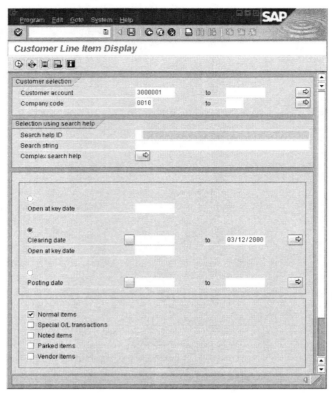.

3. The list of cleared items is displayed. The information on this list should match the information displayed on the web.

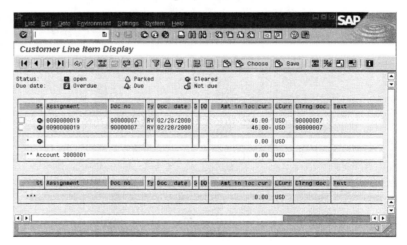

Making It Happen: Customer and Accounts Receivable Information on the Internet

In the following sections, we demonstrate how to make existing customer and A/R information available on the web. This chapter is not intended to be a thorough discussion of how A/R should be configured in your R/3 System.

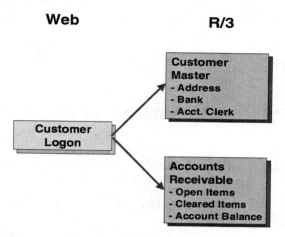

The customer logs on to this IAC with a customer number and password. Once logged on, customers can display their own master data, including their address and contact details, bank account information, and contact information for the accounting clerk assigned to them.

In addition, the customer can display A/R line items, such as open items and cleared items. If a customer receives a reminder for a payment that has been delayed in the mail, a quick check on the web site can show the customer whether a payment has been received.

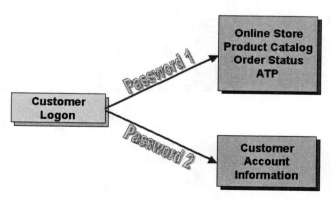

The password used for the customer account information is different from the password used for the other preconfigured IACs. The Internet user object type used for the other preconfigured sell-side IACs is *KNA1*. The object type for the customer account information is *BUS1007*. Since passwords are linked to the combination of customer number and object type, Internet customers must keep track of two passwords if they wish to access multiple IACs. The password for the customer account information IAC must be created manually in the R/3 System; it is not created through a registration process on the Internet. Please refer to chapter 16, "Internet Users: Passwords for Customers" on page 367 for details on the Internet user object types and passwords.

Some companies believe that a second password for the customer account information allows for additional security for displaying financial information. However, customers often see the need for a second password as an inconvenience. The password can be made the same for all IACs, including the customer account information, if the modification in appendix F, "Modification: Changing the Customer Type for IKA1" on page 533 is applied.

Master Data in R/3 to Support Customer Account Information

The following sections describe the steps involved in setting up sales order tracking. You must ensure that:

- All data is correctly entered into the customer master record
- The customer exists in the R/3 System and has been assigned a password

Ensure all Data Is Correctly Entered into the Customer Master Record

The first step to support the display of customer account information is to ensure that the correct data is entered into the customer master record. If the customer fields are not maintained, the data cannot be shown on the Internet.

Task

Verify the data in the customer master record

1. In the *Command* field, enter transaction **XD03** and choose *Enter* (or from the navigation menu, choose *Logistics → Sales and Distribution → Master Data → Business partners → Customer → Display → Complete*).

2. On the *Display Customer: Initial Screen*:

   a. In *Customer*, enter the number of the customer that logged on the Internet in the previous section.

   b. In *Company code*, enter the company that the customer chose on the Internet.

   c. In *Sales organization*, choose the sales organization in your company with which the customer interacts.

   d. In *Distribution channel*, choose the distribution channel you use for doing business on the Internet.

   e. In *Division*, choose the division for which the customer has been created.

f. Choose ✔ .

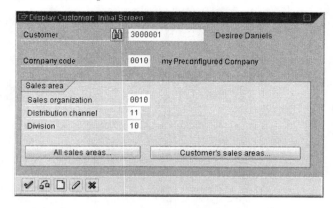

3. On the *Change Customer: General Data* screen:

   a. The address data displayed on the Internet is maintained on this screen.

   b. Scroll down to the bottom of the screen.

4. On the *Change Customer: General Data* screen:

   a. The telephone data displayed on the Internet is also maintained on this screen.

   b. Choose the *Payment transactions* tab.

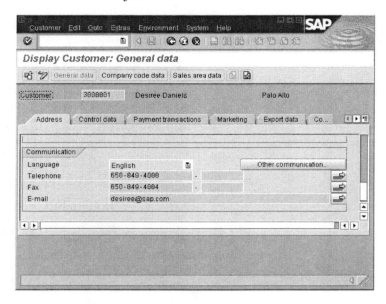

5. On the *Change Customer: General data* screen:

   a. Enter the bank information.

   b. Choose *Company code data*.

Company code data button

The bank information displayed on the Internet is maintained on this screen.

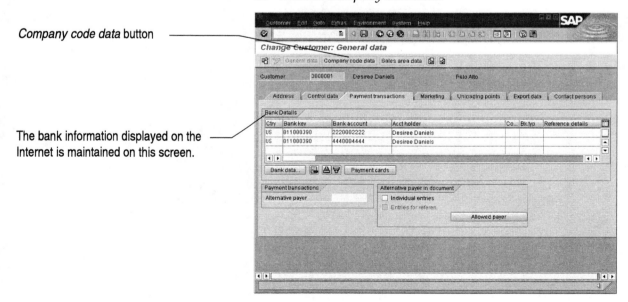

6. On the *Change Customer: Company code data* screen:

   a. Choose the *Correspondence* tab.

   b. Enter the accounting clerk information.

The accounting clerk information displayed on the Internet is maintained on this tab.

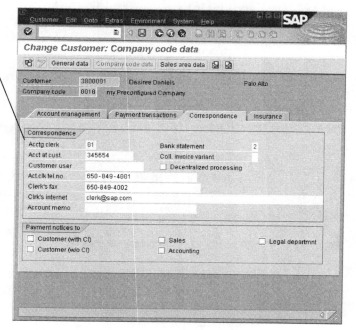

Ensure the Customer Exists in the R/3 System and Has a Password

If you wish to use object type *KNA1* for the Internet user instead of *BUS1007* to be more consistent with the other IACs, you can implement the modification documented in appendix F, "Modification: Changing the Customer Type for IKA1" on page 533. Note that this would be a modification and not a configuration change and thus would have to be maintained by your company in case of an upgrade.

You may also wish to keep the object types separate since the financial information accessible using the customer account information IAC may be sensitive.

To support the display of customer account information, you must ensure that the customer exists in R/3 and has been assigned a password. New customers are not allowed to register using the customer account information IAC. The customer must already have a customer number and password.

The customer master record must already exist for the sales area used on the Internet. To create the customer master record, enter transaction **XD01** in the *Command* field and choose *Enter* (or from the navigation menu, choose *Logistics → Sales and Distribution → Master Data → Business partners → Customer → Create → Complete*). Please refer to chapter 5, "Customers in the Online Store" on page 133 for details about customers in IACs.

The Internet user must be created using object type *BUS1007*. To create the Internet user, enter transaction **SU05** in the *Command* field and choose *Enter* (or from the navigation menu, choose *Tools → Administration → User Maintenance → Internet User*). Please refer to chapter 15, "The ITS User: Logging on to R/3" on page 349 for details about the Internet user.

Customer Account Information Configuration

Note

For changes that we deliver for the look and feel of the customer account information functionality, and instructions on how to make changes to the ITS HTML ^Business^ templates, please refer to chapter 13.

The following sections describe the steps involved in setting up the customer account information configuration. You must:

- Configure the link between your e-mail system and the R/3 System (not preconfigured)

- Check the SAPNet – R/3 Frontend notes

Configure the Link Between your E-mail System and R/3

The link between your e-mail system and R/3 has not been preconfigured. For assistance on linking your e-mail to the R/3 System, please refer to chapter 19, "E-mail and Fax" on page 416.

Check the SAPNet – R/3 Frontend Notes

To properly complete your customer account information configuration, you should check for applicable SAPNet – R/3 Frontend notes (formerly OSS). For details on SAPNet – R/3 Frontend notes, please refer to appendix A, "SAPNet Frontend Notes" on page 495.

PART TWO

Reporting

Section Overview

As an increasing number of businesses begin to integrate an online storefront with their traditional offline, brick-and-mortar stores, the ability to review and analyze the incremental sales resulting from their web presence is imperative. Fortunately, in today's digital world, we have evolved from the days of the green-barred, mainframe reports toward real-time online queries and ad-hoc reports that can be produced electronically. Companies require up-to-date, aggregated information that presents the sales activity captured from their online store in comparison to sales generated through traditional channels. The integration of an Internet solution has opened a vast amount of reporting requirements on the web.

Our goal is to provide you with the reporting methods which enable you to:

- Analyze customer behavior in order to improve product offerings and markets

- Combine customer behavior data with the customer's order in order to gain a more complete analysis

Web statistics provide invaluable information on your customer's online shopping experience and site success. To achieve these reporting objectives, you can use R/3 reports, in conjunction with outside web-intelligence technologies, to analyze correlations.

Through SAP standard reporting tools and Tealeaf™ software, business e-leaders responsible for justifying a company's Internet investment can evaluate which distribution channel sales result from and how successful their online store is. Tealeaf Technology™, a spin-off from SAP, provides the solutions for capturing and providing insights to your customer's online shopping experience. For more information on Tealeaf Technology, please refer to their web site at *www.tealeaf.com*.

We surveyed our Accelerated Internet Selling focus group to gather feedback on the reporting requirements most significant to their company's web-related business needs. In regards to e-commerce reporting, we asked our focus group several questions in the following areas:

- Customer profile

- Data mining and trends

- Sales transactions

- Technical-related issues

We broke down the questions by category and ranked them by level of importance by our focus group in the tables below. Alongside the reporting requirements, we indicated with which reporting method you could best extract the data.

Exactly who are the people visiting the online store and how often do they browse versus purchase? The results of the customer-oriented questions, in their order of significance, can be found in the table below:

Customer-Oriented Questions	R/3 Reporting	Tealeaf Auditor	Vote (%) on Importance
What % of all my customers are visiting the site and ordering product?	X		35.5
What % of all my customers are visiting the site and checking the product availability?	If ATP		28.5
Which customer or group of customers uses the site most often?		X	23.5
Which % of all my customers are visiting the site?		X	22
Which % of all my customers are visiting the site and getting order status?	X	X	19.5
Number of times each ID purchased	X	X	19
How many ID's were from the same company?	X	X	13
Number of times each ID entered a site		X	12

The customer's buying behavior and purchasing patterns can be examined through analytical report processing such as trend analysis and advanced queries. Business managers are often curious about the "what" and "why," and require the necessary reports which facilitate the decision making. The results of the data mining analytical questions can be found in the following table:

Data Mining Analytical Questions	R/3 Reporting	Tealeaf Auditor	Vote (%) on Importance
80% look but do not buy. For the 80%, what products are they looking at?		X	31
Identify the effects of price changes/discounts		X	30
For the "look but do not buy," what products are they looking at most?		X	25.5
For the "look but do not buy," what price ranges are they looking at?		X	22

Data Mining Analytical Questions	R/3 Reporting	Tealeaf Auditor	Vote (%) on Importance
For the "look but do not buy," what products are added to the shopping basket but not bought?		X	21.5
What path did visitors take through the web site?		X	16.5
What, in general, is the behavior of customers related to purchase?		X	15.5

What is the impact of introducing an online storefront? Are the company's regular customers now buying online, or has the Internet reached a new customer base and expanded market share? The results of the sales transaction questions can be found in the table below:

Sales Transaction Questions	R/3 Reporting	Tealeaf Auditor	Vote (%) on Importance
What is the average number of dollars going through the site for the product?	X		30.5
What items are most commonly ordered over the Internet? Top 100?	X		28
Average dollars spent per Web order vs. non-Web order	X		25
What % of total customer orders is taken over the web site?	X		24.5
What is the average value of order?	X		19.5
What is the quantity of each item?	X		14
What is the average number of line items per order?	X		11.5

With more and more people using the Internet today, network traffic and the load on servers has increased, affecting the desirability of the web site. Companies need the capability to analyze peak times, know the number of hits to their site receives, and respond to any problems the customer may experience. The results of the technical-related questions can be found in the table below:

Technical Questions	R/3 Reporting	Tealleaf Auditor	Vote (%) on Importance
What is my peak user load and when does it usually occur?		X	30.5
How many customers fill the cart but do not complete an order?		X	26
How many people tried to access the site but could not get through security?		X	26
How many people are not making it through registration?		X	26
What is the average response time per page for the customers?		X	25.5
How much time is it taking a person per line item to create a new order?		X	22
Where are the people dropping off in registration?		X	16.5
What is the average length of time that a user holds a session on the site?	X		15.5

To stay competitive in today's fast-paced world, companies require access to timely, accurate information regarding all facets of their organization. For example, decisions to develop a new product line or revise the business plan are based on the analysis of integrated information flowing through a company's enterprise software system. As companies expand their businesses by blending sales efforts through Internet channels, the ability to analyze the contribution of the web site and its effect on business is crucial.

Sales Activity Reports

Overview

With the integration of the Accelerated Internet Selling (AIS) solution to your R/3 System, a comprehensive suite of reports and tools are accessible to help companies extract a goldmine of real-time information. In addition to your traditional sales channel, integrating an Internet channel into your business strategy creates additional reporting requirements for analysis.

In this chapter you learn how to:

- Analyze the most frequently used R/3 Internet sales, in two categories:

  - **Document Analysis** – To view a list of sales orders, blocked sales orders, backorders, incomplete sales documents, and list of all outbound deliveries

  - **Statistical Analysis** – Reports based on standard info structures and user-defined info structures

- Configure the self-defined info structures.

In order to distinguish the sales generated from your Online Store versus those from other channels (such as retail or direct), we recommend you enter the distribution channel which identifies Internet sales transactions when executing your standard Sales Information System (SIS) reports. If you have an existing R/3 System and are implementing the Online Store, you need to create a new distribution channel for Internet sales under your organizational structure. In a fresh installation, if you implement the Online Store preconfiguration together with the Preconfigured Client (PCC), the distribution channels *10* (Retail channel) and *11* (Internet channel) are already delivered.

Also note that the PCC already has active info structures *S700, S701,* and *S703* for the purpose of analyzing the Internet sales. If you need to further modify or configure any info structure, then you can refer to "Configuration of Self-Defined Information Structures" on page 298.

Analyzing Internet Sales with R/3: Report Definitions

List of Sales Orders

By running the list of sales orders report, you can view the sales documents, sorted by sold-to party, that were generated through the Internet sales channel. With your Online Store being tightly integrated to the backend R/3 System, all orders placed through the web site are immediately passed through and stored in your R/3 System. Therefore, you can query R/3 by specifying criteria such as sold-to party, period of time, and web order number.

Blocked Sales Orders

Sometimes it is necessary to block shipment of a confirmed Internet sales order. A delivery block indicator can block the delivery of a pending sale that has been entered into R/3 as a web order. Typical reasons for a delivery block are:

- The customer postpones or changes the shipping date
- The product did not pass a QA check
- Export papers are missing
- The company decides to accept a returning customer's order even though the credit card was not authorized and performs manual follow-up with the customer

Backorders

A backordered sales order report shows all the sales placed over the Internet that are set for delivery, but are currently backlogged. The system creates the report based on the confirmed and backlogged sales documents, along with the corresponding value.

Incomplete Sales Documents

If the required fields are not filled out when creating a web sales order, the order documents are converted to incomplete sales documents. The incomplete sales documents report displays all incomplete sales documents and allows users to change the orders and complete them.

List of All Outbound Deliveries

Run the list of outbound deliveries reports to review the current delivery status of the web sales order. The report displays:

- The delivery document created for the ship-to party and the picking date of that order
- List of goods issued and their dates of delivery

Incoming Order Report

The incoming order analysis from the Sales Information System (SIS) provides information on incoming Internet orders over a period of time (for example, a month). The analysis provides information by customer, product (material), sales organization, sales employee, or sales office. The report also provides the invoiced sales activity associated with each order.

Invoiced Sales Report

The invoiced sales report analyzes the invoiced Internet sales (for example, the net value of the billing item stated in the document currency) over a period of time (a month). The analysis can be run according to customer, product (material), sales organization, sales employee, or sales office. With this report, you can use multiple selection and drilldown criteria to evaluate the invoiced sales data.

Shipping Point

The shipping point analysis is based on data that has been updated from the creation of the delivery note of the Internet order. The analysis provides information by shipping point, route, forwarding agent, and destination country. This report can be used to answer questions such as:

- Who delivers in what way (freight forwarding)?

- What was the route?

Territory Sales Report (Daily, Weekly, Monthly)

The territory sales report lists all the sales activity generated from your Online Store and can be analyzed by country, region, and sold-to party, from data aggregated based on a daily, weekly, or monthly basis.

Available Reports: Quick Reference

We have summarized the most frequently used R/3 Internet sales reports along with their corresponding menu paths in the following two categories.

- Document analysis

- Statistical analysis

The sections that follow demonstrate with step-by-step instructions how to execute the various reports. These examples acquaint you with the reporting capabilities of SAP R/3.

Document Analysis

Within each application area of the R/3 System, you can call up reports that are directly linked to tasks in the R/3. The reports in the table below enable you to evaluate and review the transaction data within the Sales and Distribution (SD) module that results from the sales activity of your Online Store.

Report Name	Menu Path
List of Sales Orders	*Information Systems → General Report Selection → Sales and Distribution → Sales → Orders → List of sales orders.* Transaction: `VA05`
List of Blocked Sales Orders	*Information Systems → Logistics → Sales and Distribution → SD Documents → Orders → Blocked sales orders* Transaction: `V.14`
List of Backorder	*Information Systems → General Report Selection → Sales and Distribution → Sales → Orders → Display Backorders* Transaction: `V.15`
List of Incomplete Sales Documents	*Information Systems→ General Report Selection → Sales and Distribution → Sales → Orders → Incomplete Orders* Transaction: `V.02`
List of All or Open Deliveries	*Information Systems → Logistics → Sales and Distribution → SD Documents → Deliveries → Deliveries List* Transaction: `VL06F`

Statistical Analysis

Online drilldown and standard analysis on aggregated transaction data is available through the Sales Information System (SIS). Reports are executed against standard and user-defined information structures that store the aggregated data by characteristics, key figures, and time periods. Statistical reports in the table below enable you to analyze the results of your Internet sales and traditional retail sales.

Report Name	Menu Path
Incoming Order Report	*Logistics → Sales and Distribution → Sales Information System → Standard analyses→ Customer* Transaction: `MCTA`
Invoiced Sales Report	*Logistics → Sales and Distribution → Sales Information System → Standard analyses → Customer* Transaction: `MCTA`

Report Name	Menu Path
Shipping Report	*Logistics → Sales and Distribution → Sales Information System → Standard analyses → Shipping point* Transaction: **MCTK**
Territory Sales Report (daily, weekly, monthly)	*Logistics → Sales and Distribution → Sales Information System → Standard analyses → user-defined info structures → Territory Sales (daily, weekly, monthly)* Transaction: **MCSI**

Document Analysis

List of Sales Orders

Task

List Internet sales documents by sold-to party

1. In the *Command* field, enter transaction **VA05** and choose *Enter* (or from the navigation menu, choose *Information Systems → General Report Selection → Sales and Distribution → Sales → Orders → List of Sales Orders*).

2. On the *List of Sales Orders* screen:

   a. Enter a *Sold-to party* or *Material* number (for example, **3000006**).

   b. In *Document date*, enter the document date range (for example, **02/28/2000** to **03/09/2000**). This range is based on the date the sales orders were created.

   c. Under *Selection criteria*, select *All orders*.

   d. Choose ✅ .

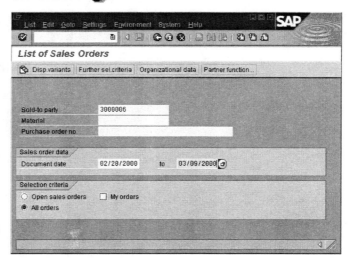

3. On the *Organizational Data* dialog box:

    a. In *Sales organization*, enter the sales organization you use for Internet orders (for example, **0010** from the Preconfigured Client).

    b. In *Distribution channel*, enter the distribution channel you use for Internet sales (for example, **11** from the Preconfigured Client).

    c. Choose ✔ .

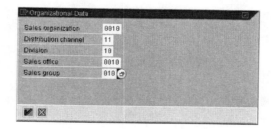

4. On the *List of Sales Orders* screen:

    a. Review the sales orders.

    b. If you wish to view only a specific range of sales orders, set the data filter by choosing 🦅 .

This screen shows the basic list of all sales orders without display variants.

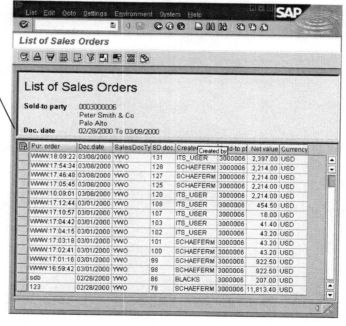

5. On the *Define filter criteria* dialog box:

    a. Under *Field list*, select *Document date* from the field list.

    b. Click ◀ to move the field to the *Filter criteria* column.

c. Choose 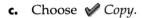 *Copy.*

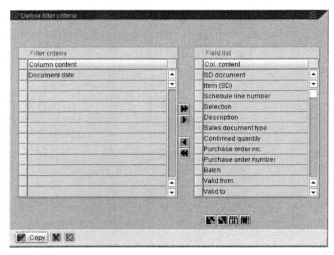

6. On the *Filter criteria* dialog box:

a. In *Document date*, enter the filter date range (for example, **02/28/2000** to **03/01/2000**).

b. Choose ✔.

7. On the *List of Sales Orders By partner* screen:

a. For numeric fields, such as net value or quantity, you can create totals. Select the *Net value* column.

b. To display the sum, choose ∑.

This screen shows the filtered output for the sales orders that occurred in the above range.

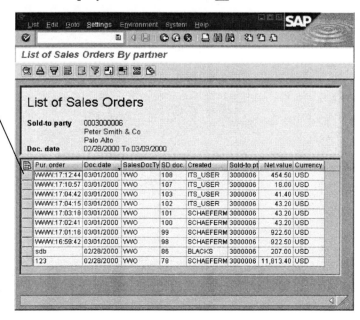

8. The screen now shows the total net value.

    a. To define the layout of your SD document list, select the display variant that determines which fields are displayed on the screen.

    b. To change the layout for the list of sales orders by partner, choose *Settings → Display variants → Choose.*

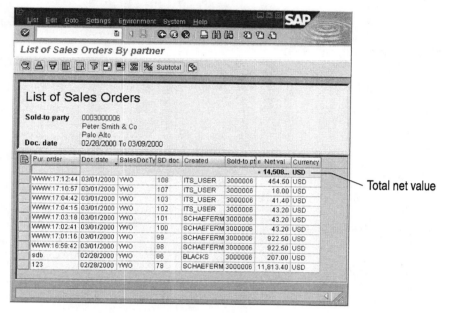

9. On the *Display variant: Choose* dialog box:

    a. To view the list of sales orders by partner and schedule lines, select the variant *3SAP*.

    b. Choose ✔ *Copy*.

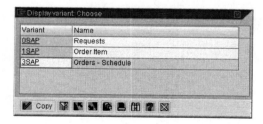

10. On the *List of Sales Orders By partner - Schedule lines* screen:

    a. Select *Standard order document 86.*

    b. Choose *Environment → Document flow* to view additional document information and master data.

This screen shows output based on display variant *3SAP.*

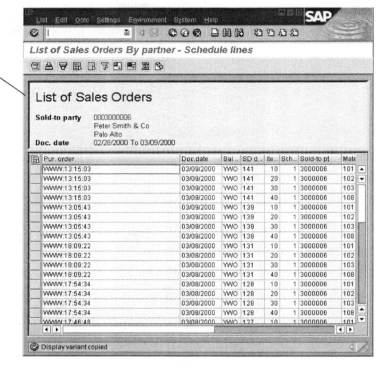

11. The *Document Flow* screen shows document flow for *e-Shop Web Order 86.*

    a. To display the individual sales document, select the *e-Shop web order* line next to the *86.*

    b. Choose ⚙ *Display document.*

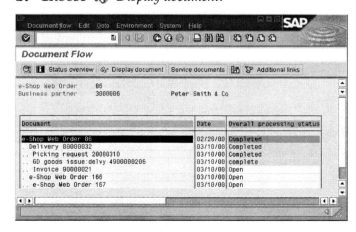

12. The *Display e-Shop Web Order 86: Overview* screen appears.

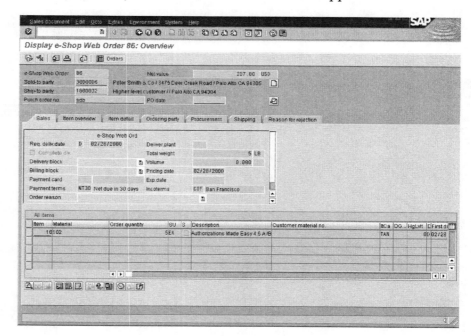

Blocked Sales Orders

Task

Display blocked Internet sales orders in the Fast display/document overview mode

1. In the *Command* field, enter transaction **V.14** and choose *Enter* (or from the navigation menu, choose *Information Systems* → *Logistics* → *Sales and Distribution* → *SD Documents* → *Orders* → *Blocked orders*).

2. On the *Sales Orders / Contracts Blocked for Delivery* screen:

   a. Under *List criteria*, select *Fast display/document overview*.

   b. Under *Organization data*, you can limit your search to Internet sales by entering the *Sales organization* and *Distribution channel* associated with Internet sales (for example, **0010** for sales organization and **11** for Internet orders).

 To limit the output, you may also want to enter other selection criteria such as sales organization, distribution channel (internet versus retail), etc.

c. To execute the report, choose ⏱

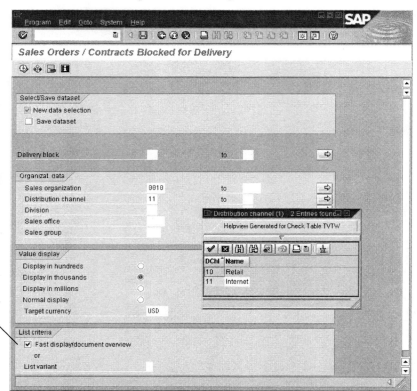

Fast display/document overview

3. On the *Sales Orders / Contracts Blocked for Delivery* report:

a. Select sales order *166*.

b. To branch into the document, choose ⊗ *Disp. doc.*

This screen shows all sales orders with a delivery block.

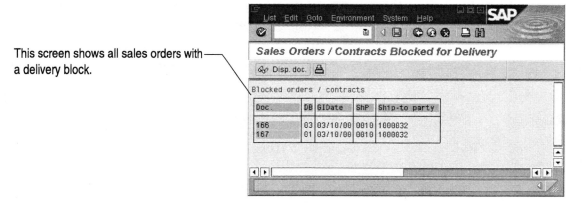

4. The *Display e-Shop Web Order 166: Overview* screen shows the standard function *Display order* (transaction **VA03**). The *Delivery block* field shows the reason for the blocked sales order.

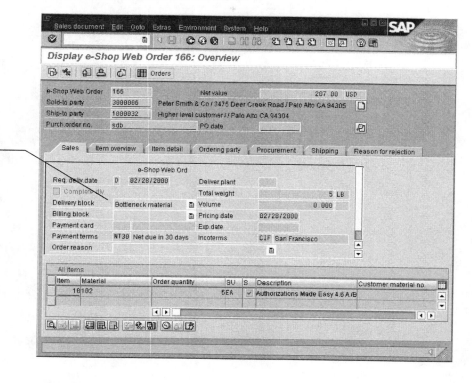

Sales order *166* is blocked due to bottleneck material.

Task

Display blocked sales orders by customer and materials

1. On the *Sales Orders / Contracts Blocked for Delivery* screen:

a. Under *List criteria*, enter **3** in *List variant* (for *Customer and material*) to view detailed information.

b. Under *Organization data*, you can limit your search to Internet sales by entering the appropriate *Sales organization* and *Distribution channel* associated with Internet sales (for example, **0010** for sales organization and **11** for Internet orders).

c. To execute the report, choose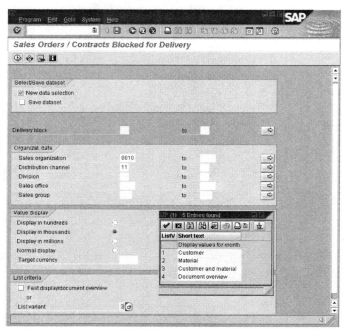

2. This screen shows all sales orders blocked by customer and materials.

Blocked sales orders by month

Blocked sales orders by customer (ship-to party)

Blocked sales orders by material

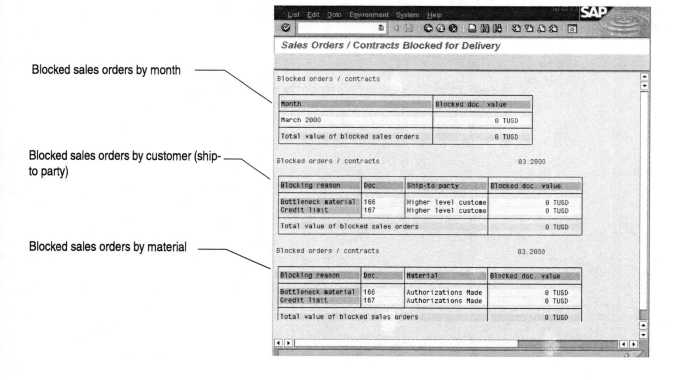

Backorders

Note

The list display of web-placed backorders can be viewed by timeframe, specific customer, or specific product.

Task

Display the backorders using Fast display/document overview

1. In the *Command* field, enter transaction **V.15** and choose *Enter* (or from the navigation menu, choose *Information Systems → General Report Selection→ Sales and distribution → Sales → Orders→ Display Backorders*).

2. On the *Backorders* screen:

    a. In *Sales organization*, enter the sales organization you use for Internet orders (for example, **0010** from the Preconfigured Client).

    b. In *Distribution channel*, enter the distribution channel you use for Internet sales (for example, **11** from the Preconfigured Client).

    c. Under *List criteria*, select *Fast display/document overview*.

    d. To execute the report, choose ⊕ .

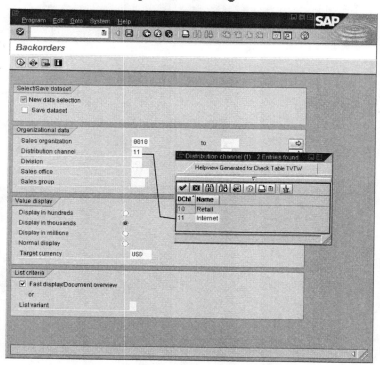

3. The next screen shows backorder documents listed by goods issue date (*GIDate*), shipping point (*ShP*), and ship-to party.

    a. To drill down to an individual backorder document (for example, *40*), place the cursor in the row of the document.

    b. To sort the documents in ascending order, choose 🖨 .

c. To view the sales document, select the document number and choose *Display document.*

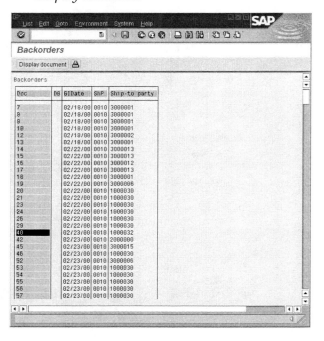

4. The *Display Web Order 40: Overview* screen shows an overview of standard order *40.* You can research the backorder by:

- Reviewing the document flow.

- Viewing the details of any action that might have been taken in shipping on the *Shipping* tab.

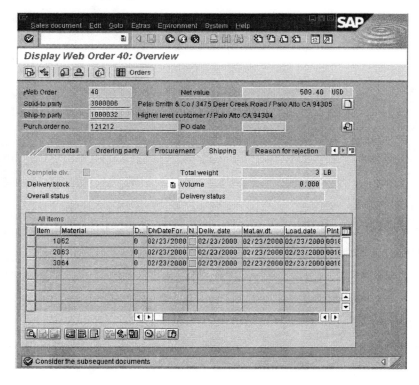

Task

Display the total value of the backorders for a particular month

1. On the *Backorders* screen:

   a. Under *Organizational data,* limit your search to Internet sales by entering the appropriate *Sales organization* and *Distribution channel* associated with Internet sales (for example, **0010** for sales organization and **11** for Internet orders).

   b. Make certain *Fast display/document overview* is deselected.

   c. Leave *List variant* blank.

   d. To execute the report, choose ⊕

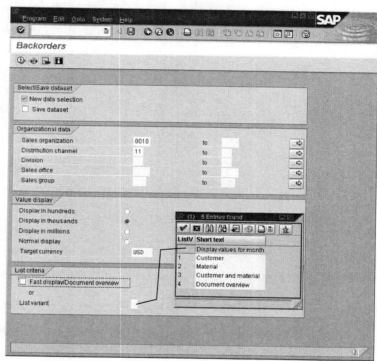

2. The next screen shows the value of the backorders per month.

   ▪ Choose ☞ *Customers* to produce a column listing by order number, customer, value, and GI date.

■ Choose &ge *Material* to produce a column listing by order number, material, value, and GI date.

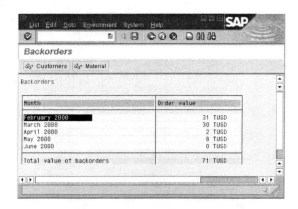

3. If you chose &ge *Customers*, the next screen shows backorders by customers.

Choose *Display document* to view the details of an individual document.

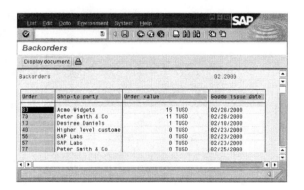

4. If you chose &ge *Material*, the next screen shows backorders by material.

Choose *Display document* to view the details of an individual document.

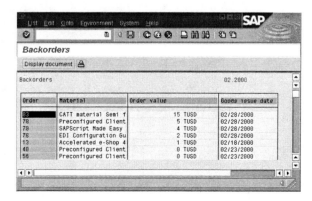

Task

Display the total value of backorders per month for customers and material

1. On the *Backorders* screen:

   a. Under *Organizational data,* limit your search to Internet sales by entering the appropriate *Sales organization* and *Distribution channel* associated with Internet sales (for example, **0010** for sales organization and **11** for Internet orders).

   b. Under *List criteria,* enter **3** in *List variant* to display customer and material information.

   c. To execute the report, choose 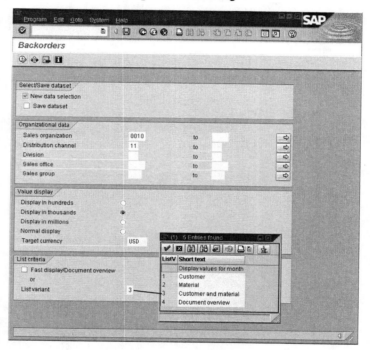 .

2. The next screen shows backorders by customer and material per month.

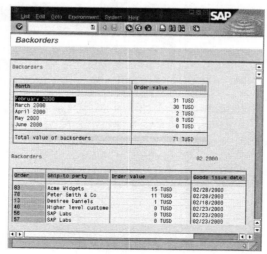

Incomplete Sales Documents

Task

Display all incomplete Internet sales documents

1. In the *Command* field, enter transaction **V.02** and choose Enter (or from the navigation menu, choose *Information Systems* → *General Report Selection* → *Sales and distribution* →*Sales* → *Orders*→ *Incomplete Orders*).

2. On the *Incomplete SD Documents* screen:

   a. Under *Incompleteness*, select all types of incompleteness you wish to analyze.

   b. Under *Organization* data, enter the *Sales organization* you use for Internet orders (for example, **0010** from the Preconfigured Client).

   c. In *Distribution channel*, enter the distribution channel you use for Internet sales (for example, **11** from the Preconfigured Client).

   d. To execute the report, choose

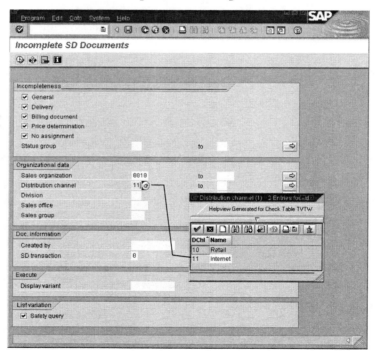

3. The next screen shows the list of incomplete sales documents. The matrix indicates the reasons for the incompleteness.

To edit a document, click on the sales order number (for example, *Order 9*).

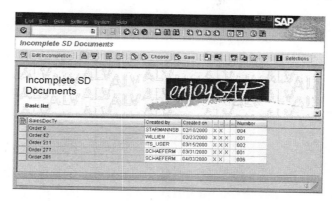

4. On the *Change e-Shop Web Order 9: Incompletion Log* screen:

   a. Select the item of the order you wish to complete.

   b. Choose *Complete data*.

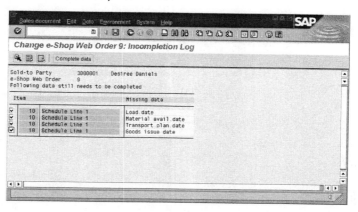

5. On the *Change e-Shop Web Order 9: Schedule Line Data* screen:

   a. Enter the missing data (for example, *Loading date*).

   b. To change the other items on this order, click ▶ (the *Edit next data* icon).

This screen shows the selected sales document and indicates missing data.

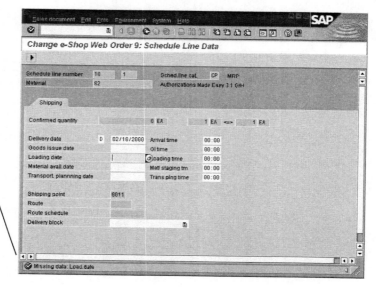

List of All Outbound Deliveries

Display all deliveries for a specific ship-to party

1. In the *Command* field, enter transaction **VL06F** and choose *Enter* (or from the navigation menu, choose *Information systems → Logistics → Sales and distribution → SD Documents → Deliveries → Deliveries List*).

2. On the *General Delivery List - Outbound Deliveries* screen:

    a. Under *Organization data*, limit your search to Internet sales by entering the appropriate *Sales organization* and *Distribution channel* associated with Internet sales (for example, **0010** for sales organization and **11** for Internet orders).

    b. Under *Time data*, enter a date range (for example, **02/28/2000** to **03/09/2000**) in *Delivery date*.

    c. To execute the report, choose ⊕

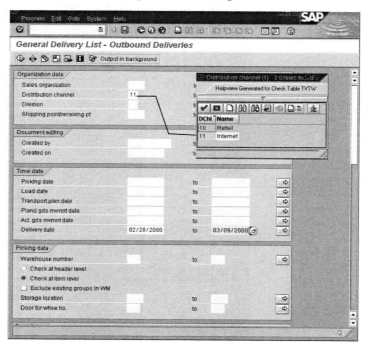

3. The *List of Outbound Deliveries* screen shows the list of outbound deliveries within the date selection entered above. From this report, you may change the layout by choosing *Setting →Display variant → Current*.

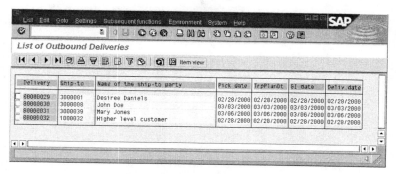

4. From the *Define Display Variant: Free selection - Header view* dialog box, you can eliminate or add other fields to change the layout of the basic output list.

   a. Under *Hidden fields*, select *Load date* from the field list.

   b. Click ◀ to move the field to *Column Content* on the left of the screen.

   c. Choose ✔ *Copy*.

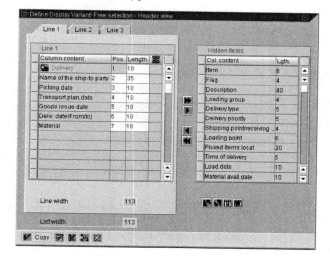

5. On the *List of Outbound Deliveries* screen, this report shows the output based on the addition of the load date field.

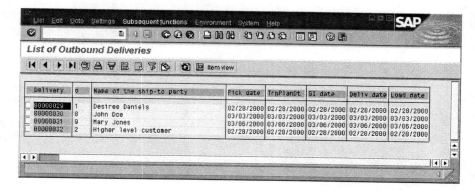

Statistical Analysis: Sales Information System

The Sales Information System (SIS) is a flexible reporting tool within R/3 that allows you to collect, consolidate, and utilize data from Sales and Distribution (SD) processing. The data stored in SIS is an aggregated subset of the data stored for your transactions and is collected and stored in information structures by characteristics, key figures, and time period.

SIS standard analyses provides an interactive analysis and drilldown feature of the data stored in these structures based on the key figures you want to analyze.

The SIS reports in R/3 are organized into the following two categories. Reports based on:

- Standard info structures
- User-defined info structures

Reports Based on Standard Info Structures

Note

Verify settings in the IMG for updating the SD information structures (transaction **OMO1**). If the information structures have not been activated, please inform your system administrator.

The information structures shown in the table below are available in SIS as **standard information structures**. These structures form the data basis for the respective standard analysis of the same name. For the purpose of demonstration, this guide provides examples of statistical analysis from data updated in the customer information structure. Please note that the following is only one example, and you have the option to execute your analysis based on any of the standard information structures.

Menu Option	For Reporting	Info Structure
Customer	Sold-to party, Material, Sales organization, Distribution channel, Division	S001
Sales office	Sales organization, Sales group, Sales office, Distr. channel, Division	S002
Sales organization	Distr. channel, Division, Material, Sales district, Sales organization, Sold-to party	S003
Material	Material, Sales organization, Distribution channel	S004
Shipping Point	Shipping point/receiving point, Route, Forwarding agent, Destination country	S005
Sales employee	Sales organization, Distr. channel, Division, Sales employee, Sold-to party, Material	S006

Incoming Order Report

Task

List and analyze the booked or incoming Internet orders for a two-month period.

1. In the *Command* field, enter transaction **MCTA** and choose *Enter* (or from the navigation menu, choose *Logistics → Sales and distribution → Sales information system → Standard analyses → Customer*).

2. On the *Customer Analysis: Selection* screen:

   a. Under *Characteristics*, enter the *Sales organization* you use for Internet orders (for example, **0010** from the Preconfigured Client).

   b. In *Distribution channel*, enter the distribution channel you use for Internet sales (for example, **11** from the Preconfigured Client).

   c. Under *Period to analyze*, enter a date range (for example, **01/2000** to **03/2000**) in *Month*.

   d. To execute the report, choose ⊕.

Note

A period is determined by the date an ordered item is changed or deleted.

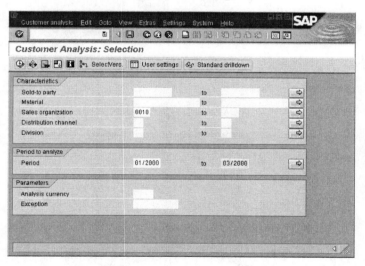

3. On *Customer Analysis: Basic List* screen, choose *Edit → Choose Key figures*, to select additional key figures or change their sequence.

This screen shows data based on the standard defaults for drilldown, key figures to be displayed, and other layout settings.

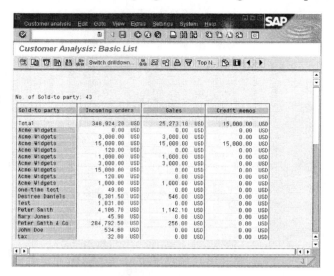

4. The *Choose Key figures* dialog box has two columns:

- *Selection criteria* lists the key figures selected for display.

- *All* lists all available key figures.

a. Select *Incoming orders qty.* from the column to the right.

b. Click ◀ to move the field to the *Selection criteria* column.

c. Choose ✔.

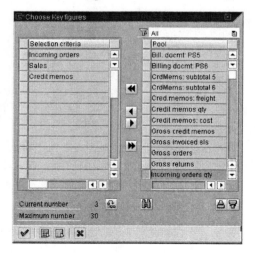

5. Continue to change the selection criteria

    a. Delete key figure *Sales* and *Credit memos* by clicking ▶ to move the field from the *Selection criteria* column back to the *Pool Column*.

    b. Choose ✔.

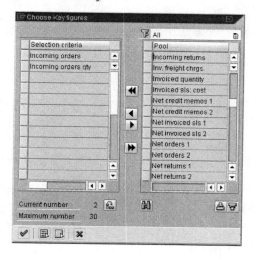

6. On the *Customer Analysis: Basic List* screen:

    a. Choose *Switch drilldown*.

    b. On the *Switch drilldown* dialog box, select *Distribution channel*.

    c. Choose ✔.

Switch drilldown button ————

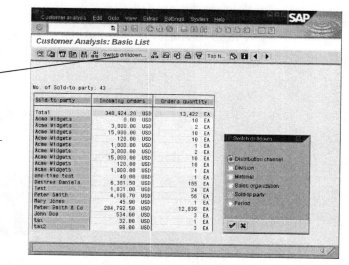

> **Note**
>
> This screen shows data based on the standard defaults for drilldown, key figures to be displayed, and other layout settings. The columns in this table correspond to the key figures chosen in step **4a**.

7. The *Customer Analysis: Drilldown* screen shows data grouped by distribution channels.

The following extract functions are available on the toolbar to further analyze the shown data:

- Sorting: ascending 🖶 and descending 🗑
- *Top N/Last N*

- Times series (periods in columns)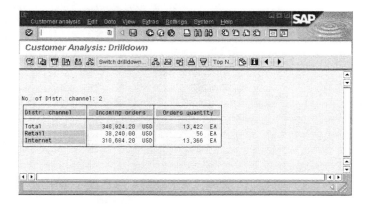
- Graphics

Invoiced Sales Report

Task

List and analyze the invoiced Internet sales of the last two months

1. In the *Command* field, enter transaction **MCTA** and choose *Enter* (or from the navigation menu, choose *Logistics → Sales and distribution → Sales Information System → Standard Analyses→ Customer*).

2. On the *Customer Analysis: Selection* screen:

   a. Under *Characteristics,* enter the *Sales organization* you use for Internet orders (for example, **0010** from the Preconfigured Client).

   b. In *Distribution channel*, enter the distribution channel you use for Internet sales (for example, **11** from the Preconfigured Client).

   c. Under *Period to analyze,* enter a date range (for example, **02/2000** to **03/2000**) in *Month*.

   d. To execute the report, choose .

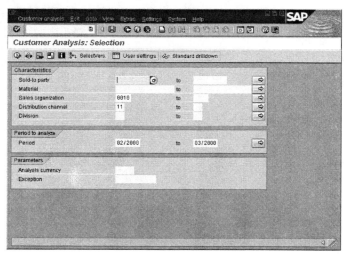

3. On the *Customer Analysis: Basic List* screen, choose *Edit → Choose Key figures,* to select additional key figures or change their sequence.

This screen shows data based on the standard defaults for drilldown, key figures to be displayed, and other layout settings.

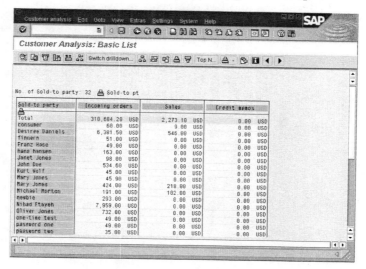

4. On the *Choose Key figures* dialog box:

a. After selecting the fields you want to analyze, choose ◀ to transfer fields from the right side of the screen to the *Selected Key figures* column.

b. To execute the report, choose ⊕.

In this example, the key figure *Invoiced quantity* is inserted and key figures *Incoming orders* and *Incoming order qty* are removed from the selection criteria list.

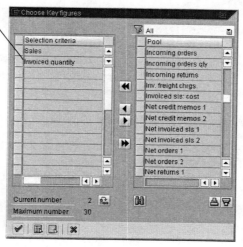

5. The *Customer Analysis: Basic List* screen shows how the above changes result in a different analysis. From this screen, you can drill down further or switch to other characteristics.

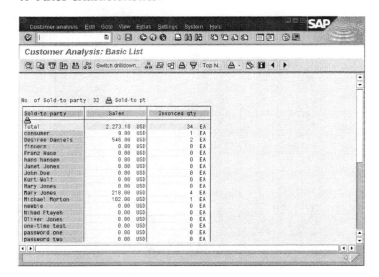

Shipping Report

List and analyze Internet shipping activity for a ten-week period

1. In the *Command* field, enter transaction **MCTK** and choose *Enter* (or from the navigation menu, choose *Logistics → Sales and distribution → Sales information system → Standard analyses → Shipping point*).

2. On the *Shipping Point Analysis: Selection* screen:

a. Enter the ten-week period you wish to analyze (for example, **2/2000** to **4/2000**) in *Period to analyze*.

b. To execute the report, choose ⊕.

> **Note**
>
> A period is determined by the date an order item is entered or changed.

3. The *Shipping Point Analysis: Basic List* screen shows data based on the standard defaults for drilldown, key figures to be displayed, and other layout settings.

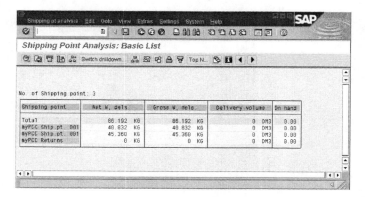

Reports Based on User-Defined Information Structures

In addition to the standard information structures, **self-defined information structures** have been created that allow you to analyze data resulting from Internet sales. For the purpose of demonstration, this chapter provides an example of statistical analysis executed against the information structure *S700* (Accelerated Internet Selling - Daily reporting). Please note this is only one example and you have the option to execute your analysis on any of the self-defined information structures below.

Menu Option	For Reporting
S700 - Accelerated Internet Selling - Daily sales	Daily reporting of sales by territory (country, region, sales district)
S701 - Accelerated Internet Selling - Weekly sales	Weekly reporting of sales by territory (country, region, sales district)
S702 - Accelerated Internet Selling - Monthly sales	Monthly reporting of sales by territory (country, region, sales district)

Territory Sales Report (Daily, Weekly, Monthly)

Task

Display Internet sales by territory for a given period.

1. In the *Command* field, enter transaction **MCSI** and choose *Enter* (or from the navigation menu, choose *Logistics → Sales and distribution → Sales information system → Standard analyses →User-defined info structures*).

2. On the *Info Structure* dialog box, to select a particular report, double-click on the appropriate line (for example, info structure *S700 - AS Daily Sales*).

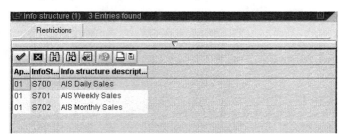

3. The *Standard analysis for info structure S700: Selection* screen prompts you for selection criteria:

   a. Under *Characteristics*, enter the *Sales organization* and *Distribution channel* you use for Internet sales (for example, **0010** and **11** from the Preconfigured Client).

   b. Under *Period to analyze*, enter a date range in the *Day* and *to* fields (for example, **08/16/2000** to **08/22/2000**).

   c. To execute the report, choose

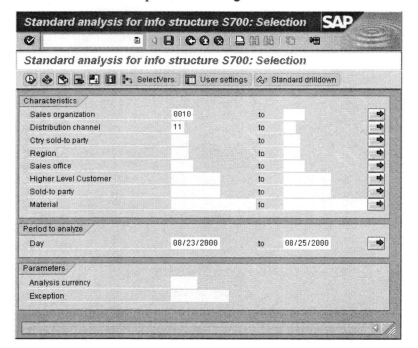

4. On the *Standard analysis for info structure S700: Basic List* screen, to analyze Internet sales activity, double-click the sales organization (for example, *myPCC Sales Org*).

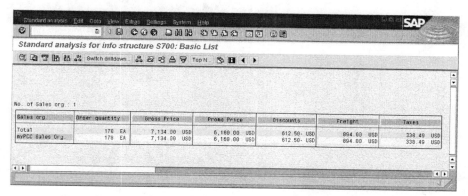

5. On the *Standard analysis for info structure S700: Drilldown* screen, double-click the distribution channel *Internet*.

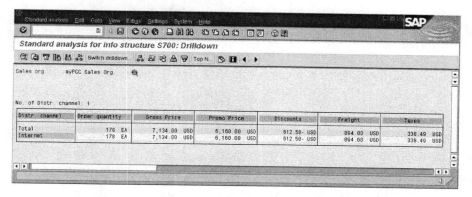

6. On the next screen, to analyze Internet sales activity for a particular country, double-click on a *Ctry sold-to* party (for example, *USA*).

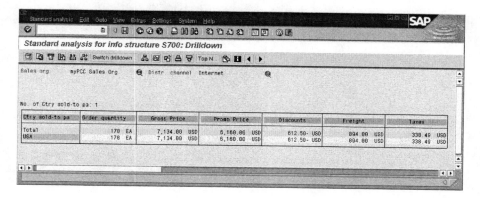

7. To analyze Internet activity for a particular region (or states), double-click on a *Region* (for example, *CA*).

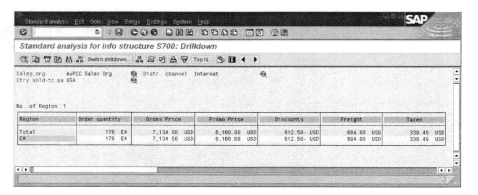

8. To analyze Internet activity for a particular sales office, double-click on a *Sales office* (for example, *myPCC Sales Office*)

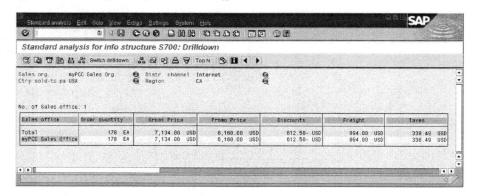

9. To analyze Internet activity for a particular higher level customer, double-click on any *Higher level customer* (for example, *SAP Labs*)

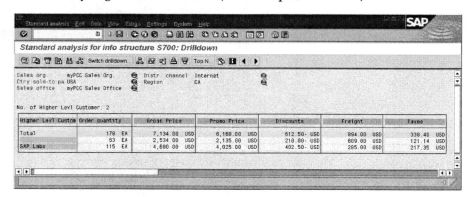

10. To analyze Internet activity for a *Sold-to party* belonging to the higher level customer, double-click on the sold-to party's name (for example, *Mary Jones*).

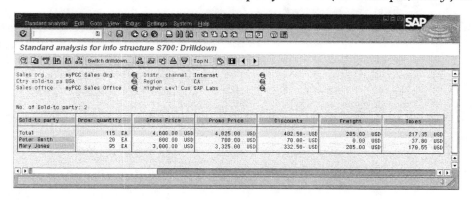

11. To analyze the material, double-click on the *Material* (for example, *Accelerated Internet Selling*).

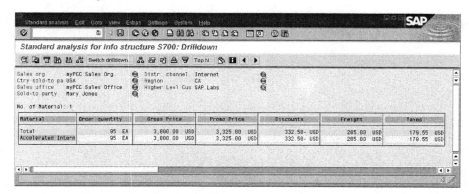

For detailed information on these topics, refer to the online documentation provided in the SAP R/3 System or to the *Reporting Made Easy* guidebooks which can be downloaded from the Simplification Group's web site *www.saplabs.com/rme*.

12. The new screen shows information relevant to your search.

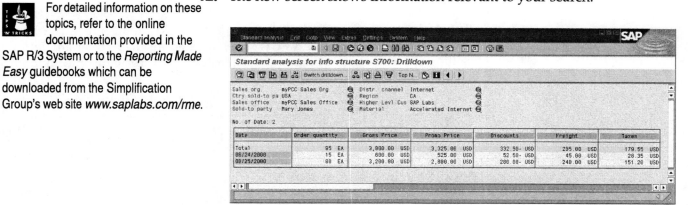

Configuration of Self-Defined Information Structures

The configuration steps listed below are for creating user-defined information structures that support the reporting requirements of the Online Store. Information structures *S700, S701,* and *S702* have been delivered with the preconfiguration. If you use the Online Store preconfiguration in conjunction with the Preconfigured Client (PCC) in a fresh installation then you need **not** configure the information structures. If you do not use the PCC, then the steps given below should be used as reference.

The steps involved in setting up self-defined information structures are to create:

- Additional fields in the append structures tables *VBAK, LIKP,* and *VBRK* (preconfigured)

- Additional fields in the table *MCVKENNZ1* (preconfigured)

- A field catalog (preconfigured)

- Information structures (preconfigured)

- Update rule 1 (preconfigured)

- Update rule 2 (preconfigured)

- Activate update for information structures (preconfigured)

Task

Create additional fields in the append structures tables VBAK, LIKP, and VBRK

This task has been preconfigured for you. The fields in the append structures tables *VBAK, LIKP,* and *VBRK* have been created for the Accelerated Internet Selling application for building the field catalogs to create the information structures.

Table Name	Component	Data Element	Field Label	Domain Name
ZAVBAK	ZKUNNR	ZKUNNR	Higher Level Customer	KUNNR
ZAVBAK	ZREG	REGIO	Region (State, Province, County)	REGIO
ZALIKP	ZKUNNR	ZKUNNR	Higher level customer	KUNNR

Table Name	Component	Data Element	Field Label	Domain Name
ZALIKP	ZREG	REGIO	Region (State, Province, County)	REGIO
ZAVBRK	ZKUNNR	ZKUNNR	Higher Level Customer	KUNNR

Task

Create additional fields in the table MCVKENNZ1

This step has been preconfigured for you. The additional fields in table *MCVKENNZ1* have been created so that user-defined field names can be used in reporting.

1. In the *Command* field, enter transaction **SE11** and choose *Enter* (or from the navigation menu, choose *Tools → ABAP Workbench → Development → ABAP Dictionary*).

2. On the *Dictionary: Initial Screen*:

   a. In the *Database table,* enter the table name **MCVKENNZ1**.

   b. Choose ⚙ *Display.*

3. On the *Choose Append for Table MCVKENNZ1* screen, choose *Append structures.*

4. On the dialog box, choose ✔ *Choose.*

5. On the *Dictionary: Display Structure* screen, enter the table name as desired and create the required fields. Below are the fields created in the append structure *ZESHOP_MCVKENNZ1:ZESHOP_ADDITIONAL_FIELDS.*

Component	Data Element	Field Label	Domain Name
ZESHOP_TAXE	ZESHOP_TAXE	Taxes	WERTV7
ZESHOP_FREI	ZESHOP_FREI	Freight	WERTV7
ZESHOP_DISC	ZESHOP_DISC	Discounts	WERTV7
ZESHOP_PROM	ZESHOP_PROM	Promo Price	WERTV7
ZESHOP_GROSS	ZESHOP_GROSS	Gross Price	WERTV7
ZESHOP_TOTVALUE	ZESHOP_TOTVALUE	Total Value	WERTV7
ZESHOP_HLEVCUST	ZESHOP_HLEVCUST	Higher Level Customer	WERTV7
ZESHOP_CRMETOTV	ZESHOP_CRMETOTV	Total Credit Memo Value	WERTV7
ZESHOP_INVSALES	ZESHOP_INVSALES	Invoiced Sales	WERTV7
ZESHOP_TOTREVAL	ZESHOP_TOTREVAL	Total Returns Value	WERTV7

Task

Create a field catalog

This step has been preconfigured for you. To define information systems using self-defined information structures, the user must clearly recognize which type of information can be used for the Logistics Data Warehouse. **Field catalogs,** which define a group of relevant fields from the application, guarantee that this information can be easily recognized.

To view the field catalog *ZEKF* (E-Shop key figures) or *ZECH* (E-Shop characteristics), enter transaction **MC18** (to create) or **MC20** (to display) in the *Command* field and choose *Enter* (or in the IMG, choose *Logistics - General* → *Logistics Information System [LIS]* → *Logistics Data Warehouse* → *Data Basis* → *Field Catalogs* and choose 🕀 next to *Maintain Self-Defined Field Catalogs*).

Below are screenshots of field catalogs *ZECH* and *ZEKF*:

Field catalog ZECH

Field catalog ZEKF

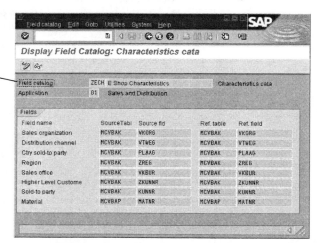

Task

Create information structures

This step has been preconfigured for you. New self-defined information structures need a four-character name, usually between *S501* and *S999*.

1. To view the information structures *S700*, *S701*, and *S702*, enter transaction **MC21** (to create) or **MC23** (to display) in the *Command* field and choose *Enter* (or in the IMG, choose *Logistics - General* → *Logistics Information System [LIS]* → *Logistics Data Warehouse* → *Data Basis* → *Information Structures* and choose 🕮 next to *Maintain Self-Defined Information Structures*).

2. In *Info struct.* (information structure), specify both a name and description for the information structure you wish to create, and assign the structure to an application.

   Self-defined information structures *S700* (Internet Sales - Daily Update), *S701* (Internet Sales - Weekly Update), and *S702* (Internet Sales - Monthly Update) are delivered in the preconfiguration of the Online Store.

   Below is a screenshot of information structure *S700*.

Note

The units of key figures should be *01* for quantities and *32* for currencies. These settings allow conversion of the units during standard analysis.

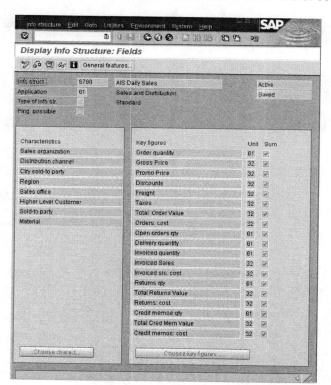

Task

Create update rule 1

This step has been preconfigured for you. Update rules help to determine how characteristics and key figures are updated from the sales transactions. For example, update rules consist of the source field, requirements, formulas, and events that trigger the update. After you define the update rules, the corresponding update programs are automatically generated.

To view the update rules for info structure *S700* and update group (stats) *1*, enter the transaction **MC24** (to create) or **MC26** (to display) in the *Command* field and choose *Enter* (or from the IMG, choose *Logistics General → Logistics Information System (LIS) → Logistics Data Warehouse → Updating → Updating Definition → Specific Definition Using Update Rules* and choose 🕮 next to *Maintain Update Rules*).

The table below shows the primary settings included in the preconfigured update *Rules for key figures* of information structure *S700* and update group *1* (sales).

Key Figure	Event	Update Type	Source table and source field name	Table for date & date field
Order quantity	VA	A	MCVBAP-KWMENG	MCVBAP-VDATU
Gross Price	VA	A	MCVBAP-KZWI1	MCVBAP-VDATU
Promo Price	VA	A	MCVBAP-KZWI2	MCVBAP-VDATU
Discounts	VA	A	MCVBAP-KZWI3	MCVBAP-VDATU
Freight	VA	A	MCVBAP-KZWI4	MCVBAP-VDATU
Taxes	VA	A	MCVBAP-KZWI5	MCVBAP-VDATU
Total Order Value	VA	A	MCVBAP-KZWI6	MCVBAP-VDATU
Orders:Cost	VA	A	MCVBAP-WAVWR	MCVBAP-VDATU
Open orders qty	VA	A	MCVBAP-OAUME	MCVBAP-ERDAT
Open orders qty	VC	A	MCLIPS-APOAUME	MCLIPS-APERDAT
Delivery quantity	VC	A	MCLIPS-LFIMG	MCLIKP-WADAT
Invoiced quantity	VD	A	MCVBRP-FKIMG	MCVBRK-FKDAT
Invoiced Sales	VD	A	MCVBRP-NETWR	MCVBRK-FKDAT
Invoiced Sales Cost	VD	A	MCVBRP-WAVWR	MCVBRP-FKDAT

The *Update rules for characteristics* can be seen by choosing the *Rules for characteristics* button.

The below screen shows the rules for characteristics for the key figures *Order quantity, Gross Price, Promo Price, Discounts, Freight, Taxes, Total Order Value, Orders:Cost*, and *Open orders qty (orders)*.

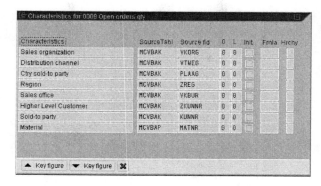

The below screen shows the rules for characteristics pertaining to the key figures *Open order qty (delivery)* and *Delivery quantity*.

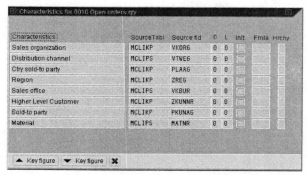

The below screen shows the rules for characteristics pertaining to the key figures *Invoice quantity*, *Invoiced Sales*, and *Invoiced sales:cost*.

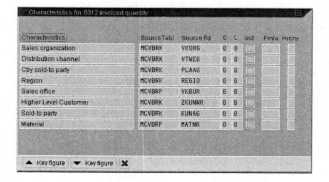

Task

Create update rule 2

This step has been preconfigured for you. The update rules for your self-defined info structures have been set for update group 2 (returns, return deliveries, and credit memos). To create the update rules, use transaction **MC24**, delete all the key figures pertaining to the update group 1 and create the update rules for the key figures pertaining to the update group 2. The update rules for the key figures for infostructure *S700* are given below:

Key Figure	Event	Update Type	Source table and source field name	Table for date & date field	Formula
Returns qty	VA	A	MCVBAP-KWMENG	MCVBAP-VDATU	100
Total Returns Value	VA	A	MCVBAP-KZWI6	MVCBAP-VDATU	100
Returns Cost	VA	A	MCVBAP-VDATU	MCVBAP-VDATU	100
Credit Memos qty	VD	A	MCVBRP-FKIMG	MCVBRK-FKDAT	100
Total Credit Memo Value	VD	A	MCVBRP-KZWI6	MCVBRK-FKDAT	100
Credit memos cost	VD	A	MCVBRP-WAVWR	MCVBRK-FKDAT	100

The characteristics for the key figures *Returns qty, Total Value,* and *Returns Cost* appear in the screen below.

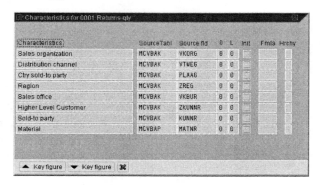

Task

Activate update for info structures

This step is preconfigured for you. Updating is triggered by an event in a logistics application (such as a sales order). An **event** is a point in time when information is created that requires recording. You can change how the information structure updates by changing the period of time (such as daily, weekly, monthly) and by changing the updating method (for example, synchronous, asynchronous, collective, or no update).

To view the settings for updating the info structure *S700, S701,* and *S702,* enter transaction **OMO1** in the *Command* field and choose *Enter* (or from the IMG, choose *Logistics - General → Logistics Information System [LIS] → Logistics Data Warehouse → Updating → Updating Control* and choose ⊕ next to *Activate Update*. On the *Choose activity* dialog box, select *Sales and Distribution* and choose ▦ *Choose*).

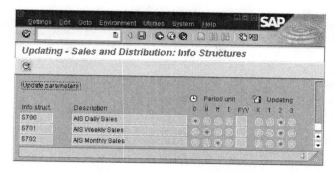

The update parameters for the self-defined information structures associated with the Online Store are shown below. A posting period has been allocated to the appropriate information structure, and all have been set for asynchronous update (a document update is made separately from the statistics update).

Info Structure	Description	Period Unit	Updating
S700	AIS Daily Sales	D	2
S701	AIS Weekly Sales	W	2
S702	AIS Monthly Sales	M	2

CHAPTER 12

Web Site Statistics

Overview

Different groups in an organization have different questions they want answered by web site statistics. For example, your IT department wants to know about the health of the site, whether the server is fast enough to handle the peak requests or whether there are dead links on the web site. Sales and Marketing want to know what content customers are interested in on the site. For example, when and where are customers dropping off, and how often do customers put items into the shopping baskets but do not buy? By analyzing products that create interest but are not purchased, marketing campaigns can target the customer and products.

In this chapter, we look at what currently is available in the market to answer such questions:

- **Log statistic tools** – Software that analyzes the logs written by the webserver that records hits, most requested pages, and downloads.

- **Web intelligence products** – Software that tracks and analyzes the total web experience of a customer in combination with data from the backend system.

Log Statistic Tools

> **Note**
>
> Dynamic pages are created from different components at the moment of the request. For example, the request for more details on a product is answered by creating a page that contains a picture, the detailed text, the current price, and current availability—all pulled from different sources. Dynamic pages allow for the most up-to-date information.
>
> Static pages, on the other hand, stay as they are (for example, the page with company address information or driving directions).

Some off-the-shelf tools are available to analyze web server log files. These tools track the number of hits, visitor sessions, and page views a web site gets over a period of time. Such tools provide a good overview of your web site's general trends, such as traffic increases over time and which of the static pages are visited the most often.

These tools also give you information about what browser and operating system your visitors are using, which is good to know when deciding whether to use new web technology. Furthermore, web tracking tools offer a list of technical statistics, such as how many requests have failed and how many hits have been cached by the server.

In an article published in July of 1999, the magazine *Network World Fusion* compares three web server log analysis tools: WebTrends Log Analyzer 4.51, Marketwave's Hit List Commerce Suite 4.0, and WebManage Technologies' NetIntellect 4.0. The article describes how the different products come to different hit results because they base their counting on different assumptions (for example, excluding or including pictures). Be sure to familiar yourself with the product's assumptions before using one of these products.

The problem with such tools starts when you want to analyze more than just general hits. The list of most visited pages in the Online Store does not necessarily give you useful information, since all of these pages are created dynamically by the ITS.

The table below shows the results of a sample log:

Most Requested Pages		
Pages	Views	% of Total Views
1 http://pal100619/iisadmin/	7	4.48%
2 http://pal100619/iisadmin/iisnew.asp	2	1.28%
3 http://pal100619/iisadmin/iihd.asp	4	2.56%
4 http://pal100619/iisadmin/iistat.asp	28	17.94%
5 http://pal100619/iisadmin/blank.htm	2	1.28%
6 http://pal100619/iisadmin/iisrvls.asp	10	6.41%
7 http://pal100619/iisadmin/iimnu.asp	8	5.12%
8 http://pal100619/iisadmin/iibody.asp	8	5.12%
9 http://pal100619/iisadmin/iis.asp	5	3.2%
10 http://pal100619/iisadmin/iitool.asp	6	3.84%

This table shows the results of running a log statistic tools against one of our test installations. It shows the most requested pages of that site. The most viewed page is a dynamically created one: *iistat.asp*. We cannot tell what the content of this page was at the time it was called. It is impossible to know what product the customers look at, the price and other details of the product available at the time, which products are the most selected ones, etc.

Web Intelligence

Aside from the number of hits, the bigger questions are:

- At what products are customers looking?

- If they drop off and leave, when and where in the shopping process?

- Are customers returning to your site repeatedly?

In short, what we are really interested in is customer behavior. *PC-Week Online* has an article covering that subject. In "E-business analysis tools are key for dot-coms," Mark Hammond gives examples of companies that have successfully improved their sales by using business intelligence tools to analyze customer behavior. Such analysis is not an easy task. The volumes of data must be captured and brought to a manageable size for analysis.

The privacy of the online customer also must be protected. Password and credit card information should not be divulged. Many customers are concerned about their information being sold, which would increase junk e-mail. Finally—especially in Europe—there laws that protect the privacy of personal transactions. It is important to let the customer know what your policies are in regards to their personal information.

Web Intelligence tools give companies the data mining capability to track visitor and customer trends. This information can help a company to better understand what draws customers to the online store, and how to encourage return visits.

By monitoring web traffic and user interaction within the web site, the company gains a clearer perspective of the visitor's shopping habits and preferences for different product offerings, services, and content.

Web intelligence tools provide more than information on the number of hits received by the site. Such tools capture the data, such as when and where in the process are shopping baskets abandoned, enables managers to analyze sales, forecast demand, optimize marketing initiatives, and tailor the site based on customer trends. Tools and reports show what attracts customers to the web site. Companies are able to respond quickly to trends in the marketplace with products that maximize profits and increase their return on e-investment. New marketing campaigns encourage return visits and purchases by their customers.

Web intelligence also allows a company to correlate the current buying behavior of customers in the online store with their prior contacts, allowing the company to focus on all aspects of the customer relationship.

The Tealeaf Solution

Note

An **event** is an action taken by a customer that leads to a response from the system. Business events relevant to capturing the customer experience to improve the product offerings include viewing product details, placing a product into the shopping basket, and saving the basket.

A new spin off from SAP, **TeaLeaf Technology**™ focuses solely on providing web intelligence. For general information about TeaLeaf Technology™ visit their web site at *www.tealeaf.com*.

Their solution tracks not only what is happening on the web server, but also captures all relevant events on the SAP R/3 side. For example, an event such as putting an item into a shopping baskets is defined and captured by their software. The results from the web site capture, which includes R/3 data, are synchronized to gather the total user experience. This complete capture can go across multiple applications, servers, sites, and sessions.

The results are saved in the TeaLeaf™ Data Store. From there they can be analyzed directly or transferred into the SAP Business Information Warehouse (BW). In BW, the Tealeaf data can be combined with R/3 Sales and Distribution (SD) data for a more complete analysis of customers and the effect of the Internet sales channel.

You are also able to replay a session step-by-step, similar to a video, which is especially helpful to locate usability problems or to get insight into the customer's buying behavior.

The TeaCommerce™ Suite includes:

- Individual and aggregate clickstream analysis

- Business event data capture

- Visual replay of complete online user interactions, much like a slide show

- Customized business reporting

- Integration with third-party reporting and analysis tools, such as SAP BW

Making It Happen

Overview

The following is a graphical representation of the TeaLeaf solution.

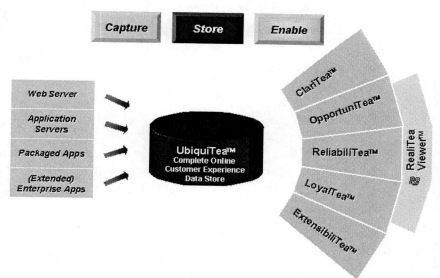

The customer experience is captured from the web server and from the application server, which in our case is an R/3 System. But it can also capture data coming from external applications.

The captured data is stored in the TeaLeaf UbiquiTea™ data store. This storage can be done on a separate server so the impact on the web and the ITS is kept to a minimum.

This wealth of information can then be analyzed by the predefined TeaLeaf ClariTea™ reports. It can also be transferred into SAP BW. You are also able to replay the total customer experience with the RealiTea™ viewer, which allows customer care to trouble-shoot problems with the web site.

Below is a diagram of how Tealeaf fits into the architecture of used by the Online Store. The primary changes include:

- The Tealeaf objects that define the business events to be captured reside in R/3, along with the IAC logic and SAP master data.

- The AGate with Tealeaf modification is used in place of the standard ITS AGate.

- Request and response files that capture the customer experience are written and stored in the Tealeaf data structure.

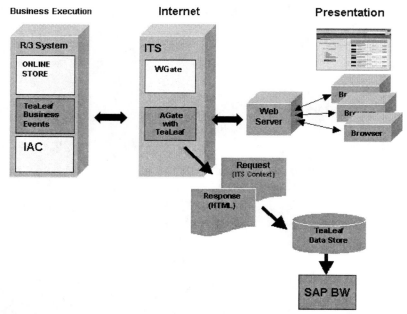

The diagram below illustrates the points at which Tealeaf captures the customer information.

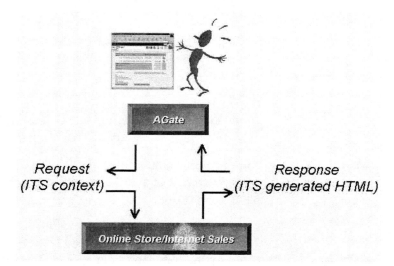

A customer puts an item into the shopping basket. The customer uses the browser and places it into the shopping basket. The web server interprets this event and sends a request to the AGate of the ITS server.

Before forwarding the request to the R/3 System, the TeaLeaf-enhanced AGate stores the ITS context including the form fields passed from the web page in a TeaLeaf request file. The R/3 System checks if this event is listed as a "TeaLeaf Business Event."

Since we want to know about visitors of our web site that put items into our shopping basket, it is a tracked event. This information, together with the response from the general R/3 System, is sent back to the AGate. Before sending the generated HTML page back to the browser, the TeaLeaf-enhanced AGate stores it in a TeaLeaf response file and inserts the business event data into the previously created TeaLeaf request file. For each interaction between AGate and the R/3 System, a pair or TeaLeaf request and response files are generated and propagated down the TeaLeaf capture pipeline.

With that, the total customer experience is captured, not only on the browser but also the relevant events on the R/3 side.

The request file stores the ITS context, the user action, and all data captured by the event. The response file stores the HTML page dynamically generated by the ITS. The figure below displays the product details captured in a sample request file.

A sample TeaLeaf request file with output of an event can be seen with product details.

```
[timestamp]
RequestTime=13:30:42 05/09/2000
RequestTimeEx=2000-05-09T13:30:42.758Z
ResponseTime=13:30:42 05/09/2000
ResponseTimeEx=2000-05-09T13:30:42.878Z

[xml1]
<appevent type="R3" app="SAP_ONLINE_STORE" event="ADD_TO_BASKET_OK">
    <var name="EVENTMSG" value="Product was put in the shopping basket"/>
    <var name="SY-CPROG" value="SAPMWWMJ"/>
    <var name="SY-REPID" value="SAPMWWMJ"/>
    <var name="SY-DYNNR" value="3000"/>
    <var name="SY-UCOMM" value="MAAD"/>
    <var name="SY-MSGID" value="W+"/>
    <var name="SY-MSGTY" value="W"/>
    <var name="SY-MSGNO" value="304"/>
    <var name="SY-MSGV1" value=""/>
    <var name="SY-MSGV2" value=""/>
    <var name="SY-MSGV3" value=""/>
    <var name="SY-MSGV4" value=""/>
    <group type="ITEM">
        <var name="CODE" value="R-1001"/>
        <var name="NAME" value="Maxitec-R 3100 Personal Computer"/>
        <var name="DESCRIPTION" value="Maxitec-R 3100"/>
        <var name="UNIT" value="PC"/>
        <var name="CURR_PU" value="USD"/>
        <var name="PRICE_UNIT" value="1,074.2900"/>
        <var name="PROMO_PRICE_UNIT" value="0.0000"/>
        <var name="QUANTITY" value="2.0000"/>
        <var name="CAMPAIGNID" value=""/>
    </group>
</appevent>
```

Delivery

As a service, the transports for the TeaLeaf Business Event Framework can be downloaded together with the transports for the Accelerated Internet Selling solution. Please contact TeaLeaf directly for the entire solution at *www.tealeaf.com*.

How It Works

Three steps are necessary for the TeaLeaf solution to work properly:

1. Install the TeaLeaf AGate.
2. Create the event framework in SAP R/3.
3. Modify the SAP Online Store program.

Install the TeaLeaf AGate

This step is required to activate the data capture. The modified AGate records each request from the web browser (the user) and records the response from the ITS (the generated HTML page).

These requests and responses are written into a compressed data format using the TeaLeaf pipeline. The TeaLeaf pipeline is a series of components that provides functionality such as filtering, compressing data, and moving it to another location.

Create Event Framework in SAP R/3

The events for customer actions are defined in TeaLeaf tables in the R/3 System. Tealeaf has already predefined the most common business events. The TeaCommerce Suite (release 1.0) comes with the following preconfigured events:

- ADD_TO_BASKET
- DROP_FROM_BASKET
- MODIFY_BASKET_ITEM
- PLACE_ORDER, VIEW_PRODUCT
- DEFINE_CUSTOMER
- CHECKOUT_BASKET
- NAME_BASKET
- USE_BASKET
- SAVE_BASKET
- DROP_BASKET
- ABANDON_BASKET
- SEARCH_STRING
- REGISTER_USER
- LOGIN

The identification of the event (program name, function code, and message number combination) is stored in the Tealeaf configuration table. These tables also give you the flexibility to add additional events. These tables and the logic all reside in the TeaLeaf namespace.

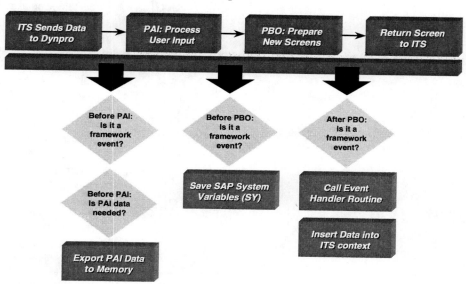

This graphic displays where in the process the TeaLeaf solution is checking for relevant events and what is written into the TeaLeaf data store.

The following is a listing of all the routines, modules, and tables the TeaLeaf solution adds to the R/3 System:

Object	Purpose
/TEALEAF/<SYS_INCLUDE>	Data definitions and form routines for event processing
/TEALEAF/<SYS_MODULE>	Process before output (PBO) and Process after input (PAI) modules
/TEALEAF/PROCESS_EVENT	Function module to dispatch handler routine
/TEALEAF/SAVE_SESSION_INFO	Function module to insert SAP data into ITS context
/TEALEAF/CUST_x tables	Event framework customizing tables
/TEALEAF/ONLINE_STORE_EVENTS	Subroutine pool for standard event handler routines

The five tables delivered as part of the TeaLeaf solution allow you to configure the events you wish to track. To display and edit the contents of these tables, enter transaction **SM31** in the *Command* field and choose *Enter* (or from the menu bar, choose *System → Services → Table maintenance → Extended table maintenance*). Enter the name of the table in the *Table/view* field, and choose *Display*.

The five TeaLeaf configuration tables include:

Configuration Table	Purpose
/TEALEAF/CUST_A	This table contains the global parameters, which allow you to turn the capture of events on and off, and specifies the location of data files in a non-ITS environment.
/TEALEAF/CUST_B	This table contains the applications for which you wish to capture events. The relevant application for all events we discuss is SAP_ONLINE_STORE.
/TEALEAF/CUST_C	This table defines the events that you wish to capture on your web site. Each event is associated with an application, and identifies the details of the event handler that is used for processing the data capture. An event may be viewing the detailed information of a product, or placing it into the shopping basket.
/TEALEAF/CUST_D	This table defines the characteristics, such as the program, screen, function code, and message number, which trigger an event. A catch-all for all messages that are not defined explicitly is also available.
/TEALEAF/CUST_E	This table defines the properties of an event, or the data that should be written to the log file for each event. Examples of data include product number, price, and unit of measure.

Modifying the Online Store

For the TeaLeaf solution to work properly in an R/3 System, you have to modify the program *SAPMWWMJ* and the flow logic of two collection screens. Please contact Tealeaf Technology directly for information on making these changes.

References

- Randi Barshack, "Shades of Gray: Privacy and Online Marketing," *E-Commerce Times*, 28 August 2000.

  www.ecommercetimes.com/news/special_reports/privacy.shtml

- Dan R. Greening, "Data Mining on the Web," *Web Techniques*, January 2000.

  www.webtechniques.com/archives/2000/01/greening/

- Mark Hammond, "E-business analysis tools are key for dot-coms," *PC Week Online*, 13 March 2000.

  www.zdnet.com/pcweek/stories/news/0,4153,2459218,00.html

- Thomas Powell, "When the hits just keep on coming," *Network World Fusion*, July 1999.

  www.nwfusion.com/reviews/0712rev2.html

- Bradley Shimmin, "Tracking the Web in real time," *Network World*, 22 November 1999.

  www.nwfusion.com/reviews/1122rev.html

- Beth Stackpole, "Targeting on buyer—or a million," *Datamation.com*, March 2000.

  www.datamation.com/dataw/0003web1.html

PART THREE

Overview of the ITS

Section Overview

In an integrated Internet scenario, the customer should be able to purchase products from the Internet without knowing the order is being directly entered into an R/3 System. For this reason, it is not enough to Internet-enable a normal R/3 transaction. There are too many fields that require knowledge of how the system is configured. Instead, the look and feel should allow the customer to place an order as easily as possible, without having to fill in a myriad of fields.

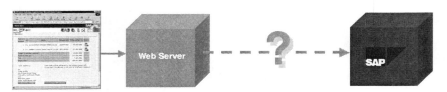

The R/3 System, however, cannot understand the HTML sent from the browser. For this reason, something needs to interpret the HTML and make it understandable to R/3. In turn, the R/3 screens must be generated into an HTML format that can be understood by the browser.

The ITS (Internet Transaction Server) is therefore needed to allow the R/3 System and browser to understand one another. The ITS has two parts, the AGate (application gateway) and the WGate (web server gateway). These two portions contain different files that allow the interaction between R/3 and the web browser to take place.

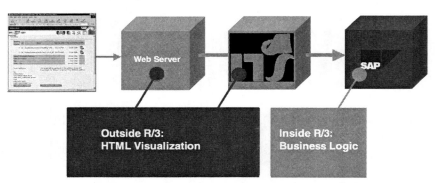

The files that control the look and feel of the Online Store, for example, are stored on different parts of the ITS. The MIME files (product thumbnails, images, and spec sheets) are stored on the WGate of the ITS. This location improves performance, since the image and sound files do not need to be retrieved from R/3, but are available on the same server accessed by the Internet customer. The service files are unique to the ITS and are stored directly on the ITS's AGate. These files are the mechanism by which the R/3 data and the look and feel of the web browser are merged.

The logic of the transaction resides within R/3. This location allows the processes accessibility. The configuration of the Online Store, and how the Internet orders and received sales and distribution processes are handled, resides in R/3. The benefits are no duplication of data, and orders taken are ready for the remaining fulfillment and invoicing processes.

The ITS brings together the look and feel with the R/3 logic of the Online Store. The chapters in this section provide an overview of the ITS, how the look and feel can be changed, and how the customers log on to the Online Store without directly logging on to R/3 itself.

Online Store Preconfiguration Technical Overview

Overview

This chapter introduces and discusses the three major components of the Online Store preconfiguration, namely the:

- Web server

- Internet Transaction Server (ITS), which itself is made up of two components: the WGate and AGate

- R/3 System

These three components are highlighted in gray in the following graphic.

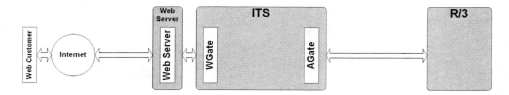

You will learn about these major technical components and their significance to the configuration of your Online Store preconfiguration. The information in this chapter provides the foundation that the following chapters will build upon.

The above diagram shows the three major (logical) components with the detailed components that compose it. This diagram serves as the basis for most of the diagrams in Part Three and Part Four of this guidebook. Other illustrations will build upon this one.

The sections within this chapter describe the conceptual layout of these components. Chapter 17, "ITS Installation and Configuration" on page 381 describes the physical layout and installation.

Web Server

The web server is the interface between the Internet and the ITS. Web users connect to your web server, where your web site is located.

For the purposes of this guide, we will use the Microsoft Internet Information Server (IIS).

Internet Transaction Server (ITS)

The Internet Transaction Server (ITS) is a program which functions as a gateway between the web server and the backend R/3 System. The ITS allows communication between the web server and the R/3 System, overcoming their technical differences. The ITS thus allows a user on the Internet or Intranet to connect to R/3.

The current version of the ITS can be downloaded from SAP at *www.saplabs.com/its*.

The ITS is made up of the:

- Web Gateway (WGate)

- Application Gateway (AGate)

Web Gateway (WGate)

The WGate connects the web server (for example, Microsoft IIS) to the main component of the ITS, the AGate.

Application Gateway (AGate)

The AGate, the main component of the ITS:

- Manages communication from the ITS to and from the backend R/3 System

- Converts HTML from the web page into SAP GUI to communicate to the R/3 System and back again

- Dynamically generates the HTML pages seen by the end user, using the Internet browser, templates, and data from R/3

R/3 System

The R/3 System provides the backend functions for the Online Store preconfiguration, such as:

- Sales order processing

- Accounting and finance

- Shipping and delivery processing

How It Works

The following sequence describes how the data from a web customer goes from the Online Store, to the backend R/3 System, and back to the web customer.

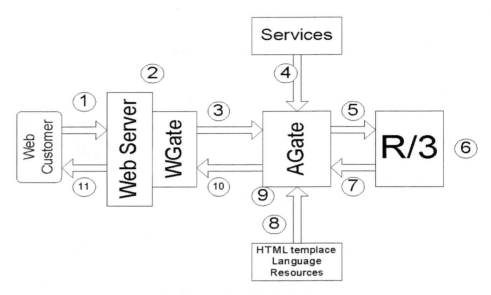

1. The web customer sends a request to the web server.

2. The web server calls the WGate.

3. The WGate sends the request to the AGate.

4. The AGate loads the service file.

5. The result is sent to the backend R/3 System.

6. The backend R/3 System processes the transaction.

7. The results or output is sent from the R/3 System to the AGate.

8. The AGate loads the HTML template and language resources.

9. The HTML template is a map or translation of the R/3 transaction to a web page.

10. The AGate generates the HTML page.

11. The HTML page is sent from the AGate to the WGate, to the web server, and then to the web customer.

Any images, sounds, and videos included in the web page are retrieved from the web server.

ITS Templates

Overview

This chapter explains the changes made to the Online Store templates and how you can adjust them according to your design plans. Templates contain everything that is visible to the end user through a web browser. All templates are based on the standard templates of theme 99. Themes are instances of Internet Transaction Server (ITS) services that differ only in their look and feel (appearance, graphics, layout, or language) and have a two letter name. All new Online Store templates can be found in theme SG. The changes made are based on the improved look and feel, and the additional functionality of the services.

The main changes are:

- New frame design

- Language-independent buttons (based on R/3 language)

- An included style sheet to make changes on all templates globally

- A display of product availability (see appendix B, "Technical SAP Enhancement: ATP in the Product Catalog" on page 499), and different taxes and special offers (see chapter 3, "Prices in the Product Catalog" on page 77)

- Single sign-on

- Selection of different shipping methods (see chapter 3, "Prices in the Product Catalog" on page 77)

- Display of the current content of the shopping basket, including price (see appendix C, "The Shopping Basket" on page 511)

- The saving and retrieval of the shopping basket (see appendix C, "The Shopping Basket" on page 511)

- Easier credit card data input

- Usage of a default credit card

- The inclusion of purchase order number and date entry for easier identification

- A new transaction to store personal data as default credit card, default shipping type, and address maintenance (see appendix B, "Technical SAP Enhancement: ATP in the Product Catalog" on page 499)

HTML [Business] is an SAP-specific macro language that allows you to merge R/3 data dynamically into HTML [Business] templates.

In Release 4.6, all frequently used design elements such as the button functionality are designed using HTML [Business] functions. For more information on HTML [Business] functions, refer to the SAP@WebStudio documentation by choosing *R/3 library → SAP@Webstudio → HTML Business Language Reference → HTML Business Language Description → HTML Business Function Specification.*

Mapping R/3 Screens to Web Templates

All HTML templates are generated through *SAP@Webstudio* from R/3 screens. Those templates are then modified with *SAP@Webstudio* using HTML^Business, HTML, and JavaScript. After modification, the templates need to be published to the ITS server, where they are accessible through a standard web browser.

The first graphic demonstrates a service in R/3. The second graphic shows *SAP@Webstudio*, which generates the template code. The third graphic displays what the end user views through the browser. For this example, we take the login procedure from transaction *WW20*. The R/3 screens are 4100 for the header frame and 8120 for the body frame. *SAP@Webstudio* generates a file called *saplwwcc1_8120.html* with the basic appearance of the R/3 screen. This template can then be modified to your needs. Not every function provided on the R/3 screens has to be used.

R/3 screen 4100 for the header

R/3 screen 8120 for the login screen

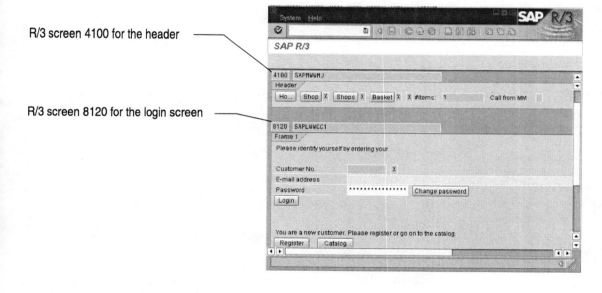

The generated template in SAP@Webstudio

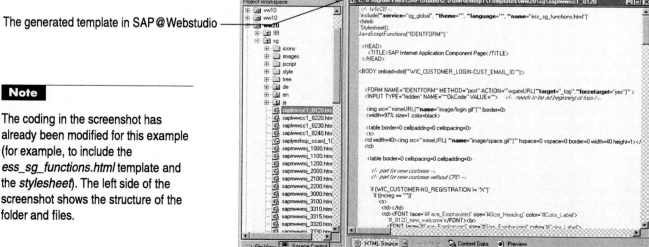

Note

The coding in the screenshot has already been modified for this example (for example, to include the *ess_sg_functions.html* template and the *stylesheet*). The left side of the screenshot shows the structure of the folder and files.

The header (screen 4100) does not use any buttons. Instead the images used provide the same functionality as buttons on the R/3 screen.

This is the login screen displayed in the browser.

Note

Notice that only three buttons from the original R/3 screen (8120) are displayed in the body frame.

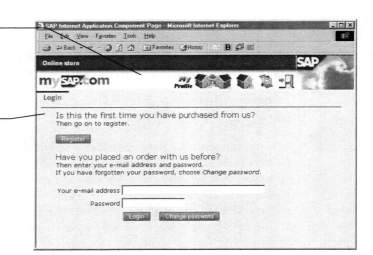

SAP@Webstudio Overview

You can download the complete documentation from *www.saplabs.com/its.*

We strongly recommend you know HTML, HTML[Business], and JavaScript if you are going to make any changes to the templates.

To change the coding of the templates, we highly recommend you use *SAP@Webstudio.* This tool handles the HTML[Business] functions that are advanced functions of HTML. With *SAP@Webstudio* you can:

- Generate templates from the R/3 screen

- Import templates and files

- Publish them onto your ITS server

The following sections provide a brief overview about the SAP@Webstudio design.

The *SAP@WebStudio* documentation can also be accessed in the R/3 Online documentation under *R/3 Library → SAP@Webstudio → HTML Business Language Reference → HTML Business Language Description → HTML Business Function Specification.*

SAP@Webstudio Screen

The following graphic gives you an overview about the *SAP@Webstudio* screen.

Source code window — Current project — Publish file

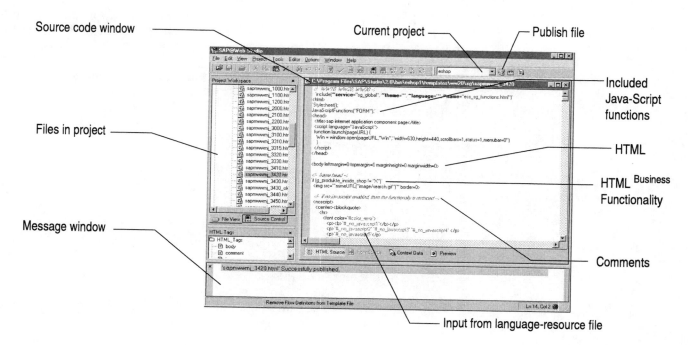

Files in project

Message window

Included Java-Script functions

HTML

HTML Business Functionality

Comments

Input from language-resource file

Working with *SAP@Webstudio* involves different types of files:

- Service files
- HTML template files
- Language-resource files
- MIME files

These different file types are described below.

Service File

The service file contains the service description, which is the set of parameters that determines how a service runs. If this information is incomplete at runtime, the ITS may derive some details from the global service file, or require the user to enter logon information. In any case, there must be one service file for each application.

Each service can be divided into one or more themes. Themes are instances of services that differ only in look and feel (appearance, graphics, layout, or language). Each theme has its own set of HTML^Business templates, flow files (if applicable), language resources, and Multipurpose Internet Mail Extension (MIME) files, but the functionality of the service is identical. In the *SAP@WebStudio*, themes are stored in subdirectories of the service directory. A typical service filename is *ww20.srvc*.

The service files are located on the AGate.

HTML Template File

HTML^{Business} templates are used by the ITS to display application screens in a Web browser. For each R/3 screen, there must be one HTML^{Business} template. Each template contains standard HTML code and HTML^{Business} statements.

HTML^{Business} is an SAP-specific macro language, which allows you to merge R/3 data dynamically into HTML^{Business} templates. A typical template filename is *sapmwwmj_3420.html.*

The template files are located on the AGate.

Language-Resource File

Language resources are language-independent files used by the ITS to run a service in a particular language.

Instead of hard-coding the language-specific texts into HTML^{Business} templates, you specify placeholders and store the text in the relevant language-resource file. At runtime, the ITS looks for placeholders in the templates and replaces them with text from the language-resource file. A typical language-resource filename is *ww20_en.htrc.*

For ease of maintenance, it makes sense for a service to keep HTML^{Business} templates language-independent by creating language resources. However, not all templates use language-resource files since these files are not mandatory.

The language files are located on the AGate.

MIME File

Multipurpose Internet Mail Extension (MIME) files contain the image, sound, and video elements included to enhance the visual appearance and effectiveness of your Internet applications. Like language resources, MIME files are optional.

The MIME files are located on the WGate.

The SG Templates

All general design and navigation standards are stored in the service *sg_global*.

There is a central SG HTML[Business] function library, called *sg_ess_function.html*. Any changes you make to *sg_ess_function.html* will affect all templates.

In the SG theme, we used a special design to show you what is possible. Everything displayed on the templates can be changed to fit your needs. For some changes, such as exchanging the company logo or navigation bar icons, you do not need to access the HTML templates. For other changes, you need to access the templates and change the coding.

As you can see from earlier chapters, the new templates look different than the standard-delivered templates. The most noticeable changes are the header, background color, and buttons. In the following section, we explain the different screen items. The screen is displayed using frames. On some screens, we use two frames and on other screens we use three, as in the standard. Frame 1 is the header frame and frame 2 is the body frame. The body frame itself can contain one or two frames, called frame 3 and frame 4 in the templates.

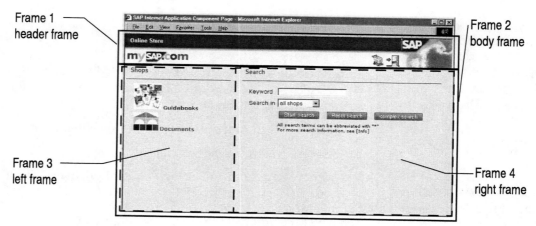

The Header Frame

The header frame is built out of multiple tables with several different images that can be changed without accessing the source code. You can replace those files on the ITS server with your own files, provided that the names do not differ from those in the template.

In the following graphic, we highlight the table borders with different colors to demonstrate how the header is built.

Inserted table 1
(displayed in yellow)

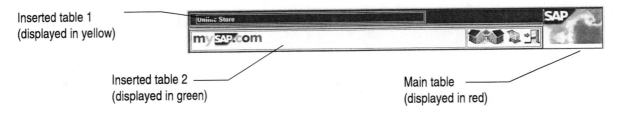

Inserted table 2
(displayed in green)

Main table
(displayed in red)

In the following graphic, we explain the displayed images; not all images that can appear are shown.

logo1.gif

bgroundstripe.gif

shadow.gif

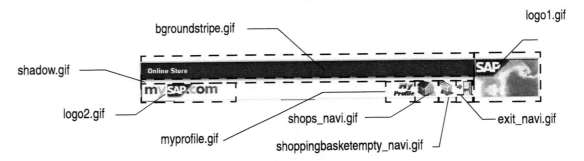

logo2.gif

myprofile.gif

shops_navi.gif

shoppingbasketempty_navi.gif

exit_navi.gif

 In order to keep the delivered images, you must copy and rename the SG images. Otherwise you cannot access them anymore after you replace them with new ones.

 It is important that you replace the correct files and give them exactly the same names. You also need to be aware of the dimensions (height, width) of the images. Differences in the dimensions of new images may require additional changes to the HTML code.

Changing an Image

To replace the upper-right SAP logo (called logo1.gif) with your own logo you must create an image, give it the same name (logo1.gif), and copy it to the server in the correct directory.

1. Select the web root directory on the WGate portion of the ITS server.

2. Select *sg_global/sg/images/topnav*.

3. Copy your new image or logo as *logo1.gif*, overwriting the existing *logo1.gif*.

The next time you call the service through your browser, the new images will be displayed.

To change the other images, proceed in the same way by replacing the images with new ones. Not all images are stored in the same directory on the ITS server, but all of them are under *sg_global/sg*.

The Body Frame

In the body frame, the different shops and products are displayed. The shop overview and product categories are displayed in frame 3, the left frame. The product catalog is displayed in frame 4, the right frame.

The images for the products are stored in the product catalog in R/3 and cannot be changed from the templates.

To change the appearance and functionality of the body frame, you have to change the templates. To do this, you should have an understanding of HTML, JavaScript, and HTML[Business], since these three programming languages are used to create the templates. Some changes, such as changing the background color, are simple to accomplish, while others require more in-depth programming knowledge.

To change the appearance of colors and fonts, you can use the style sheet located on the AGate portion of the ITS server under *sg_global → sg → style → ess.css*.

To change the background color, open the style sheet *ess.css* in *SAP@Webstudio* (or any other editor), and change the value for the background color to the desired one.

```
body {
font-family: arial,verdana,sans-serif;
font-size: 10pt;
background-color: #EFEFE7;
}
```

After making the changes, save and publish the file to the ITS server.

The *ess.css* style sheet provides additional unused parameters since it originates from the Employee Self-Service (ESS) templates.

Changing the Background Color of the Templates

Changing the background color of the templates can be tricky because of the three-dimensional shadows for the legend in the Online store. These shadows are graphics with a color that matches the tan background color. If, for example, you choose to change the background color to blue, the three-dimensional shadows will remain tan. In the following sections, we provide two suggestions to resolve this issue:

Creating New Graphics

You can create new background graphics that match your new color scheme. Save them under the web root directory on the WGate portion of the ITS-server:

1. Select *sg_global → sg → images → bevels*
2. Select one of the following:

   - *bottom_new.gif*

   - *top_new.gif*

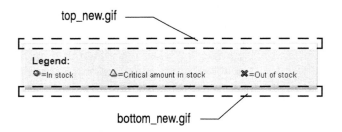

top_new.gif

Legend:
=In stock   =Critical amount in stock   =Out of stock

bottom_new.gif

Exchanging the 3D Graphics with 'SpaceImage()'

You also can modify the three-dimensional function graphics and exchange the bevel images with transparent gifs:

1. On the AGate portion of the ITS instance, select templates *sg_global → sg → ess_sg_functions.html*.

2. Go to the function *'Topshadow'*.

3. In the first cell of the second table row, exchange *'mimeURL(~service="sg_global",~language="", "images/bevels/top_new.gif")'* with `'mimeURL(~service="sg_global",~language="", "images/spacer.gif")'`

4. Do the same for the functions *'Bottomshadow()'* and *'Shadowbox()'*. For the former, replace the bevel image with the transparent gif *bottom.gif*. For the latter, replace the bevel with *left_side_new.gif, right_side_new.gif,* and *top_new.gif*.

In addition to the style sheet fonts, tables and headings are defined in the language-resource file *ww20_en.htrc*.

> **Note**
>
> This procedure removes all of the three-dimensional effects from the templates.

> The templates are only maintained in English. If you would like to use a different language, you have to maintain the individual language files yourself. You can find other language files under theme 99 that are not adjusted to the new templates from theme SG yet. Compare them to *ww20_en.htrc* in the theme SG and add the missing entries to your specific language-resource file.

Architecture of the Buttons

To make it easier to add new functions or a different language to your templates, we created the buttons in a different manner than those in the standard templates. The buttons in the standard templates are static GIF images that need to be created in the same style for each new button and language. To avoid re-creating GIFs, we implemented a dynamic button function. This function takes the original R/3 button text and displays it on the button in the HTML template.

The button consists of:

- The left border image
- A hyperlink (which is the button text that comes from R/3) with a background image
- A right border image
- Several JavaScript handlers

Whenever the button text changes in R/3—for example, due to a different language—you do not have to change the template since the button is created dynamically. The graphic below demonstrates what images are used for the buttons. The style of the button can be changed in the same way as described with the images in the header frame. The only differences are:

- The images to build the button are stored in a different directory on the ITS server (*sg_global/sg/images/button*)

- The image in the middle is a background image

Button as displayed in the browser:

Button as built up in the table (we set the borders to viewable for this example):

button_left.gif ——————

button_tile.gif ———

——— button_right.gif

To change all buttons:

1. Select the WGate portion of the web root directory in the ITS server.

2. Select *sg_global/sg/images/button*.

3. Copy your new images, overwriting the existing files (they must have the same names).

Current Shopping Basket

To provide a better overview of the contents of the shopping basket, we added functionality to continuously display the current contents of the shopping basket. This view of the contents appears in the same frame as the product hierarchy. If the basket is empty, an empty shopping basket is displayed with the words *Shopping basket is empty*. These words can be changed in the language-resource file *ww20_en.htrc*. To change it replace the words in the right column of the table next to word *currentbasketempty*.

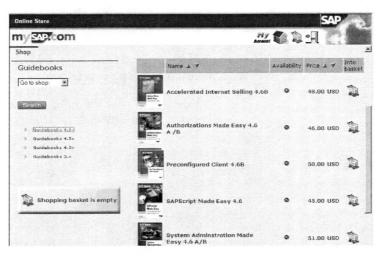

If there are items in the basket, a filled shopping basket icon is displayed with the words *Current basket content*. These words can be changed in the language-resource file *ww20_en.htrc*. To change it, replace the words in the right column of the table next to word *currentbasket*.

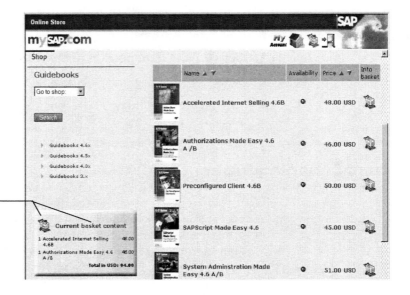

To get to the shopping cart, you can click the shopping cart icon or the words *Current basket content*.

The shopping basket overview is displayed in the browser using multiple tables. There is a separate table for the top and bottom image, which creates the 3D effect. One table is used for the shopping basket icon and text, and another table for the actual items. The table for the item description has an image as the background picture. See the next graphic for the names of the images.

To set up the R/3 side of this shopping basket, see appendix C, "The Shopping Basket" on page 511.

Creating and Changing Graphics

You can create new graphics that match your new color scheme. Save them under the web root directory on the WGate portion of the ITS server:

1. Select *sg_global* → *sg* → *images* → *bevels*

2. Select *curr_bask_top.gif* or *curr_bask_mid.gif* or *curr_bask_bottom.gif*

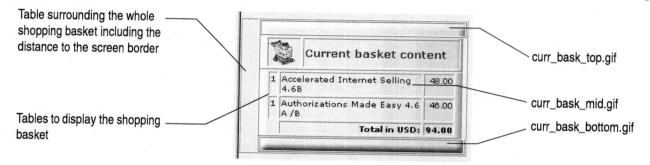

Table surrounding the whole shopping basket including the distance to the screen border

Tables to display the shopping basket

curr_bask_top.gif

curr_bask_mid.gif

curr_bask_bottom.gif

The customer can access the actual shopping basket screen to review the complete content by clicking on either the shopping cart icon or the heading.

For the necessary changes on the R/3 side, refer to appendix C, "The Shopping Basket" on page 511.

Credit Card Data Input

To make it easier for the customer, we simplified the input for credit card data. In the former version, you had to enter the expiration date in exactly the same manner as it was displayed in an input field next to your actual date input field. The expiration date input has been changed to a drop-down menu for the month and year. This method avoids improper data entry, converting the information automatically into the format required by R/3.

Old data input for credit card information:

Simplified input fields for credit card information:

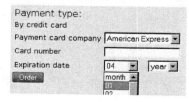

If customers store a default credit card in their profile, they can use the default credit card instead of entering the credit card data manually.

My Profile

The new *My Profile* functionality is a separate transaction (**ZOSA**) that allows customers to create and maintain their personal profiles. In this profile, individual customers are able to maintain their addresses, passwords, store multiple credit cards, and define a default credit card. In addition, a default shipping type can also be selected. To use the templates described in this section you need to make changes to R/3. See appendix E, "My Profile Service" on page 529 for information on what to adjust. All templates are stored in the directory *zosa/sg*.

MyProfile can be accessed from the home page link and from the header frame by choosing the *My Profile* icon. If a user has already logged on to the system, he or she does not need to log on to the profile since a temporary cookie for storing the logon information is used. See "Single Sign-on" on page 348 for a description of this functionality.

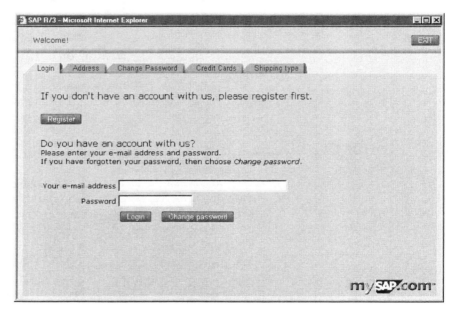

To access the different features of this function, we created tabstrips. The functionality of the tabstrips comes from R/3 and is handled in template *saplyeshop_account_1000.html*. The tabstrips are build up from different images that can be changed to meet your color scheme. The images to build the tabstrips are stored on the ITS server *sg_global/sg/images/tabs*. We deliver two color sets for the tabstrips, tan and blue. If you prefer a different color, use one of the sets and change the color using a graphic program. The two sets are in the directory *sg_global/sg/images/tabs/blue* and *sg_global/sg/images/tabs/tan*.

These directories function as a storage place to use for modifications. The files actually used by the program are in the directory *sg_global/sg/images/tabs*. The following illustration lists the filenames for the tabstrips.

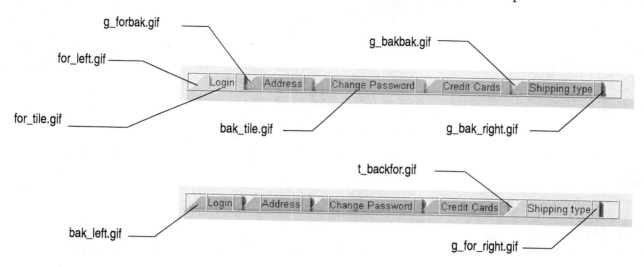

If you would like to add tabstrips with additional functionality, you need to add that functionality to the template *saplyeshop_account_1000.html*.

The picture below demonstrates how the *okcode* and the right image order of the tabstrips, active and inactive, is being handled in Webstudio.

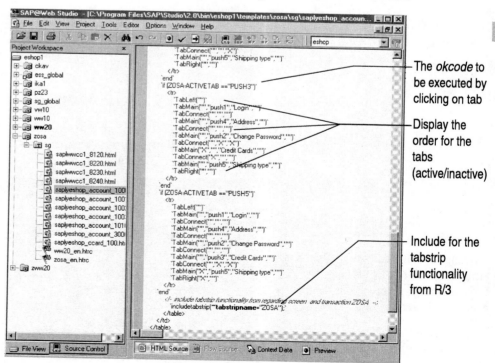

In addition, you may need to change the background color of the tabcards accordingly. These changes are made in the language-resource file, stored in the template directory *zosa/sg/zosa_en.htrc*. The default color is tan. Change the color code next to the entry *tabbground* to the same color as the active tabcolor (*tabbground = #DED7C6*).

In the same file *(zosa_en.htrc)*, you can also change the size of the tab cards under *_tabcard_height* and *_tabcard_width*. The delivered values for the size are height = 410 and width = 99%.

Changing the Form of Address

On the registration screen we provide two different settings which depend on the salutation. If a individual salutation of Mr. or Ms. is being selected you will be asked for a first and last name, the date of birth, and the address. The last name is the only mandatory field. The same applies to the registration screen in service *ww20*.

If a personal form of address is selected, the system asks for a first and last name and the date of birth.

When you select company as the form of address, you get only two input lines for the company and the address line. In this case the first and last name and the date of birth are suppressed.

If a company form of address is selected, the system asks only for the company name but provides a second line for the name of an individual.

These form-of-address selections help to avoid wrong input data in the case of a personal or company address. The changes for this are in template *saplwwcc1_8120.html*, service *zosa*, and service *ww20*. The code checks if a company name is selected and refreshes the screen with the new values.

To check if your R/3 settings in table *TSAD3T* are set to *0003* (company) for the form of address, enter transaction **SM30** in the *Command* field and choose *Enter*. Then in the field *Table/view* enter **V_TSAD3** and choose *Display* or *Maintain*. The coding in the template checks for '*if (WIC_CUSTOMER-TITLE_KEY != "0003")*'. If your settings in R/3 are not *0003* for company, the functionality is not given.

You can change your R/3 settings, but remember it can affect other areas or change the template coding.

To change the code of template *saplwwcc1_8120.html* in service *zosa* and *ww20*, search in the template for the line '*if (WIC_CUSTOMER-TITLE_KEY != "0003")*' and change *0003* to the value that your company salutation has.

Search for these lines and change *0003* to the desired value for the company salutation if you do not change it R/3.

The company value needs to be the same as the code in this template though.

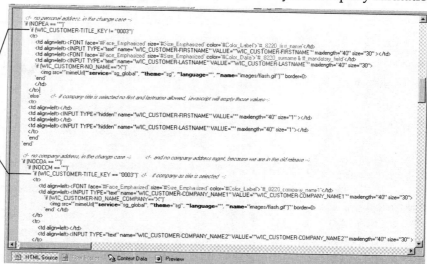

Customer Experience: My Profile

This section provides an overview of what customers experience using the *My Profile* functionality. *My Profile* can be accessed from the home page of the preconfigured Online Store by selecting *My Profile*. The image below shows the SAP-delivered homepage; your homepage will probably look different. The name of the home page file is *OnlineStore_en.html* and it is located in the root directory of the WGate.

1. In the Internet browser, our customer, Christina, enters the URL of the home page you configured as part of the ITS installation.

2. She chooses *My Profile* from the home page.

Tips & Tricks

My Profile can also be accessed by clicking on the *My Profile* icon in the header frame.

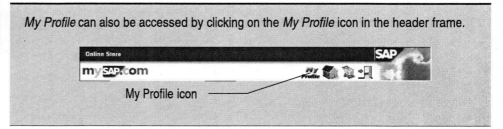

My Profile icon

If you do not want a new window to open, for example if you used an additional frame, where you start all the services, you need to modify the JavaScript that opens the new window. This JavaScript can be found on every template where the link to the *My Profile* functionality exists.

3. A new window opens, allowing Christina to log on or register.

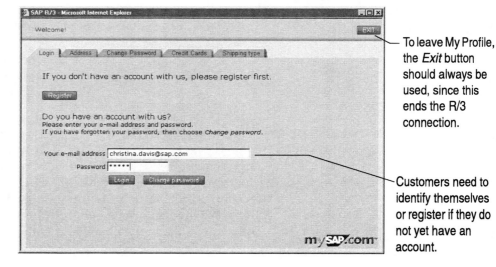

To leave My Profile, the *Exit* button should always be used, since this ends the R/3 connection.

Customers need to identify themselves or register if they do not yet have an account.

If customers have used their login information before, they do not need to log in again, because the system uses a temporary cookie to identify users automatically.

Note

On this screen, users can use all the functionality provided with *My Profile*, such as:

- Maintaining address data
- Changing password
- Storing multiple credit cards with the selection of a default credit card
- Selecting a default shipping

4. Christina logs on. The system greets her with her name and customer number.

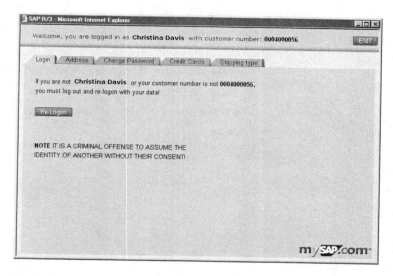

5. Christina wishes to change her address information. To do this, she chooses the *Address* tab. Not all fields are mandatory.

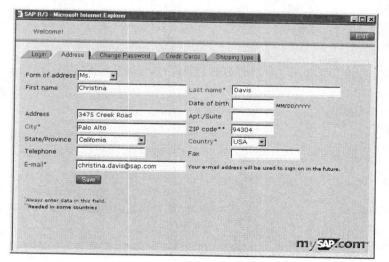

6. Christina can now change her password.

    a. Christina chooses the *Change password* tab.

    b. Christina enters the password twice. She then chooses the *Change password* button to save the changes.

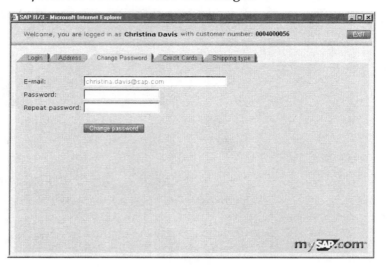

Note

After saving, the input fields for the card type and card number become disabled and only the last four digits of the credit card number become visible. This occurs so the card type and number cannot be changed, only the expiration date.

7. Christina wishes to store her credit card information.

    a. She chooses the *Credit Cards* tab.

    b. She then enters her credit card information, such as card type, cardnumber, expiration date, and card-holder name.

    c. Christina chooses *Save*.

    d. If Christina wishes to delete a credit card, she can choose the trash can next to that particular card.

    e. If Christina wants to assign a card as the default card, she can select the card by clicking on the radio button in the default column. It is still possible to use a different credit card other than the default in the Online Store.

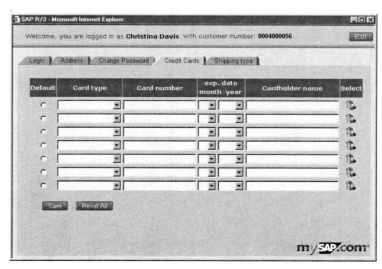

8. Christina wishes to set a default shipping type.

> **a.** She selects the *Shipping type* tab the shipping method she wants as her default. It is still possible to use a different shipping type in the store than the default.
>
> **b.** After selecting the shipping type, she chooses *Save*.

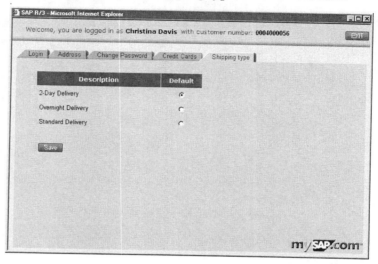

Forgotten Password

> **1.** Christina has forgotten her password. She chooses the *Change password* button on the initial *My Profile* screen.

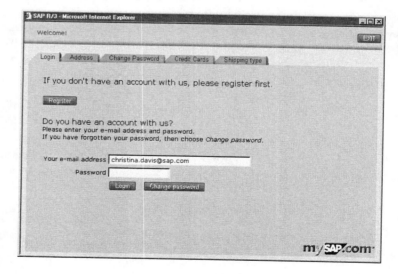

2. The system displays a new screen.

   a. She enters the e-mail address where she wants the new password to be sent.

   b. She then choose *Enter*. A new password is then sent to her e-mail address.

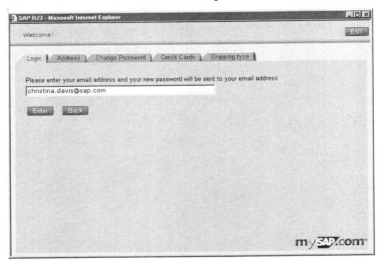

Single Sign-on

The cookie is only stored in memory and not on the hard drive. It will be removed when the browser is closed.

We implemented a cookie function into some templates so that users only have to log in once during their current session. If users go to the next login screen, they do not have to log in again, since their e-mail address (or customer number) and password are stored temporarily in a cookie. This cookie is only valid during the browser session and is removed from memory when the browser window is closed.

Let us assume a user logged on to the Online Store successfully. The user now enters a different service that requires a logon. The template recognizes that a related cookie exists and takes the logon data from the cookie, places it into the input field on the screen, and proceeds automatically to the next screen. The table below shows the templates involved in single sign-on.

Transaction	Template
Online Store (WW20)	SAPLWWCC1_8120.html
Sales Order Status (VW10)	SAPMV45X_101.html
Available to Promise (CKAV)	SAPMAVCK_500.html

The cookie function itself is stored in the service *sg_global* in the *sg_ess_function.html* template.

The ITS User: Logging on to R/3

Overview

Since the logic of the Internet Application Components (IACs) resides within R/3, a transaction within the system must be executed that sends information to the Internet. In order to start a transaction, an R/3 user with authorization to start IAC transactions must be logged on.

From an overhead and security perspective, it is not desirable to create a "normal" R/3 user for each customer that wishes to make a purchase. Instead, a single R/3 user logs into the system in the background for all customers that access the IAC from the web. This R/3 user is hidden from the customer; the customer is not aware that a logon to an R/3 System occurs in the background. The R/3 System and ITS user information is stored in a service file located in the directory structure of the ITS AGate. This R/3 user should only have limited authorizations, so that only the appropriate Internet transactions can be executed.

During the setup of the ITS, a decision must be made whether a different R/3 user will be created for each IAC transaction, or whether the same R/3 user is used for all IAC transactions and services.

What We Deliver

In the Online Store preconfiguration, we provide the following deliverables:

- Preconfiguration of one generic ITS user

- Preconfiguration of one activity group for the generic ITS user

- Documentation about the functionality of the generic user for the ITS logon

Logging on to R/3 Using the ITS

ITS User

When a customer accesses an Internet Application Component (IAC) from the web browser, a request is sent to the ITS. When the initial request is received, the ITS must log on to the R/3 System to start a transaction within R/3. The user information for this generic ITS user is stored in the service files in the ITS AGate. Each service file points to the appropriate transaction, or IAC, within R/3.

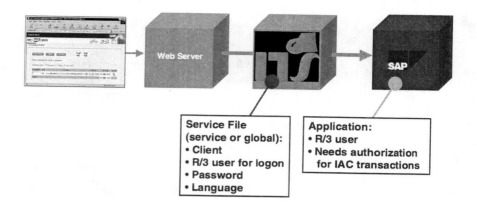

When a service is requested from the browser, the service file is checked for user information. For example, when a user enters the Online Store from the Internet (service *WW20*), the ITS checks the service file *ww20.srvc* for the ITS user information. If no user information is stored in the individual service file, the user in the *global.srvc* file is used for the logon. In this way, for each IAC, a decision must be made for whether to use a service-specific user or a global user.

The generic user remains logged on for the entire visit of the customer to the Online Store. It may be desirable to add a timeout parameter to the service file, which controls how long a session remains open. A timeout feature ensures that if a customer leaves the web site, the R/3 session closes within a designated time frame, which enhances the performance of the ITS. However, this timeout parameter should not be too short so that a customer is not disconnected while browsing the store. Especially for customers who browse the Internet from home, there may be distractions that cause them to leave their computer and return later to continue shopping.

Default Languages and Parameters

If multiple languages are required for the Online Store, the customer should be given the opportunity to choose the preferred language. To make this option available, the generic ITS user must also log on in the language chosen by the customer.

The simplest solution is to create two (or more) buttons on the web site through which the customer can enter the store. Each button has a hyperlink to the URL of the Online Store. Each hyperlink contains a different language specified as the *~language* parameter in the URL. The language should not be specified in the service files

Language	URL
English	http://<home URL>/scripts/wgate/ww20/!?~language=EN
German	http://<home URL>/scripts/wgate/ww20/!?~language=DE

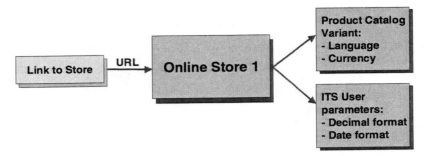

http://<homeURL>scripts/wgate/ww20/!?~language=EN

Once the ITS user has logged on to the R/3 System using the sample URL above, a list of the available Online Stores is displayed, in the language specified in the URL. The descriptions of the Online Stores should be maintained in every language that the customer can choose.

After the customer chooses an Online Store, the language and currency are determined by the product catalog variant specified in the Online Store configuration. The product catalog variant determines the language and currency used for data display in the product catalog. The language used to log on by the ITS user should match the language specified in the Online Store configuration.

The date and decimal format displayed in the product catalog are determined by the parameters in the ITS user, who logs on to start the service (transaction).

Finally, text variables referenced in the HTML [Business] templates on the web site in the Online Store also need to be displayed in the specified language. An appropriate language-resource file must exist in the ITS AGate directory, and the corresponding language-dependent MIME files must exist in the ITS WGate directory. The language specified in the URL determines the correct language-resource file that must be used.

Scenarios for Multilanguage Web Sites

For consistency, how should the configuration look if a customer chooses a U.S. setting? The language, currency, date, and decimal format must all be consistent. At the same time, if a customer chooses German, how should the configuration look? One solution is as follows:

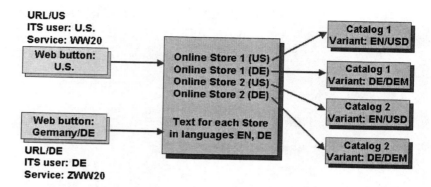

The following data setup is required:

- Two different ITS users should be created—one with U.S. parameters, the other with German parameters.

- The Online Store service needs to be copied on the ITS side, for example to a *ZWW20* service. Each service still starts the same transaction for the Online Store, *WW20*, but is assigned a different ITS user with the appropriate defaults.

- Each web-accessible product catalog must have two variants maintained. Each variant contains language, currency, and texts in each language.

- The list of Online Stores must be maintained in both languages (using the translation tool in the Online Store configuration). Each Online Store links to each product catalog/variant combination.

- The customer, once U.S. is chosen, should choose a U.S. Online Store, meaning a U.S. variant of the product catalog, using the correct defaults. It may be desirable to limit the list of Online Stores displayed based on the language chosen by making a change in the ITS templates.

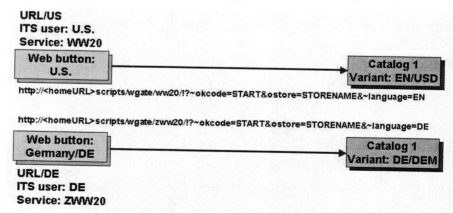

If only one product catalog should be accessible from the web, the U.S. and German web buttons can immediately start the appropriate Online Store, using the URL shown above.

The steps involved in setting up the ITS user are described in the following sections. You must:

- Create the activity group that limits the authorization of the generic ITS user (preconfigured)

- Create or change the user for the ITS general logon (preconfigured)

- Assign the ITS user to the activity group

- Place the ITS user into the appropriate service file

Master Data to Limit the ITS User Authorization

Create the Activity Group that Limits the Generic ITS User's Authorizations

The first step to configuring the logon to R/3 through the ITS is creating an activity group that limits the ITS user's authorizations. The activity group *YESHOP_ITS_USER* has been preconfigured for you. You may wish to change some of the authorizations, such as limiting the sales area to which the ITS user has access. Creating this activity group ensures that the generic ITS user does not have access to perform internal company functions.

Task

Create the activity group that limits the generic ITS user's authorizations

1. In the *Command* field, enter transaction **PFCG** and choose *Enter* (or from the navigation menu, choose *Tools → Administration → User Maintenance → Activity Groups [User Roles]*).

2. On the *Activity Group Maintenance* screen:

   a. In *Activity group*, enter the name of the activity group to be assigned to the ITS user. Activity group **YESHOP_ITS_USER** is delivered with the Online Store preconfiguration.

   b. Choose 🖉 *Change.*

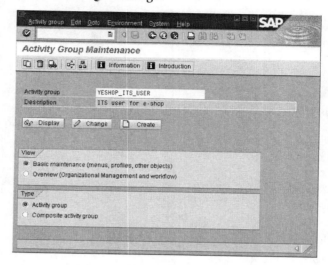

3. On the *Change Activity Groups* screen:

   a. Review the activity group's description.

   b. Choose the *Menu* tab.

A more detailed description of the activity group may be entered at the bottom of this tab frame.

4. On the *Menu* tab:

a. Review the allowed transactions.

b. Choose the *Authorizations* tab.

 The following transactions are allowed: **WW10** (IAC product catalog), **WW20** (IAC Online Store), **VW01** (SD Scenario–Incoming Orders), **VW10** (SD Scenario–Order Status), **CKAV** (Check availability), and **IKA1** (IKA–Customer account information). These transaction, with the exception of **VW01**, are IACs included in the Online Store preconfiguration. These transactions generated the objects for which authorizations need to be determined.

In addition, transactions **XD01**, **XD02**, and **XD03** are allowed (create, change, and display customer), because they contain the objects required for the customers to be created through the Online Store registration process.

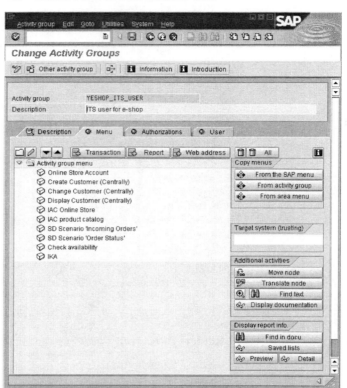

5. On the *Authorization* tab, at the bottom of the screen, choose 🖊 *Change authorization data*.

6. On the *Change Activity Group: Authorizations* screen:

   a. If changes are made to these authorizations, choose 💾.

   b. Choose 🌐 to generate the authorizations.

The following authorization objects is generated based on the transactions that the ITS user should be allowed to run. The table below documents the details of the preconfigured authorizations. The *Customer: Central Data* authorization object is added manually, since it is required for the customer account information, but is not generated based on the transaction code. The *Classification System* object was also added manually, to support the scenario in which a customer is only allowed to display particular product groups within the catalog.

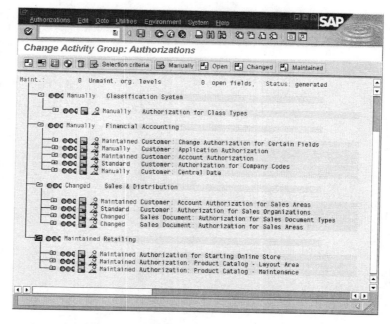

The activity group is transported in the configuration transport without the add-on transaction *ZOSA*. It is transported again with the transport containing the add-ons, this time including transaction *ZOSA*.

The following authorizations are included in the preconfigured activity group:

Authorization	Detail	Values
Cross-application Authorization Objects		
Authorization Check for Transaction Start	Transaction code	CKAV, IKA1, VW01, VW10, WW10, WW20, XD01, XD02, XD03, ZOSA
Classification System		
Authorization for Class Types	Class type	011, 060
Financial Accounting		
Customer: Change Authorization for Certain Fields	Field group	* (all)
Customer: Application Authorization	Activity	Create or generate Change Display Print Edit messages Display change documents Maintenance of payment cards Display of payment cards Confirm change

Authorization	Detail	Values
	Customer and Vendor Master Data	* (all)
Customer Account Authorization	Activity	Create or generate Change Display
	Authorization group	* (all)
Customer: Authorization for Company Codes	Activity	Create or generate Change Display
	Company code	* (all)
Customer: Central Data	Activity	Create or generate Change Display Display change documents Maintenance of payment cards Display of payment cards Confirm change
Sales & Distribution		
Customer: Account Authorization for Sales Areas	Activity	Create or generate Change Display
	Authorization group	* (all)
Customer: Authorization for Sales Organizations	Activity	Create or generate Change Display
	Division	* (all)
	Sales organization	* (all)
	Distribution channel	* (all)
Sales Document: Authorization for Sales Document Types	Activity	Create or generate Change Display
	Sales document type	* (all)
Sales Document: Authorization for Sales Areas	Activity	Create or generate Change Display Print Edit messages
	Division	* (all)

Authorization	Detail	Values
	Sales organization	* (all)
	Distribution channel	* (all)
Retailing		
Authorization for Starting Online Store	Authorization group for online store	* (all)
Authorization: Product Catalog – Layout Area	Activity for product catalog layout	Display/read
	Authorization for group for layout	* (all)
Authorization: Product Catalog – Maintenance	Activity for product catalog	Display/read
	Authorization group product catalog	* (all)

For details about activity groups and authorizations, please refer to the *Authorizations Made Easy 4.6A/B* Guidebook. You can find information about this guidebook at *www.saplabs.com/auth*.

Create or Change the User for the ITS General Logon

The next step to configuring the R/3 logon through the ITS is creating or changing the user for the ITS general logon. The steps below illustrate how to add the parameters to the ITS user. This step has been preconfigured for you when you run CATT procedure *ZESHOP_ITS_USER*. These steps do not need to be performed unless you choose to make a change to the parameters.

Only the fields critical for the IACs are discussed in this section. Fields necessary for "normal" users are not addressed.

Task

Create or change the user for ITS general logon

1. In the *Command* field, enter transaction **SU01** and choose *Enter* (or from the navigation menu, choose *Tools → Administration → User Maintenance → Users*).

2. On the *User Maintenance: Initial Screen:*

   a. In *User*, enter the name of the user you wish to use for the ITS logon.

b. Choose ☐ (or ✏ if the user already exists).

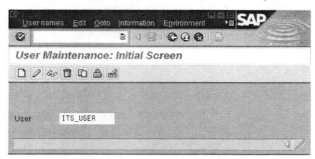

3. On the *Maintain User* screen:

   a. An entry in the *Internet mail* address field is required for the e-mail confirmations to be sent to a customer.

   b. Choose the *Defaults* tab.

Preconfigured e-mail confirmations are sent when an order is created from the Internet, when a delivery is shipped, and when the customer's credit card is charged.

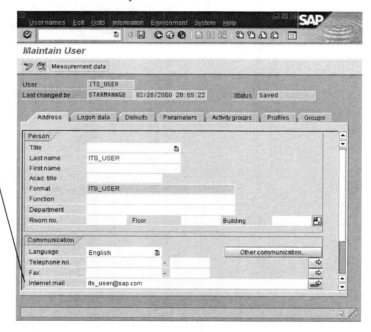

4. On the *Defaults* tab:

   a. Review the information on screen.

b. Choose the *Parameters* tab.

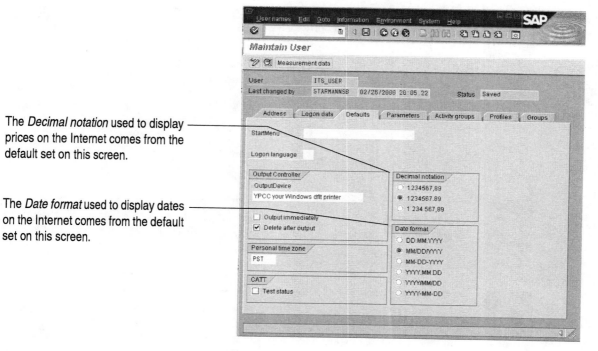

The *Decimal notation* used to display prices on the Internet comes from the default set on this screen.

The *Date format* used to display dates on the Internet comes from the default set on this screen.

5. On the *Parameters* tab:

a. For the *VKO* parameter, enter the sales organization you use for Internet orders.

b. For the *VTW* parameter, enter the distribution channel you use for Internet orders.

c. For the *SPA* parameter, enter the division you use for Internet orders.

d. For the *WKR* parameter, enter the plant for which you wish to do availability checking in the ATP service.

e. Choose 🖫 .

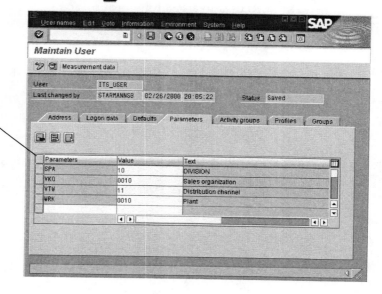

These memory parameters are used for processing in certain IACs. Both the *Parameters* and *Value* columns are manually entered.

Caution

If you are upgrading from a previous release, it may be necessary to include the following parameter to the ITS user: `ITS_PING_SWITCH_ON`, with a value of `YES`. This suppresses the navigation menu when the ITS user logs in.

The SAPNet – R/3 Frontend note (formerly OSS) *195318* discusses this parameter.

In our tests using a new install of R/3 and ITS, we did not find this parameter to be necessary for the functionality. However, setting this parameter should increase the performance of the ITS.

TechTalk

The parameters for the sales area are used primarily for the sales order status IAC (`VW10`). The plant parameter is used primarily for the available-to-promise IAC (`CKAV`).

Caution

CATT procedure `ZESHOP_ITSUSER` is run as part of the installation. The procedure creates the sample ITS user master record if it does not already exist, and adds Get/Set parameters. You need to determine whether you will create a different ITS user for each sell-side service, or use the same ITS user for all ITS services.

Additional security should be implemented, such as limiting this user to only the sell-side Internet applications. A sample activity group, which contains only authorizations for the sell-side Internet applications, is delivered with the Online Store preconfiguration. This activity group will be assigned to the ITS user in the next step.

Assign the ITS User to the Activity Group

The next step in configuring the logon to R/3 through the ITS is assigning the ITS user to an activity group. You need to perform this step manually.

Task

Assigning the ITS user to the activity group

1. In the *Command* field, enter transaction **PFCG** and choose *Enter* (or from the navigation menu, choose *Tools → Administration → User Maintenance → Activity Groups [User Roles]*).

2. On the *Activity Group Maintenance* screen:

    a. In *Activity group*, enter the delivered activity group **YESHOP_ITS_USER**.

b. Choose 🖊 *Change*.

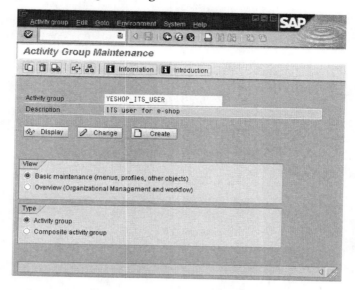

3. On the *Change Activity Groups* screen:

   a. Choose the *User* tab.

   b. Under *User ID*, enter the ITS user.

   c. Choose 🖫 .

   d. Choose 🔲 *User compare*.

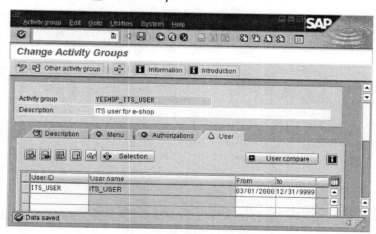

4. On the *Compare User Master Record of Activity Group* dialog box, choose
🔠 *Complete compare*.

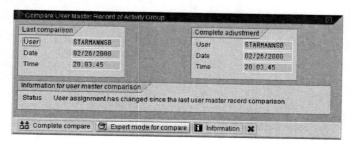

It may be necessary to activate each of the three activity groups within the composite activity group *SAP_BC_EVERY_EMPLOYEE* before the authorizations function correctly.

5. Back on the *Change Activity Groups* screen, choose 🖫 .

6. Perform steps 1–5 again, for activity group *SAP_BC_EVERY_EMPLOYEE*. This activity group allows basic navigation for the ITS user.

7. To verify that the assignments have been made, enter transaction **SU01** in the *Command* field and choose *Enter* (or from the navigation menu, choose *Tools → Administration → User Maintenance → Users*).

8. On the *User Maintenance: Initial Screen*:

a. In the *User* field, enter the ITS user name.

b. Choose 🖧 .

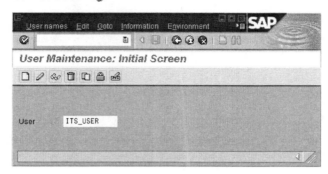

9. On the *Display User* screen:

a. Choose the *Activity groups* tab.

b. Review new activity groups.

c. Choose the *Profiles* tab.

The two activity groups, *YESHOP_ITS_USER* and *SAP_BC_EVERY_EMPLOYEE* were added in the prior steps. Since the group *SAP_BC_EVERY_EMPLOYEE* is a composite group, the activity groups within it were also assigned to the user.

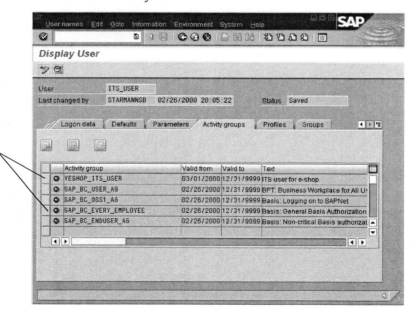

10. On the *Profiles* tab, the profiles generated for the activity groups are displayed.

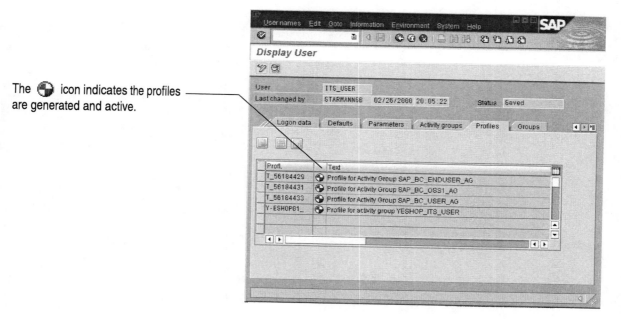

The 🌐 icon indicates the profiles are generated and active.

Place the ITS User into the Appropriate Service File

The final step to configuring the R/3 logon through ITS is to place the ITS user into the appropriate service file. Using SAP@Webstudio, you need to open the appropriate service file *xxxx.srvc*, located under the directory structure *<its_root>\services*, where the *<its_root>* is your virtual ITS installation.

The service file requires the parameters shown below in order to log on to R/3 when starting an IAC. A blank for the language allows the hyperlink from the web site to the IACs to define the language.

Parameter Name	Value
~client	300
~login	ITS_USER
~password	********
~language	

The password can be typed normally. It will be masked in SAP@Webstudio. Although the service file is stored as a text file, the password is encrypted.

The individual service files (such as *ww20.srvc* for the Online Store) are checked first for this logon information. If these parameters do not exist there, the default ITS user—stored in the *global.srvc* file—is used instead. The language is not entered as a parameter, but is passed from the URL.

Internet Users: Passwords for Customers

Overview

A customer must have an ID before a purchase can be made through the Internet Application Components (IACs). This customer ID may already exist in R/3, otherwise the customer registers in the Online Store and the ID is created at that time. In the configuration of the customer administration profile, a determination is made on whether a customer must sign in before or after browsing the product catalog. An additional setting determines whether a customer can register online or must already have a customer ID before being allowed to make a purchase. Please refer to chapter 1, "Creating the Online Store with the Catalog" on page 5 for additional information about the customer administration profile.

When a customer registers on the web site, the R/3 System creates a customer master record. In addition, a password is stored in an encrypted format. This password is stored for an "Internet user," which is created at the same time as the customer master record. This Internet user number is the same as the customer number. The customer number is used to identify the Internet user, even if the logon is configured to use an e-mail address.

The only information stored in the Internet user is the password and validity period. A customer cannot log on to the R/3 System using the Internet user. The Internet user is validated by the IACs when the customer logs on. Logic is included in each IAC to ensure that a customer can only see his or her own address, order, account status, and so on, as part of these transactions.

If customers are not allowed to register on the web site, or if existing customers should be allowed to order from the Internet, a process must be put in place by which Internet users are created for these customers. One of the biggest issues is whether an e-mail address has been maintained for the customers. If not, a campaign to obtain this information must be undertaken. This could include mail campaigns and phone calls. If this e-mail address information does not exist, the Online Store should not be configured to allow logons using an e-mail address. Without an e-mail address, order, delivery, and billing confirmations cannot be sent out electronically.

If customers already exist within R/3, their existing customer numbers should be used. If an existing customer creates a new customer number cover the Internet, consolidation of the two customers numbers can only occur in reporting.

What We Deliver

In the Online Store preconfiguration, we provide the following deliverables:

- Data load program for Internet users.

- Documentation on the functionality of the Internet user for customers.

Customers as Internet Users

When a customer registers on the web site for the first time, the customer number and Internet user are created. No manual intervention is necessary. Online registration is only possible if it is allowed in configuration by the customer administration profile. The customers do not log on to the R/3 System directly; a generic user logs on in the background. Although several customers may be browsing the web site, only one R/3 user is logged on. Please refer to chapter 15, "The ITS User: Logging on to R/3" on page 349 for information about the generic user.

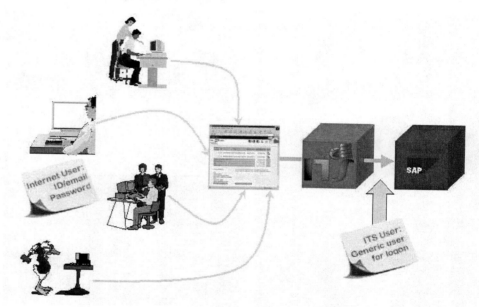

Once the customer ID and password exist, a series of validations take place in the background of the IAC before the customer can place an order. The Internet user, again, is not an R/3 user, but is simply used to store the password for the customer number.

For example, in the Online Store, the customer may log on with either an e-mail address or a customer ID. This option is determined in the customer administration profile. Since the Internet user is based on the customer number, if the customer logs on with an e-mail address, the customer number must be found. The customer number is then used for two verifications. The customer master record must exist for the sales area stored in the product catalog master data, since the sales order will be created with this sales area. If the customer exists, then the Internet password is validated. Only one Internet password is created for a customer, regardless of the sales area.

WW20: Logon

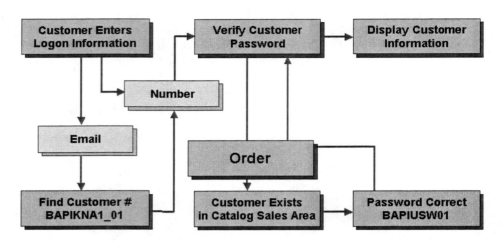

An object type is associated with the Internet user. These object types are stored in table *BFUSER_TYP*. The types delivered with the standard system include:

Internet User Type	Description
APPLICANT	Applicant
BUS1006001	Business partner employee
BUS1007	Debitor
BUS1008	Creditor
BUS1065	Employee
KNA1	Customer
PDOTYPE_PT	Attendee
SCUSTOMER	Flugkunde (SAP Schulungen) – for SAP training courses

The Internet users are stored in table *BAPIUSW01*. A password is associated with the combination of a customer number and Internet user type. As a result, a different password can be associated with the same customer number for different object types.

For example, the following table shows that a different password (encrypted) is used for object type *KNA1* (used by the Online Store, sales order status, and most other sell-side IACs) and object type *BUS1007* (used by the customer account information IAC).

CLIENT	OBJTYPE	OBJID	PASSWORD	...
400	KNA1	1234567890	BDC3238AB8651EF	...
400	KNA1	5566778811	AAAAGB12F4G5R6T	...
400	KNA1	9991231231	ALIK8675J11K1UZ	...
400	BUS1007	1234567890	HGD234HDS134GFT	...

The following table identifies the ITS service and Internet user type used for this service.

ITS Service	Description	Internet User Object Type
WW10	Product catalog	KNA1
WW20	Online Store	KNA1
VW01	Sales Order Entry	KNA1
VW10	Sales Order Status	KNA1
CKAV	Available-to-Promise	KNA1
IKA1	Customer Account Information	BUS1007

The passwords **PASS** and **SAP** are not allowed for Internet users. Also, all e-mail addresses and passwords are case-sensitive.

Since the customer account information IAC uses a different object type, the password for the same customers may be different for ordering than for monitoring their address and financial data. This difference could provide a level of security if your customer is a company and access to the account information should be limited. However, in a consumer-oriented scenario, this may also be confusing, since customers would need to keep track of multiple passwords for your site, in order to access all the functionality that you make available. If you decide that the customer type should be the same for all preconfigured services, you may wish to implement the modification in appendix F, "Modification: Changing the Customer Type for IKA1" on page 533.

The following sections describe the steps involved in setting up Internet users:

- If you are configuring an early logon for your customers, you need to create an Internet user for each customer (this step occurs automatically when customers register themselves on the Online Store).

- If you are using e-mail logon for your existing customers, you will need to collect this information from them and enter it into the customer master records.

Internet User Master Data

Create an Internet User for Existing Customers

Internet users that contain the password for customers must be created. This step may be performed manually. It is also part of the data load program.

Task

Create an Internet user for existing customers

1. In the *Command* field, enter transaction **SU05** and choose *Enter* (or from the navigation menu, choose *Tools → Administration → User Maintenance → Internet User*).

2. On the *Maintain Internet user* screen:

   a. In *ID*, enter the customer number. You must use the customer number, even if you use e-mail addresses for logging on to the Internet services.

   a. In *Type*, enter **KNA1** if you are creating a customer for the Online Store, product catalog, sales order entry, sales order status, and available-to-promise services. Enter **BUS1007** if you are creating a customer for the customer account information service.

   b. Choose 🗋 .

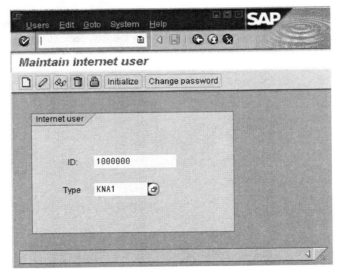

3. On the *Restrict validity* dialog box:

   a. In *Valid until,* either enter a date to which the Internet user will be valid or leave the field blank.

   b. Choose ✔ .

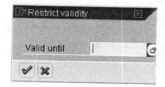

Note

The password is generated automatically.

4. On the *Information* dialog box, choose ✔ .

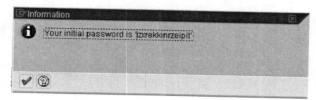

5. On the *Maintain Internet user* screen, if you wish to change the password for the Internet user, choose the *Change password* button.

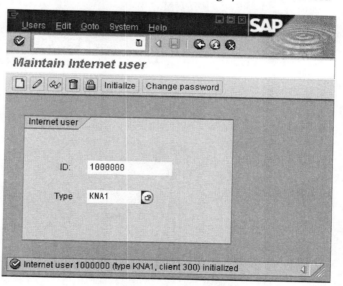

When customers initially log on to an Internet service for the first time, they are **not** required to change the password. For this reason, you may not want to choose a generic password, such as **INIT**, since initializing all Internet user passwords the same way may be a security risk.

6. On the *Change password* dialog box:

   a. In *New password,* you can enter a new password for the Internet user.

   b. Choose ✔ *Transfer.*

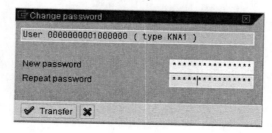

The password has been reset.

Caution

> The Internet user is created automatically through the Online Store customer registration (service WW20). The user type in this case is **KNA1**. However, for a customer to log on to the customer account information service (IKA1), the user type must be created as type **BUS1007**, or debitor. If the customer type should be the same for all preconfigured services, you may wish to implement the modification in appendix F, "Modification: Changing the Customer Type for IKA1" on page 533.

Enter the Customer E-mail Address Information into the Customer Master Record

Note

These steps can be performed using the Internet user data load program. Please refer to *Data Load Program for Internet Users* later in this chapter for details.

Customer e-mail address information must be entered into the customer master record. This step may be performed manually. It is also part of the data load program.

Task

Enter customer e-mail addresses into the customer master record

1. In the *Command* field, enter transaction **XD02** and choose *Enter* (from the navigation menu, choose *Logistics → Sales and Distribution → Master Data →Business partners → Customer → Change → Complete*).

2. On the *Change Customer: Initial Screen*:

   a. In *Customer*, enter the customer number.

   b. In *Company code*, the company code in which the customer was created is optional for changing the e-mail address, since this information does not change for each company code.

   c. In *Sales area*, the sales area information is optional to change the e-mail address, since this information does not change for each sales area.

   d. Choose ✅ .

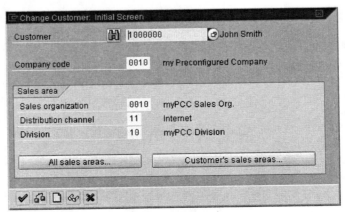

3. On the *Change Customer: General data* screen:

   a. Scroll to the bottom of the *Address* tab.

   b. In *E-mail,* enter the e-mail address of the customer.

   c. Choose 💾.

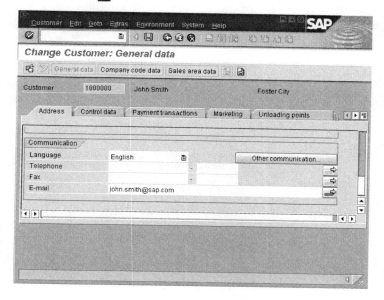

Data Load Program for Internet Users

As explained in the earlier sections of this chapter, an Internet user is necessary to access any of the Internet Application Components (IACs) available in R/3. By definition, the Internet user is different than the R/3 user. Usually, the Internet user is created in R/3 when a customer registers through any of the services available in the Online Store.

However, for those companies who have implemented R/3 and already have customer master entries, an alternate solution is required to speed up the creation of Internet users. This data load program has been developed to create Internet users en masse for all qualifying existing customers. The load program needs an input file with all the customers for whom an Internet user needs to be created.

The load program goes through the following steps for every entry in the file:

1. It checks if the customer numbers provided exists in the customer master. If not, it logs an error and skips that entry.

2. The load program creates an Internet user entry with object type *KNA1*.

3. It sets the initial password to *init*.

At each step, it does sufficient validations to ensure that only correct data passes into the system.

To further ease the loading experience, we added this load program in the Data Transfer Workbench (transaction *SXDA_OLD*).

As of R/3 Release 4.6, the transaction **SXDA** initiates the Data Transfer Workbench. However, for this object, we would recommend you use the **SXDA_OLD** transaction since it is simple and straightforward.

If you plan to use this load program a number of times, we recommend you use **SXDA** transaction.

Task

Start the load program

1. In the *Command* field, enter transaction **SXDA_OLD** and choose *Enter*.

2. On the first screen, in *Object number*, enter **330**.

3. On the *Data Transfer Workbench* screen:

   a. In *Phys file name,* enter the filename that has the list of customers.

   b. Choose ⊕. This action launches the actual load program.

   c. Choose ▯.

   d. Choose ✎.

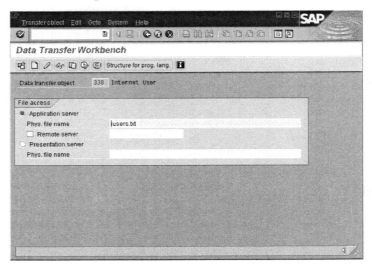

4. On the *File: _Transactions* screen, choose ✎.

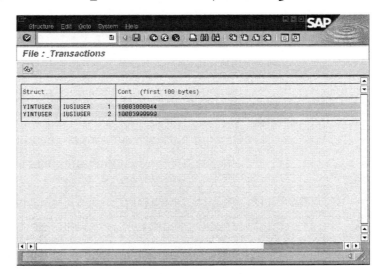

The details of the structures and format of the data to be provided is documented in program documentation of ABAP report *ZESHOP_IUSER_LOAD*.

5. After reviewing the structures on the *Generic structure editor* screen, in which the product catalog data has to be provided, choose 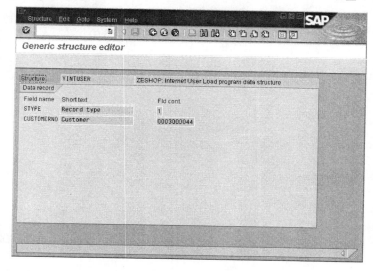 twice.

6. On the *Data Transfer Workbench* screen:

a. Once the input file is created, enter that name in *Phys file name* under *Application server*.

b. Choose ⊕.

7. On the ZESHOP: *Internet User Load program* screen:

a. In *Internet Users: Input File*, the system asks you to confirm the filename.

b. In *Internet Users: Error File*, enter the filename in which you want the system to log all error messages.

c. Choose ⊕ to load.

 Please note that the *Customer number* field must exactly match the R/3 System. For example, if the customer master has customer number *0003000044*, then the load file also should have *0003000044*. If the value is **3000044**, the number would not be recognized and would log the error – "...customer not found."

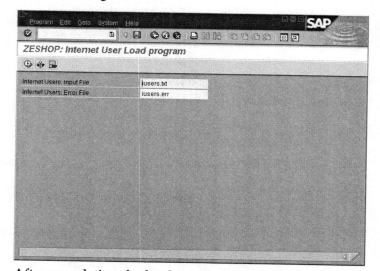

 For details about the Data Transfer Workbench, please refer to the *Data Transfer Made Easy Guidebook*. You can find information about this guide at *www.saplabs.com/dx*.

After completing the load process, please review the error file for all errors, warnings, and information logged, and take the necessary action.

For the technical details about the load program, see the table below:

Description	Technical Object
Name of load program	ZESHOP_IUSER_LOAD
Name of structure used for input file	YINTUSERS

PART FOUR

Technical Infrastructure

Section Overview

Managing the technical infrastructure in an environment that includes e-commerce must take into account a variety of systems, from an R/3 System, to the ITS server, to the web server. Furthermore, the number of additional systems required depends on the complexity of the business processes in place and the service your customers expect from your company. For example, if customers receive an e-mail confirmation when their orders and deliveries are processed, this notification requires integration between the Internet, R/3, and an e-mail server. If taxes are to be calculated real-time using software that is external to R/3, integration to this system is required. If credit cards are allowed for payment, real-time authorization protects your company from accepting invalid credit cards.

The following section focuses on the high-level landscape and the integration issues between the different systems. Depending on the hardware and software chosen in an implementation, some of the detailed processes may differ, so our aim is to be impartial to different vendors. The chapters in this section focus on the settings that need to take place within the R/3 environment to handle such topics as security. We heavily focus on the Internet Transaction Server (ITS), which is the key new component added to the system landscape when IACs (Internet Application Components) are implemented. Other portions of the landscape, such as R/3, a web server, and so on, are often already in place, and must be integrated into the IAC solution.

ITS Installation and Configuration

Overview

This chapter discusses issues related to the installation and configuration of the basic technical infrastructure in the Online Store preconfiguration. We do not reprint installation instructions except where necessary.

The installation guide referenced in this chapter is the "SAP@Web Installation Guide," for ITS Release 4.6B.

In this chapter you learn about some of the issues involved in the installation and configuration of the ITS. In chapter 13, we discussed the logical layout of the landscape. In this chapter, we discuss the physical implementation of the components from chapter 13.

Sizing

Sizing the system (or how much equipment you need) is a major issue with every installation of software. With a system that interfaces with the Internet, it is even more important because of the potential for substantial traffic from the web. We discuss some of the issues you should be aware of and plan for. You need to take into account:

- There is no "magic formula"

- Expected web traffic

- Browsing versus purchasing ratio

- Benchmarks

- Sizing of the backend R/3 System

One of the first things to realize is that there is no "magic formula" in sizing a system. There are many variables that must be considered. Unfortunately, some of these variables are difficult to estimate.

Because the real world is dynamic, sizing must be done continuously whenever there are changes that could affect the system.

Sizing issues must continually be reconsidered because:

- Decisions during the development phase of the project that significantly affected the sizing of the system might need revisiting.

- A sizing that is correct in June may be grossly inadequate to handle the Christmas sales volume, which in turn is grossly oversized for the rest of the year.

- New products, acquisitions and mergers, advertising, and similar events could change sizing requirements.

Expected Web Traffic

Estimating the web traffic is very similar to a restaurant manager trying to determine how many waiters to have on staff on a particular night.

If too much staff is present, the customer will get fast service. But the extra waiters will stand around without anything to do, costing the restaurant their salary without the revenue of additional customers.

With too few staff, the customers will become frustrated with slow service. The few waiters will be overworked. Some customers might not return for repeat business.

The number one issue is to obtain a good estimate of the web traffic you expect to hit your site. Specifically, you need to estimate the number of concurrent (at-the-same-time) users that will connect to your site and browse or purchase products using the Online Store.

Web traffic numbers are very difficult to estimate. Yet estimated web traffic affects all your sizing decisions, and as a result has significant financial impact. Your marketing and sales departments must provide realistic estimates of expected web traffic.

If you underestimate the web traffic, the response time for customer and internal user will degrade because of extra traffic into the:

- Limited bandwidth network
- Web severs
- ITS
- Backend R/3 System

If you overestimate the web traffic, you will spend more money for equipment than necessary.

Seasonality

Another factor to consider in estimating web traffic is seasonal traffic, such as Christmas, Valentines Day, Mothers Day, etc. Seasonal traffic could be 2–10 times the "nonseasonal" traffic, or more. If you do not plan and size for the surge (or peak) of seasonal traffic, performance and customer response time will be slow. If the majority of your business (revenue) is in a peak season, such as Christmas, then the answer is to design for the peak.

A business decision must be made on how to balance the requirement to handle peak traffic versus idle resources during the period (or valley) when traffic is low. This dilemma is the "peaks and valley" concept.

A grower of red roses would have its peak on Valentines Day, whereas a tulip grower would have its peak on Easter.

A retail store may have its peak at Christmas, and a hotel or vacation resort may have its peak during the summer or winter months.

Seasonal traffic is different for different industries and even companies within the same industry. The example to the right shows this difference in similar industries.

The Backend R/3 System

The single largest cost item is the effect on the backend R/3 System, especially if it involves high-end or expensive UNIX servers and disk subsystems. NT web and ITS servers are relatively inexpensive compared to the backend R/3 servers. Therefore, in order of cost, the sizing effort should concentrate on the backend R/3 System first.

Browsing Versus Purchasing Ratio

The browsing versus purchase ratio is the number of web users who browse the catalog of items versus those who purchase items. The specific ratio of customers who browse versus purchase depends on the specific site. This ratio has an effect on sizing as follows:

- Customers who browse read from the R/3 database. When browsers read from the R/3 database and the data is in one of the buffers or caches, no physical disk access occurs. This case is not so taxing on the database.

- Customers who purchase need both read and write access to the R/3 database. When customers enter their orders, they write to the database, which requires physical disk access. Physical disk access takes more time than reading the data from the buffer or cache. It is this disk-writing access that impacts performance.

Benchmarks

Benchmarks are used to assist in sizing a new system. An estimate is made by comparing an input value (for example, the number of Sales and Distribution [SD] users) to the benchmark table and looking up the recommended sizing for acceptable performance.

Frontend ITS Server

Thus far no documented benchmarks are available for the current ITS. SAP is currently conducting these benchmarks.

An older sizing document (for ITS version 2.0) exists called *Sizing the Internet Transaction Server (ITS), version 2.0*, which you can download from SAPNet (it can be found under the alias *sizing*). This document can be used as a starting point.

Sizing the Backend R/3 System

A major issue is how to size the backend R/3 System. Because of the potential large number of web customers, and the probable situation that the number of web customers is many times the number of internal R/3 users, a good estimate of web traffic is critical to size the backend R/3 System.

A "rough" ratio for calculating load and sizing is 1.0 external web user to 0.75 internal Sales and Distribution (SD) users (1: 0.75).

When sizing the backend R/3 System, you must also consider other standard R/3 sizing issues. Some variables to consider include:

- The different types of users and their needs (for example SD, MM, FI, CO, transactional, query, etc.)

- Volume of transactions

Example

If the expected number of concurrent external web users is 4,000 (this number is equivalent to 3,000 internal SD users), and the number of concurrent internal users is 300, the backend R/3 System must be sized for 3,300 users.

- Background (batch) jobs that need to be run

- Number of items in the various master files

- Amount of history to keep (one year, two years, or more)

- For the various "information systems," the detail or summary level for which they are configured

For these variables and more, the values are not fixed. In fact, during the development process, a decision could be made that affects the sizing of the system. Thus sizing is not a "one time" event or task. It needs to be reviewed periodically or any time a decision is made that could affect it.

The sizing of the backend R/3 System primarily takes place with the hardware vendor, where the customer provides the necessary input. Using experience with other customers, hardware vendors will recommend a hardware configuration.

You can use the preliminary sizing tool, the *Quick Sizer*. It is available on SAPNet under the alias *sizing*.

Internet Transaction Server (ITS)

Operating System

The Internet Transaction Server (ITS) is currently only available for Windows NT.

The ITS WGate must be installed on the same computer as the web server. Therefore, the web server must be an NT web server.

What About LINUX and UNIX?

Note

The ITS 4.6D WGate for LINUX is now available. Please see the ITS web site at *www.saplabs.com/its.*

LINUX . SAP is currently porting the ITS to LINUX. Availability date is still to be determined. For current information and status, please go to the ITS home page at *www.saplabs.com/its.*

UNIX. Availability of individual UNIX versions depends on the various UNIX vendors porting the LINUX ITS to their version of UNIX. Please check with your UNIX vendor for availability.

ITS Root Directory

Other chapters make reference to *<its_root>*. The default path of *<its_root>* is *C:\SAP\ITS\2.0\<sid>*.

Installation Options

In the installation of the ITS, there are two major options:

- **Single Host**: Install the WGate and AGate together on a single server.
- **Dual Host**: Split the WGate and AGate, and install on separate servers.

Single Host

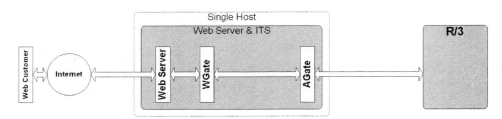

The WGate and AGate can be installed together on a single server when performance, scalability, or security is not an issue (for example, in a testing environment). The installation of a second server is eliminated, thus saving cost and administration effort.

For further instructions, see the section "Single Host Installation" in "SAP@Web Installation Guide."

Dual Host

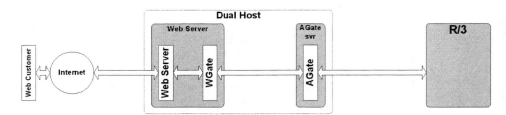

The WGate and AGate can be installed on separate servers to enhance performance, scalability, and security.

By having both on a separate server, a firewall can be inserted between the WGate and AGate, thus adding an additional layer of security to the AGate. In this way, the processing requirements of the AGate are separated from the web server and the WGate.

For further instructions, see the section "Dual Host Installation" in "SAP@Web Installation Guide."

Virtual ITS

A virtual ITS is a computer with more than one ITS instance installed.

Virtual Web Server

An important item in a virtual ITS is the virtual web server, where two or more web servers are installed on a single computer. Each web server is addressable individually by the combination of an IP address and port number.

Each virtual ITS links to a virtual web server. This link is shown in the following diagram.

A virtual ITS can be made on both a single and dual host environment. The following diagram shows a virtual ITS on a single host installation. This example is a development environment where the two ITS instances are for the DEV system (client 100) and the QAS system (client 100).

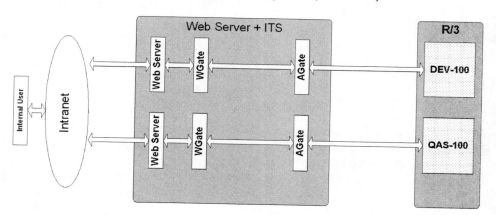

Virtual ITS allows the use of a single computer for nonproduction systems where performance, scalability, and security tend not to be issues. These systems would include development, QA, test, sandbox, and training systems.

Virtual ITS is recommended when installing the web-based ITS Administration tool. This keeps the administration instance separate from the production ITS instance.

Hint

To make administration easier, we recommend the files for the various instances be separated as follows:

Default directories created in the IIS installation:
```
c:\inetpub
    wwwroot
    scripts
```

Prerequisite: To install virtual ITS on a single computer, a matching number of virtual web servers must be installed before the virtual ITS installations can begin.

Add the following directories:

```
c:\itspub
    esh_100    <sid>_<client>
        wwwroot    (the home directory)
        scripts    (the scripts directory)
    dev_100    <sid>_<client>
        wwwroot
        scripts
    qas_100    sid>_<client>
        wwwroot
        scripts
    adm        (this is for the html administration tool)
        wwwroot
        scripts
```

These directories must be created at the operating system level before the IIS and ITS installations that require them.

For the **ITS install**, see the section "Single Host Installation" in "SAP@Web Installation Guide."

Specific Items

HTTP Port. When installing a virtual web server, in order to specify which web server to connect to, you need to specify the web server using a unique IP and port number combination. You need to have either a different IP address for each web server (multiple Network Interface Cards or NICs), or specify a different port for each web server (single NIC).

To specify an IP address:

Web Server	ITS Instance	Computer Name	IP	HTTP
Web Server 1	ITS instance 1	Webserver1	128.128.128.30	80
Web Server 2	ITS instance 2	Webserver2	128.128.128.31	80

When you install virtual ITS, you need to specify the matching IP address as:

`http://<computer_name>:<http_port>` (for example, *http://webserver1:80* or *http://webserver2:80*)

To specify a port number:

Web Server	ITS Instance	HTTP port
Web Server 1	ITS instance 1	8001
Web Server 2	ITS instance 2	8002

With **//web1:80** (port 80 is the default if you do not enter a port number) and **//web1:8001**, the difference is the port number, 80 versus 8001.

With **//web1:80** and **//web2:80**, the difference is the IP address, web1 versus web2.

Example

If the default port 80 is used, it is not necessary to enter the port number in the URL (for example **//webserver1**).

When you install virtual ITS on the same IP address, you need to specify the matching ports as:

```
http://<computer_name>:<http_port>
```

(for example, *http://webserver:8001 or http://webserver:8002*)

Creating Multiple Web Servers on Microsoft IIS

The web server for this documentation, the Microsoft Internet Information Server, is installed from the Windows NT 4.0 Option Pack.

The tasks required to create multiple web servers are:

- Install the NT option pack

- Add the web server

- Create the virtual directory

- Set memory usage

- Start the web site

The last four tasks are repeated for each additional web server to be created.

Task

Installing the NT option pack

1. Choose *Typical* installation.

2. Accept all defaults.

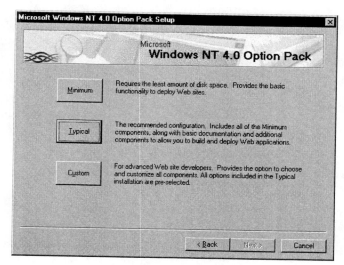

3.   After the NT option pack is installed, on the desktop, choose *Start → Programs → Windows NT 4.0 Option Pack → Microsoft Internet Information Server → Internet Service Manager*.

4.   On the *Microsoft Management Console* screen:

    a.   Expand the node *Internet Information Server*

    b.   Expand the server node (for example, *palle10108*).

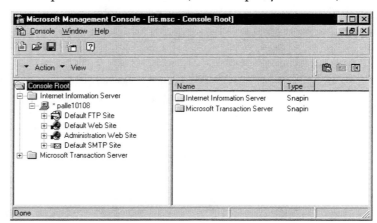

5.   To stop the installed default server:

    a.   Right-click on *Default Web Site*.

    b.   Choose *Stop*.

Task

Add your web servers

1.   On the *Microsoft Management Console* screen:

    a.   Right-click on the server (for example, *palle10108*).

    b.   Choose *New → Web site*.

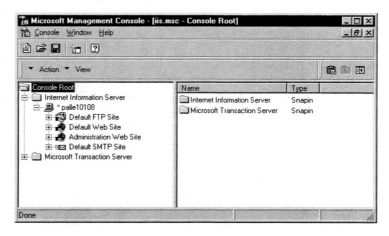

2. On the *New Web Site Wizard* screen:

    a. In *Web Site Description,* enter the name of the new web site. Use the following format wherever possible to reduce confusion:

        `<sid>_<client-number> <short description>`

    (for example, `ESH-100 eShop development`)

    b. Choose *Next.*

3. On the next screen:

    a. In *Select the IP Address to use for this Web Site,* use the list box arrow to select the IP address. If there is only one IP address assigned to the server, select *All Unassigned.*

    b. In *TCP Port this Web Site should use,* enter the TCP port. This step is critical for virtual web sites.

    The TCP port number is used in the ITS installation. See step **2b** in the section "Installation Notes for Virtual ITS Installation" on page 397.

    c. Choose *Next.*

Note

Where web sites share the same IP address, the only way to differentiate between them is the TCP port for each site (for example, enter 8001).

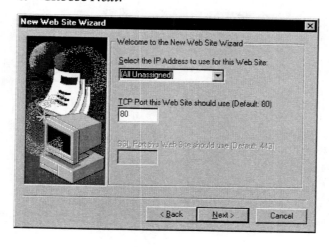

4. On the next screen:

   a. Choose *Browse*, then navigate through the directory structure to select the proper home directory for the web site (for example, `c:\itspub\esh_100\wwwroot`).

   b. Choose *Next*.

5. For permissions access:

   a. Select *Allow Read Access*.

   b. Choose *Finish*.

Task

Create Virtual Directories

1. On the *Microsoft Management Console* (MMC) screen:

   a. Expand the node *Internet Information Server*.

   b. Expand the server node (for example, *palle10108*).

   c. Right-click on the virtual web site (for example, *ESH-100*).

   d. Choose *New* → *Virtual Directory*.

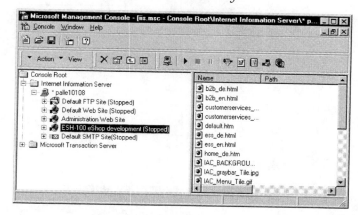

2. On the first screen of the *New Virtual Directory Wizard*:

   a. In *Alias to be used to access virtual directory*, enter **scripts**.

   b. Choose *Next*.

 The alias will allow the user to enter scripts in the URL rather than the actual directory structure (for example, //palle:8001/scripts/... rather than //palle:8001/itspub/esh-100/scripts/...).

This alias makes it easier to enter the URL.

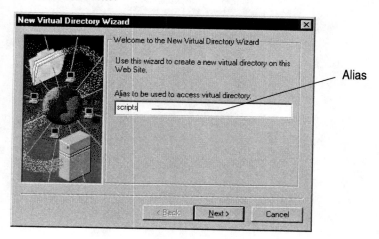

Alias

3. On the next screen:

    a. Choose the *Browse* button. Then navigate and select the scripts directory (for example: `c:\itspub\esh_100\scripts`).

    b. Choose *Next*.

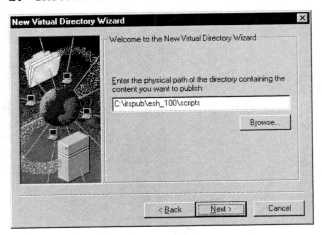

4. On the next screen:

    a. Set the security by selecting:

        • *Allow Script Access*

        • *Allow Execute Access*

    b. Choose *Finish*.

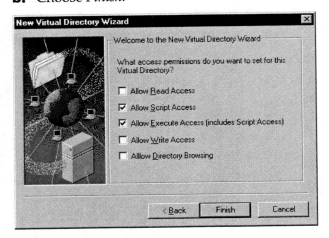

5. The virtual scripts directory has been created.

Virtual scripts directory

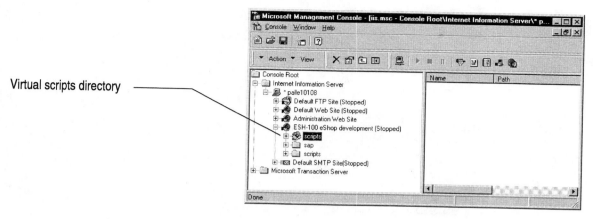

Task

Set memory usage

Note

Setting the memory usage is important because if it is not set, none of the virtual ITS instances can be accessed. For example, you will be able to access the ESH instance but you cannot access the ITS Administration tool to manage the ITS server over the web.

1. On the *Microsoft Management Console* screen:

   a. Right-click on the virtual directory scripts under the web site.

   b. Choose *Properties*.

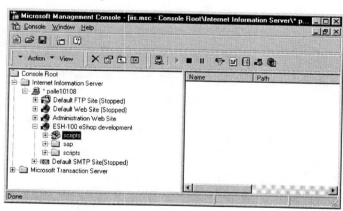

2. On the *scripts Properties* screen:

   a. Choose the *Virtual Directory* tab.

   b. Select *Run in separate memory space (isolated process)*.

c. Choose *Apply.*

d. Choose *OK.*

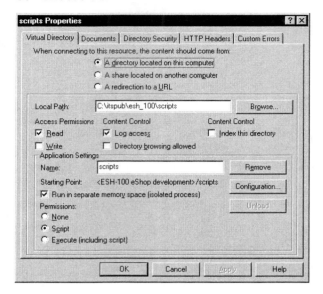

Task

Start the web site

1. On the *Microsoft Management Console* screen:

a. Note that the new web site shows *Stopped* in parenthesis.

b. Right-click on the new web site.

c. Choose *Start.*

The new web site shows *Stopped.* After starting the web site, the information in parenthesis disappears.

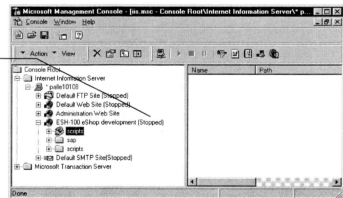

2. The new web site no longer shows *Stopped.*

3. Now you can install the ITS.

Installing the ITS

The Employee Self-Service (ESS) manual can be ordered from *www.saplabs.com/ess.*

The ITS software, documentation, and other information can be obtained from the ITS web site at:

www.saplabs.com/its.

Please see the *SAP@Web Installation Guide* for detailed installation steps.

- Single-host, begin on page 25

- Dual-host, begin on page 49

Please note that there are installation prerequisites that must be met before the ITS can be installed. See the "ITS Installation Requirements" in "SAP@Web Installation Guide."

Installation Notes for Dual Host ITS Installation

The AGate must be installed before the WGate. To install the WGate, you need to know what TCP ports the AGate is using. After the AGate is installed, to find the specific port number to enter, look in the *services* file:

c:\winnt\system32\drivers\etc\Services

Look for this entry:

sapavw00_<virtual ITS>

Example

In this example, instance ESH is on port 3900:

- sapavw00_ESH   3900/tcp   # automatically created by install

- sapavwmm_ESH   3901/tcp   # automatically created by install

In the next example, instance ADM is on port 4000:

- sapavw00_ADM   4000/tcp   # automatically created by install

- sapavwmm_ADM   4001/tcp   # automatically created by install

The ports you will use start from the port number in the services file to nine ports above that. For example, 3900 plus nine ports is 3900-3909.

Installation Notes for Virtual ITS Installation

In this section, we expand on a few selected steps for the installation of a virtual ITS instance.

Before the virtual ITS installation, you must create a matching virtual web site for each virtual ITS instance you will install.

For an ITS Administration instance installation, select *ADM administrative web site*.

The name of the site depends on what you named it when you created the web site. See page 390, "Add your web servers."

Task

Install the ITS

1. On the *Web Server Selection* screen, select the web server to which to link the ITS (for example, *ESH-100*).

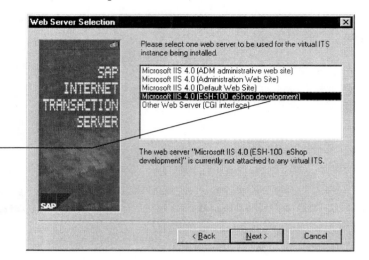

2. On the *Web Server URL* screen:

a. In *Hostname and Domain*, enter the host name of the web server.

b. In *Port*, enter the appropriate TCP port number for that web server.

The port number used is the port number assigned when the web site was created. See page 390, "Add your web servers."

In this example with host **palle10108**, port **80** is the default and would be used for the production instance.

If you have more than one virtual ITS server and a single network interface card, then the port numbers must be different (for example, host = **palle10108** and port = **8001**).

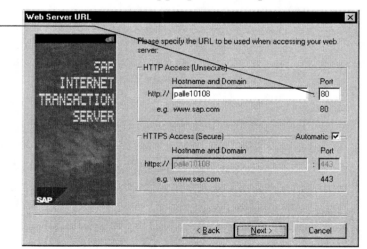

3. On the *Installation Package* window, select the default where the install window shows *46b_all*.

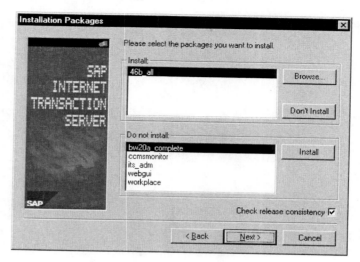

For an ITS Administration instance, the install option *its_adm* would appear under *Install* (or this window would be skipped).

4. On the *Memory Configuration* window, choose one of two options:

- *Default configuration* – used for a production system

- *Minimize memory usage* – used for anything other than a production system.

In this example, we selected *Minimize memory usage.*

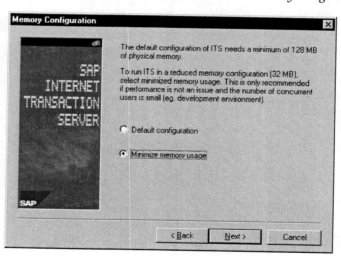

5. On the *R/3 Login* window:

a. In *System Name* enter the <SID>.

b. In *Client* enter the client number.

c. In *R/3 User* enter the user ID for the ITS user (normally `its_user`). The ITS user should have been created in the target R/3 System in advance. See Chapter 15, "The ITS User: Logging on to R/3" on page 349 for more information about ITS users.

d. In *Password,* enter the password for the user.

e. In *Confirm password,* reenter the password.

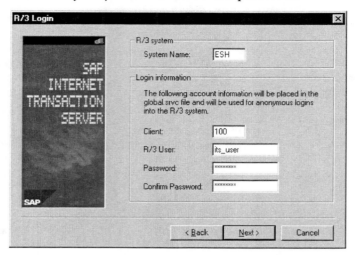

Load Balancing

Similar to SAP GUI load balancing with R/3, the ITS server can connect to a logon group rather than a specific server. The logon group assigns the next available application server to the ITS connection.

Load balancing also provides the ability to scale the number of R/3 application servers to accommodate increased web processing requirements.

Single Application Server

With this option you specify the specific application server or central instance to which you wish to connect.

Unlike load balancing, if the specific application server is "down" the ITS does not connect to any other application servers. It is also not able to scale, since you are connecting to one specific application server.

6. On the *R/3 Connection* window, select one of the following options:

- *Load Balancing*

- *Single Application Server*

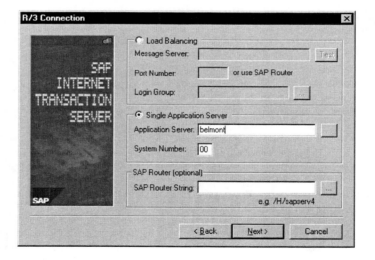

7. On the *Windows NT Security* window, select the appropriate security mode (for example, we selected *ITS Administration Group and ITS Users*):

- *Everyone* – for early development or sandbox.

- *ITS Administration Group and ITS Users* – for a development or QA system.

- *ITS Administration Group Only* – for the production system.

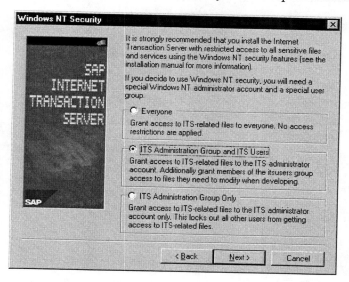

For the next step, the *ITS Admin Group* and the *ITS Users Group* that you enter **must** have been created before beginning the ITS installation (see section "Creating the ITS Administrator Account" in "SAP@Web Installation Guide."

8. On the *Windows NT Accounts* screen (which appears if either *ITS Administration Group and ITS Users* or *ITS Administration Group Only* is selected in the previous window):

a. In *Password* and *Confirm Password*, enter the password for the *ITS Administrator*.

b. In *ITS Admin Group*, enter the group name.

c. In *ITS Users Group*, enter the group name.

The *ITS Administrator* is the user ID that logged in to install the ITS.

Double-check the spelling of the groups; it is easy to make a mistake. As shown in the ITS Admin Group, it was entered as `istadmins` rather than `itsadmin`. The ITS install will fail if the install program cannot find the groups.

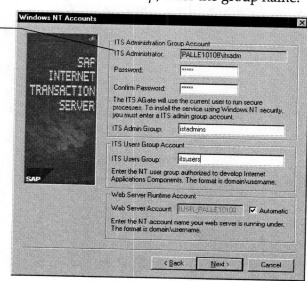

9. On the *Homepage* window, enter the URL for the home page of the web site (for example, `http://palle10108`).

The port number used is the port number assigned when the web site was created. See "Add your web servers" on page 390. The same port number was entered on page 397 in "Installation Notes for Virtual ITS Installation."

 For virtual sites using other than the default port 80, you also need to enter the port number in the format `<host-name>:<port>` (for example `http://palle10108:8001`).

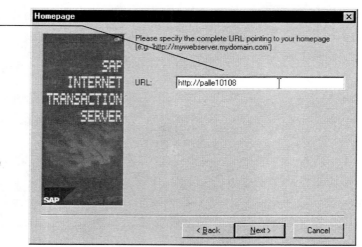

Reference

SAP@Web Installation Guide, Release 4.6B, Material #51007411, Walldorf, SAP AG, 1999.

CHAPTER

18

Infrastructure Security

Overview

In this chapter, we discuss infrastructure security issues that affect installation for Online Store preconfiguration. These issues include:

- Firewalls

- Encryption

Sensitive data is located on and transmitted between the various components of your Online Store and the R/3 System. This important information includes user IDs, passwords, company financial information, and more.

SAP is not a network security company. We leave the details of network security setup to specialists. What we discuss in this chapter are the major security items you should consider. For firewalls, we provide basic information, but a network specialist needs to configure the firewalls.

Firewalls

What Is a Firewall?

A firewall separates network segments from each other, for example it separates the Internet from your internal network. A firewall only allows permitted network traffic (by protocol and port number) to pass from one segment to another. A firewall prevents something on the exposed side of the firewall from getting to the protected side of the firewall.

Example

In home construction, a wall constructed of a special material can slow down the spread of a fire, giving you time to get out of the house.

In your car, the firewall prevents an engine fire from spreading quickly into the passenger compartment, giving you time to get out of the car.

In ships, the watertight compartment restricts flooding in a ship to the one compartment that flooded, thus saving the ship from sinking.

Other Sources of General Firewall Information

SAP does **not** endorse any particular products. The following listing is provided for your convenience. This list shows just a few of the firewall books on the market; please check various technical books for additional sources. We have **not** reviewed the books listed below.

- D. Brent Chapman and Elizabeth D. Zwicky, *Building Internet Firewalls,* (O'Relly, 1995), ISBN: 1565921240 (old but still useful for background information on firewalls)

- William Cheswick and Steven Bellovin, *Firewalls and Internet Security: Repelling the Wily Hacker,* (Addison-Wesley, 1994), ISBN: 0201633574, (2nd edition: July 2000, ISBN: 020163466X)

- Marcus Goncalves, *Firewalls: A Complete Guide,* (Osborne, 1999), ISBN: 0071356398.

  ___ *Firewalls Complete (Complete Series),* (McGraw-Hill, 1998), ISBN: 0070246459

- Marcus Goncalves and Vinicius Goncalves, *Protecting Your Web Site with Firewalls,* (Prentice Hall, 1997), ISBN: 0136282075.

- Mathew Strebe, *Firewalls: 24seven,* (Sybex, 1999), ISBN: 0782125298.

How to Configure Your Firewall

Firewalls should be installed in layers, according to a concept known as "defense-in-depth." What is a defense-in-depth? This concept is a defense where each firewall provides a layer of security, so an intruder penetrating one layer has to penetrate additional layers to get to the R/3 System.

Example

A medieval castle's defense-in-depth is composed of the following sequential levels of security:

- Moat

- Outer castle wall

- Inner castle wall

If attackers pass through the moat, they still have to penetrate the outer castle wall. If attackers get past the outer castle wall, they still have to penetrate the inner castle wall. This sequence of barriers gives the defenders more time to detect and prevent an attack. If the only defense is the moat, once past the water barrier, the attacker would be free to inflict immediate damage.

Placing the Proper Firewalls

You need to know where each firewall should be placed in relation to the various components, and what the pass-through parameters are for the firewalls. The pass-through parameters (protocol and port number) are required by network security personnel to configure the firewall. In addition, the network specialist needs to know the IP address of the source system(s) and the target system(s). The IP addresses are specific to your installation.

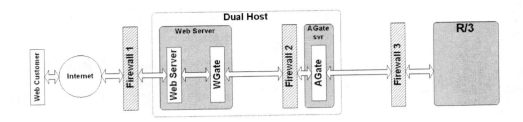

Firewall 1

The first firewall should be installed between the Internet and the web server (see above). It represents the first layer of defense. In most environments, a firewall protects the web server, so it should already exist in the system landscape.

The pass-through parameters are as follows:

Protocol	Ports
HTTP	80
HTTPS	443

Firewall 2

Penetrating the second firewall (Firewall 2), an invader could access sensitive transaction information, such as user ID and passwords, sent from the ITS AGate to the R/3 System.

The second firewall should be installed between the ITS WGate and the ITS AGate. This firewall restricts access to the ITS AGate server from the web server. Specific to the ITS, this firewall may require a separate installation. If the ITS is installed on a single host, as in a development environment, a second firewall is not needed.

This firewall may exist in companies that put their web servers outside a corporate firewall, separating the internal network from any external traffic.

The pass-through parameters are as follows:

Protocol	Ports
TCP/IP	xxxx - yyyy

For the ports, xxxx is a starting port address (the default is 3900) and yyyy is the ending port number, nine ports above the starting port number. For example, the default ports run from 3900–3909. Ten ports are used for each ITS installation.

For virtual ITS installations, the port number depends on the installation. For example:

ITS	Ports
ITS #1	3900-3909
ITS #2	3910-3919

The ITS install program looks in the services file for available ports before configuring the AGate and writes the port number that it configures into the services file.

To find the specific port number for entry, after the AGate is installed, look in the services file:

c:\winnt\system32\drivers\etc\Services

The entry to look for is:

sapavw00_<virtual ITS>

Example

In this example, instance ESH is on port 3900

- sapavw00_ESH   3900/tcp   # automatically created by install

In the next example, instance ADM is on port 4000

- sapavw00_ADM   4000   # automatically created by install

Firewall 3

Install the third firewall between the ITS AGate and R/3 System. This firewall restricts the network traffic from the ITS AGate server to R/3. Only SAP GUI protocol is allowed through this firewall.

The third firewall can be either another commercial firewall or the SAProuter. The SAProuter, part of the standard R/3 installation, also allows only certain protocols through particular ports.

The pass-through parameters are as follows:

Protocol	Ports
SAP GUI	32xx

For the ports, xx is the system number for the R/3 installation. For example, if the R/3 System number is 00, the port would be 3200.

If the SAProuter is used, the same SAProuter used for the SAP service connection and internal users can also be used for the web connection. If your network security policy requires a second SAProuter, one can be installed to handle only the web traffic to R/3.

Encryption

For additional security, encryption can be implemented. Encryption has two goals:

- Protect the customers data on the Internet from being viewed by unauthorized parties.

- Protect the data within your network from being viewed by unauthorized parties.

Protecting the Customers Data on the Internet

When you protect customer data on the Internet, you are securing the link between the web customer and your web server. You do this to protect the security of sensitive customer data, such as credit card data, from being viewed and used by unauthorized persons. The encryption is done by using secure HTTP protocol or HTTPS from the customer's browser.

Protecting the Data Within Your Network

Encrypt network traffic because:

- Sensitive data is being transmitted on an internal network and you want to prevent unauthorized internal personnel from accessing it.

- The data link is external to your facility, thus at risk of being tapped.

  If the Accelerated Internet Selling system is partially outsourced to an Application Service Provider (ASP), where the web server and ITS AGate are outsourced and the rest of the system is located in-house, the link between the ITS WGate and ITS AGate could be encrypted. This link goes over a possibly insecure WAN between the ASP and the customer. See Chapter 20, "Outsourcing" on page 425 for more information on outsourcing.

To protect data within your network, secure one or two internal network links. This is done to:

- Prevent internal users from viewing customer or other sensitive data on the internal network.

- Protect data on the network from outside attacks that penetrate the firewalls.

Encryption can be done using various commercial encryption programs to encrypt the message on one side and then decrypt it when it gets to the destination.

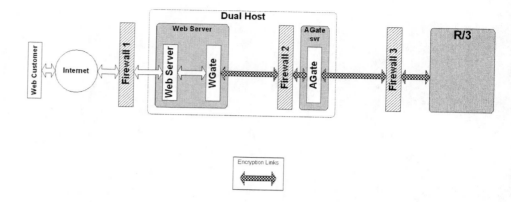

The above diagram shows where encryption can be implemented for an Online Store's system landscape. The network links can be secured using encryption such as SNC between the:

- ITS WGate and ITS AGate

- ITS AGate and R/3 System

See the online documentation for more information about SNC at:

SAP Library → Basis Components → Security (BC-SEC) → Secure Network Communications (SNC)

Reference

SAP@Web Installation Guide, Release 4.6B, Material #51007411, Walldorf, SAP AG, 1999.

Interfacing with Third-Party Components

Overview

In this chapter, we discuss four of the other components to which the Online Store preconfiguration interfaces. These four components are:

- Credit card verification

- Tax calculation

- Freight calculation

- E-mail and Fax

Third-party products that interface with R/3 fill specialized needs beyond the scope of R/3. These third-party products aid Accelerated Internet Selling by performing needed tasks—all while the web customer remains online.

When we state that the installation of third-party components is part of the R/3 installation project, we mean that it is not an additional system installation specifically for the Accelerated Internet Selling component. These installations need to be interfaced and configured as part of the initial configuration of the Sales and Distribution (SD) module.

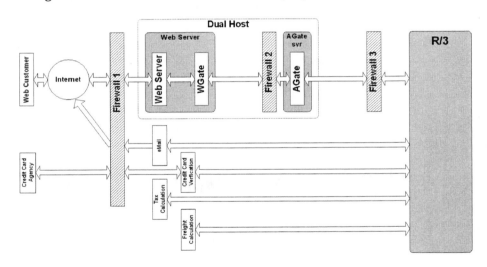

Note

Not all components fit into the firewalls as shown above. Those such as credit card verification, tax calculation, and freight calculation can be connected to the vendors in various ways. Others such as direct or dial-up phone connections or physical disk and CD-ROM updates would not go through the firewall.

The above diagram shows the additional components (e-mail, tax calculation, credit card verification, and freight calculation) and how they fit into the system landscape with the network firewalls.

Credit Card Verification and Authorization

Credit card verification and authorization services allow you to process credit card orders online.

With a verification and authorization component, the web customer's credit card can be checked while the customer is online. If any authorization problems occur, the customer can be immediately informed before the sales process is complete. The customer can then use a different card. This immediate verification reduces manual authorization handling and prevents product shipment if the bank will not honor the charge.

The credit card verification and authorization software must be installed on a separate computer and connected to R/3 over the network. Your network connection to the verification and authorization service must be either dial-up (on demand) for limited traffic, or an always-on connection if you are a company with significant credit card transactions.

The SD module is configured to interface and R/3 is configured to communicate with the credit card verification system.

These configurations are set up during the R/3 installation.

> **Note**
>
> In future releases, if a credit card is declined, the web customer can save the order, resolve the issue with their bank, and return to complete the order, without having to reenter the order from the beginning.

Setting up the Credit Card Interface

SAP has defined an interface—CA-PCI (Payment Card Interface)—with which you can achieve seamless integration with any third-party software or service that supports this interface. Many popular vendors are already certified or are in process of certification. On SAPNet use the alias CSP (for Complementary Software Providers) for a list of vendors who are certified for this interface.

For more information on interfacing for credit cards, see chapter 7, "Credit Card Authorizations and Settlement" on page 195.

Tax Calculation

There are two options for calculating tax:

- Calculate tax within R/3
- Use an external third-party tax calculation package

Third-party tax calculation packages calculate sales tax based on the web customer's tax jurisdiction (for example, state = California, county = Santa Clara, city = Palo Alto) and add the appropriate sales tax to the order.

Sales tax rates differ based on where the customer is located (their tax jurisdiction). Some states have no sales tax, and others peak over 8%. At 8%, the sales tax could be a significant portion of the sale, and an even more significant portion of the gross margin.

If the sales tax is not computed at time of sale, you would have to either:

- Make a second charge to the web customer's credit card. If a customer is charged twice in error, they may not return to your site.

- Pay the tax out of the gross margin of the sale

  If the margin is small, paying the tax out of the gross margin might leave the sale as a loss.

The tax packages also prepare the tax reports for the various tax jurisdictions, in terms of who you have to pay and how much.

The SD module is set up to interface to external tax packages, but R/3 must be configured to communicate with a particular external tax package. This configuration occurs during the original R/3 installation project.

For more information on tax calculation, see chapter 3, "Tax Calculation" on page 91.

> An open question still remains as to whether sales over the Internet are taxable by various states. We recommend you consult with your accountants or tax department to determine if Internet sales are taxable for you. The penalties for not paying these taxes, wherever due, could be severe.

Freight Calculation

A freight calculation component allows your Online Store to calculate freight charges based on the item being ordered and adds the freight charge to the order.

The ability to calculate the freight charge and add it to the sales order allows the web customer to get the complete cost, including freight, while still online. Similar to taxes, if you do not compute the freight at the time of the sale, you have to either:

- Make a second charge to the web customer's credit card for freight

- Pay the freight out of the gross margin of the sale

For more information of freight calculation, see chapter 3, "Freight Calculation" on page 90.

When to Calculate Freight

There are two times at which you can calculate and charge freight, either at the time of sale or after the product is packed and ready for shipping.

At Time of Sale

Advantages. Assessing freight at the time of sale allows the freight charge to be presented to the web customer and charged to their charge card with their purchase, all in one transaction.

Issues. Charging freight at the time of sale requires that the material master record for each item be maintained with the data required to calculate the freight charges (weight, size, shipping restrictions, etc.).

Limitations. The packaging overhead (such as packing materials, size of box, and orders packed into more than one box) sometimes does not get calculated into the freight calculation. Thus the actual freight may be different from what you charged the customer.

Charging Freight after Packed for Shipping

Advantages. After the purchase is packed, measured, and weighed, a more accurate freight charge can be assessed. At this point the unknown variables of packaging overhead are no longer unknown. Your employees can enter data into a freight company's terminal or web page to determine the exact freight charge.

Issues. This method of assessing freight is an after-the-fact calculation. An adjustment would need to be made to the order, or a second charge made against the web customer's charge card.

Limitations. Your customer must deal with an updated bill. The shipping cost may dramatically affect the price of the order and may result in late order cancellations.

Setting up the System for Freight Calculation

The R/3 System needs to be configured to interface with particular freight vendors and their freight calculation packages. Each freight calculation package has its own processes to interface with their company and update their rate tables.

The installation of a freight system is often done as a part of the R/3 installation.

SAP created the Express Shipping Interface (XSI) interface specification for integrating the freight service provider solutions. With the help of this interface, you can:

- Generate the tracking number per service provider

- Print the labels using the templates provided in the system

- Pull in the freight rates from flat files to the condition tables using the ALE IDocs

Note

We have not made use of the XSI interface in this release but hope to provide solutions around it in the subsequent releases. Meanwhile, we recommend you look at this interface and consider the solutions that can be developed around it.

- Send out the manifest using the ALE IDocs or XML documents using the Business Connector.

E-mail and Fax

E-mails and faxes come under the topic of business communication. SAP has developed a technical layer to allow easy and open integration with popular third-party messaging application software such as Microsoft Exchange™, Topcall™, and sendmail™. This integration gives tremendous capability to the R/3 System, enabling R/3 applications and users to send and receive documents from a communication server mailbox. Documents can also be sent and received in the R/3 System through other connectors connected to the server, for example, through the Internet or as a fax. Attachment files (for example, R/3 documents, Microsoft Office™ documents, and fax bitmaps) can be transmitted in both directions. However, please note that in this release, we focus on the outbound flow of business documents. SAP provides two different technologies:

- **SAPcommunications** – The communication server is a stand-alone software suite that connects to R/3 through CPI-C links

- **SAPconnect** – It uses the RFC technology of R/3 and expects the application software to provide the RFC server.

In this chapter, we discuss one solution using SAPconnect, Microsoft Exchange Connector, and Microsoft Exchange. Many other scenarios are possible and need to be considered based on your company's communication policy.

Integration of SAPoffice and Microsoft Exchange Using SAPconnect

The illustration immediately below explains the interactions between different components of SAP systems. The document starts at the application side making use of SAPscript, message control, and address management, and finally goes to SAPconnect layer. Once the document arrives at the

SAPconnect layer, it makes use of RFC protocol and connects to various supported messaging applications and exchanges business documents as shown in the second figure.

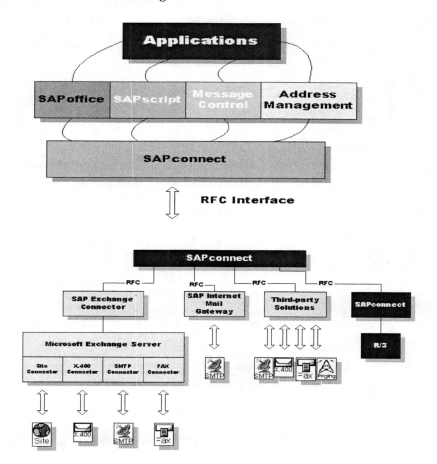

The integration requires the:

■ Availability of Microsoft Exchange with appropriate SMTP mail gateway software (the installation of Microsoft Exchange and its setup to send e-mails is outside the scope of this document)

■ Installation of SAP Exchange Connector software.

■ Creation of RFC destination in SAP

■ Maintenance of the user master with Internet e-mail address

■ Configuration of the SAPconnect software

Installing SAP Exchange Connector

The SAP Exchange Connector connects the Microsoft Exchange server to the R/3 System. The SAP Exchange Connector controls message receipt, message conversion, and message transport between the Microsoft Exchange server and SAPconnect, the R/3 System's communications interface.

There are two options for installing the SAP Exchange Connector. You can install on either:

- A separate computer system under Microsoft Windows NT workstation/server (variant A)

- A Microsoft Exchange Server itself (variant B)

Please use the online documentation of SAP Exchange Connector:

SAP Library → Basis Components → Basis Services / Communication Interfaces (BC-SRV) → Communication Interfaces (BC-SRV-COM) → BC-SAP Exchange Connector

The online documentation explains all aspects of the Exchange Connector installation and its relationship with Microsoft Exchange. Ensure at the time of installation that the system administrator has global authorizations. During the installation of the connector, you should have already decided on:

- Program IDs for the Exchange Connector services *RFCin* and *RFCout*

- RFC username for *RFCin service*

- Routing address patterns such as "*.com," "*.org," or "*.de"

In R/3 you have to make necessary settings. Perform the following tasks.

Task

Create CPIC-user

1. In the *Command* field, enter transaction **SU01** and choose *Enter*.

2. Create a CPIC user with the name as specified in the Exchange Connector.

Task

Create RFC Destination

Since we focus mainly on the outbound e-mails, we need only one RFC destination for *SXC_RFCout*.

1. In the *Command* field, enter transaction **SM59** and choose *Enter*.

2. On the *Display and maintain RFC destinations* screen, choose *Create*.

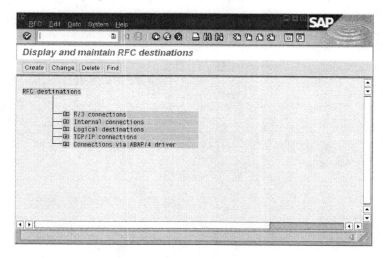

3. On the *RFC Destination SXC_OUT* screen:

a. In *RFC destination*, enter **SXC_OUT**.

b. Under *Registration*, in *Program ID*, enter the program ID as specified on the SAP Exchange Connector.

c. Choose *Gateway*.

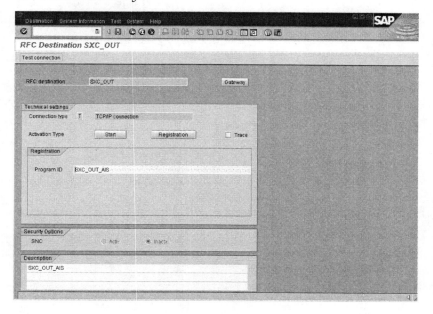

4. On the *RFC Destination SXC_OUT* dialog box:

    a. In *Gateway host*, enter the gateway host. This entry should again match the gateway information you provided in the Exchange Connector.

    b. Choose *O.K.*

The gateway host and service fields show sample values. Your values will be different.

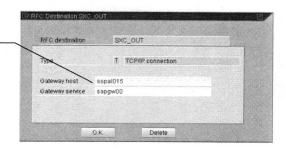

5. On the *RFC - Connection Test* screen:

    a. Choose 💾 .

    b. Choose 🏠 .

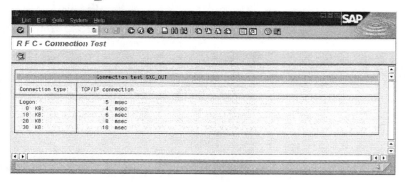

Task

Configure SAPconnect nodes

1. In the *Command* field, enter transaction **SCOT** and choose *Enter*.

2. On the *SAPconnect:Administration (system status)* screen, choose ▯ .

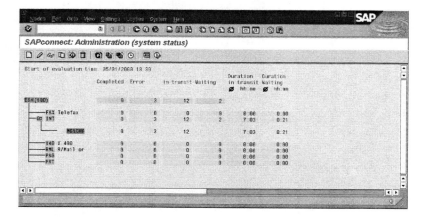

3. A wizard prompts you for the following information across multiple screens:

a. Node name and description

b. *RFC destination* – It should match the name of *SXC_RFCout* destination. Please note that this entry is case-sensitive.

c. *Address type* – The address type supports FAX, INT, X400, etc. You could choose a different address type based on the components supported by your environment. For our case, choose *INT*.

d. *Address area* – This entry would be based on the number of exchange servers in the environment. In our case, since we have only one exchange server, we entered an asterisk (*) indicating all addresses need to be sent through this node.

e. A set of selections prompts you for the supported document formats as part of the messages. For simplicity, select *All formats*.

f. In *Device type*, keep the default as proposed by the system.

g. The system prompts you to provide any other address type. You could make other selections such as *FAX* and give the relevant information.

h. On the last screen, select the checkbox that asks if the node is ready for use.

Task

Set up "send" scheduling

After completing the node, you need to set the frequency at which SAP should check whether any mails need to be sent out. You need to plan this properly based on your needs and performance considerations.

1. After planning the schedule, on the *SAPconnect: Administration (system status)* screen, choose *View → Jobs*.

2. On the *SAPconnect: Administration (jobs)* screen, choose ⬜ .

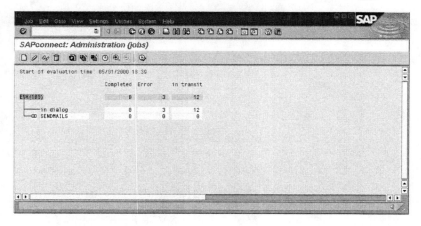

3. On the *Schedule send process* dialog box:

    a. In *Job name*, give any name of your choice.

    b. Choose ✓ .

4. On the *SAPconnect send process: Variants* screen:

    a. Select the standard variant *INT*.

    b. Choose the *Schedule job* button.

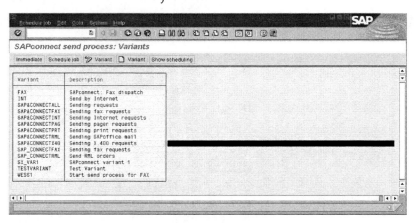

5. On the *SAPconnect send process Scheduling: Start Time* screen, with the help of the various options available, set the scheduling plan.

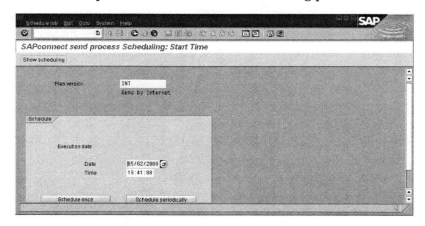

Task

Maintain the SMTP e-mail addresses

For all the SAPoffice users who need to send Internet e-mail messages, they must have an Internet address in the user master as shown in the accompanying screenshot.

1. In the *Command* field, enter transaction **SU01** and choose *Enter*.

2. On the *User Maintenance: Initial Screen*:

   a. In *User*, enter the ITS user.

   b. Choose ✎ .

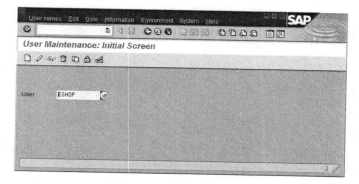

3. On the *Maintain User* screen:

   a. Scroll down and enter in *Internet mail* the SMTP e-mail address. This e-mail address becomes the return address.

   b. Choose 💾 .

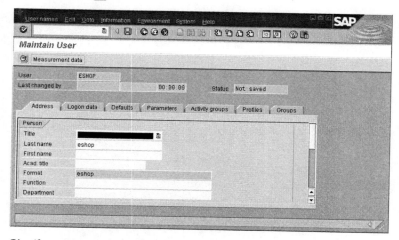

Similar to e-mail integration using the Exchange Connector with Microsoft Exchange, you could also think of a sendmail-based solution. Again, the SAP Online help gives complete procedures to set up the interface between SAP and the sendmail software. Please note that in the UNIX environment, sendmail is free software, but in the Windows NT environment it is not.

The application side of the configuration that actually initiates the SAP documents as e-mail is discussed in chapter 1, "Creating the Online Store with the Catalog" on page 5.

CHAPTER 220

Outsourcing

Overview

Outsourcing involves locating some or all of your computing equipment at a third-party hosting company. This hosting company is also known as an Application Service Provider (ASP). Outsourcing is not a new phenomenon, having existed since the early days of computing in the form of time-sharing and data processing service bureaus. Outsourcing is a way for smaller companies to reduce the cost of running and maintaining a complex system landscape.

ASPs operate and maintain the servers, networks, and related equipment. They are responsible for system upkeep to an agreed-upon level (a service-level agreement or SLA).

Why Outsource?

Outsourcing is a business decision. There are several reasons to outsource the system. The two primary reasons are:

- Financial cost savings
- Difficulty in finding and keeping the specialized personnel required to operate and maintain the system

Financial Savings

Note

A leasing arrangement can also reduce the initial cash outlay.

One reason for outsourcing is the financial savings you get from managing your cash flow. If you purchase all the equipment to run in-house, you face significant upfront cash outlay. In an ASP situation, the cost for the service is billed monthly, avoiding a large upfront cash outlay for equipment purchase.

By sharing costs, the price of the specialized equipment and personnel is not borne by you alone. These costs are spread among the various other customers of the ASP, such that each is only bearing a portion of the cost.

Note that cost savings apply where all or most of the infrastructure does not exist and must be put in place. If adequate infrastructure already exists, the savings would decrease because you would be duplicating infrastructure you already have.

Example

If you already have a backup power generator of sufficient output to handle the additional equipment, the backup generator at the ASP would not be an additional benefit. If however you did not have a backup power generator, and you kept the installation in-house, you would have to purchase and install a generator. In that case, if you outsource, the generator at the ASP would then be a benefit.

Personnel

For certain specialized skills, it could be difficult to find personnel at the level you need. For a small company, it may be difficult to financially justify such hiring, and it may be difficult to attract such a person to a small company. An ASP allows you to have access to these skilled people and share the cost with other customers of the ASP.

Example

One Database Administrator (DBA) could support three or four small customers. This arrangement would save each customer the full cost of a DBA, who would not be fully utilized. People with this kind of specialized skill might demand a high salary. A small company may have difficulty justifying and staffing a full web and R/3 organization. Each person would either be underworked or have to fill many roles to keep fully busy.

Establishing Equipment Location

There are three options for equipment location. Not all ASPs provide you with all options. The pro and con discussions assume that the specific R/3 and Online Store preconfiguration equipment must be acquired.

Your equipment can reside:

- Onsite, where the ASP "takes over" your IT operation

Pro	Con
The equipment is onsite where you have physical control over it and the data.	You need to finance the purchase of the equipment and required infrastructure.
Security issues of having equipment and data physically outside of your facility and control are eliminated.	The resource sharing benefits would be minimal, as there would not be the economies of scale that a shared data center would have. You would still have access to the pool of expertise that an ASP would have to maintain your in-house data center.

- Offsite, but with your own equipment (You would own the equipment located at the ASP; essentially, you are renting space at the ASP facility for your equipment)

Pro	Con
You would save because of the infrastructure that exists at the ASP.	You need to finance the purchase of the equipment.
	There might be security issues with your equipment and data being outside of your physical control.

- Offsite, ASP-provided equipment (You would be renting the equipment from the ASP)

Pros	Cons
You do not have to finance the purchase of equipment.	There might be security issues with your equipment and data being out of your physical control.
You would save on the equipment and infrastructure that exists at the ASP.	

System Landscape Outsource Options

You can also consider outsourcing from a system landscape perspective, deciding exactly what is outsourced. There are three options:

- Partial – web server and WGate
- Partial – web server, Wgate, and AGate
- Everything

Partial Outsource – Web Server and WGate

In this system landscape option, the web server and the ITS WGate get outsourced to the ASP.

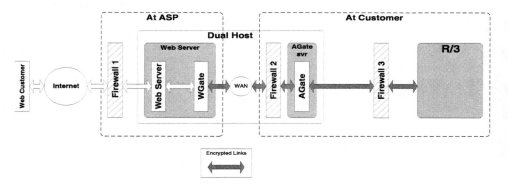

With **minimal outsourcing,** only the web server is outsourced. Everything else is kept "in house."

Problems and Issues

The problem with a partial outsource of the web server and WGate may be security. The WAN link between the WGate (at the ASP) and the AGate (at the customer site) is potentially an unsecured link. The data going over this link should be encrypted to reduce your exposure.

Partial Outsource – Web server, WGate, and AGate

In this system landscape option, the web server and the ITS WGate and AGate are outsourced to the ASP.

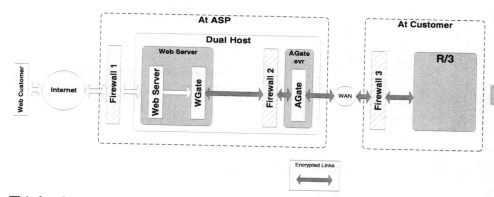

This landscape option is known as **medium outsourcing**. The web server and the ITS are outsourced, while the R/3 System is kept "in house."

Problems and Issues

The problem with this partial outsource is again security. The WAN link between the AGate (at the ASP) and the R/3 System (at the customer site) is potentially an unsecured link. The data going over this link should be encrypted to reduce your exposure.

Outsourcing Everything

With this system landscape option, the entire system (web server, ITS WGate, ITS AGate, and R/3 itself) is outsourced to the ASP.

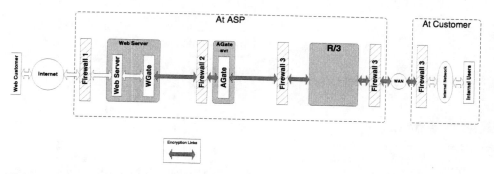

This option is called **full outsourcing**, where the web server, ITS, and R/3 Systems are all outsourced.

Problems and Issues

Network . With full outsourcing, an additional network issue becomes how to connect your users to the R/3 System at the ASP. With either of the two partial options, the network connection was not an issue as the R/3 System was in-house.

Security . On a fully outsourced system, **all** your data is at a site outside your immediate influence and control. This setup poses security risks to your data. You are completely reliant on the security of the ASP to secure your data.

Other Programs. Running programs other than R/3 on this remote equipment may require operating system access or access of a different kind. You may need to work through such issues with the ASP.

General Problems and Issues

Before outsourcing, check with your legal and sales departments. You may have contracts (such as defense department-related contracts) which have clauses that prohibit or prevent you from outsourcing all or part of your system.

Direct operating system access may be required to perform certain tasks. You may need to access the operating system yourself, or have the ASP perform the required tasks. To get images for your products into the ITS WGate, you need FTP access into the operating system, or you must e-mail the files to the ASP who then copies the files into the appropriate locations.

As you have seen there are several reasons and options for outsourcing. You need to decide if it makes business sense to outsource. If you decide to outsource, you need to look at your situation and evaluate which of the different outsource options make best business sense for you.

The following table shows the different options:

	Web Server/WGate	Web Server/WGate + AGate	Everything
Onsite, your equipment	n/a	n/a	X
Offsite, your equipment	X	X	X
Offsite, rented equipment	X	X	X

References

Justin Newton, "Designing a Data Center," *Web Techniques*, August 1999, volume 4, issue 8, page 46-55.

Yvonee Lee, "The Challenge of Web Hosting," *Web Techniques*, August 1999, volume 4, issue 8, page 57-59.

System Administration for Accelerated Internet Selling

Overview

Every system needs to be administered and maintained to keep it running well. The Accelerated Internet Selling system is no different. You need to administer and monitor your system so your web customers have reasonable response time.

In this chapter, we do not repeat information published in the SAP standard documentation. We discuss the HTML-based ITS Administration tool that comes with the ITS and makes monitoring and managing the ITS easier. We also discuss system monitoring and some of the items that need to be monitored. This chapter touches on two other system administration topics:

- Document management of images for the web site

- Upgrading the ITS

SAP Standard Documentation

Rather than restate material documented elsewhere, we refer you to the specific source documentation, in most cases the online documentation. The online documentation for the ITS is:

SAP Library → Basis Components → Frontend Services (BC-FES) → ITS/SAP@WebStudio (BC-FES-ITS) → ITS Administration Guide

Under *ITS Administration Guide* are the following topics:

- *ITS Administration*

  - *Installing and Starting ITS Administration*

  - *User Management*

  - *ITS Instance Monitoring*

    ITS Configuration Parameters

    Log Files

- *ITS Administration in R/3*

  - *Maintaining Internet Users*

- *ITS Service Parameters*

The information in the online documentation and the ITS installation guide is more extensive than what we could include in this guide. We recommend you review that documentation and familiarize yourself with it for easier reference.

Also available is *ITS Administration Guide, Release 4.6 D* (283 pages), available for download from *www.saplabs.com/its*.

> **Note**
>
> In addition to the online documentation is the installation guide for the ITS SAP@Web Installation Guide, which is available for download from the ITS web site at *www.saplabs.com/its*.

ITS Administration Web Interface

The ITS Administration tool is an HTML-based administration tool used to monitor, control, and configure the ITS instances using a web interface.

Installation

We recommend you install the ITS Administration tool as a separate virtual ITS specifically for this tool. Such a setup is more secure, with the added advantage that you can stop other ITS instances whenever you need. See the installation process for virtual ITS in the *"SAP@Web Installation Guide."* Also see the online documentation:

SAP Library → Basis Components → Frontend Services (BC-FES) → ITS/SAP@Web Studio (BC-FES-ITS)→ ITS Administration Guide

Then choose *ITS Administration Guide → ITS Administration → Installing and Starting ITS Administration*

Log On to the ITS Administration Tool

Log on to the ITS Administration tool with the following URL:

`http://<host-name>:<port>/scripts/wgate/admin/!`

For example:

`http://itssvr:8001/scripts/wgate/admin/!`

We recommend you bookmark the URL to the ITS Administration tool, since the URL is not intuitive.

The default user ID is `itsadmin` and the default password is `init`. As with all default passwords, it should be changed as soon as possible after the installation. See the procedure to change the password in the online documentation.

SAP Library → Basis Components → Frontend Services (BC-FES) → ITS/SAP@Web Studio (BC-FES-ITS) → ITS Administration Guide

Then choose *ITS Administration Guide → ITS Administration → User Management → Changing the Password*

Using the ITS Administration Tool

Note

With the ITS Administration tool, you monitor and administer the server where the AGate component of the ITS is installed (see chapter 17, "ITS Installation and Configuration" on page 381 about where the AGate is installed).

On a dual host installation, you need to use the standard NT monitoring tools or other tools to monitor the server where the web server and WGate are installed. The ITS developers are aware of this issue. A work-around is to install a third ITS instance as a single-host installation on the web server. The ITS Administration tool on the third instance would then be able to administer the system with the web server and WGate.

 The term "flush log files" may be confusing. This process flushes the log information from the cache (memory) to the log file. The purpose of this action is to get the log data from the cache (volatile memory) into the log file (nonvolatile memory/storage). It does **not** mean flushing the data from the files.

Please refer to the online documentation for detailed information on using the ITS Administration tool.

The major functions of the ITS Administration tool are:

- User Management
  - Managing users
  - Changing passwords
- ITS Instance Monitoring
  - Monitoring the ITS instances
  - Starting and Stopping the ITS instance
  - Monitoring ITS performance
  - Reviewing the log files
- ITS configuration
  - ITS configuration parameters
  - Setting up file security
  - Setting up network security
  - Displaying ITS service templates
- Other ITS maintenance tasks
  - Flushing log files
  - Clearing the template cache
- Monitoring system information

Monitoring

Like any system, you need to monitor the Accelerated Internet Selling systems. You need to monitor the various components of your Online Store (web server, ITS server, R/3, and network infrastructure) for the following:

Issue	Questions
System problems	■ Are the systems running properly?
	■ Are there any processing errors?
Security	■ Has there been a security breach?
	■ Is someone trying to break into your system?

Issue	Questions
Performance	■ What is the load on the system?
	■ Is performance adequate or is it below a desired threshold?
	■ Where is the performance bottleneck?
Statistics	■ How many sessions are active at once?
	■ What is the traffic pattern of web customers?
	■ How many users are accessing your system?
	■ What is the CPU usage?
	■ What is the memory usage?
	■ What is the disk usage?

For monitoring, you need **reference points**. Some of these reference points are definite, and others are specific to your installation.

Reference points are necessary to assess and define "normal" conditions. "Normal" can be specific to your installation.

Specific references for monitoring:

Reference	Definition
ITS	See the online documentation for *ITS Instance Monitoring*:
	SAP Library → Basis Components → Frontend Services (BC-FES) → ITS/SAP@Web Studio (BC-FES-ITS) → ITS Administration Guide
	Then choose *ITS Administration Guide → ITS Administration → ITS Instance Monitoring*
R/3	See the guidebook *System Administration Made Easy* (Release 4.6A/B).
Your web server	See the documentation (or various third-party books) for your web server.
Network security	Work with your network security specialist.
Operating system	See the Windows NT documentation and various third-party NT administration books.

Example

A definite **reference point** is the maximum number of sessions available, for example 64. A specific reference point is the "normal" number of session active, for example 35.

Example

Following the maximum and normal values from the example above, if the number of active sessions is 61, you have not reached the maximum number of sessions (of 64), but you are 74% above the "normal" number of sessions (of 35). This number is an indicator that you may need to investigate why the number of active sessions increased.

Security

The security logs of all systems (web server, routers, firewalls, R/3) should be reviewed on a regular basis. By regular we mean **at least** daily, preferably several times a shift. If any kind of security problems or security breaches occur, you want to minimize the problem by minimizing the amount of time that you are unaware of the problem.

Automated Alert

For fast notification of alerts, one procedure is to program a system monitor (or script) to review the contents of the various security logs regularly (for example, every five minutes), and generate a pager alert if a problem is found. This alert reduces considerably the duration of time that you are unaware of a security problem. The various security logs and scripts still need to be reviewed periodically for new problems should be programmed into the script to generate an alert page.

Firewall Logs

Please work with your network specialist to learn where the firewall logs are and how to read them.

Performance and Statistics

In chapter 14, we said that estimating (or guessing) web traffic with any accuracy is **very** difficult. Because of this problem, web traffic must be monitored and compared to original estimates to determine if the system sizing must be adjusted to handle the actual web traffic. If the system sizing must be adjusted, you may need all the lead-time you can get. While some components can be scaled easily, other components could be difficult (in terms of time, effort, cost, etc.). For more information on gathering statistics, see chapter 12, "Web Site Statistics" on page 307.

The ITS Administration tool provides statistics related to the ITS, such as sessions used versus maximum number of sessions, workthreads used versus maximum number of workthreads, and CPU% usage.

Web Server

Like any system, the web server must be monitored on a regular basis for problems and performance issues. Please review the documentation for your specific web server to see what and how different monitoring tasks should be performed.

Document Management

Document management is the tracking and management of documents. For your Online Store preconfiguration, document management refers to the publishing and managing of graphic images for your web page, most importantly, the images of your products. When graphics are copied to the web server, change control discipline is required. The graphics on the production system should be the same as that on the QA system and the development system. If not, the wrong images could appear when a web customer looks at a page.

To publish, images, one option is to go through source control. This step is part of the *SAP@Web Studio* process:

> Choose *SAP Library → Basis Components → Frontend Services (BC-FES) → ITS/SAP@Web Studio (BC-FES-ITS)*

> Then choose *SAP@Web Studio → ITS Service Publishing*

Please see chapter 14, "ITS Templates" on page 327 for more information on SAP@Webstudio.

A second option bypasses source control. Bypassing is done primarily for images. However all controls are now manual.

Problems

If the system has been outsourced, you normally do not have access to the directories at the operating system level. The ASP has to copy or move the files into the appropriate directories for you.

Upgrades

The ITS **must** be upgraded before you upgrade the R/3 System to either the same release to which you are upgrading or to a higher release. Like the SAP GUI, the ITS is backward compatible but not forward compatible.

CHAPTER 222

Performance

Overview

In this chapter, we discuss the various ideas and options for improving the system performance of the Online Store preconfiguration.

Performance is important because if system performance is poor, the response time for both the web customer and internal R/3 user will be long, resulting in customer dissatisfaction.

This chapter covers different performance issues and helps you decide how to define and improve performance, and scale your Accelerated Internet Selling system.

Performance Tuning Process

Performance tuning of the Online Store preconfiguration utilizes the standard problem solving process. As a prerequisite, you must have performance statistics for comparison to determine if you indeed have a problem. To analyze the performance:

1. Measure relevant performance statistics.

    *   Quantify the picture to determine whether you really have a problem.

    *   Create reference points so you can tell when performance is improving or worsening.

2. Look for the bottleneck.

    Be aware that what you see might only be a "symptom" of the problem, not the problem itself. This step requires research using various tools to find the root problem.

3. Evaluate the alternatives to eliminate or reduce the bottleneck.

4. Eliminate the bottleneck.

5. Measure the relevant performance statistics again.

6. Evaluate the new performance against the reference performance.

    Did the performance improve or did it worsen? If it got worse, you may need to "undo" whatever you did.

7. Repeat the cycle as needed until the performance is satisfactory or is economically unjustifiable to continue.

Target Customer

When thinking about performance, the question is "performance for who"? Ask yourself: Who are your target customers? The primary web customer groups are consumers and businesses. Although each group can be further broken down to fine-tune the target, we are interested in general performance issues for each target group. As a vendor selling on the web, the characteristics of your target web customer should drive the design of your web site.

Performance for Consumers

Consumers normally have phone access to Internet Service Providers (ISPs). The data transfer rate of a phone connection is typically much slower than the connections that a business has. Most customers do not have ISDN, cable, DSL, or other high-speed connections to their ISP. Web pages with lots of data and high-resolution graphics take longer to load over the phone line.

Customers might wait for content, but there is a limit to how long they will wait before becoming dissatisfied. You need to work with your marketing department to determine the maximum allowable wait time for web site design.

If you design your web site specifically for the current 28.8–56k modems, you need to monitor the technology and be ready to change when a sufficient percentage of your customer base has high-speed Internet access.

Because of the slow performance using a standard telephone line modem at home, many consumers do much of their web surfing at work where the Internet access is much faster.

Performance for Businesses

Businesses normally have high-speed connections to their ISP or directly to the Internet. Because of the high-speed connection, the amount of data on a web page has minimal impact on the load time.

Example

A buyer in the purchasing department is looking for a chair. If a vendor's web site takes several minutes to load long pages full of pictures, finding the right chair and ordering it may take more than 15 minutes. The buyer's company may switch to vendors with faster web sites where the buyer can complete the search and place an order in a few minutes.

If your target customers are other businesses, then the amount of web page data is not much of an issue. Your customers should have a sufficiently fast connection.

However, in the business world, time is money. If the business customer has to wait, they may switch to a vendor with a faster web site. People have more and more work to do, and the faster they can do it, the less work backs up on their desk.

Web Page Performance

In this section, we discuss some of the specifics that affect the performance of a web page, such as graphics, page size, and traffic.

Graphics

With graphics, performance improvements depend on the amount of data sent to the web customer over the Internet. The issue is bandwidth. How fast is the connection between the web customer and their ISP? In order to improve the speed that a web page loads, you must keep the amount of data to a practical minimum, balancing the speed of loading the page with content. To minimize web page data:

- Reduce the amount of graphics on the page

  - Display image on demand. Click on the text name of an item to display the graphics.

  - Use thumbnails of images that the web customer can click on to get a full-size graphic, rather than put all the full-size images on the page.

- Lower the graphics resolution or color depth of images on the page

  Most web applications do not need to show an item with a color depth of over 65,000 colors. If this depth is required, have the web user click on the smaller and lower color depth image to get a full size, deep color image.

Page Size

Another way to improve web page performance is to reduce the page size. Rather than have a web page many screens long, break up the page into several smaller pages linked to a higher-level page.

Smaller pages load faster, although the customer will have more pages to go through.

Traffic

Traffic has a direct influence on performance. The more traffic on the web site, the greater the effect on performance. If your system is not adequately sized for the traffic you get, the response time for the web customers will increase to an intolerable amount. At that point, you will start losing customers.

The problem, as discussed in "Expected Web Traffic" on page 383, is to accurately estimate the web traffic that will hit your site, and more specifically, the web traffic that will access your online store. Estimating web traffic is extremely difficult, but you are dependent on this number to size your system. For performance, you must keep track of:

- Total volume of web traffic

- Browse versus buy customers

System Configuration

Sizing of the Backend R/3 System

A single web user is roughly equivalent to 0.75 internal SD users. Thus if you have 4000 concurrent web customers browsing or buying, this amount is equivalent to approximately 3000 internal SD users. The backend R/3 System must be appropriately sized for this load.

Scaling

Evaluate the Current Servers

Example

Your CPU utilization at peak hours is steady at over 95%. Your current ITS server has two CPUs and the provision to increase to four processors. Consider adding the additional two processors.

If the existing Network Interface Card (NIC) is a 10baseT card, consider replacing the NIC with a 100baseT card (your network must be able to support 100baseT).

Unnecessary Work

Check the servers to determine if programs or services that do not need to be running on the web or ITS servers are using processing, memory, and disk space. These items are "excess baggage." Over time, programs and other tasks may have been added to the server that diminish server performance. Such "excess baggage" should be removed from the web or ITS servers and moved to another server.

Upgrade the Servers

Determine if the processors and memory (RAM) or other components can be scaled.

Example

Your current ITS server has a dual 166MHz Pentium ® which is significantly behind the current top CPU speed for Intel-based servers at 500MHz. In this case, you might consider upgrading the server itself.

Perhaps the memory in your server can be increased to only 512MB, and the memory is the slower 66MHz. Current servers can be configured with more than 1GB of RAM and memory speed over 100MHz.

Replace the Servers

There comes a point where the old, slower equipment creates more of a performance bottleneck than can be worked around. The cost of upgrading older equipment may not make business sense anymore. At that point, the equipment should be replaced with current technology.

Determine if the existing server is "dated." Is the performance of the server components significantly slower or has considerable limitations that can be overcome by current products?

Scaling the Systems

We discuss various options to scale the performance of the system. You can:

- Separate the WGate from the AGate
- Scale the WGate
- Scale the AGate
- Scale R/3
- Have a dedicated R/3 System

Be sure to scale the correct component, the one causing the bottleneck. Otherwise you will see little improvement in performance.

The options for scaling the WGate and AGate both assume that the existing hardware is maximally configured—four processors, 1 GB or more of RAM. Scaling applies to the scaling of the production system, not a virtual ITS for a nonproduction system.

Separate the WGate from the AGate

One option for scaling is separating the WGate from the AGate. The following illustration shows the dual host ITS installation.

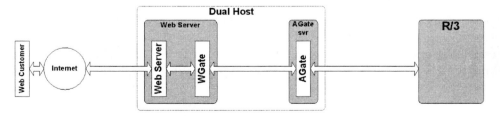

In this configuration, the WGate and AGate are installed on separate servers. Because the WGate must be installed on the same computer as the web server, separating the WGate and AGate separates the web server from the AGate. This distribution shifts the processing load of the web server and the AGate onto separate servers.

Scale the WGate

Another option for scaling involves the WGate. In this configuration, multiple web servers and WGates are linked to a single AGate.

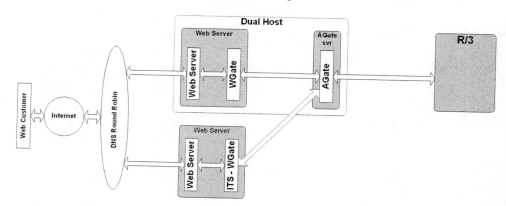

The *DNS Round Robin* masks the web server landscape from the web customer. When the customer enters a web site URL (such as *www.sap.com*), the *DNS Round Robin* routes the web customer to the next available web site (for example, *www1.sap.com* or *www2.sap.com*). Web customers are usually unaware when they are routed to a web server other than the URL they entered.

On a dual host installation, you need to monitor the web server and WGate server with other tools, such as the standard NT administration tools. The ITS Administration tool monitors the system where the AGate is installed.

You should watch the CPU utilization of the web and WGate server. If CPU utilization is consistently high, or high during peak periods:

- Above 80% would be a warning point

- Above 90% you are probably CPU-bound; if utilization averages 90% or more, that means you might be reaching 100% during periods of higher activity because so little ceiling remains

Issues

Keep in mind that change control is important. The web pages and images must be maintained identically on both web servers. Otherwise, web customers see different pages or images depending on the web server to which they are connected.

Scale the AGate

Another option for scaling involves the AGate. In this configuration, multiple web servers with their own WGate and AGate are linked to a single R/3 application server.

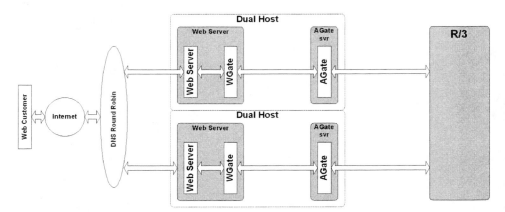

Every AGate requires a separate web server, because currently the WGate can only communicate with one AGate.

Indicators of AGate bottleneck include:

- Sessions

  If the used or maximum number of sessions is the same or close, you may be running out of sessions.

- Work threads

  If the used or maximum number of threads is the same or close, you may be running out of work threads.

- CPU utilization of the AGate server

  Consistently high, or high during peak periods.

  - Above 80% would be a warning point

  - Above 90% would be when you are probably CPU-bound.

Issues

Keep in mind that change control is important. The web pages and images must be maintained identically on both web servers, or web customers will see different pages or images depending on the web server to which they are connected.

The request from one user must **always** be directed to the same web server where that user started the session. Data cannot be transferred between web servers.

If an AGate server crashes, the session is lost. There is no failover capability to move the web customer's session from one path to another; in other words, there is no way to move the session from web server A to web server B.

Scale R/3

Another option for scaling involves the R/3 System. In this configuration, the AGate or AGates are configured to link to a "logon group" of multiple R/3 application servers dedicated to web customers. Other logon groups would exist for the internal R/3 users. Additional application servers can be added to the logon group as needed to handle additional processing requirements.

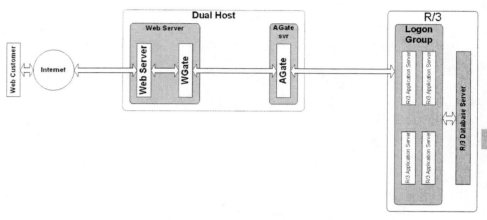

By monitoring the CPU utilization of the application servers, you can determine when you need to add additional application servers to the logon group. As with sizing the R/3 System, work with your hardware vendor to determine the R/3 application server configuration needed to support your needs.

Issues

Additional application servers do not address a bottleneck problem at the database server.

Dedicated R/3

An R/3 System can be dedicated to web service. This option would address the problem of a bottleneck at the database server. This configuration separates internal processing requirements from external (web) processing requirements.

This dedicated R/3 System would be coupled to the main R/3 System using ALE.

Example

Month-end processing would create significant load on the backend R/3 System. This activity could then affect response time for your web customers.

Issues

Dedicating an R/3 System is an expensive option as the production system is essentially duplicated, or enough of it is to satisfy the requirements of the web.

Scaling Summary

Many of the scaling methods can be combined in different configurations, such as the following combination:

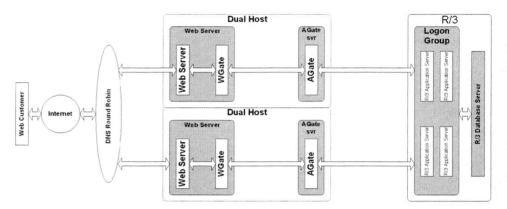

In the above diagram, scaling methods are used to:

- Separate the WGate and AGate
- Scale the AGate
- Scale R/3 with application servers

The ability to combine scaling methods allows you to tailor the configuration to your needs.

References

ITS Tuning Guide, Release 4.6 D (Palo Alto, CA: SAP Labs Inc., 2000). Available for download from *www.saplabs.com/its*.

PART FIVE

Starting an E-commerce Project

Section Overview

Managing an e-commerce project should be based on the same criteria as any other project in your organization. Although e-commerce is receiving much attention in the press as a new means of marketing and attracting new customers, businesses are realizing that these criteria are not enough. Customers should not just be attracted to a web site because it is attractive and glitzy. They should also be able to find the information they are looking for and use this information to make informed purchasing decisions—preferably from your Internet store. Graphics should draw attention to a particular point and should not to be overused or distract the customer.

Most importantly, taking an order over the Internet is just the first step of the process. These orders must be integrated into your sales and fulfillment processes. Many other business decisions must be made, including how to handle pricing, product promotions, commissions, freight, and reporting.

Some of the more common organizational issues that need to be addressed while undertaking any business and IT project are even more important when it comes to e-commerce project, because e-commerce is more visible to the customers. For example:

- Critical success factors should be defined before beginning a project.

- Costs and timelines must be planned and monitored.

- E-commerce projects should be undertaken to fulfill a business need, not just to implement technology for technology's sake.

- The project should fit with the company's overall e-commerce strategy.

- More importantly, the project should fit with the company's overall business strategy.

In order to facilitate the planning of your e-commerce project, we are providing project and cost planning templates. We also discuss how the value-add of e-commerce to your company can be measured, either in hard or soft benefits.

Finally, once you have an Internet store, remember that such a store requires constant attention. Once you have an Internet presence, you must also use it in your marketing. Let you customers know about it. Use it in advertising. Register with search engines. Participate in the SAP Marketplace or other marketplaces.

CHAPTER 23

Project Planning

Overview

When a company decides to implement an e-commerce solution such as the Online Store, it is not just a simple matter of putting up an Internet site and waiting for the customers to find your site. Just as any other project, be it driven by business or IT reasons, the Online Store implementation must be thoroughly planned. Such planning requires careful consideration of the scope, timeline, and available resources and skills on your project team.

Online Store implementations fall into two categories:

- Companies who are implementing the R/3 System and the Online Store at the same time. Essentially, the Online Store is part of the scope of the R/3 implementation.

- Companies who already have an R/3 System and now wish to add the Online Store functionality. In this approach, the Online Store implementation is a new phase of an R/3 implementation.

The project plans for each of these approaches are different. While adding the Online Store to an existing R/3 System can essentially be considered a small implementation, many of the larger issues—R/3 landscape, initial familiarity with the R/3 System and training, change management—have already been addressed, and only the incremental changes require more careful planning.

Project Plan for a Complete Implementation

Companies who do not currently have an R/3 System may wish to include the Online Store as part of their initial scope. In this case, the normal project plan provided by Accelerated SAP should be used.

This plan contains all of the phases and tasks that are part of an R/3 implementation. The project plan provided by Accelerated SAP does not go into component-level detail. As part of the implementation, the scope of the project must be defined. In this situation, the scope includes the Online Store and the sales and distribution processes that support the Internet order and order fulfillment processes, and thus becomes part of the entire implementation.

The additional areas that need to be considered over and above the normal R/3 implementation include:

- When determining the technical landscape, the ITS server, web server, and additional firewalls must be considered.

- In the material master configuration and data transfer, enough time should be spent on determining which products will be sold on the Internet, and the texts and images that should be displayed in the Online Store.

- In order to identify orders placed through the Internet, an additional distribution channel may be used. If this is the case, additional views for customer and material master will need to be created.

- If products sold on the Internet will be priced differently than those sold through other distribution channels, additional conditions or pricing procedures may be required.

- For the look and feel of the Online Store, additional time needs to be allocated for changes to incorporate your corporate identity into the HTML Business templates, and to integrate the store into any existing web site you may have.

For details on the tasks that must be considered during an Online Store implementation, please refer to the separate project plan provided for companies implementing the Online Store in a subsequent phase. Such detailed tasks are not included in the Accelerated SAP project plans, because these high-level plans are only used as a starting point for all companies. In addition, we did not wish to create confusion by providing an "altered" Accelerated SAP project plan.

 As part of the Accelerated Internet Selling solution, we provide a copy of the Accelerated SAP project plan templates for small and medium-sized businesses. There is a 6-month and a 9-month implementation plan, in Microsoft Project™ and Microsoft Excel™ format. The project plans have not been changed. These files are contained in the file *ASAP ProjPlan Templates.zip*, which is delivered as part of the transport download and on the CD that accompanies this guidebook.

Project Plan for Implementing Sell-Side IACs as an Add-On

Companies who already have a live implementation of an R/3 System may wish to expand their system to include the Online Store and related sell-side applications on the Internet. These companies can use the Accelerated SAP project plan, or define a new, more limited project plan.

If a company chooses to use the Accelerated SAP project plan, the scoping should be defined to include only the Online Store. The implementation time needs to be condensed, since many of the larger issues of an R/3 implementation have already been addressed. The benefit to using the Accelerated SAP plan is that all phases of a business and IT project are considered. The drawback is the plan may be too all-encompassing for what is essentially an expansion to a company's current R/3 implemented functionality.

The company may also choose to use a project plan that addresses only the Online Store implementation in a more detailed manner. The benefit of such a plan is it immediately addresses the tasks at a more detailed level, and cuts out some of the extensive organizational issues that should have been addressed when R/3 was first implemented. The drawback is it may still be necessary to address these issues, since going forward with an Internet presence, and an Online Store, requires rethinking the strategic direction of the company.

As part of the Accelerated Internet Selling solution, we provide an implementation plan for companies implementing the Online Store as an add-on to an existing R/3 System. The plan is in Microsoft Project format, and is contained in *AIS_OnlineStore.zip*, which is delivered as part of the transport download and on the CD that accompanies this guidebook.

We provide an outline of such a detailed plan, intended for use by companies implementing the Online Store in a subsequent phase. This plan should be used as a starting point for an add-on implementation of the Online Store.

Monitoring Project Costs

Overview

This statement by META Group emphasizes an often neglected task: when investing in e-commerce solutions, IT organizations can get the most from their investments and partnerships if they effectively track and manage ongoing costs.

The purpose of this chapter is therefore to point out the importance of proper cost and time recording or tracking, and to raise awareness among the project management team for this issue. To assist you, this chapter introduces a template based on the ASAP for Small and Midsized Businesses (SMBs) project plan that allows proper cost and time recording for the Accelerated Internet Selling implementation project.

What We Deliver

Together with Accelerated Internet Selling, we provide a template that enables you to record the time and money planned versus spent per task and application area. The template is based on the Microsoft Project™ plan that is also delivered with this package.

The Benefit of Proper Cost Tracking

Prior to implementation, one of the most important tasks is to make all return-on-investment calculations and business justifications. Many companies fail to make hard return-on-investment (ROI) calculations for ERP applications projects, too enamored by the technology. Consulting firms now advocate that a business justification be a critical success factor for enterprise-wide IT projects. The purpose of new technologies should be to support business needs.

META Group also stresses the implications of not tracking costs in one of its latest reports. This well-known research institution had a hard time finding suitable participants for its analysis; the vast majority of potential respondents declined to participate because they had not tracked costs and therefore could not provide detailed information. This lack of cost tracking is alarming, given that best practice suggests organizations that track such information are better equipped to manage, contain, and reduce costs. By properly tracking and actively managing costs, companies could lay the groundwork for continuous planning and improvement.

But applying such lessons is not easy. Therefore, we provide a template that enables you to record this important information.

We recommend you avoid the example of those organizations that embarked on implementations because they felt they had no choice, regardless of the total cost of the implementation (TCI) or total cost of ownership (TCO), return on investment (ROI) or net present value (NPV) calculations. The template we provide allows you to perform these calculations.

Hopefully, cost reduction, productivity gains, business process improvements, and increased revenues will be the driving force behind your implementation, not just by-products.

The Cost&Time Template

The Cost&Time template has been developed based on the 4.6B ASAP project plan for SMBs. This project plan is a trimmed-down version of the standard ASAP project plan, which dramatically reduces the number of lines.

Note

The project plan from ASAP for SMBs includes several tasks for the sales cycle of the Value Added Reseller (VAR) or Certified Business Solutions (CBS) Provider. We left the project plan intact since the VARs and CBS Providers use this tool too. These tasks—shaded in purple—can be disregarded by customers using this plan and template. These tasks are:

- 1.1 Prospect Qualification (including all subtasks)
- 1.2.1 Sign Professional Service Engagement for Blueprint (including all subtasks)
- 2.4.3 Sign Contract (including all subtasks)

Where to Obtain the Template

The Cost&Time Template zip file is included on the CD that accompanies this guidebook or can be downloaded from the Simplification Group's web page at: *www.saplabs.com/ecom*.

How to Use the Template

Note

You must have Microsoft Project installed to use this template.

The following sections provide technical assistance in using Microsoft Project with the template. Explanations show how to record the money and time spent per task.

Technical Setup and Hints

Task

Download and view the Cost&Time template

The template has been developed by adding 45 columns to the project plan. Since it is not very easy to scroll around with this number of columns, five custom forms have been created for usability reasons.

1. Download the Cost&Time template from *www.saplabs.com/ecom*.

2. Open the project plan file.

3. Choose *View → Gantt Chart*. The screen should now look similar to the one below.

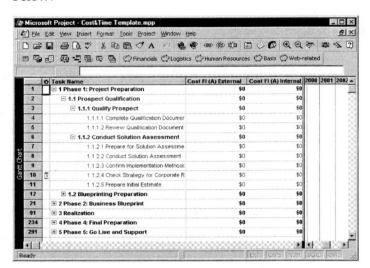

Unfortunately, not all Microsoft Project settings are downloadable. Therefore, a few settings need to be set up once the project plan has been opened. Those settings include the custom forms and buttons created for the template. Please see the instructions below.

Furthermore, the number of field names for custom columns is very limited within Microsoft Project. Therefore, field names with identifiable data format settings—such as the dollar sign ($) and appropriate number formats on the cost side, and "dys" for the time side—have been chosen for the *Actuals* columns and simple number settings for the *Budget* columns.

Task

Open the Custom Forms toolbar

The *Custom Forms* toolbar allows you to easily use the custom entry forms.

1. To open the *Custom Forms* toolbar, choose *View → Toolbars → Custom Forms*.

2. Click 🔲.

3. The *Custom Forms* dialog box appears, from which a variety of forms can be chosen. We set up the following forms for your convenience:

- *Basis – Cost and Time Entry*

- *Financials – Cost and Time Entry*

- *Human Resources – Cost and Time Entry*

- *Logistics – Cost and Time Entry*

■ *Web-related – Cost and Time Entry*

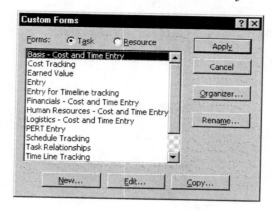

Creating the Custom Button Bar

Since many numbers have to be entered into the template, a custom button bar would allow you to call up the appropriate entry form quickly.

Task

Create custom button bar.

To create a button bar like the one above:

1. Choose *View → Toolbars → Customize.*

2. On the *Toolbars* tab, select *Custom Forms.*

3. On the *Commands* tab:

   a. In the *Categories* column, select *All Forms.* The titles of all custom forms appear in the right window.

   b. Drag and drop each of the following custom forms to a desirable location on the toolbar at the top of your screen:

- *Basis – Cost and Time Entry*
- *Financials – Cost and Time Entry*
- *Logistics – Cost and Time Entry*
- *Human Resources – Cost and Time Entry*
- *Web-related – Cost and Time Entry*

4. Right mouse click on each new button (this step only works with the *Customizing* window still open) and choose *Change Button Image*.

   a. Choose an image (for example, the piggy bank).

   b. Right mouse click on each new button again and choose *Name: <title of custom form>* to shorten the names to just the phrase before the dash.

5. Choose the *Close* button.

Exporting to Microsoft Excel™

As Microsoft Project does not allow you to analyze the entered data you can export the data to Microsoft Excel for further steps. The export of the data to Excel from Project can be started at any time during the project.

Task

Export to Microsoft Excel

To export a table to Excel in the appropriate format:

1. Choose *File → Save As*.

2. On the *Save As* dialog box:

   a. Enter the desired filename.

   b. Use the list box to choose *MS Excel Workbook (*.xls)* as the file type.

   c. Choose *Save*.

3. On the *Export Format* dialog box, choose *New Map*.

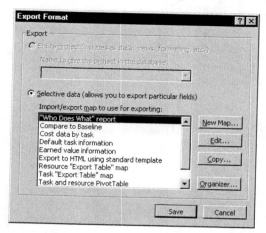

4. On the *Define Import/Export Map* screen:

  a. In *Import/Export map name*, enter the desired map name.

  b. On the *Options* tab, under *Data to import/export*, select *Tasks*.

  c. Under *Microsoft Excel options*, select *Export header row/Import includes headers*.

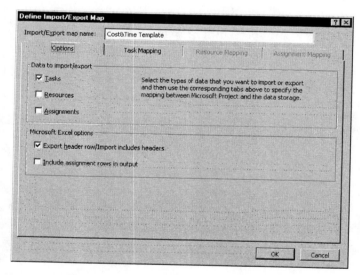

5. On the *Task Mapping* tab:

  a. Choose the *Base on the Table* button.

   b. On the *Select Base Table for Field Mapping* dialog box, select *Entry* and choose *OK*.

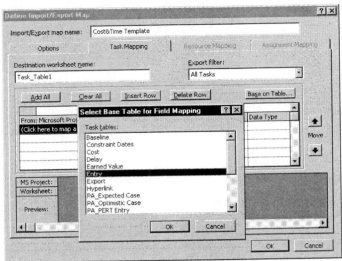

6. Back on the *Task Mapping* tab:

   a. Place your cursor in the first row.

   b. Choose *Insert Row* to insert one row at the top of the table.

   c. Under *From: Microsoft Project Field*, using the list box for the first row, select *WBS*.

   d. Select the rows starting with *ID* and *Indicator* and click *Delete Row*.

   e. Choose *OK*.

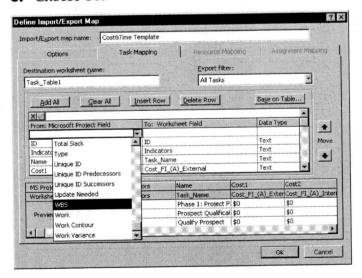

When you first open the table in Excel, it may still look unmanageable. To clean it up, use the *Pivot table* functionality to group the tasks according to task level and the columns by application area. Then you can start the autoformat *Accounting 3* to receive a table with a better layout.

 Make sure you enter the data in a nonconflicting manner. Microsoft Project does not allow you to set up a macro that could prevent data from being entered on lower and higher levels of tasks within the same branch. Therefore, you need to make sure data is entered for tasks of the same level within one branch. For example, data can be entered for task 1.1.1.1 and 1.1.1.2 but not for task 1.1.1 at the same time. If you enter data across multiple branch levels, the data will not add up correctly due to this double entry.

Even though the *Details/Comments* field appears small, lots of text can be entered to capture meaningful information for the particular task. When typing, the cursor moves to the right until the maximum number of 250 letters has been reached.

Since the template does not capture the cost for software licenses and hardware purchased, you should record these in a separate spreadsheet. These costs are needed for complete calculations of ROI (Return on Investment), and NPV (Net Present Value), and TCO (Total Cost of Ownership) or TCI (Total Cost of Implementation).

7. On the *Export Format* dialog box, select the newly created map and choose *Save*.

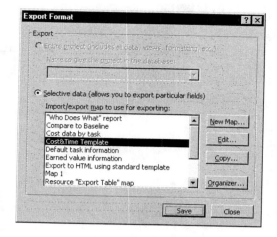

Filling Out the Template

Having completed the technical setup of the template, you are ready to enter data into the *Actuals and Budget* columns of the appropriate application areas.

Task

Fill out the template.

1. Position the cursor in line of the desired task and press a button on your customized button bar for the appropriate application area.

2. The *<Application area> - Cost and Time Entry* dialog box appears.

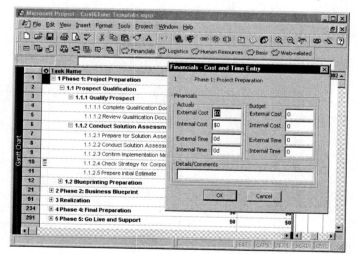

What the Template Captures

When developing the template, all possible setups were discussed. We decided to follow the approach META Group takes and set up the following categories for the cost and time entry for the Actuals and Budget numbers:

- **Resource Type** – Internal staff members and external professional services might be deployed for the implementation project. Therefore, it is important to track the cost incurred and time consumed by these resource types separately.

- **Application Area** – Separating the numbers also by the major application areas—such as Financials, Logistics, Human Resources, Basis, and web-related—as their place of occurrence provides detailed insight for further analysis. By short-listing the major issues, problems or invoice numbers will enable you to track the numbers entered back to its origin.

References

- "Enterprise Application Ongoing Support Costs Unveiled," META Group, 1999.

- Jeff Sweat, "Learning Curve - Savy Companies Apply the Painful Lessons Learned from Implementing Enterprise Resource Planning Software to Next-Generation Applications," *Informationweek*, 2 August 1999.

CHAPTER 25

The Value-Add Side

Overview

This chapter discusses the anticipated benefits and enhanced value of implementing an Internet sell-side application. To assist you during your project undertaking, this chapter presents some of the "soft" benefits, measurable components, and critical success factors you should be aware of throughout the course of your e-project. Whether you are undergoing a full-scale ERP and e-commerce implementation or just an extension to your existing R/3 System, a good grasp of the value-add side will increase your awareness of the benefits of implementing an Internet storefront.

Competitive pressures and uncharted opportunities have influenced companies to rethink their current business models and embrace the potential of an integrated e-commerce strategy. E-commerce has reoriented IT projects with new goals and expectations.

With IT funds being allocated toward launching an online business solution, it has become imperative for organizations to justify these budgets and gauge the future business prospects fueled by this investment. IT executives or e-business leaders are responsible for identifying the key drivers and "value added" by adopting an e-initiative. As with any system implementation, the challenge is to assess the competitive advantages and tangible **return on investment (ROI)** the company can anticipate based on the technologies and best practices applied. This chapter reviews the benefits of integrating an Internet sell-side application with your ERP system.

The Business of E-shopping

A global marketplace has become a reality through a virtual network of buying and selling over the Internet. People across the globe are logging on to their computers and purchasing a wide range of merchandise and services over the Internet. The enthusiasm and fascination of the World Wide Web has propelled online sales to reach record numbers. According to Forrester Research Inc., Internet sales tripled in 1999 to over $20 billion.

Note

According to Shop.org, in a study conducted by the Boston Consulting Group in the year 2000, the online retail market is expected to grow 85% and surpass $61 billion in revenues. With such tremendous growth, the opportunities in e-commerce are immense.

In today's fast-paced digital world, the business paradigm has shifted. The traditional "brick-and-mortar" retailer, the "mom and pop" shop around the corner, and the new "upstart" all recognize that providing a web-based storefront in conjunction with the current sales distribution can contribute to the company's future growth and survival. Companies selling products directly on web sites can achieve significant sales and revenue opportunities and operational savings. Offering self-service through online ordering, order tracking, and fulfillment status are attractive options for new and existing customers. The retail possibilities through this channel are not limited by geographic boundaries, time zone restrictions, or language barriers (if multilingual versions exist). The Internet allows a collaborative network of trade, communication, and shared information between the various market players—manufacturer, wholesaler, retailer, and customer—around the globe.

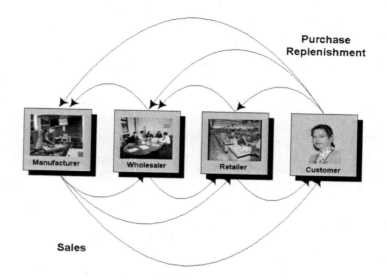

Internet selling encompasses the entire process chain of selling over the web. Through online selling, businesses use the Internet channel to increase sales opportunities with consumers (business-to-consumer), other businesses (business-to-business) and resellers (business-to-reseller). With an online store, the customer is presented with an interactive "virtual" shop where they view a comprehensive product catalog, select their desired goods or services from that catalog, and have purchases delivered directly to their home or office. While the customer partakes in this shopping experience, companies can monitor shopping activities and behavior. With web-technology, it is possible to track the web site the customer visits and how much time they stay on each page. This data can provide powerful market research for future product development and improved customer relationships through better service and one-to-one personalization.

Evaluating the Benefits of your E-business

In this age of e-business, companies not only associate value based on cost reductions and efficiencies, but also by the revenue captured based on customer relationship management and business partner networks. Companies and customers can seize the benefits and advantages of an Internet sell-side application. Let us look at the "value added" and the benefits that a company may realize by implementing an online store.

Company Benefits

Early-to-Market Advantage

Early adopters of Internet strategies can gain the advantage of web presence and branding over their respective competition. There is a first-to-market advantage for those who deploy their products or services over the Internet, gaining market exposure and capturing the loyalty of e-shoppers early on. With so many choices, customers tend to remember the pioneers who set the pace.

In today's Internet economy, if companies are late to present their product or service online, they may experience increased competition, narrow pricing flexibility, and an inability to compete in their specific market space. They may find themselves squeezed out of their market segment. Therefore, to remain competitive in this time-sensitive market, companies must be able to respond quickly to customer requirements by altering their current infrastructure and processes.

Reduced Barriers of Entry

With e-commerce, smaller companies can compete in the same market space as their larger competitive conglomerates. The Internet has leveled the playing field and reduced the barriers of entry for these businesses. Companies of any size have the same opportunity to trade their goods over the Internet because of the low cost of entry to set up an online store. The Internet has refined the value supply chain, creating new markets and new sellers.

Streamlined Business Processes

Every business process requires a transaction. Systematic and repetitive tasks that are paper-based and transaction-intensive, are the best scenarios for automation. A company can realize cost savings and efficiencies if their online business process transactions are tightly integrated with a backend fulfillment system. By web-enabling the sales process with an online order form, customers can register and enter their own sales order, which is input directly into the backend ERP system. A proficient one-phase sales transaction results. Limiting the manual intervention reduces redundancy, excessive paper flow, and errors by having the order entered only once into the system. Eliminating manual processes and waste is one of the top goals for companies initiating an Internet strategy.

Online self-service reduces the need for a large call center where customers call in or fax an order, check the status, or ask questions. The company can then focus energies on expanding customer relationships, improving the fulfillment process, and working with the channel suppliers to ensure that the inventory is available for on-time delivery and quality service.

Customer Acquisition through Multichannel Distribution

Customers expect to have a choice in the method for selecting and purchasing products. They would like to purchase items online and have the option of going to the physical store. To comply, companies may wish to consider multichanneling as a way to boost productivity, cut operating costs and increase revenue through corporate identity, customer acquisition, and repeat business.

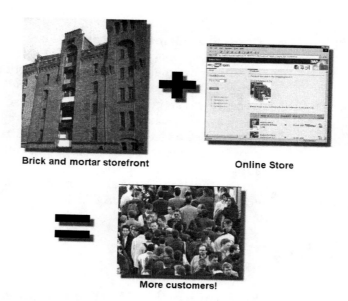

Brick and mortar storefront + Online Store

= More customers!

For smaller companies who want to expand but cannot afford to spend millions on building a physical storefront, hire sales peoples, print and distribute product catalogs, and carry inventory, using the web channel is optimum. An online store can work in parallel with an existing "brick-and-mortar" storefront by expanding the reach to prospective and existing customers.

Increased Market Share through Global Operation

An Internet storefront allows you to connect with potential customers worldwide. Manufacturers, wholesalers and retailers can communicate with one another on an international level because web sites can support multiple languages and offer product catalog versions produced with country standards (language and currency). Companies can sell in the global marketplace without having to move their headquarters or operations to another country. Market opportunity is not restricted to the region of the traditional store. The online store can reach the masses anywhere in the world where connectivity is available, which in turn can increase market share and profit.

Customer Insights

With the Internet, companies are able to track the shopping behavior of their existing and prospective customer. Companies can no longer push products to the customer. Instead, the customer is an integral part of a company's research and development, impacting the product designs and offerings. The Internet provides insights to who the customers are, what they are buying, and any feedback customers wish to provide. Customers will most likely return to your online store if it is easy to use and navigate through.

Central Information Portal – mySAP.com

Part of an Internet user's online satisfaction comes from smooth navigation, personalized product marketing, and individualized customer content. Companies can benefit from Web browser tools that allow for a centralized gateway where shopper and seller meet in an open, collaborative marketplace that enables business relationships. Centralized portals such as mySAP.com provide an electronic hub, bringing together a community of customers and suppliers for one-stop shopping, increased communication, and quick and easy navigation. Companies can take advantage by being listed as a partner company within the mySAP.com network.

Customer Benefits

Self-service: 24/7 for Convenience

With an easy–to-use web interface, the customer can shop twenty-four hours a day, seven days a week, in the convenience of his or her own home. There are no haggling sales people or long lines at the register. The Internet is perfect for an e-shopper with insomnia because the virtual shop never closes. Customers can take their time and browse through the product catalogs of multiple web shops. Shoppers can fill and save the products in a shopping basket and check out at any time.

Whether the Internet shopper is a consumer purchasing for personal consumption or a business partner purchasing for corporate supplies, the benefit of saving time and money through the convenience of electronic product catalogs is significant.

Increased Communication

Note

With the Internet, communication and services are enhanced because real-time information can be passed to the customer regarding product introductions, product information, and price changes.

With the Internet, customer and company can communicate more effectively and more rapidly. When customers can find out what products are available, what the price of the product is, and the status of their order, they feel more empowered. Customers can avoid spending hours on the phone between predefined times to speak to a customer service representative. If they have a question for the company, with online interaction, they can send an e-mail with comments or questions.

Price Transparency and Value for Money

Note

The company's web store gets marked as a favorite if it provides good customer service, personalization, and presentation.

The Internet provides the means for customers to conduct price comparisons from multiple sources. Prospective buyers search the Internet to acquire a target price range. Instead of having to drive from shop to shop looking for the best prices, customers can gain valuable information at their fingertips. With pricing information readily available, customers benefit by the discounts companies may offer to stay competitive.

Measuring your Return on Investment

The previous sections covered some of the "anticipated" benefits and added value that an online store can produce. However, a successful system implementation still requires a properly managed project plan and careful attention to quantifiable metrics to help you gauge and evaluate the cost of your investment and anticipated returns. Because the use of the Internet channel is relatively new, it is difficult to measure the expected return on investment (ROI) based on preset formulas or mathematical models. This section takes the benefits described earlier and categorizes them according to measurable components, where you can attach a quantified value or establish process performance targets.

As a guideline, we refer you to the performance-measurement model created by well-known business strategists and authors, Dr. Robert S. Kaplan and Dr. David P. Norton. They created a method for companies wanting to gauge the measurements that drive an organization's performance. In their book, *The Balanced Scorecard*, they provide a scorecard that captures the critical value-creating activities. They translate an organization's mission and strategy into a comprehensive set of performance measures that provides the framework for a strategic management system. The scorecard measures organizational performance against four perspectives:

- Financial
- Customer
- Internal processes
- Employee learning and growth

Using Kaplan and Norton's *The Balanced Scorecard* as a guide, we provide you with cost and profit metrics, and information on the tools you can use to determine and compare your company's ROI.

Financial Considerations

You can expand your whole business by adopting an online store along with your traditional sales channel. As a multifaceted organization, your company can provide the customer with a choice when it comes to shopping. The revenue buckets should be separated based on multichannel distributions of your product strategy so you can measure the incremental sales that the online sales contribute versus those of the traditional stores.

With an online order fulfillment process, the company can realize cost savings and improved use of resources. With this automated process, increased productivity can be achieved and cost reductions tracked. The company can track the reduction in capital investment against the increase of a technological investment

Monthly financial and income statements that report the state of business in terms of sales versus operating expenses and investments can be used as a tool to measure increased sales revenue, a reduction in operating costs, and asset utilization.

Customer Considerations

The cost of acquiring and retaining an existing customer can quickly exhaust company resources and funds. With an online store, the goal is to captivate the customer with personalization, great product offerings, and outstanding customer service.

With an Internet shop, you can easily track the purchases and profitability an individual customer contributes to the bottom line. By studying the purchasing habits and statistics of the various customers, the company can gauge if new service offerings need to be put into place. The company can track the ROI based on increased customer service and support, repeat customer rewards and incentive plans, and product offering personalizations that may contribute to web site ease.

Consider measuring the repeat business that a customer contributes to revenue based on the addition of an online store. Also consider measuring the influence of initiating a proactive customer service strategy. What impact to profitability does increased customer service and customer satisfaction provide to the company?

Internal Business Processes

With an online store, the traditional business processes are re-engineered. The company can measure the cost savings and increased value provided to the customer by streamlining the business operations and throughput time. An online, automated sales process can:

- Increase customer satisfaction

- Decrease response time

- Transform existing internal job roles

- Lead to increased profitability by reducing overhead.

The company can track ROI by analyzing the cost savings and increased profit generated by these business process improvements.

Note

The "virtual" store allows companies to expand their business without expanding their pocket books on real estate.

Note

The Internet allows easy tracking of customer visits and purchases made on the Web, information that can serve as a potential profitability metric.

Conduct an Activity Based Cost analysis (ABC) to determine from where the cost efficiencies and savings originate. Measure the cost per transaction to see what impact an automated process has on the number of transactions and cost savings.

Employee Learning and Growth

After implementing an Internet initiative, companies can assess the impact of this technology on their employees. Companies can learn about the skills and competencies of their employees and measure the change in productivity influenced by newly acquired skills and enhanced business processes. Companies should consider measuring employee productivity before and after the introduction of Internet technology to determine the impact.

Employee satisfaction and retention is very important to the long-term objectives of an organization. When employee morale and satisfaction are high, organizations can expect an increase in productivity and customer service, leading to increases in sales revenue. Employee turnover can be very costly to an organization. The cost to recruit and retrain a new employee effects productivity during the learning curve. Companies can monitor and measure the impact of employee retention after implementing an Internet strategy.

An IT Project represents a radical change for any organization when it influences a change in the existing corporate culture. In some cases, the mention of a new system implementation translates to layoffs, shifting of job duties, and unclear expectations. Companies must be prepared to initiate **change management** in order to relieve and prevent the workforce from feeling left behind, provide workforce development opportunities that enhance current duties, and provide meaningful work to replace administrative activities. You can measure the impact the new implementation has on employee growth and learning by gauging the number of training classes the employees enroll in and the initiative they take to develop their skills.

Critical Success Factors to Manage your E-project

A triumphant "Go Live" is the ultimate goal of your system implementation and e-project. There are key areas that are critical to the success of your project that should be taken into consideration and not overlooked.

The Internet May Be a Competitive Requirement

In today's digital economy, the Internet has emerged as a universal communication network. The wave of the future is toward online interaction for communicating and conducting business activities. Converging an Internet strategy along with a traditional business model can help companies seeking to reinvent themselves within this new economy. Companies who wish to ignore the impact and power of the Internet may find themselves out of business. The Internet could become more a competitive requirement than a competitive advantage.

ERP System Integration

A successful Internet business expands beyond an attractive web-based storefront. To accommodate the large quantity of data passing through your Internet site, an ERP backend system should be tightly integrated with your web storefront. An attractive web site without the system infrastructure to support customer demand and the volume of orders in a timely manner could cause customer dissatisfaction, and ultimately reduced profits.

Project Management

It is critical to have a clear vision and mission for your IT project. Management involvement and a clearly defined project plan contribute to the success of the implementation. Preparing a project plan with definable activities, milestones, and deliverables can keep a project within scope and according to schedule. The decision-making hierarchy and the roles and responsibilities of each project participant should be defined from the onset. Once the project plan is put into place and roles are defined, the team must be empowered to execute the plan within the given timeframes.

Cost Tracking and Recording

In order to determine the total cost of ownership and the projected ROI for your system implementation and e-project, a mechanism for capturing and tracking actual cost should be maintained. Using a cost worksheet, broken down by the various project stages, enables the project manager to analyze where the money is being allocated throughout the implementation and make timely decisions if it is determined the project is moving off course. Tracking can be especially critical for projects on a set time schedule and fixed budget.

Engaging in this discipline of tracking and recording actual costs provides the company a benchmark with which to compare returned value. It is difficult to determine the ROI if a cost metric has not been in place. A high-level cost worksheet used in a *META Group Research* study, tracks cost based on three categories—Software Fees, Application Configuration, and IT infrastructure—and separates them by implementation and ongoing support phase. We have included a cost-tracking template based on the Accelerated Internet Selling project plan in Chapter 24, "The Cost&Time Template" on page 457.

Security

Some customers may be hesitant to shop online due to the fears about sending credit card numbers over the Internet. A company must have a solid security landscape and plan in place. Make sure your credit card processing is secure using the latest encryption technology. To ease the apprehension, companies should stress security with their customers to foster a relationship of trust. When customers feel the company has taken the precautions to make their shopping experience secure, they are more likely to feel comfortable enough to shop online.

Customer Relationship Management

Note

The battle for customer retention and loyalty increased in 1999 by 15%. In a report by Jupiter Communication research, customers ranked customer service 37% as part of their purchasing incentive on the web.

Provide end-to-end customer service. Whether your customer is a consumer or business, offer them an online shopping experience with a rich product mix, personalized information, and a complete online sales process. Offer incentives and rewards for repeat business and loyalty. The shopping experience for the customer should be so satisfying that they bookmark your online store in their favorites menu.

Customers should have the comfort and confidence that online shopping is a simple, secure, and convenient method to purchase and receive their merchandise in a timely manner. It is critical that the inventory is available to promise in order to complete the order fulfillment process. If backorders occur, inform the customer of the delay and offer them a discount on their next purchase. Respond immediately to customer inquiries online through e-mail or by phone. Have an 800 number available in case of immediate technical issues. If you make a promise to the customer on your web site, make sure you follow through and fulfill the promise. Customer relationship management should be the heart and soul of your business.

Content Management

Not only should your web-based storefront be easy to use, but also provide the content and service the customer demands. New content should be updated on a regular basis, drawing customers back to your online store not only for product information, but also for the value-enhancing information. Along with selling products and services, companies can provide information as a way to educate and invite customers to return to your online store. A prospective customer may be surfing the web to gather information about a specific topic or product and come across your web page.

Reducing the Risk with Accelerated Internet Selling

A successful e-commerce strategy requires more than just a desire to sell goods and services online. Companies taking the leap into e-business must understand the integration between their frontend application and their back-office applications that reside in ERP systems. SAP Accelerated Internet Selling provides a seamless integration with your SAP R/3 System by utilizing the functional processes within the Sales and Distribution (SD) module and supporting multiple business scenarios. With Accelerated Internet Selling, all data is stored and processed in R/3, eliminating redundancy and providing the most up-to-date transactional and master data.

The packaged sell-side Internet solution provides a head start to companies wanting to sell online. The time, cost, and complexity to implement a web storefront can be significantly reduced with the accelerated solution.

References

- Dr. Robert S. Kaplan and Dr. David P. Norton, *The Balanced Scorecard*, Harvard Business School Press, Boston, MA, 1996.

- "The SAP Online Store," SAP AG White Paper, 1999.

- "Enterprise Application Ongoing Support Costs Unveiled," META Group Research, 1999.

- "E-Reality Sets In: Separating E-Fact from E-Fiction for the Second Phase of E-Business," META Group Research, November 1999.

- Dr. Howard Rubin, "Electronic Commerce: Strategy Formulation, Management/Measurement and Benchmarking," META Group Research, 1999.

Selling on the mySAP.com Marketplace

Overview

This chapter provides a brief overview about the mySAP.com™ Marketplace and how you can use the SAP Online Store and related functionality in your R/3 System to sell goods using the Marketplace.

In this chapter, you learn about the three main ways to sell on the mySAP.com Marketplace, by:

- Signing up on the Marketplace

- Offering your goods in your catalog using the Open Catalog Interface (OCI)

- Exchanging documents with customers using the Marketplace

You also learn about obtaining the SAP Business Connector (SBC) and where to get additional information.

mySAP.com Marketplace Overview

Marketplaces

Marketplaces on the Internet allow sellers to do marketing for their companies at a centralized place, offer their goods, and engage with customers in business transactions. There are closed marketplaces where only "members" trade, and open marketplaces where every interested company can sign up. There are vertical marketplaces where companies of related industries deal with each other, and marketplaces that do not focus on certain industries. Some marketplaces are designed for commerce between companies, and others allow the public to engage in transactions.

Currently, marketplaces are one of the hottest Internet-related topics. Trade journals constantly report about new marketplaces and new services as many e-commerce players try to establish a presence in this dynamic field. Only one thing seems to be certain: as the number of companies seeking Internet solutions grow, more and more implementation-related questions will need to be addressed.

mySAP.com Marketplace and Other SAP Marketplaces

Note

The mySAP.com Marketplace is not industry-specific. It is designed for business-to-business trade with over 4,800 registered companies.

SAP offers several marketplaces that are distinctive entities. The general **mySAP.com Marketplace** at *http://marketplace.mysap.com* is open to any company interested in participating and can be accessed by the general public. Additionally there are a number of other, more specialized marketplaces.

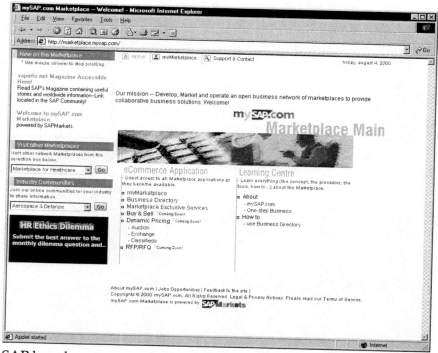

SAP has also announced other marketplaces. Among these marketplaces are ones for health care supplies, chemical companies, and the SAP services industry. Recent press announcements from SAP include:

- The launching of a mySAP.com Marketplace for the SAP Community (announced on Feb. 24, 2000)

- Deutsche Bank and SAP joining forces to bring an online financial services marketplace to mySAP.com (Feb. 23, 2000)

- Statoil and SAP teaming up to create the first open online marketplace for the oil and gas industry (Jan. 20, 2000)

- Global chemical and pharmaceuticals companies to build mySAP.com industry marketplace (Dec. 15, 1999)

- Neoforma.com and SAP partnering to create health care marketplace (Dec. 15, 1999)

Note

For more information on what SAP has to offer for Marketplaces, go to SAPNet at *www.sapnet.sap.com*:

- As a customer or partner, click *mySAP.com Marketplaces* under *SAP Solutions* for a comprehensive set of white papers, brochures, and presentations.

- As a user from the general public, click on *Solutions* on the left pane and then *Marketplaces* on the following screen.

SAP's marketplace technology is evolving rapidly. In the April 2000 release of the Marketplace software, SAP started to support auctions and RFQ/RFP business processes.

The remainder of this chapter covers only the mySAP.com Marketplace.

Selling on the mySAP.com Marketplace

To sell on the Marketplace you have two options:

- **The simple way:** Just register your company on the Marketplace. A link to your web site is placed in the Marketplace's *Business Directory*. Customers will find your company on the Marketplace, follow the link, and buy in your Online Store.

- **The integrated way:** Register as above, but allow customers to read your catalogs electronically and then exchange electronic business documents with you.

The following sections discuss:

- Registering on the Marketplace

- Enabling your product catalogs to be read electronically

Registering on the mySAP.com Marketplace

By registering your company on the mySAP.com Marketplace you allow other companies to find you in the Marketplace's Business Directory. This directory is a listing of all Marketplace participants. Users of the Marketplace can browse the directory alphabetically by business name or by product category. Users can also use a search feature.

Task

Registering on the mySAP.com Marketplace

1. Obtain a D-U-N-S number (a Dun & Bradstreet number).

2. In your Internet browser, enter `http://marketplace.mysap.com`.

3. Click *One-step business*.

4. Follow the instructions on the screen.

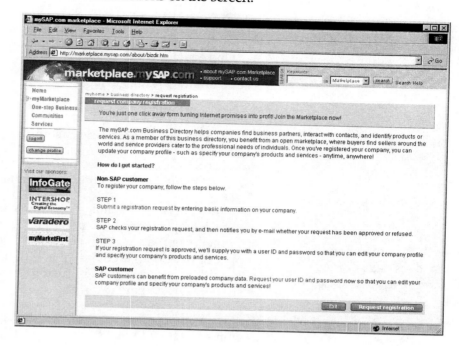

Reading the Product Catalog Electronically

A customer can manually browse your product catalog on the Internet, select a product, note the material number and price (and perhaps availability information), and then manually enter that data into the customer's procurement system. But a vendor could benefit most if a customer could bypass the use of pencil and paper and transfer all the data electronically into the company's procurement system.

There are several ways a vendor could distribute and allow access to their catalog data:

- A customer may choose to have electronic catalogs of some key vendors stored in their in-house network for fast and easy access.

- There may be an intermediary company housing the catalogs of many vendors and giving access to this data to many customers.

- A vendor may have their catalog on their own systems and allow customers to access the catalog over the Internet.

The first two scenarios are fairly customer-specific, so only the last scenario is described in this chapter.

Customer-Vendor Data Exchange

Using the mySAP.com Marketplace, a customer may want to:

- Find a vendor

- Browse a vendor's catalog

- Select products

- Retrieve the data into the customer's procurement system

The following discussion assumes that the vendor has an SAP system and uses the Online Store and the SAP Internet Transaction Server (ITS).

To allow access to the catalog and move the data into the procurement system, SAP provides the Open Catalog Interface (OCI). OCI allows the customer to embed a return address (to where the product data is later supposed to be delivered) into the URL used to access the catalog system. The return address allows the product information to be returned to the customer's procurement system.

OCI is an interface on the vendor side. The vendor has to instruct the customer on how to make use of the OCI interface.

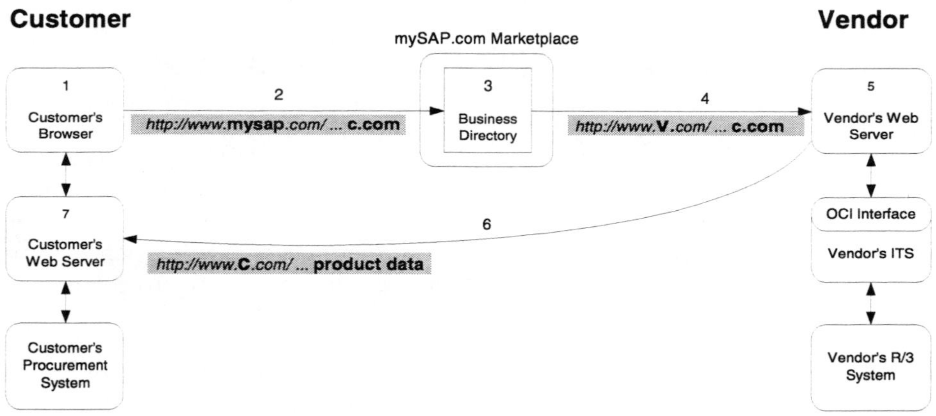

Note

SAP's Business-to-Business Procurement (BBP) product is a product with a built-in access mechanism to retrieve data from a vendor's catalog using OCI.

Task

Retrieving catalog data using OCI

1. The customer starts a new shopping session in their procurement system (for example, by opening a shopping basket).

2. The customer accesses the mySAP.com Marketplace. The URL with which the Marketplace is called (for example, `marketplace.mysap.com`) contains the return address where the customer would later like the product data to be delivered (in the above graphic called *c.com*, "c" for customer).

3. The customer browses on the Marketplace for a fitting vendor and selects that vendor.

4. The Marketplace links to the vendor's web site. The return address piece *c.com* is forwarded to the vendor's web site.

5. On the vendor's system, the customer browses the catalog, selects items, gets pricing, and clicks on a checkout button to indicate the shopping process is finished.

6. The ITS collects the data for the selected products, strips the return address out of the incoming URL, and constructs a new URL starting with the return address, followed by the product data.

7. The customer's procurement system parses the URL for the product data and enters the data into the procurement system.

SAP BBP OCI Requirements

For detailed descriptions on how the URLs need to be constructed for SAP BBP, refer to SAP's OCI 1.0 description.

Task

Obtaining the OCI 1.0 description

1. In your web browser, enter `www.sap.com/csp/scenarios`.

2. In the navigation menu on the left, scroll down and select *SAP B2B Procurement*.

3. In the table on the right, select *B2B-OCI*.

4. At the bottom of the page, use the link to download the documentation.

Exchanging Business Documents With Customers

The electronic exchange of standardized business documents streamlines the sales process. Documents such as orders arrive in the vendor's SAP R/3 System and are automatically dealt with, and responses such as order confirmations are sent out immediately without human interaction.

Business Processes

A complete cycle of business interactions can include:

1. Product selection by customer

2. Inquiry by customer

3. Quotation by vendor

4. Purchase order creation on customer side, triggering a sales order creation on vendor side

5. Order confirmation by vendor

6. Shipment notification by vendor

7. Goods receipt notification by customer

8. Invoice by vendor

9. Payment by customer

Of the above actions, it is likely that the product selection, inquiry, and quotation are performed manually. Many of the other processes can be triggered electronically.

In this chapter, we show how a sales order and order confirmation are created.

SAP Business Connector Overview

The selection of the vendor's products is done using the Online Store in R/3, but the following exchange of business documents does not involve the ITS or Online Store. Business documents are exchanged directly with the seller's R/3 System. R/3's technology to receive and send business documents is called **Application Link Enabling** (ALE). The exchanged documents are called **IDocs**.

IDocs cannot be sent directly over the Internet but require a conversion into an Internet-enabled format. The format of choice is XML. To convert IDocs into XML documents and vice versa, SAP offers a tool called the SAP Business Connector (SBC).

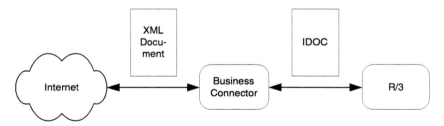

Sample Business Document Exchange

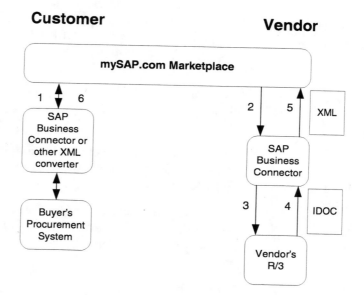

This sample document exchange is shown from a vendor's perspective:

1. The customer places an order.

2. The Marketplace routes the order as a XML document to the vendor.

3. The SBC converts the XML order document into the IDoc *ORDERS*.

4. The order is processed in R/3 and the IDoc *ORDERSP*—an order confirmation—is created.

5. The order confirmation is transported using the vendor's SBC to the Marketplace.

6. The Marketplace routes the order confirmation to the customer.

SBC Access, Information, and Support

Obtaining the SBC

The SAP Business Connector (SBC) can be obtained in two ways:

- It is shipped free of charge with any R/3 or mySAP.com component product. It is included in the mySAP.com build 2 CD package.

- It can be downloaded from SAPNet (for customers and partners). Go to *www.sapnet.sap.com/connectors* and then click on *Business Connector*. At publishing time, the current version is 3.01.

Getting More Information and Documentation on the SBC

As an SAP customer or partner, to get more information on the SAP Business Connector, go to the same place where you downloaded the software (*www.sapnet.com/connectors*, then click *Business Connector*). Among other helpful documents, you will find three very comprehensive documentation files:

- **SAP Business Connector Integration Guide**: Information on how to install, configure, and develop applications for the SAP BC Integration Module.

- **SAP Business Connector Administration Guide**: Information about using the Server Administrator to configure, monitor, and control the SAP Business Connector Server. This book is for server administrators.

- **SAP Business Connector Developers Guide**: Information about creating and testing SAP BC services and client applications. This book is for application developers.

SBC Training

There is an SBC training course as part of the R/3 Release 4.6C curriculum. Its course number is BC635

SBC Support

You can file problems on SAPnet – R/3 Frontend Notes (SAP's support system) under component BC-MID-BUS.

Technical Implementation Tasks for Business Document Exchange

SBC Server and Developer Installation

Note

This section is only intended as an overview of the necessary tasks to enable the communication between R/3 and the SBC. For detailed information, refer to the documentation accompanying the SBC.

The system requirements for SBC are:

- Windows NT 4.0 (at the time of this writing, NT was the only platform; Unix platforms are under development)

- More than 128MB of physical memory

- More than 60MB of disk space (plus space for storing the messages)

Apart from downloading the SBC (see at the beginning of this section), the following software is needed:

- Sun Java Development Kit (JDK) 1.1 (can be downloaded at *http://java.sun.com/products/jdk/1.1/*)

- Microsoft Internet Explorer 4 or 5 (can be downloaded at *http://www.microsoft.com*)

The SBC runs against R/3 Systems of Release 3.1H or higher.

SBC Database Configuration

By configuring a database for the SBC, all the transactions and logs can be saved and examined.

ALE/IDoc Configuration

Perform the usual steps of setting up your ALE system:

1. Set up a logical system.
2. Create an RFC destination.
3. Maintain a distribution model.
4. Set up your partner profile.
5. To verify the results, enter transaction **WE20** in the *Command* field and choose *Enter*.

R/3 SD Configuration

Verify that several items have been set up:

- The customer
- The materials the customer is buying
- Output determination

  For the output type identified in the ALE configuration, set up a master data record for a key combination of at least document type *EC*. The medium of this record needs to be identified with an *A* for Distribution (ALE).

Setting Up The SBC - R/3 Communication

The communication between R/3 and the SBC works using RFCs. To communicate with R/3 RFCs and BAPIs, the SBC needs to be set up as an RFC client to send data to R/3 and as an RFC server to receive data from R/3. For IDocs, tRFCs are used. The following steps need to be performed:

1. Set up the proxy information.
2. Set up an R/3 server for which to send documents.
3. Set up a listener to receive documents from an R/3 System.

Routing an IDoc to the Marketplace

The portal (the mySAP.com Marketplace) needs to be defined in the SBC. In the SBC, you can determine to where documents are delivered by use of routing rules.

Note

If you need more information about R/3's ALE features, please consult the online help. It contains four well written sections on ALE:

- Quickstart Guide (about 19 pages)
- Application scenarios
- Programmer's guide
- IDoc Maintenance (if you want to alter IDocs)

Retrieving XML Documents from the Marketplace

In the SBC, you can determine how often the Marketplace should be polled for new documents.

CHAPTER 27

Internet Selling Information

Web sites

The links below provide additional information on topics related to the Accelerated Internet Selling preconfiguration. The Accelerated Internet Selling solution is located on the site *www.saplabs.com/ecom.*

Web site	Topic
www.sap.com/e-commerce	Information about sell-side Internet scenarios (choose *Selling* from SAP's e-commerce site)
www.saplabs.com/its	Information about the Internet Transaction Server (ITS), plus software and documentation downloads. Can also download *ITS Administration Guide, Release 4.6D* (283 pages) and *ITS Tuning Guide, Release 4.6D* (57 pages)
www.saplabs.com/ess	Information about Employee Self-Service (ESS).
www.cybercash.com/ www.paylinx.com/ www.trintech.com/ www.trustmarque.com www.xitcorp.com/	Information about certified partners that provide credit card authorization and clearing processing (in alphabetical order): CyberCash, PaylinX, Trintech, TrustMarque, and XiTechnologies.
www.taxware.com/ www.vertex.com/	Information about certified external tax packages (in alphabetical order): Taxware and Vertex.
www.saplabs.com/pcc/	Information about the Preconfigured Client, which may be used in conjunction with the Accelerated Internet Selling product.
shop.sap.com/	Shop for SAP-brand merchandise and educational items in the SAPshop.
www.saplabs.com/ess	Employee Self-Service information and book.
www.tealeaf.com	Company that offers web statistics solutions.

Other References

- Randi Barshack, "Shades of Gray: Privacy and Online Marketing," *E-Commerce Times*, 28 August 2000.

- D. Brent Chapman and Elizabeth D. Zwicky, *Building Internet Firewalls*, (O'Relly, 1995).

- William Cheswick and Steven Bellovin, *Firewalls and Internet Security: Repelling the Wily Hacker*, (Addison-Wesley, 1994), ISBN: 0201633574, (2nd edition: July 2000).

- "Enterprise Application Ongoing Support Costs Unveiled," META Group Research, 1999.

- "E-Reality Sets In: Separating E-Fact from E-Fiction for the Second Phase of E-Business," META Group Research, November 1999.

- Marcus Goncalves, *Firewalls: A Complete Guide,* (Osborne, 1999).

  ___ *Firewalls Complete (Complete Series),* (McGraw-Hill, 1998).

- Marcus Goncalves and Vinicius Goncalves, *Protecting Your Web Site with Firewalls,* (Prentice Hall, 1997).

- Dr. Robert S. Kaplan and Dr. David P. Norton, *The Balanced Scorecard,* (Harvard Business School Press, Boston, MA, 1996).

- Dr. Howard Rubin, "Electronic Commerce: Strategy Formulation, Management/Measurement and Benchmarking," META Group Research, 1999.

- "The SAP Online Store," SAP AG White Paper, 1999.

- *SAP@Web Installation Guide, Release 4.6B,* Material #51007411 (Walldorf, SAP AG, 1999).

- Mathew Strebe, *Firewalls: 24seven,* (Sybex, 1999).

- Jeff Sweat, "Learning Curve - Savy Companies Apply the Painful Lessons Learned from Implementing Enterprise Resource Planning Software to Next-Generation Applications," *Informationweek,* 2 August 1999.

PART SIX

Appendixes

SAPNet Frontend Notes

Overview

During an implementation of the Online Store, you may need to apply one or more notes to get the R/3 System functionality to work correctly. For the Internet Application Components (IACs), many notes have been written for informational purposes, providing you with configuration recommendations.

The list of SAPNet Frontend Notes below is not intended to be a comprehensive list, but represents the notes most commonly required during an Online Store implementation.

Product Catalog

The IAC for the product catalog is WW10.

Note	Description
135661	This note describes how to customize the euro. It also provides an update program that verifies all settings are correct and makes any missing entries. This note is required when the product catalog should be displayed in multiple currencies.
91481	This note contains additional information about customizing the euro.

Product Catalog with Integration to Procurement

 The IAC for the product catalog called from a procurement application is *WW30*. This IAC has not been preconfigured, but may be valuable for customers who wish to use the Online Store in such a scenario.

Note	Description
172340	This note describes the parameters that need to be passed when the product catalog is called from the BBP (business-to-business procurement) application.

Online Store

 The IAC for the Online Store is *WW20*.

Note	Description
138684	This note describes the configuration necessary for prices to be displayed on the Internet.
99816	This note describes the required product catalog structure for displaying products.
113481	This note lists all data required for creating the product catalog.
139471	This note describes an error encountered in creating customer numbers, and describes why customer number ranges must be internal.
190536	This note describes the required configuration for the data carrier, so that all products can be displayed.
169091	This note allows subtotals from the pricing procedure to be passed to the Internet, so that price breakouts can be displayed in the Online Store.
212783	This note corrects a problem with the tax calculation when a different delivery address is entered, or when a one-time customer is used. The correct tax calculation requires the user exit for tax jurisdiction code determination to be in place (the user exit is preconfigured).
196608	This note enables the screen display of the region (state) field for the sold-to customer just prior to placing the order.
213898	This note enables the screen display of the region (state) field for the ship-to customer just prior to placing the order.
187143	This note solves an error in the address management of the one-time customers created from the Online Store.
150650	This note discusses how the availability check should be configured to obtain the desired results on the quotation screen.
315142	This note corrects the partner determination in orders when consumers are used in the Online Store.
197819	This note allows partner determination based on the customer hierarchy to be configured in SD.

Note	Description
210298	This note allows partner determination based on the customer hierarchy to be performed in the Online Store.
314819	This note allows partner determination based on the customer hierarchy to be performed in the Online Store.
197511	This note corrects a problem with saving consumers when personal data is not maintained.

Sales Order Status

 The IAC for the sales order status is *VW10*.

Note	Description
179338	This note adds the display of the region (state) field.
182633	This note corrects a security issue in which a customer could display another customer's order. This problem only occurred when the order number was specified during the initial order selection.
188482	This note discusses the Y2K date format for shipping data.
143145	This note discusses the URL length for the sales order status. The URL cannot exceed 132 characters.
206887	The customer and password combination are verified before displaying orders. This note corrects an error in which the wrong customer is displayed when multiple customers have the same e-mail address but different passwords.

Available to Promise

 The IAC for the available-to-promise check is *CKAV*.

Note	Description
168837	This note discusses reasons why the ATP IAC does not work with Netscape Navigator 4.0.

General

 These notes apply to multiple IACs.

Note	Description
99166	This note describes the get/set parameters required in the ITS user master record that support the IACs.
86334	This note provides general recommendations on where to find information about ITS.
195318	This note discusses a get/set parameter for the ITS user in 4.6, after going through an upgrade.
183845	This note provides a technical overview of IACs and lists other SAP Front-End notes that are available to solve specific problems.

Technical SAP Enhancement: ATP in the Product Catalog

Overview

This enhancement could easily be extended to assign some meaning to the threshold quantity of the material master, such as "his product ships normally in 3–4 eeks," by adding new values for the reshold code and threshold escription.

In the standard Online Store, the availability of products is not displayed while browsing the product catalog; a different Internet Application Component (IAC) is provided for this functionality. Due to customer requests, the capability to display product availability is included in the Online Store preconfiguration as an enhancement. For information about the Online Store, please refer to chapter 1, "Creating the Online Store with the Catalog" on page 5.

Stock availability for the products in the Online Store is displayed on two web pages in the Online Store:

- On the product listing page, the availability is displayed using status icons. An icon indicates whether the item is currently in stock (green = in stock, yellow = fast moving item, red = out of stock).

- On the product detail page, the availability is displayed as the available quantity in stock.

The availability status is based on the new product-specific field *Threshold quantity* in the material master. The following icons are used in our preconfiguration:

- ⚪ (green) – Available quantity is greater than the threshold quantity, or the threshold quantity is not maintained.

- △ (yellow) – Available quantity is greater than 0 and lower than, or equal to, the threshold quantity.

- ✖ (red) – Available quantity is zero.

You must make two decisions with regards to the availability check:

- Displaying the availability for one plant or across all plants

- Using a static or a dynamic availability check

Customer Experience: Display Product Availability in the Online Store

While browsing the product catalog in the Online Store, the availability of the product can be displayed in two ways:

- As a "traffic-light" icon

- As the actual quantity in stock

The quantity is determined based on the parameter settings for the plants, the type of availability check, and the threshold in the material master record.

Traffic light icon

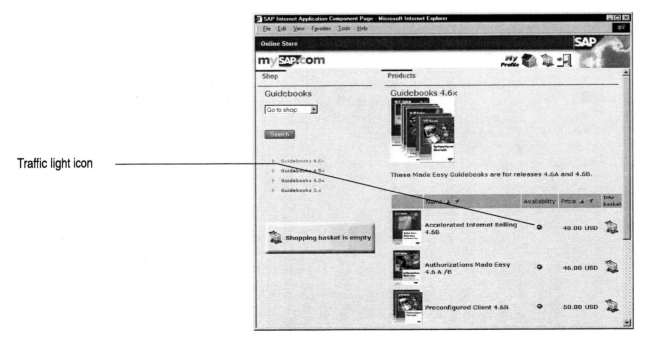

The detail screen of the product displays the quantity remaining in stock.

Quantity in stock

Options for Displaying Availability

Displaying the Availability for One Plant or Across All Plants

You must decide whether to display the availability of the product using the delivery plant or across all your plants. The system initially looks for the delivery plant information in the customer master record. If it is not maintained there, the system looks for the information in the material master record.

Keep in mind that when individual customers register on the Internet, the delivery plant is copied from the reference customer. Since the plant information is copied, a determination is not made as to which plant is closest to the customer. A finer distinction is possible in a scenario in which you sell to business partners with whom you have a business relationship, and can enter this plant based on the customer's location.

At the time the order is placed in the standard Online Store functionality, the availability check is based on only the delivery plant. For this reason, if you choose to display the availability of a product across all of your plants while browsing the catalog, the R/3 System may determine that an item you show as in stock is actually unavailable in the delivery plant. Internally, this result means that the item is available in another plant. Customer orders are accepted independent of the stock availability. If the order quantity could not be confirmed, the customer is not provided with a delivery date when the order is placed in the Online Store. Internally, the order is proposed to a sales

Note

The transports for the Online Store preconfiguration do not include changes to the standard programs of the Online Store. In the case of the availability information, a standard user exit and corresponding enhancement project are transported. All other "hooks" into the standard material master data structure and workflow must be created manually. Instructions are provided in the Installation Guide.

agent using workflow. The responsibilities of the sales agent should then include contacting the customer with a firm delivery date, based on the plant in which the product is available.

In making the determination of which plants should be used to show availability of products while browsing the catalog, the following situations should be considered:

- Are most products produced at only one plant or multiple plants? If most of your products are produced at only one plant, a cross-plant availability check may not make sense.

- How far apart are your plants? If you have one plant in the U.S. and another plant in Asia, and a customer orders a product in the U.S., would shipment of a product from Asia to the U.S. be cost-prohibitive? Would the time it takes to ship the product be longer than producing the item in the U.S. (local) plant? On the other hand, if all your plants are located in different cities in Texas, a cross-plant check would allow the customer to receive the product more quickly, without a cost impact for freight on your company.

- Are your plants in different countries? If you do a cross-plant check, how will this impact your taxes, shipping documents, customs, and so on? If all of your plants are in Europe, there is less of an impact than if you have one plant in the U.S. and another in Europe.

- How often do you expect the sales agent to be required to contact the customer with an updated delivery date? The response time is very important for customers ordering on the Internet.

Using a Static or a Dynamic Availability Check

You must also decide whether to base the availability check on the quantity of material remaining in stock at the time the order is placed, or on the available-to-promise quantity configured in the Sales and Distribution module (SD). The quantity of material is based on the unreserved stock in inventory (static check). The ATP stock is based on the default ATP rule configured in SD (dynamic check). Within this rule, you may determine the quantities included in the availability calculation. The ATP rule can be configured to include reservations on inventory from other customers, planned receipts based on purchases and production schedules, and so on. ATP is also the check used at the time the order is placed through the Online Store. The default rule is also used for the ATP service, and is discussed in chapter 9, "Available to Promise" on page 223.

When determining whether to show product availability while browsing the catalog, the following situations should be considered:

- Are most of your customers business partners or consumers? For business partners, it will be more important to process a delivery check based on ATP rules and a delivery date the customers enter, while consumers generally visit another web site if the product is not currently in stock.

- How long is the lead time on obtaining (buying or producing) your products? If the lead time is short, a complex ATP calculation does not make sense and will only reduce performance of your Online Store.

- Are the products fast-moving? If there is a high probability that product availability may change in the course of a day because of high demand, you may wish to use ATP since the orders placed by other customers are taken into account during the processing of the availability information.

- How often do you expect the sales agent to be required to contact the customer with an updated delivery date? The response time is very important for customers ordering on the Internet.

Implementation of the Modification

For the extensions to SAP standard that need to be implemented, you must:

- Create the Online Store preconfiguration parameters (preconfigured).

- Enter the delivery plant in the appropriate master data.

- Extend the material master with the *Threshold quantity* field.

- Calculate and transfer the stock availability to the web pages for display (preconfigured).

- Create a workflow for orders that could not be confirmed (preconfigured).

- Update the ITS templates to work with the modifications (preconfigured).

Create the Online Store Preconfiguration Parameters

This table has been preconfigured for you. Create a new table that contains the parameter names and parameter values required by the user exit. The table contains a parameter with a value to represent whether the stock availability should be summed up across all plants or just reflect the main delivery plant of the customer. If the delivery plant is not maintained for the customer, the delivery plant of the material is used. Another parameter identifies sales document types being used for orders generated through the Online Store preconfiguration.

The table *ZESHOP_CFGPARAMS* is delivered with the Online Store preconfiguration. It contains the configuration parameters used in the delivered enhancements. The following table entries are delivered:

Char (parameter)	+ (value)	Description (not in table)
PCAT_BROWSER_STOCK_AGGREGATE	N	Aggregate across plants?
PCAT_BROWSER_STOCK_DYNAMIC	Y	Dynamic check?
PCAT_BROWSER_STOCK_DYNAMIC_RULE	02	Checking rule to use if ATP is used
PKAT_BROWSER_DEBUG	Y	Allows debugging through the ITS
PKAT_BROWSER_ORDER_TYPE1	YWO	First order type used for selling on the Internet
PKAT_BROWSER_ORDER_TYPE2	YWRE	Second order type used for selling on the Internet

To change the values in this table, in the *Command* field, enter transaction **SM30** and choose *Enter* (or from the menu bar, choose *System → Services → Table maintenance → Extended table maintenance*). In the *Table/view* field, enter **ZESHOP_CFGPARAMS** and choose *Maintain*. You can also run the install wizard, as documented in the Installation Guide. In the *Command* field, enter transaction **SA38** and choose *Enter* (or from the menu bar, choose *System → Services → Reporting*). Then run the program **ZESHOP_WIZARD**.

Enter the Delivery Plant in the Appropriate Master Data

If the availability check should occur for only one plant, the plant is determined by finding the delivery plant entered in the master data, first in the customer master record and then in the material master record

To enter the delivery plant in the customer master, in the *Command* field, enter transaction **XD02** and choose *Enter* (or from the navigation menu, choose *Logistics → Sales and Distribution → Master Data → Business Partners → Customer → Change → Complete*). Enter the customer number and sales area. Choose *Sales area data* in the customer master, then choose the *Shipping* tab. In the *Delivering plant* field, enter the plant from which most products will be delivered for this customer.

To enter the delivery plant in the material master, in the *Command* field, enter transaction **MM02** and choose *Enter* (or from the navigation menu, choose *Logistics → Materials Management → Material Master → Material → Change → Immediately*). Choose the *Sales: Sales Org. Data 1* view. Enter the plant, sales organization, and distribution channel used for your Internet business. In the *Delivering plant* field, enter the plant from which this product will be delivered most often for your Internet business.

Example

Table *ZESHOP_CFGPARAMS* contains two fields: *FNAME,* 40 characters for the parameter name, and *FVAL,* 128 characters for the parameter value.

As table content, enter parameter name **PKAT_BROWSER_STOCK_AGGREGATE** and parameter value **Y** if you want to aggregate the stock availability across all plants, or parameter value **N** if you want the stock availability to reflect only the main delivery plant of the customer.

Set parameter value **Y** for **PKAT_BROWSER_STOCK_DYNAMIC** if the available quantity should be calculated dynamically based on checking rule **A** or whatever is specified under parameter **PKAT_BROWSER_STOCK_DYNAMIC_RULE**, or **N** if the unrestricted-use stock should be used.

Enter parameter name **PKAT_BROWSER_ORDER_TYPE1** and parameter value **YWO** for your Online Store preconfiguration order type. If you use additional order types, enter **PKAT_BROWSER_ORDER_TYPE2**, its value, and so on.

Extend the Material Master with the Threshold Quantity Field

Note

In the Online Store preconfiguration, we provide structure *ZAMARA* and data element *ZTRES*.

ZTRES is based on the domain *MENG13V* and references the basic unit of measure *MARA-MEINS*.

This step has been preconfigured for you if you followed the instructions in the Installation Guide. The modification delivered with the Online Store includes a structure and subscreen that can be used to extend the material master. The *Threshold quantity* field is added to the material master and allows you to enter the threshold value. When the stock reaches the threshold value or drops below it, a yellow icon appears. If no threshold value is entered, a green light will be displayed.

Task

Add a threshold quantity field to the material master

1. Extend the material master table *MARA* by creating an append structure that holds the new field for threshold quantity.

2. Include the new field in the material master maintenance transaction by creating and inserting a new subscreen for the screen container *BASIC DATA.*

See the online documentation in the IMG to configure the material master. Choose *Logistics - General → Material Master → Configuring the Material Master → Here's How [Quick Guide Using an Example]).*

Task

Add the structure and subscreen to the material master

1. In the *Command* field, enter transaction **OMT3B** and choose *Enter* (or in the IMG, choose *Logistics – General → Material Master → Configuring the Material Master → Define Structure of Data Screens for Each Screen Sequence*).

2. Please refer to the Installation Guide for step-by-step instructions. You may choose to add the delivered structures elsewhere in the material master.

Calculate and Transport Stock Availability to Web Pages for Display

This step has been preconfigured for you. Two user exits are available that allow additional fields to be displayed in the product list and in the detail view of the product catalog. The changes made to implement the user exit are described below. To deactivate the user exit, simply deactivate the enhancement project. Enhancement project *YE_PC* is delivered with the Online Store preconfiguration.

In the *Command* field, enter transaction **CMOD** and choose *Enter* (or from the navigation menu, choose *Tools → ABAP Workbench → Utilities → Enhancements → Project Management*). The project is active in the Online Store preconfiguration.

Project	Enhancement	Function Exit	Include
YE_PC	WOSX0001	EXIT_SAPMWWMJ_001	ZXWOSU01
	WOSX0002	EXIT_SAPMWWMJ_002	ZXWOSU02

- SAP enhancement *WOSX0001* with function module *EXIT_SAPMWWMJ_001* is available to transport the quantity of the unrestricted-use stock to the product detail screen of the Online Store.

- SAP enhancement *WOSX0002* with function module *EXIT_SAPMWWMJ_002* is available to determine the stock availability status icon and to transport it to the product-listing screen of the Online Store.

Detail Specification

Determine stock parameters:

- Read table *ZESHOP_ZFGPARAMS* with the parameter for the delivery plant aggregation indicator *PCAT_BROWSER_STOCK_AGGREGATE*.

If parameter value requests main plant only, determine main delivery plant:

- Read product catalog using function call *ADV_MED_READ* to retrieve sales organization and reference customer.

- If a customer has logged on and enhancement parameter *PI_CUSTOMER* has been specified, determine ship-to party through customer hierarchy using function call *SD_PARTNER_DETERMINATION* (see function *VIEW_KUAGV* on how this function can be used). If no delivery plant has been specified in the ship-to customer master, use the delivery plant from the material master.

- If *PI_CUSTOMER* is not specified, read the delivery plant from the reference customer master specified in the Online Store profile, available through enhancement parameter *PI_TWICOSTORE-KUNNR*. If it is not available, the customer master in the product catalog basic data is used. If the delivery plant information is not maintained in the customer master,

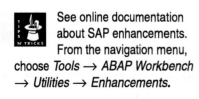

See online documentation about SAP enhancements. From the navigation menu, choose *Tools → ABAP Workbench → Utilities → Enhancements*.

the delivery plant is read from the material master record linked to the product catalog. If no customer-specific delivery plant is available, use the delivery plant specified in the material master.

Calculate unrestricted-use stock for the material master:

- Read the threshold quantity *ZTRES* and the basic unit of measure *MEINS* from the material master *MARA*.

- If the delivery plant of the material master is to be used as main delivery plant, read *DWERK* from *MVKE*.

- The configuration parameter *PKAT_BROWSER_STOCK_DYNAMIC* determines how the available quantity is calculated. If the unrestricted-use stock is checked, the quantity *LABST* is read from *MARD*. If the SD setting for ATP is checked, a function call to *BAPI_MATERIAL_AVAILABILITY* is made. Use only positive quantities without decimals.

- If the unit of display specified in the layout area of the product catalog, available through enhancement parameter *PI_PRODUCT-UNIT*, is different from the material master base unit of measure, convert the stock quantity using function call *MATERIAL_UNIT_CONVERSION*.

Transfer availability flag and quantity to the web pages:

- Determine the stock availability flag by comparing available and threshold quantities.

- Convert the available stock quantity to a character field according to the display unit of measure and with no leading zeros.

- Set the context fields per product using macro *FIELD-SET*. Transport the context space per screen or web page using macro *FIELD-TRANSPORT*.

Since these routines are processed frequently, it is advisable to reduce database accesses (for example, by determining the main delivery plant and the available or threshold quantities) by storing the results from the database in the internal program buffer and refreshing these only when needed.

The new fields are not displayed on the SAP screens *SAPMWWMJ_3420*, *SAPMWWMJ_3430*, and *SAPMWWMJ_4260*. If you want to display the new fields on the SAP screens for debugging purposes, you need to make changes to the layout and flow logic of these screens and to the screen structures *WIC_PRODUCT* and *WIC_DETAIL*. These changes are modifications without SAP-provided user-exits.

These changes are delivered with the HTML ^Business^ templates in the Online Store preconfiguration.

Note

The new fields are now available for the HTML template but are not displayed yet. The HTML templates must be enhanced with HTML ^Business^ commands. The following changes must be made in the templates:

- Template *SAPMWWMJ_3420* must be modified to display the status icon.

- Templates *SAPMWWMJ_3420* and *SAPMWWMJ_4260* must be modified to display the available quantity.

The HTML ^Business^ templates delivered with the Online Store preconfiguration already contain these modifications.

Create a Workflow for Processing an Unconfirmed Order

This step has been preconfigured for you if you followed the instructions in the Installation Guide.

Note

Before you start, you need to plan a few things:

- Plan the PD organization for the workflow processing. Please note that it is not necessary to configure the Human Resources (HR) module to make use of the PD organization.

- Who is going to be the workflow administrator in case of technical errors?

- Do you want the tasks to be general tasks? Please note that having general tasks would send a work item to all members of an organization and therefore is not recommended.

- Who are going to be processors for the application-level errors? The best practice is to assign positions or jobs rather than individuals, making it easier to maintain workflows.

1. Create a user *WF_BATCH* of type *CPIC*. In the *Command* field, enter transaction **SU01** and choose *Enter* (or choose *Tools → Administration → User Maintenance → Users*). Please refer to the Installation Guide for the detailed steps to do this.

2. Run the workflow customizing wizard with transaction **SWU3**. Perform all the steps of the wizard. Without this customization, the workflow will not work. Each step of the wizard provides explanations. We recommend reviewing the initial chapters of Workflow online help (at *help.sap.com*,choose *SAP Library in HTML format → Release 4.6B English →* Basis *Components → Business Management → SAP Business Workflow*) to understand the concepts and take advantage of workflow.

3. Review the task. In the *Command* field, enter transaction **PFTC_CHG** and choose *Enter* (or choose *Tools → Business Workflow → Development → Definition Tools → Tasks/Task Groups → Change.*)

4. In the *Task Type* field, choose *Standard Task*. In *Task*, enter the task **90100003**. Choose ✏ .

5. To assign the message agent who will process the work item, choose the *Default Roles* tab. We recommend you assign job positions, rather than actual individuals, as message agents. In the PD organization, you would have assigned the users to the position.

6. In the *Triggering Events* tab of the task view, check that the event is displayed. Save the task.

7. In the *Command* field, enter transaction **SWETYPV** and choose *Enter.* Search for the combination of the object type *BUS2032* and event *Created*. Double-click the listing you have found to display the detail view of the event linkage. Ensure that the function *ZSWE_CHK_DPLANTSPLIT_WF_REQD* is assigned in the *Check function* field.

Detail Specification

Create standard task:

We created the standard task *90100003* that sends a message to the assigned agent. Please ensure that the relevant agents are assigned as per your organizational structure.

Create check function module:

We have already provided the check function *ZSWE_CHK_DPLANTSPLIT_WF_REQD*. This check function determines whether to proceed with the workflow, based on the availability of the product ordered at the specified delivery plant.

Restrict processing to Online Store orders:

Retrieve sales document type of the sales order and check against parameter *PCAT_BROWSER_ORDER_TYPE%* in table *ZESHOP_ZFGPARAMS*. If it is not an Online Store order, raise *ANY_EXCEPTION*.

Determine the unconfirmed order items:

- Call the new custom function module *Z_YESHOP_ATP_CHECK* that expects the sales order number *I_VBELN* as input and returns a table *O_VBAP* with unconfirmed order items.

- The called function checks for each order item *VBAP* if it could be confirmed by comparing the cumulated ordered quantity *KWMENG* with the cumulated confirmed quantity *KBMENG*. If *KBMENG* is smaller than *KWMENG*, return the item in the parameter table *O_VBAP* to the calling program.

- If the order has no unconfirmed items, the function returns an empty table *O_VBAP* and the program raises *ANY_EXCEPTION*. In these cases, the workflow will not be triggered as no action needs to be taken.

- Once the workflow starts, e-mails are sent to all agents assigned to the task. For the first processor of the work item, it brings up the sales order in change mode and has the *VBAPD-EPMEH* field checked for all the items that needs to be reviewed for unconfirmed quantities.

Update the ITS Templates to Work with the Modifications

For the availability of products to be displayed on the quotation screen, changes need to be made in the ITS templates. This step has been preconfigured for you.

The template files in the AGate directory structure of ITS have been modified to allow customers to display availability in the product catalog. The template files are located in the ITS AGate directory, under the directory structure *<its_root>\templates\ww20\sg*, where the *<its_root>* is your virtual ITS installation, and *sg* is the theme delivered with the Online Store preconfiguration. In addition, the language-resource file has been changed so variables could be added for the availability icons and text.

The following files are modified to support the availability logic:

Template	Change
SAPMWWMJ_3420.HTML	Display traffic-light icons in product list
SAPMWWMJ_3430.HTML	Display quantity in product detail screen
WW20_EN.HTRC	Variables for descriptions of the quantity and icons

Task

Modify the ITS templates

The following changes have been made in the HTML ^{Business} templates:

- In template *SAPMWWMJ_3420.HTML*, the traffic light icons are displayed, along with a legend that describes the icons.

- In template *SAPMWWMJ_3430.HTML*, the quantity is added to the display of the detail information.

Task

Modify the language-resource file

The file *ww20_en.htrc* is the language-resource file that contains values for the language-specific variables used for the IACs. The following variables have been added to support the availability logic:

Parameter	Value
_3420_header_stock	Availability
_3430_stock	In stock:
notinstock	Out of stock
instock	In stock
stock_trashhold	Critical amount in stock

The Shopping Basket

Overview

This appendix provides a detailed functional description and step-by-step instructions concerning the technical changes for two add-on functionalities we provide:

- Displaying the current basket content
- Saving the current shopping basket

The first enhancement displays the current contents of the shopping basket in the left frame. It allows users to see an overview of the items in their basket and the total price of their selections.

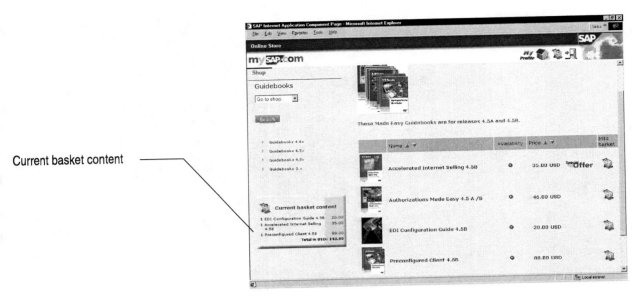

Current basket content

The second add-on function gives shoppers the choice of saving the current shopping basket and retrieving it at a later time.

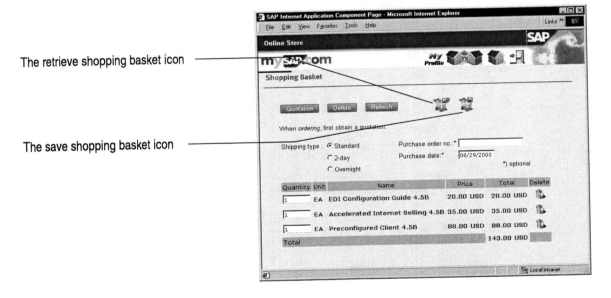

The retrieve shopping basket icon

The save shopping basket icon

Customer Experience: Displaying Current Shopping Basket Content

The display of the shopping basket gives the user the ability to view on screen what items have been added to the shopping basket, including the total price.

The shopping basket is always displayed while the customer is browsing the product groups.

This shopping basket only displays a message when it does not contain any items.

A running total is displayed when products are added to the shopping basket. However, the freight and tax are not calculated in the window. The customer might not have logged in, provided a shipping address for the tax calculation, or chosen a shipping method for freight calculation.

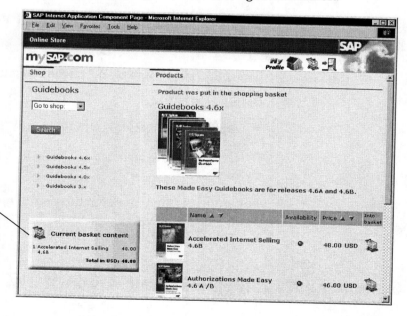

You can go to the shopping basket by choosing the shopping basket icon or header text.

Implementation of the Modification

To implement the modification to the SAP standard system and obtain this functionality, you must:

- Create the include program with the logic to display the shopping basket (preconfigured)

- Extend the Online Store program to include processing for displaying the shopping basket

- Update the ITS templates to work with the modifications (preconfigured)

Create the Include Program with the Logic to Display the Shopping Basket

This include program has been preconfigured for you. It contains the logic to maintain an internal table that contains all the items a customer has placed into the shopping basket. This internal table contains a the relevant fields that are displayed in the basket window.

Extend the Online Store Program to Include Processing for Displaying the Shopping Basket

The following program and screen must be changed:

- SAPMWWMJ

- SCREEN 3000 of program SAPMWWMJ

Please refer to the Installation Guide for instructions on making these modifications.

For more information about this shopping basket, see chapter 14, "ITS Templates" on page 327, sections "Current Shopping Basket" and "Changing Graphics."

Update the ITS Templates to Work with the Modifications

This step has been preconfigured for you. For the functionality to be for displaying the shopping basket, changes need to be made to the ITS templates.

The template files in the AGate directory structure of ITS have been modified to display the shopping basket. The template files are located in the ITS AGate directory, under the directory structure *<its_root>\templates\ww20\sg*, where the *<its_root>* is your virtual ITS installation, and *sg* is the theme delivered with the Online Store preconfiguration. In addition, the language-resource file has been changed so variables could be added for the basket text.

The following files are modified to support the display of the shopping basket:

Template	Change
SAPMWWMJ_3310.HTML	Added the display of the shopping basket
WW20_EN.HTRC	Variable for descriptions of the basket

Task

Modify the ITS templates

Template *SAPMWWMJ_3310.HTML* has been modified to include the display of the shopping basket.

Task

Modify the language-resource file

The file *ww20_en.htrc* is the language-resource file that contains values for the language-specific variables used for the IACs. The following variables have been added to support the basket texts:

Parameter	Value
currentbasket	Current basket content
currentbasket_empty	Shopping basket is empty
totalin	Total in

Saving the Shopping Basket

The store-and-retrieve shopping basket functions could also be the base for an enhancement that enables a user-specific, wish-list functionality.

Users can store their shopping baskets and retrieve them at a later session. This functionality is common on many web sites, and allows customers to return to your shop at a later time to place an order, without needing to repeat a search to find the desired products.

Customer Experience: Saving and Retrieving the Shopping Basket

For the save-and-retrieve shopping baskets to work, the customer must be logged in. If the customer is not logged in when calling these functions, the logon screen is called by the enhancement.

The functionality of saving the shopping basket allows customers to:

- Save a shopping basket

- Retrieve a saved shopping basket

- Replace a saved shopping basket (when a customer saves a shopping basket, all old items in the basket are replaced by the new items)

Note

Items that are added to a basket are overwritten when the customer retrieves a saved basket.

The icon indicates that the shopping basket shown below can be saved.

The icon allows the customer to retrieve a shopping basket.

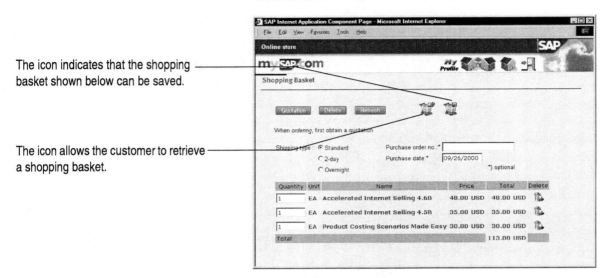

When the customer chooses to save the basket on the previous screen, the message on the screen below indicates that the items have been saved in the customer shopping basket. If the customer is not logged on, the customer is prompted to log on before the shopping basket can be saved.

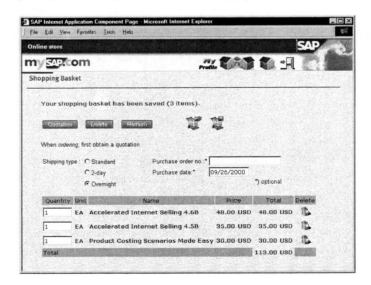

Note

If a customer has already placed items into the basket, the items will be overwritten when the customer retrieves a saved basket.

Once the customer has entered the store, the saved items can be retrieved by choosing the shopping basket icon.

To retrieve a saved shopping basket, the customer goes to the shopping basket.

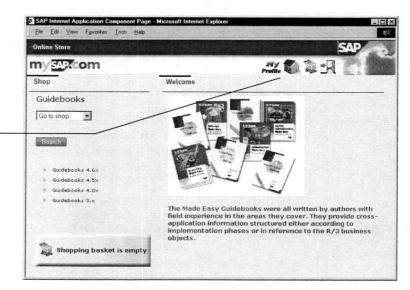

Although a message displays saying that the shopping basket is empty, the template has been modified to allow the customer to retrieve the shopping basket on the following screen by clicking the icon.

The same icon is used here to allow the customer to retrieve the saved basket.

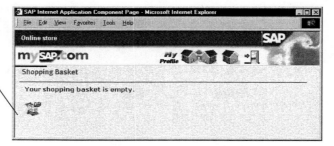

The retrieved shopping basket is displayed. The customer can continue shopping.

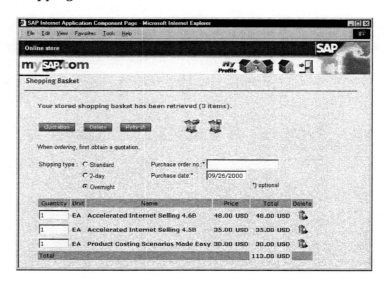

Implementation of the Modification

To implement the modifications to the SAP standard system and obtain this functionality, you must:

- Create a shopping basket table in SAP (preconfigured)

- Create a program that maintains the SAP shopping basket table (preconfigured)

- Extend the SAP Online Store program to include processing for the store-and-retrieve shopping basket function

- Update the ITS templates to work with the modifications (preconfigured)

Create a Shopping Basket Table in SAP

This table has been preconfigured for you. The table *ZYESHOP_BASKET* is created that works as the repository for the shopping baskets. Key fields are customer ID, product catalog ID, material ID, and unit of measure. Nonkey fields are basket quantity, catalog layout identification, and creation information. The structure of the table is as follows:

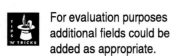

For evaluation purposes additional fields could be added as appropriate.

Field Name	Key	Field Type	Data Type	Length	Decimal	Short Text
MANDT	X	MANDT	CLNT	3		Client
KUNNR	X	KUNNR	CHAR	10		Customer number
WMINR	X	WMINR	CHAR	10		Product Catalog number
MATNR	X	MATNR	CHAR	18		Material Number
MEINH	X	MEINH	UNIT	3		Unit of Measure for display
MENGE_D		MENGE_D	QUAN	13	3	Quantity
AREA		LAYPOSNR	NUMC	10		Layout Area number
ITEM		LBPID	NUMC	10		Layout area item identifier
ERDAT		ERDAT	DATS	8		Creation Date
ERZET		ERZET	TIMS	6		Creation Time

Create a Program to Maintain the SAP Shopping Basket Table

This function module has been preconfigured for you. Create a function module that reads or updates the table entries. Input parameters are customer ID, product catalog ID, the selection of the functions *RETRIEVE* or *STORE*, and a table parameter based on the structure of the shopping basket table.

Detail Specification. Function module *Z_YESHOP_BASKET_MAINTAIN*:

- Check the input parameter. The customer and product catalog should exist in SAP and the requested function can only be *RETRIEVE* or *STORE*; for the *STORE* function, check also the data consistency of the input table *O_BASKET*.

- For the function *RETRIEVE*, select the stored shopping basket data from table *ZYESHOP_BASKET* based on *KUNNR* and *WMINR* and pass it onto the table parameter *O_BASKET*.

- For the function *STORE*, check the data consistency of table parameter *O_BASKET*, delete any existing shopping basket data for *KUNNR* and *WMINR*, and insert the new data.

Extension for the Function Store and Retrieve Shopping Basket

There are two code changes that must be made to incorporate the add-ons into the Online Store. The following programs must be changed:

- SAPMWWMJ

- MWWMJF03_USER_COMMAND_4000

Please refer to the Installation Guide for instructions on making code changes.

Update the ITS Templates to Work with the Modifications

For the functionality to be available for saving and retrieving the shopping basket, changes need to be made in the ITS templates. This step has been preconfigured for you.

Generic articles and components are currently not processed. These types of materials can only be used in an IS-Retail installation.

The template files in the AGate directory structure of ITS have been modified to allow customers to save and retrieve a shopping basket. The template files are located in the ITS AGate directory, under the directory structure *<its_root>\templates\ww20\sg*, where the *<its_root>* is your virtual ITS installation, and *sg* is the theme delivered with the Online Store preconfiguration. In addition, the language-resource file has been changed so variables could be added for the save-and-retrieve functions.

The following files are modified to support the saving and retrieving of the shopping basket:

Template	Change
SAPMWWMJ_4220.HTML	Save and retrieve the shopping basket
SAPMWWMJ_4210.HTML	Retrieve the shopping basket

Task

Modify the ITS templates

The following changes have been made in both templates:

- Both templates have been modified to allow the retrieval of the shopping basket.

- Template *SAPMWWMJ_4220.HTML* has been modified to allow the saving of the shopping basket.

Detail Specifications

General Flow Logic

- The flow logic for the new function code processing for *ZBRO* (the retrieve shopping basket) and *ZBSA* (the store shopping basket) is modeled after the SAP standard function code *QUOT* in *USER_COMMAND_4000*.

- Check that the program runs in sales order status without errors, and that the user invokes the function code from inside the shopping basket.

- If the customer has not logged on yet, process the customer logon first, and then continue with the function code processing.

Customer Processing

- Prepare the logon by initializing the customer processing and set the logon screen *SAPLWWCC_8120* for *FRAME_2*.

- Store the requested function code as the next action to be performed.

- Process the customer function codes and skip the SAP standard processing of the customer function codes in *USER_COMMAND_SAPLWWCC*. This routine is modeled after SAP standard, only that it processes as next actions the new function codes instead of the SAP standard ones as defined in *CUSTOMER_SAPLWWCC_LEAVE*.

- Determine the customer number; this number is either the logon customer ID or the one-time customer reference number.

Function Code ZBRO Processing

- Retrieve the stored shopping basket for the customer and the product catalog using function call to *Z_YESHOP_BASKET_MAINTAIN*.

- Retrieve the current product catalog items using function call to *BAPI_ADV_MED_GET_ITEMS*.

- Filter out products from the stored basket that are no longer available in the current catalog and update the stored basket items with the current catalog layout identification.

- Delete the current shopping basket.

- Fill the new shopping basket based on the stored basket; this routine can be modeled after *BASKET_ITEM_ADD*, including the reread of the item to retrieve pricing data using *BAPI_PRODCAT_GETITEM* and *BAPI_PRODCAT_GETPRICES*, propose the requested delivery date using *OSTORE_REQDATE_PROPOSE*, format quantities, and increase index and counters.

- Issue a message that the stored shopping basket has been retrieved. If the new shopping basket contains no items, set the empty basket screen *SAPMWMMJ_4210*. Otherwise set shopping basket screen *SAPMWMMJ_4220* for *FRAME_2*.

Function code ZBSA processing:

Note

The HTML template *SAPMWMMJ_4100* must be enhanced with HTML ^{Business} commands to display and invoke these function codes.

- Fill current shopping basket items into parameter table *O_BASKET* and call function *Z_YESHOP_BASKET_MAINTAIN* for updating the SAP table.

- Inform the user that the shopping basket has been stored, and set screen *SAPMWWMJ_4220* for *FRAME_2*.

Tips & Tricks

The new function codes are not displayed as buttons on the SAP screens *SAPMWWMJ_4100*, *SAPMWWMJ_4210*, or SAPMWWMJ_4220. However, these functions can be triggered on the appropriate SAP screens by typing the function code into the *Command* field and choosing *Enter*.

The store-and-retrieve function, currently available only on the shopping basket page, could however be implemented for other pages too (for example, the stored shopping basket could be automatically retrieved and displayed right after logon).

At this time, the retrieve function overwrites any existing shopping basket of the current session, but it could be enhanced so that the stored and current shopping basket are merged (for example, after the users select items of the stored basket they want to bring over into their current basket).

Technical SAP Enhancement: Purchase Order Entry

Overview

For many business-to-business scenarios, the system-generated purchase order (PO) number is not appropriate. In the standard R/3 System, the Online Store generates the PO number *WWW*, followed by the current time stamp.

In our enhancement, the fields *Purchase order number* and *Purchase order date* are open for input on the Internet and transferred to the order. The current date defaults as *Purchase order date*, but this can be overwritten. If the user does not enter a purchase order number, the standard PO number, described above, is generated.

The PO data is held for the duration of one order creation and initialized for the next order, even if the customer has not left the store to place the order.

Customer Experience: Entry of Purchase Order Number

The PO number may be entered by the customer on the screen that displays the contents of the shopping basket and allows the customer to request a quotation.

Purchase no. is an optional field. The current date defaults as the purchase order date.

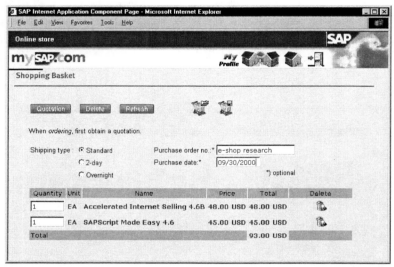

If a PO number is entered, the number and date are displayed on the screen that contains the customer-specific quotation. If no PO number is entered, the PO number and PO date are not displayed.

Purchase order number and date ——

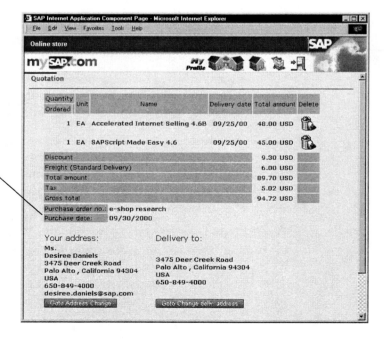

Once the order is confirmed, and a PO number is entered, both the PO number and PO date are displayed. As on the previous screen, if a PO number is not entered, neither PO field is displayed.

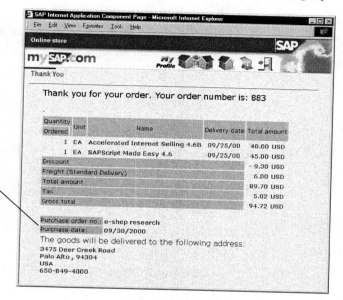

Purchase order number and date

The PO number is transferred into the order created in R/3. To display the order, in the *Command* field, enter transaction **VA03** and choose *Enter* (or from the navigation menu, choose *Logistics → Sales and Distribution → Sales → Order → Display*). Enter the order number, and choose ✅ to display the screen below.

The purchase order number and date are transferred to the R/3 sales order.

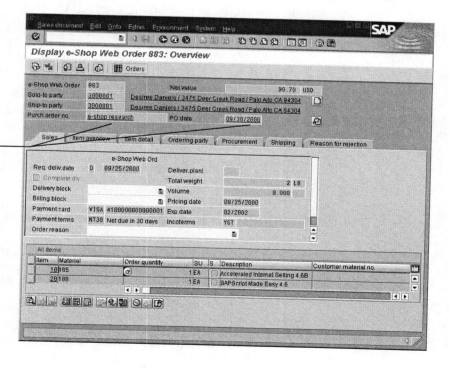

Implementation of the Modification

To implement extensions to SAP standard, you must:

- Create the three subroutines to process the purchase order data (preconfigured)

- Link the subroutines to the Online Store programs

- Update the ITS templates to work with the modifications (preconfigured)

Create the Three Subroutines to Process the Purchase Order Data

This step is preconfigured for you. For purchase order data to be process, three subroutines have been created.

1. Retrieve user input from the web.

    a. Retrieve the PO data from the web and convert the date into its internal format using *CONVERT_DATE_TO_INTERNAL*.

    b. Store the data in global variables.

    c. If the user input is not a valid date, issue a warning message and propose today's date in the correct format.

2. Transfer the PO data to the web.

    a. If the date is initial, use today's date.

    b. Transfer the purchase data from the global variables to the web.

    c. At subscreen *4235*, order confirmation, clear the global variables.

3. Pass the data to the order creation BAPI.

    a. If the user has entered a value for the PO number fill it into the sales document header structure. Otherwise, use SAP standard *WWW* and current time.

    b. Fill the purchase order date into the sales document header structure.

Link the Subroutines to the Online Store Program

This step has been preconfigured for you if you followed the instructions in the Installation Guide. Linking subroutines to the Online Store program involves modifying the appropriate flow logic and source code of all required programs.

- The routine for retrieving the PO data needs to be called when the carrier screen for quotation and order is being processed after input.

- The routine that sets the PO data has to be included in the PBO flow logic of the common carrier screen or the order and quotation subscreen.

- The routine that fills the internal structures of the sales document BAPI is included in the routines for creating a quotation and an order.

Example

Subroutines *ZZ_PURCHASE_DATA_GET*, *ZZ_PURCH_DATA_SET* and *ZZ_PURCHASE_DATA_FILL* have been created in include *ZMWWMJFZY*.

Form *ZZ_PURCHASE_DATA_GET* is being called in *USER_COMMAND_4000* at the beginning of the block that processes the function code. *ZZ_PURCH_DATA_SET* has been created as a module in the PBO flow logic of screen *SAPMWWMJ_4000* right before the module *FIELD_TRANSPORT*. Form *ZZ_PURCHASE_DATA_FILL* has been included at the beginning of form *QUOTATION_CREATE* and *ORDER_CREATE*.

The programs specified in this step have been created for you.

Task

Modify the appropriate flow logic

The detailed code is documented in the Installation Guide, which is delivered with the preconfiguration transports. The flow logic of screen *4000* in program *SAPMWWMJ* must be changed. In the *Command* field, enter transaction **SE51** and choose *Enter* (or from the navigation menu, choose *Tools → ABAP Workbench → Development → User Interface → Screen Painter*).

Task

Modify the source code of all required programs

The detailed code is documented in the Installation Guide, which is delivered with the preconfiguration transports. Five programs must be changed. In the *Command* field, enter transaction **SE38** and choose *Enter* (or from the navigation menu, choose *Tools → ABAP Workbench → Development → ABAP Editor*). The following programs must be changed to incorporate the purchase order field functionality into your Online Store.

After saving your modifications, you must activate and generate the programs.

- *SAPMWWMJ*

- *MWWMJTOP*

- *MWWMJF03_USER_COMMAND_4000*

- *MWWMJF03_QUOTATION_CREATE*

- *MWWMJF03_ORDER_CREATE*

Note that these changes to the function modules are not configuration changes; they are modifications to the R/3 System. Please thoroughly document and test these changes if you choose to apply them.

Update the ITS Templates to Work with the Modifications

For the PO number and date to be passed from the Internet to the R/3 sales order, changes need to be made in the ITS templates. This step has been preconfigured for you.

The template files in the AGate directory structure of ITS have been modified to allow customers to enter a PO number and date. The template files are located in the ITS AGate directory, under the directory structure *<its_root>\templates\ww20\sg*, where the *<its_root>* is your virtual ITS installation, and *sg* is the theme delivered with the Online Store preconfiguration. In addition, the language-resource file has been changed so variables could be added for the PO logic.

The following files are modified to support the PO number and date logic:

Template	Change
SAPMWWMJ_4220.HTML	Enter the purchase order data
SAPMWWMJ_4230.HTML	Display the p.o. number and date
SAPMWWMJ_4235.HTML	Display the p.o. number and date
WW20_EN.HTRC	Variables for descriptions of the purchase order data

Task

Modify the ITS templates

The following changes have been made in the HTML ^{Business} templates:

- Allow the entry of the purchase order number and purchase order date, defaulting the current date, in template *SAPMWWMJ_4220.HTML*.

- In templates *SAPMWWMJ_4230* and *SAPMWWMJ_4235*, display the PO number and date if the PO number is not zero

Task

Modify the language-resource file

The file *ww20_en.htrc* is the language-resource file that contains values for the language-specific variables used for the IACs. The following variables have been added to support the PO logic:

Parameter	Value
_4230_footnote	*)
_optional	optional
_purchno	Purchase no.
_purchdate	Purchase date
_colon	:

APPENDIX

E

My Profile Service

Overview

Note

The customer experience for the My Profile service are discussed in Chapter 14, "My Profile" on page 340.

The My Profile service is a new Internet Application Component (IAC) that gives customers the ability to maintain their personal data. Customers can set a default credit card number and default shipping mode.

The new service can be called directly from a web page on your corporate web site.

My Profile link from web page

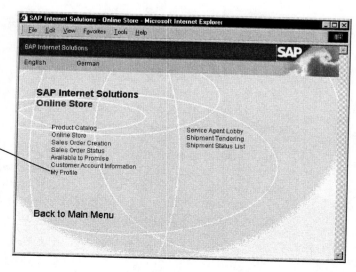

It can also be called from within an existing IAC, such as the Online Store.

The My Profile icon from within the Online Store

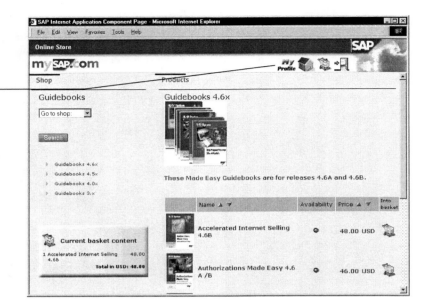

Note

The transaction for My Profile is *ZOSA*.

When the service is called, a new window is opened. The new window ensures that if the service is called from within the store, the Online Store session is not interrupted.

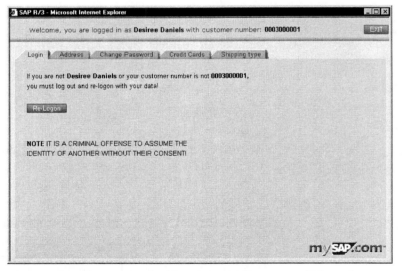

Note

Please refer to chapter 5, "Making it Happen: Customers in the Online Store" on page 147 for details on the different types of customers available in the Online Store.

The My Profile service has been created to consolidate the management of customer information. The customer can register or log on, maintain address data, change the account password, obtain a password reminder, maintain credit card information, and maintain a default shipping method.

To use the entire functionality of this service, a full customer master must be used for your Internet business. If a consumer is used, no sales area data is maintained, so no shipping method can be stored. If a one-time customer is used, no master record exists since customer data is stored within the sales order, so the My Profile service should not be used.

Enabling the My Profile Service

Note

The preconfiguration of the ITS templates for the My Profile service are discussed in chapter 14, "My Profile" on page 340.

To enable the My Profile service, you need to make changes to the following programs, modules, and screens:

- *SAPMWWMJ*
- *MWWMJF03_USER_COMMAND_4000*
- *MWWMJF01_USER_COMMAND_1000*
- *MWWMJF03_SUPPORTED_PAYMENT_TYP*
- *MWWMJF03_ORDER_CREATE*
- *MWWMJO30_FILL_CCARD_TYPE-SCREE*
- *SCREEN 4220*
- *FUNCTION MODULE SD_CCARD_READ_DB*

Please refer to the Installation Guide for instructions on making these modifications. After saving your modifications, you must activate and generate the programs.

The new components (function groups *YESHOP_CCARD* and *YESHOP_ACCOUNTS*) contain the transaction logic for the My Profile service and have been preconfigured for you.

APPENDIX

F

Modification: Changing the Customer Type for IKA1

Overview

Note that changing this object type is not a configuration change; this is a modification to the R/3 System. Please thoroughly document and test this change if you choose to apply it.

Note

For additional information about the Internet user, please refer to chapter 15, "The ITS User: Logging on to R/3" on page 349.

In the Internet Application Component (IAC) *IKA1* (customer account information), the object type for the Internet user is *BUS1007*. This type is inconsistent with the object type for the users in all other IAC services in the preconfigured sell-side functions, and requires customers to maintain two different passwords.

The code modifications below allow you to change the customer object type for the Internet user from *BUS1007* to *KNA1* for the customer account information IAC. Object *KNA1* is used for all other preconfigured IACs. If you choose to implement this modification, your customers will no longer need two different passwords to carry out different functions on your web site.

Note that although the password can now be the same between this and other IAC services, it is still not possible to log on to the customer account information transaction with an e-mail account in the standard R/3 System.

Program Changes

The object type must be changed in two function modules. In the *Command* field, enter transaction **SE37** and choose *Enter* (or from the navigation menu choose *Tools → ABAP Workbench → Development → Function Builder*).

BAPI_DEBTOR_CHECKPASSWORD

```
FUNCTION BAPI_DEBTOR_CHECKPASSWORD.
*"----------------------------------------------------------------
------
*"*"Lokale Schnittstelle:
*"      IMPORTING
*"              VALUE(DEBTORID) LIKE  BAPI1007-CUSTOMER
*"              VALUE(PASSWORD) LIKE  BAPIUID-PASSWORD
*"      EXPORTING
*"              VALUE(RETURN) LIKE  BAPIRETURN STRUCTURE  BAPIRETU
*"----------------------------------------------------------------
------
* value of id_type corresponds to name of business object in the
BOR
>>>>BEGINNING OF DELETION
CONSTANTS IDTYPE_ LIKE BAPIUSW01-OBJTYPE VALUE 'BUS1007'. "object
IDyp
>>>>END OF DELETION
>>>>BEGINNING OF INSERTION
CONSTANTS IDTYPE_ LIKE BAPIUSW01-OBJTYPE VALUE 'KNA1'. "object ID
>>>>END OF INSERTION
```

BAPI_DEBTOR_CHANGEPASSWORD

```
FUNCTION BAPI_DEBTOR_CHANGEPASSWORD.
*"----------------------------------------------------------------
------
*"*"Lokale Schnittstelle:
*"      IMPORTING
*"              VALUE(DEBTORID) LIKE  BAPI1007-CUSTOMER
*"              VALUE(PASSWORD) LIKE  BAPIUID-PASSWORD
*"              VALUE(NEW_PASSWORD) LIKE  BAPIUID-PASSWORD
*"              VALUE(VERIFY_PASSWORD) LIKE  BAPIUID-PASSWORD
*"      EXPORTING
*"              VALUE(RETURN) LIKE  BAPIRETURN STRUCTURE  BAPIRETU
*"----------------------------------------------------------------
------
* value of id_type corresponds to id of business object in the BO
```

```
>>>>BEGINNING OF DELETION
CONSTANTS IDTYPE_ LIKE BAPIUSW01-OBJTYPE VALUE 'BUS1007'. "object
ID
>>>>END OF DELETION
>>>>BEGINNING OF INSERTION
CONSTANTS IDTYPE_ LIKE BAPIUSW01-OBJTYPE VALUE 'KNA1'. "object ID
>>>>END OF INSERTION
```

Miscellaneous Utilities

Overview

In this appendix, we explain two utilities we developed for internal use but feel our customers could benefit from. The following sections explain how to:

- Get data from the frontend to the application server using FTP

- Change the screen field text

- Change messages

- Display the delivery address on the Internet, even when it is the same as the billing address

FTPGET

The *ZFTPGET* program is useful for getting data from the frontend to the application server. In tasks such as data transfer, loading a large file to the application server is desirable. Although the Data Transfer Workbench has similar functionality, it works only for those objects and formats supported by the workbench. Therefore, it is useful to have a generic utility—the *ZFTPGET* program—to upload files to the application server.

Task

Use ZFTPGET to load data from the frontend to the application server

1. In the *Command* field, enter transaction **SE38** and choose *Enter*.

2. On the *ABAP Editor: Initial Screen*:

   a. In *Program*, enter the report name **ZFTPGET**.

   b. Select *Text elements*.

   c. Choose ⊕.

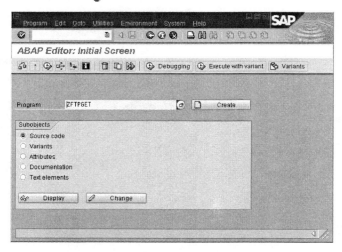

3. On the *ZFTP Program* screen:

   a. In *PServer Source File*, enter the source file on the presentation server (parameter *SFILENM*).

   b. In *AServer Destination File*, enter the path on the application server where the file needs to be copied (parameter *DFILENM*).

   c. Choose ⊕.

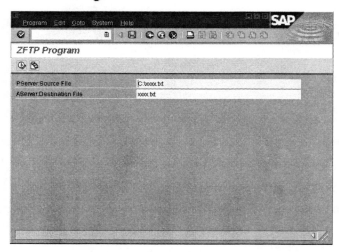

The file uploads from presentation server to the application server.

Field Text Modification

Note

To learn how field text is handled in the preconfigured Online Store templates, see "Architecture of the Buttons" on page 336

During the development process, we noticed that many choices of field text wording for the standard Online Store IACs could have been better. These texts are directly used in the buttons in HTML templates.

You might want to modify the text, and SAP allows modification of these texts to better suit your requirements. However, if you are building a German web site and need to change the text, then it is not possible to change this text since German is the original source language of development. Therefore, if you are building a German web site, you need the following report.

Task

Modify the field text for German web sites

1. In the *Command* field, enter transaction **SE38** and choose *Enter*.

2. On the *ABAP Editor: Initial Screen*:

   a. In *Program*, enter the report **ZFIELD_TEXT_CHANGE**.

   b. Choose ⊕ .

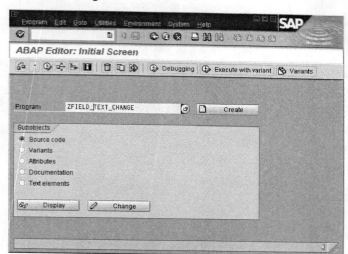

Note

Currently, we are only supporting changes using *DE* (German) because for all other languages, standard SAP provides a change-of-text capability. It is much better to use the standard method since it is CTS-enabled. The changes made by this report are transportable.

3. On the *ZESHOP – Translation Program for Field display text* screen

   a. In *Program Name*, enter the module pool name.

   b. In *Screen Number*, enter the screen number.

c. In *Field Name*, enter the field name as shown in the F1 technical help.

d. In *Display Text*, enter the new text you want for this field.

e. Choose ⊕.

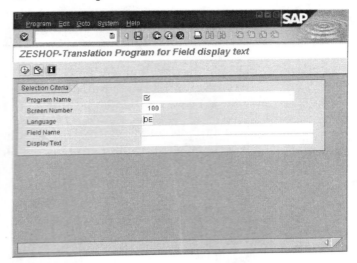

How to Change Messages

Task

Change message text

To change messages, you first need to locate the message class for the messages. Perform the following steps:

1. To locate the message class, double-click on the message.

n the status bar

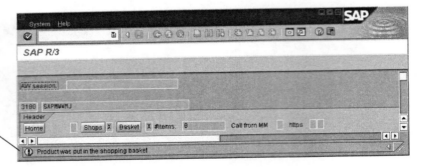

2. On the *Help - SAP R/3* dialog box, choose *Technical Info*.

3. On the *Technical Information* dialog box:

    a. *Appl. area* tells you the message class. Below that is the message number.

    b. Choose ✖ twice.

Within the *Appl. area* field is the message class, which in this case is *W+* and the messages number is *304*.

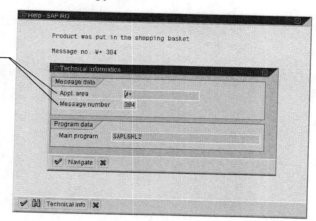

4. To change the message text, enter transaction **SE91** in the *Command* field and choose *Enter*.

5. On the *Maintain Message Class* screen:

    a. In *Message class*, enter the message class.

    b. Choose 🖉 *Change*.

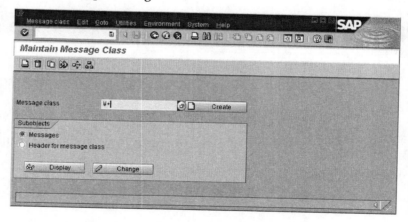

6. On the *Display Messages: Class <XX>* screen:

    a. All the messages relevant for the message class are displayed.

    b. Choose *Maintain all*.

    c. Choose *Maint. in logon lang*.

d. Change the message according to your needs.

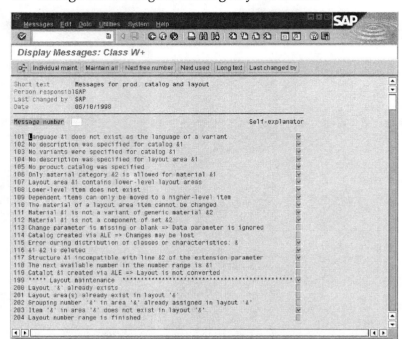

How to Change the Text on the Button

Task

Change the text on a button

1. Locate the program name and screen number of the button that you want to change.

2. On the transactional screen, place you cursor in a field and choose (or *F-1*).

3. On the *Help -SAP R/3* dialog box:

a. Choose *Technical info* (or *F-9*).

b. Note the program name and screen number.

c. Choose ✖ twice.

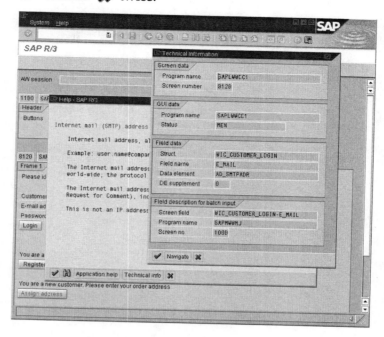

4. In the *Command* field, enter transaction **SE80** and choose *Enter*.

5. On the *Object Navigator* screen:

   a. Use the list box to select *Program*.

   b. Enter the program name in the entry field.

   c. Choose 🔍.

   d. Under *Object name*, click ▶ next to the *Screens* line.

   e. Double-click on the screen you want to change.

   f. Choose ➡ *Layout*.

The overall screen name changes after you double-click on the screen in step **5e**.

List box with which you select *Program*

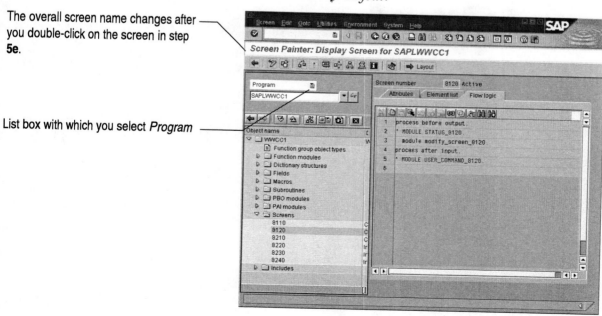

6. On the *Screen Painter: Display Screen <XXXXXXXXX>*:

   a. Double-click on the button you want to change (for example, *Change password*).

   b. The *Screen Painter: Attributes* dialog box appears.

   c. Choose 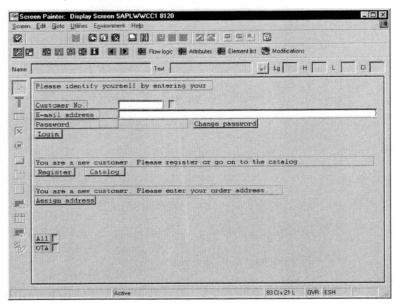.

   d. If the system asks for the object access key and you do not have one, check with your administrator. Enter the object access key and proceed.

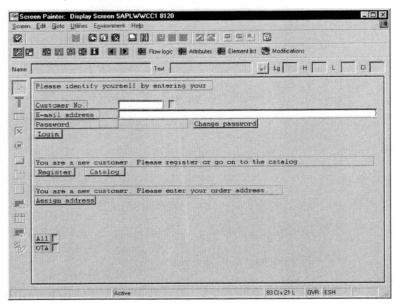

7. On the *Screen Painter: Attributes* dialog box, enter the new button text in *Text*.

8. Back on the *Screen Painter: Display Screen <XXXXXXXXXXX>*, choose to save and activate.

Displaying the Bill-To Address as the Delivery Address

In most cases, the delivery address is the same as the bill-to address. To display the bill-to address as the delivery address, the following program and screen must be changed:

- *MWWMJF05_CUSTOMER_ADDRESS_READ*
- *MWWMJF03_MODIFY_SCREEN_4230*

To implement these code changes, please refer to the Installation Guide.

Introduction to Computer-Aided Test Tools (CATTs)

Overview

The Online Store preconfiguration includes a set of Computer-Aided Test Tools (CATTs), organized into test catalogs. We provide two test catalogs.

The test catalogs have been developed to:

- Install master data into your system, if you are using the Online Store preconfiguration in conjunction with the Preconfigured Client (PCC)

- Validate the preconfiguration

  We use the CATTs to guarantee the quality of what was preconfigured within R/3. For the Online Store preconfiguration, only the new sales document flow can be tested. All other procedures can only be tested manually because the data comes from the Internet. The sections in each chapter that discuss "The Customer Experience" and "The View from Within your Company" can be used to manually test the preconfiguration.

Additional CATT procedures are delivered that are not included in the catalogs. These CATTs should be run manually during the installation process, in cases in which the Online Store preconfiguration is not used in conjunction with the PCC. Please refer to the *Installation Guide* for details on these CATT procedures.

What Is a CATT?

To illustrate what a CATT is, consider a basic Sales and Distribution (SD) sales process in R/3 with the following steps:

1. Create a customer master.
2. Create a material master.
3. Create a price.
4. Create a promotional price.
5. Create an order.
6. Deliver the order.
7. Bill the order.
8. Print the invoice.
9. Post the payment.
10. Create a return order.
11. Create a return delivery.
12. Release the credit block from the return order.
13. Create the credit memo.

The CATT *ZESHOP_SALES_TAXABLE* performs these steps automatically by invoking R/3 transactions, populating screen fields, and then driving the transactions with menu or icon button input equivalents (BDC OK codes). If you run the CATT in *Foreground* mode, you actually see the entire process, screen by screen. You can change field values as the CATT runs, and can rerun the CATT as often as you like. Running CATTs in foreground mode is a good way to become familiar with new business processes and to discover what the preconfiguration lets you do.

Some Things to Know Before You Proceed

All the CATTs in this document run with the properly installed Online Store preconfiguration implemented in conjunction with the PCC, just after the installation. However, if you change the configuration, the CATTs may run

The first time some transactions are invoked in a newly installed system, they do not run normally. Rather, they generate a screen. Of these transactions, some only generate the screens (if run manually), but not if the transaction is called from a CATT. If one of the CATTs results in an error, try to rerun it. If the error persists, manually call up the transaction (often, calling the first screen is enough) and then rerun the CATT. The problem should not reoccur.

with some errors. CATTs are especially sensitive to customizing that changes screen sequences and field selections. They also expect PCC organizational structures and customizing to be present.

Many of the CATTs discussed in the Online Store preconfiguration *Installation Guide* can be run individually even when the Online Store preconfiguration is used as an add-on to existing configuration, or with a modified PCC. The CATTs you run are those that install master data, such as condition records, based on Online Store preconfiguration transports. The organizational structures used in your company, such as the sales area, must be entered as the parameters before running these CATTs. However, when the Online Store preconfiguration is used as an add-on, the CATTs that create the sample master data, such as the product catalog, should not be run, because of the potential conflicts when screens have been modified in the course of an implementation.

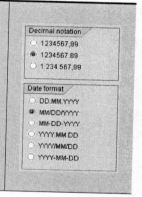

Caution

CATTs are sensitive to the user default date and decimal formats that you set under *System → User profile → Own data*.

The CATTs delivered with the e-commerce preconfiguration expect the date format to be **MM/DD/YYYY** and the decimal notation to be **period**, as shown at right.

Example: Executing the Test Catalogs

Note

For details about the CATT procedures that should be run when the Online Store preconfiguration is used as an add-on to existing configuration, please refer to the *Installation Guide*.

The Online Store preconfiguration CATTs have been organized into test catalogs from which you can run individual CATTs, groups of CATTs, or the entire catalog.

The Online Store preconfiguration comes with two test catalogs:

- *e-Shop: Install Catalog (**use only with the PCC**)* consists of the installation CATTs that create master data required to complete the configuration, such as condition types. It also creates sample data, such as a product catalog. This install catalog should only be run when the Online Store preconfiguration is used in conjunction with the PCC. For details about this catalog, please refer to the *Installation Guide*.

- *e-Shop: Test Catalog (**use only with the PCC**)* consists of all the test processes that can be run automatically with no user interaction. This catalog should only be run when the Online Store preconfiguration is used in conjunction with the PCC.

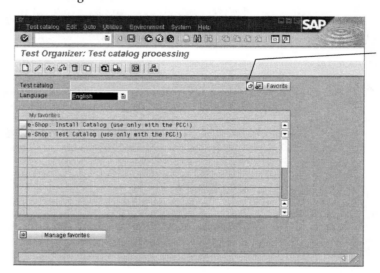

The Online Store Test Catalog

Task

Run a test catalog

1. In the *Command* field, enter transaction **STWB_1** and choose *Enter* (or from the navigation menu, choose *Tools* → *ABAP Workbench* → *Test Workbench* → *Test Organizer* → *Manage test catalog*).

2. On the *Test Organizer: Test catalog processing* screen, use *possible entries* in the *Test catalog* field.

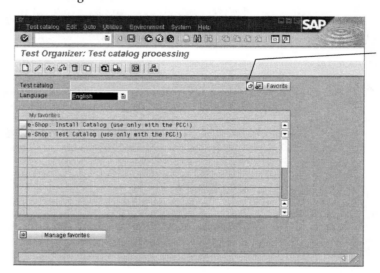

Possible entries button

3. On the *Find test catalogs* dialog box:

    a. In *Title*, enter **e-Shop:*** to find all test catalogs delivered with the Online Store preconfiguration. You can also choose to leave this field blank to display all catalogs.

    b. Choose ⊕.

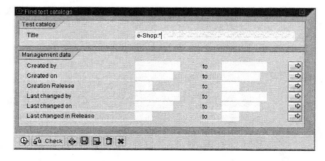

4. On the *Find structure* dialog box, double-click on the line *e-Shop: Test Catalog (use only with the PCC!)*.

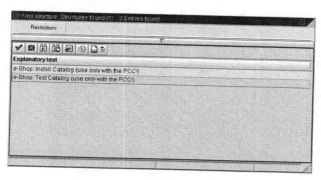

5. Back on the *Test Organizer: Test catalog processing* screen, choose 🔧.

6. On the *Display test catalog e-Shop: Test Catalog (use only with the PCC!)* screen:

   a. Place your cursor on the top node if you want to execute the entire test catalog or on individual nodes.

   b. Choose ▦ *Test Case*.

This action creates master and transactional data. **Never** run this in a future production client.

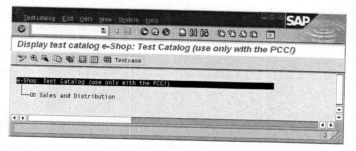

7. On the *Start CATT test cases Local* dialog box:

   a. Under *Processing mode*, select *Background*.

   b. Choose ✔.

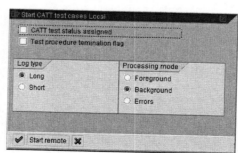

The test CATTs create master data. **Never** run them in a production environment.

Some of the CATTs in the test catalog will not run properly on weekends or public holidays as defined in the factory calendar for the U.S. If the factory is closed, the SD module will not allow deliveries.

8. On the final screen, a blue log indicates that the test catalog has been run successfully.

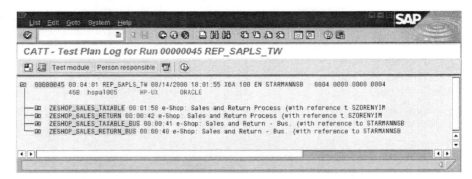

Example: Executing a CATT

The following sample CATT session helps you to become familiar with CATT transactions by creating a vendor. Run it several times in *Foreground* and *Background* and view the log at the end of the session to see what information it contains.

Task

Execute an individual CATT procedure

1. In the *Command* field, enter transaction **SCAT** and choose *Enter* (or from the navigation menu, choose *Tools → ABAP Workbench → Test → Test Workbench → SCAT – CATT Extended*).

2. On the *Computer Aided Test Tool: Initial Screen*:

a. Enter the name of the CATT to test (for example, **ZPCCXD01_CREATE_CUSTOMER**).

b. Choose 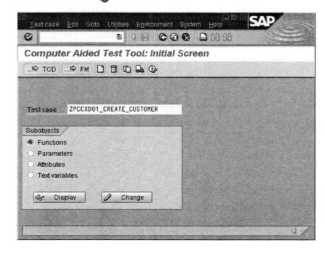.

3. On the *CATT: Execute Test case ZPCCX01_CREATE_CUSTOMER* screen, before you run the CATT, choose the execution options and assign values for the CATT's parameters.

   a. Under *Log Type*:

Log Type	Result
Long	During the execution, the system writes log data that is displayed in a log tree.
Short	If the test run is error free, no log data is written during the process. The log tree only displays the test run that was started and the import and export parameters of the specific test modules. When the CATT is finished, test-run errors are displayed in *Long*.
W/o (log type without display):	The log data is written like a short log, but the log tree is not automatically displayed.

   b. Under *Processing mode*:

Processing Mode	Result
Foreground	The transaction flow appears on the screen where the input values are visible. The parameter values are not hard-coded and can be changed.
Background	The CATT parameter values cannot be changed during processing.
Errors	This transaction displays only errors and runs without dialog until the first error. After that first error, the transaction continues to run in dialog so that corrections can be made.

   c. Under *Variants*, select *W/o*.

   d. In the *Parameter value* column, change the CATT parameter's default values **before** you run it.

e. Choose ⊕ .

4. On the *Create Customer: General data* screen:

   a. Review the default data you just entered. You can still make changes.

   b. Choose ✅ when you finished any changes on this screen.

5. Continue to enter through all the following screens. The dialog box at the bottom right contains the function code recorded in the CATT procedure. Choose ✅ to continue moving through both screens and dialog boxes.

6. The final screen shows a log of a successful CATT.

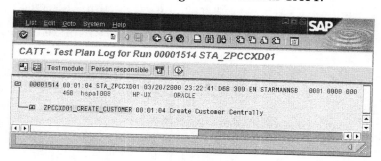

Example: Executing a CATT with Variants

The following sample CATT session helps you to become familiar with variants in CATT procedures by creating a series of vendors for the freight carriers.

Task

Execute a CATT with variants

1. On the *Computer Aided Test Tool: Initial Screen*:

   a. Enter the CATT procedure **ZESHOP_FREIGHT_CARRIERS** in the *Test case* field.

   b. Choose 🖫 .

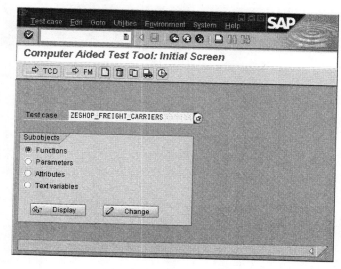

2. On the *CATT: Execute Test case ZESHOP_FREIGHT_CARRIERS* screen, choose *Goto → Variants → Edit.*

3. On the *CATT: Maintain variants for test procedure ZESHOP_FREIGHT_CARRIERS* screen:

    a. The list of variants is displayed.

    b. Place your cursor on the first variant, and choose 🔲 .

Each variant creates a different vendor.

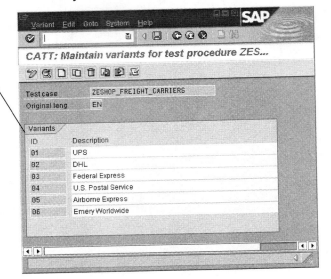

4. On the *CATT: Maintain variant 01 for test procedure ZESHOP_FREIGHT_CARRIERS* screen:

    a. The parameters are filled in for the variant.

    b. Choose 🔙 twice.

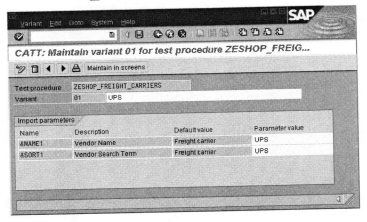

5. On the *CATT: Execute Test case ZESHOP_FREIGHT_CARRIERS* screen:

    a. Under *Processing mode,* choose *Background.*

    b. Under *Variants,* choose *All.*

c. Choose ⊕.

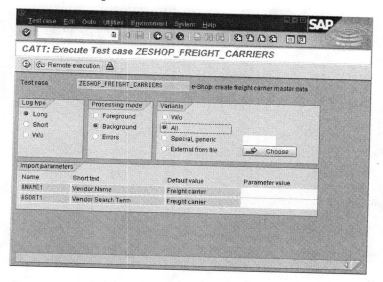

6. On the *CATT - Test Plan Log for Run 00001510 REP_SAPMSCAT* screen, the log is displayed, with the log of the last variant expanded.

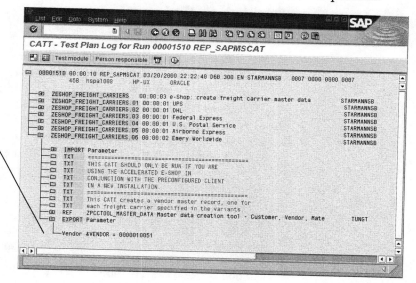

The vendor number created for the freight carrier is exported.

CATT Procedures Delivered with the Online Store Preconfiguration

Do **not** run CATT procedures that create master data in a production environment!

The following CATT procedures are delivered with the Online Store preconfiguration. Some of these CATT procedures create configuration data, while others create sample master data.

Tips & Tricks

To own the CATTs delivered with the Online Store preconfiguration:

1. In the *Command* field, enter transaction **SE38** and choose Enter.

2. in the *Program* field, enter report **RDDTADI7** and choose ⊕ .

3. In the field *Request/task,* enter the transport request number with which you imported the CATTs. In the field *New original system,* enter your **<SID>**.

4. Choose ⊕ .

CATT as a "Transport Helper"

The CATT procedure *ZESHOPXXXX* is provided to consolidate all procedures transported as part of the Online Store preconfiguration. Since not all CATT procedures are used in a catalog, this CATT is a simple mechanism to keep track of all the high-level CATTs included in the transport.

CATTs in the Installation Catalog

The following table summarizes all CATT procedures contained in the Installation Catalog, which is run when the Accelerated Internet Selling solution is used in conjunction with the PCC. To access the catalog, enter transaction **STWB_1** in the *Command* field and choose *Enter* (or from the navigation menu, choose *Tools → ABAP Workbench → Test → Test Workbench → Test Organizer → Manage test catalog*). Please refer to the *Accelerated Internet Selling - Online Store 4.6B Installation Guide* for details. The Installation Guide is delivered with the download file that contains the transports.

CATT Procedure	Description
Configuration	
ZESHOP_PRICE_DET	Configures the pricing procedure determined for Internet orders.
ZESHOP_CUSTOMER_HIERARCHY	Configures the customer hierarchy type and corresponding partner functions. The customer hierarchy type is used for business scenarios in which multiple employees from one company make purchases in your store.
Master Data	
ZESHOP_ITSUSER	Creates the generic ITS user for logging on to the ITS if it does not exist. If this user already exists, the CATT adds the appropriate Get/Set parameters.
ZESHOP_INCOTERMS	Creates the Incoterms, which determine the pricing for the type of delivery selected by the customer.

CATT Procedure	Description
ZESHOP_OUTPUT_RECORDS	Creates the condition records that allow e-mail to be sent for the order types used for the Online Store.
ZESHOP_CLASSES	Creates the classification system data that provides the functionality for limiting access to a catalog based on the customer ID.
ZESHOP_FREIGHT_CARRIERS	Creates vendor master records for the freight carriers for which order tracking is configured.
ZESHOP_ONETIME_CUST	Creates the customer master record used as a reference for the Online Store that uses one-time customers.
ZESHOP_PROD_CATALOG	Creates a sample product catalog, including the basic data, reference customer, structure, products, and documents.
ZESHOP_MULT_PASSWORDS	Creates the customer master records used in a customer hierarchy, when multiple employees of a company make purchases in your store.

CATTs in the Test Catalog

The following table summarizes all CATT procedures contained in the Test Catalog, which is run when the Accelerated Internet Selling solution is used in conjunction with the PCC. To access the catalog, enter transaction **STWB_1** in the *Command* field and choose *Enter* (or from the navigation menu, choose *Tools → ABAP Workbench → Test → Test Workbench → Test Organizer → Manage test catalog*). Please refer to the *Accelerated Internet Selling - Online Store 4.6B Installation Guide* for details. The Installation Guide is delivered with the download file that contains the transports.

CATT Procedure	Description
ZESHOP_SALES_TAXABLE	Process flow that creates a sales order, delivery, and invoice, and then returns the items. Uses the sales document types delivered for the consumer scenarios. The sale in this process is taxable.
ZESHOP_SALES_RETURN	Process flow as described above, but the sale is not taxable.
ZESHOP_SALES_TAXABLE_BUS	Process flow as above. The sales document types are the ones delivered for the business scenario. The sale in this process is taxable.
ZESHOP_SALES_RETURN_BUS	Process flow for the business sales document types as above. The sale in this process is not taxable.

CATTs for the Product Catalog

The following CATT procedure provides you with a sample product catalog. The structure of the product catalog is discussed in detail in chapter 2, "Creating the Product Catalog" on page 43.

ZESHOP_PROD_CATALOG. This CATT creates the sample product catalog. The sample products include documentation and guidebooks developed by the Simplification Group. This CATT should only be run if the Online Store preconfiguration is used in conjunction with the PCC.

 The CATT that creates the sample product catalog should only be run if you are using the Online Store preconfiguration in conjunction with the PCC in a new implementation. The CATT cannot anticipate changes to field settings and values that normally occur during an implementation. If you are not using the Online Store preconfiguration with the PCC, please create your own product catalog, keeping in mind the requirements in the step-by-step instructions.

This CATT should **never** be run in a productive environment.

CATT Procedure	Description
ZPCCTOOL_MASTER_DATA	Creates the customer master record of the reference customer in the basic data of the product catalog and for consumers.
ZESHOP_CONSUMER	Assigns the customer master as the reference for consumers.
ZESHOP_PROD_CAT_BASIC	Creates the basic data of the product catalog.
ZESHOP_PROD_CAT_LAYOUT	Creates the layout of the product catalog, including the shop and product group levels.
ZESHOP_PROD_CAT_BASIC	Creates the basic data of the product catalog.
ZESHOP_PROD_CATALOG_MATS	Creates the master data for the 4.6 guidebook product group. This CATT is called six times, once for each product created.
ZESHOP_PROD_CAT_LAYOUT_46	Assigns the guidebooks to the layout for the 4.6 guidebooks.
ZESHOP_PROD_CATALOG_MATS	Creates the master data for the 4.5 guidebook product group. This CATT is called five times, once for each product created.
ZESHOP_PROD_CAT_LAYOUT_45	Assigns the guidebooks to the layout for the 4.5 guidebooks.
ZESHOP_PROD_CATALOG_MATS	Creates the master data for the 4.0 guidebook product group. This CATT is called ten times, once for each product created.
ZESHOP_PROD_CAT_LAYOUT_40	Assigns the guidebooks to the layout for the 4.0 guidebooks.

CATT Procedure	Description
ZESHOP_PROD_CATALOG_MATS	Creates the master data for the 3.x guidebook product group. This CATT is called eight times, once for each product created.
ZESHOP_PROD_CAT_LAYOUT_3X	Assigns the guidebooks to the layout for the 3.x guidebooks.
ZESHOP_PROD_CATALOG_MATS	Creates the master data for the HR documents product group. This CATT is called two times, once for each product created.
ZESHOP_PROD_CAT_LAYOUT_HR	Assigns the guidebooks to the layout for the HR documents.
ZESHOP_PROD_CATALOG_MATS	Creates the master data for the technical documents product group. This CATT is called one time, once for each product created.
ZESHOP_PROD_CAT_LAYOUT_TECH	Assigns the guidebooks to the layout for the technical documents.

ZESHOP_PROD_CATALOG_MATS. This CATT creates the master data for the products in the product catalog. It is called from CATT procedure *ZESHOP_PROD_CATALOG*. This CATT should only be run if the Online Store preconfiguration is being used in conjunction with the PCC.

CATT Procedure	Description
ZPCCTOOL_MASTER_DATA	Creates the material master record of the product that will be assigned to the product catalog.
ZPCCVK31_PRICE_COND_MATERIAL	Creates the price for the product that will be assigned to the product catalog.
ZPCCVK11_SALES_PRICE_MAT	Creates a sales price for the product that will be assigned to the product catalog, if required.
ZESHOP_DMS	Creates the document to be linked to the product. The document contains the references to the image files for display on the web.

CATT Procedure	Description
ZESHOP_DMS_ONEDOC	Creates an additional document that will be linked to the product, if required. The document contains the references to the data file for display on the web.
ZESHOP_PROD_CATALOG_MM02_DOCS	Links the created documents to the material master record.
ZESHOP_PROD_CATALOG_MM02_TEXT	Creates the sales order text that will be copied from the material master into the product catalog.

ZESHOP_ONETIME_CUST. This CATT creates the reference customer for stores using one-time customers. This CATT should only be run if the Online Store preconfiguration is being used in conjunction with the PCC.

CATT Procedure	Description
ZESHOP_ONETIME_CUST	Creates a one-time customer master used as a reference for the Online Store in which only one-time customers are used.

CATTs for Product Catalog Authorizations

The following CATT procedure provides you with the master data in the classification system, which allows you to limit customer access to the catalog. The method of using classification as an authorization mechanism is discussed in detail in chapter 4, "Limiting Access to Product Groups Within a Product Catalog" on page 109.

ZESHOP_CLASSES. This CATT creates the classes used to limit the access to the product catalog.

CATT Procedure	Description
ZESHOP_CHAR	Creates the characteristic that defines the type of customer
ZESHOP_CLASS	Creates the class that may be linked to the customer master; the characteristic is assigned
ZESHOP_CLASS	Creates the class that may be linked to the product catalog layout; the characteristic is assigned

CATTs for Multiple Employees Purchasing

The following CATTs support the scenario in which multiple employees in the same company purchase from your store. For information about this scenario, please refer to chapter 6, "Multiple Employees Making Purchases for One Corporation" on page 165.

ZESHOP_CUSTOMER_HIERARCHY. This CATT creates the configuration for the business partner scenario. A CATT is used instead of a transport, to ensure that existing customer hierarchy configuration is not overwritten.

CATT Procedure	Description
ZESHOP_OVH1_CH_TYPE	Creates the hierarchy type used for the customer hierarchy.
ZESHOP_VOPA_CUSTHIER	Creates the partner functions YA, YB, YC, and YD, to be used for the customer hierarchy.
ZESHOP_VOPA_CUSTHIER_AG	Assigns the newly created partner functions to the account groups 0001, 0012, and YWEB.
ZESHOP_OVH1_CH_TYPE_2	Assigns partner function YA to hierarchy type Y.
ZESHOP_VOPA_SLSORDER	Creates the partner determination procedure YWB, and assigns it to order type YWB.
ZESHOP_VOPA_SLSORD_SP	Adds the sold-to partner to the partner determination procedure. This must be done in a separate step due to technical difficulties with the CATT procedure.
ZESHOP_VOPA_DELIVDOC	Adds the new partner functions to the existing partner procedure determination rules for delivery documents.
ZESHOP_VOPA_BILLDOC	Adds the new partner functions to the existing partner procedure determination rules for billing documents.
ZESHOP_OVH2_AG	Assigns the account groups to hierarchy type Y.
ZESHOP_OVH3_CUSTHIER	Assigns the sales area used for Internet processing to hierarchy type Y.
ZESHOP_OVH4_AUART	Assigns the customer hierarchy type to sales order type YWB.

The CATT that creates the sample customer master records should only be run if you are using the Online Store preconfiguration in conjunction with the PCC in a new implementation. This CATT cannot anticipate changes to field settings and values that normally occur during an implementation. If you are not using the Online Store preconfiguration with the PCC, please create your own customer master records, keeping in mind the requirements in the step-by-step instructions.

This CATT should **never** be run in a productive environment.

ZESHOP_MULT_PASSWORDS. This CATT creates sample customers that use a customer hierarchy. The last step, creating the actual hierarchy, must be performed manually, since there are technical problems in creating the hierarchy with a CATT procedure.

CATT Procedure	Description
ZPCCTOOL_MASTER_DATA	Creates the customer master that represents the company to which the employees are linked.
ZESHOP_CREATE_INET_CUSTOMERS	Creates the employees which will be linked to the company.
ZESHOP_CUSTHIER_DISC	Creates a discount for the company, for which each of the employees is eligible.
ZESHOP_CUSTHIER	Displays the documentation that provides the instructions for creating the customer hierarchy, using the customer master records that were just created.

ZESHOP_CREATE_INET_CUSTOMERS. This CATT creates the master data for the employees that will be linked the company.

CATT Procedure	Description
ZPCCTOOL_MASTER_DATA	Creates the customer master that represents the company to which the employees are linked.
ZESHOP_INET_USER	Creates the Internet user for the customer master records just created. The password is automatically generated.
ZESHOP_INET_USER_CHPW	Changes the password for the customers, using the last name of the customer.

CATTs that Support Sales Order ProcessCATTs for Pricing

The following CATT procedures assist you in pricing the products in your product catalog. Pricing is discussed in detail in chapter 3, "Prices in the Product Catalog" on page 77.

ZESHOP_PRICE_DET. This CATT assigns the pricing procedure used to calculate taxes for the product catalog and orders received through the Internet. If you are not using the Online Store preconfiguration in conjunction with the PCC, you need to enter your own sales area as parameters. The default document pricing schema is *X*. For internal taxes, the pricing procedure parameter should be set to *ZWAJUS*. For taxes with an external package, pricing procedure *ZWAXUS* should be assigned.

CATT Procedure	Description
ZPCCTAX_OVKK	Assigns the pricing procedure, based on the parameters entered at runtime

ZESHOP_INCOTERMS. This CATT facilitates the calculation of sample freight rates. It creates the master data (rates) that can be used to demonstrate the freight calculation. The Incoterms allow this calculation for overnight shipping, two-day shipping, and standard shipping.

CATT Procedure	Description
ZESHOP_INCOTERMS	Creates the master data for the three delivered Incoterms: **YST**, **Y2D**, and **YOV**

CATTs for Sales Order Status

The CATT that creates the sample vendor master records should only be run if you are using the Online Store preconfiguration in conjunction with the PCC in a new implementation. This CATT cannot anticipate changes to field settings and values that normally occur during an implementation. If you are not using the Online Store preconfiguration with the PCC, please create your own vendor master records, keeping in mind the requirements in the step-by-step instructions.

This CATT should **never** be run in a productive environment.

The following CATT is for the scenario to display customer orders and link to the carrier web site for tracking. This scenario is explained in detail in chapter 8, "Sales Order Status" on page 207.

ZESHOP_FREIGHT_CARRIERS. This CATT creates the vendor master data used to demonstrate the sales order status tracking with URL links. This CATT should only be run if the Online Store preconfiguration is used in conjunction with the PCC.

There are six variants for this CATT, one for each vendor. When executing the CATT, do **not** enter a value for the freight carrier name and search term in the import parameters.

CATT Procedure	Description
ZPCCTOOL_MASTER_DATA	This CATT creates the vendor master for six freight carriers, using variants for each carrier. The CATT is run once initially before reading the variants. In order to facilitate changing the variants, the first run-through of the CATT creates a "generic" freight carrier that can be copied to create others, if required.

CATTs for the ITS User

The following CATT creates the generic ITS user that logs on to R/3 when a customer accesses a sell-side IAC. The generic ITS user is explained in detail in chapter 15, "The ITS User: Logging on to R/3" on page 349.

ZESHOP_ITSUSER. This CATT creates the generic user that should be used to log on to ITS. If the user already exists, which usually occurs if the Online Store preconfiguration is used in conjunction with the PCC's optional ESS configuration, an e-mail address and the appropriate get/set parameters are added to the user master record. If the user does not exist, it is created. The activity group is not assigned; this must be done in a manual step.

CATT Procedure	Description
ZPCCTOOL_CHECKUSER	Determines whether the ITS user already exists; the user ID **must** be in capital letters
ZPCCSU01_01	If the user does not already exist, this CATT creates the ITS user with U.S. defaults for number and date displays; parameters are assigned that will be necessary for the IAC services to function correctly
ZESHOP_ITSUSER_EMAIL	Adds the e-mail address to the user master of the ITS user

CATTs that Support Sales Order Processing in the Online Store

The following CATTs create SD master data, and test the new sales document types delivered with the Online Store preconfiguration. The Online Store configuration is described in chapter 1, "Creating the Online Store with the Catalog" on page 5.

ZESHOP_OUTPUT_RECORDS. This CATT creates the master data for the output types, which allows the confirmation e-mail to be sent to the customer when an order is created, a delivery is shipped, and the invoice is processed.

CATT Procedure	Description
ZPCCVV11_ORDER_OUTPUT	Creates the output condition type that designates the sales document type, delivered with the Online Store preconfiguration, that generates a confirmation e-mail to the customer when the sales order from the Internet is created. This CATT is run twice, for the two different order types delivered with the preconfiguration.
ZPCCVV21_SHIPPING_OUTPUT	Creates the output condition type that designates the delivery type, delivered with the standard R/3 System, that generates a confirmation e-mail to the customer when the delivery is shipped.
ZPCCVV31_BILLING_OUTPUT	Creates the output condition type that designates the billing type, delivered with the Online Store preconfiguration, that generates a confirmation e-mail to the customer when an invoice, receipt, or credit memo is processed. This CATT is run twice, the first time to create the output conditions for the billing document for the invoice/receipt, and again to create the conditions for the credit memo. This CATT is run twice, for the two different billing types delivered with the preconfiguration.

ZESHOP_SALES_TAXABLE. This CATT tests the sales document flow of the document types delivered with the Online Store preconfiguration for the consumer scenario. The sales in this procedure is taxable.

CATT Procedure	Description
ZPCCTOOL_MASTER_DATA	Creates the material master of the product to be sold, the customer master record, and the price of the product
ZPCCVK11_CREATE_ZDP1	Creates a percentage discount for the product using the material pricing group
ZPCCVK11_SALES_PRICE_MAT	Creates a sale price for the product
ZPCCVK11_CREATE_K007	Creates a discount for the customer
ZPCCVA01_STD_ORDER	Creates an order with the newly created product and customer
ZPCCVL01N_DELIVERY	Creates the delivery and posts the goods issue for the order
ZPCCVF01_BILLING	Creates the invoice for the order based on the delivery document
ZPCCVF03_ISSUE_BILLING_DOC	Prints the invoice for the document
ZPCCTOOL_VBRK	Finds the billing amount from the invoice header to facilitate the payment process
ZPCCFBZ1_PAYMENT2	Posts the incoming payment for the invoice
ZESHOPVA01_YWRE	Creates a return order with reference to the invoice
ZPCCVL01N_RET_DELIVERY	Creates the return delivery document and posts the goods receipt
ZPCCVKM3_RELEASE_SO	Releases the sales order with credit block
ZPCCVA02_SO	Change the credit block in the sales order
ZPCCVF01_BILLING	Create the credit for the return

ZESHOP_SALES_TAXABLE_BUS. This CATT is the same as the CATT *ZESHOP_SALES_TAXABLE,* but is run for the order type used for the business partner scenario.

ZESHOP_SALES_RETURN. This CATT tests the sales document flow of the document types delivered with the Online Store preconfiguration for the consumer scenario. This procedure is similar to *ZESHOP_SALES_TAXABLE*, but the sale is not taxable.

CATT Procedure	Description
ZPCCTOOL_MASTER_DATA	Creates the material master of the product to be sold, the customer master record, and the price of the product
ZPCCVK11_CREATE_ZDP1	Creates a percentage discount for the product using the material pricing group
ZPCCVK11_SALES_PRICE_MAT	Creates a sales price for the product
ZPCCVK11_CREATE_K007	Creates a discount for the customer
ZPCCVA01_STD_ORDER	Creates an order with the newly created product and customer
ZPCCVL01N_DELIVERY	Creates the delivery and posts the goods issue for the order
ZPCCVF01_BILLING	Creates the invoice for the order, based on the delivery document
ZPCCVF03_ISSUE_BILLING_DOC	Prints the invoice for the document
ZPCCTOOL_VBRK	Finds the billing amount from the invoice header to facilitate the payment process
ZPCCFBZ1_PAYMENT2	Posts the incoming payment for the invoice
ZESHOPVA01_YWRE	Creates a return order with reference to the invoice
ZPCCVL01N_RET_DELIVERY	Creates the return delivery document and posts the goods receipt
ZPCCVKM3_RELEASE_SO	Releases the sales order with credit block
ZPCCVA02_SO	Change the credit block in the sales order
ZPCCVF01_BILLING	Create the credit for the return

ZESHOP_SALES_RETURN_BUS. This CATT is the same as the CATT *ZESHOP_SALES_RETURN,* but it is run for the order type used for the business partner scenario.

INDEX

A

SAP R/3 Made Easy Guidebook™ Order Form

fatbrain.com {☆}

For a faster turnaround, visit *http://shop.sap.com*, or *www.fatbrain.com/sap* and order online!
If you do not have access to the Internet, you can order the SAP R/3 Made Easy Guidebooks by completing and faxing this form to fatbrain.com

Fax: +1 408.752.9919 (U.S. Number)   Phone: (+1) 800.789.8590 or (+1) 408.752.9910
E-mail: orders@fatbrain.com

Ship To Information (* indicates required information)

Company*: _____   Phone: _____

Contact Name*: _____   Fax: _____

Address*: _____   E-Mail: _____

_____

Order Information

	Release	ISBN	Price	Qty.	Total
Authorizations Made Easy	☐ **4.6A/B**	1-893570-24-X	$46.00 each	x_____	= $ _____
	☐ 4.5A/B	1-893570-23-1	$46.00 each	x_____	= $ _____
	☐ 4.0B	1-893570-22-3	$46.00 each	x_____	= $ _____
Data Transfer Made Easy (English)	☐ **4.0B/4.5x**	1-893570-04-5	$32.00 each	x_____	= $ _____
	☐ 3.1G/H	1-893570-02-9	$45.00 each	x_____	= $ _____
Data Transfer Made Easy (German)	☐ **4.0B/4.5x**	1-893570-05-3	$32.00 each	x_____	= $ _____
MRP Strategies Made Easy	☐ **3.0D–3.1I**	1-893570-81-9	$36.00 each	x_____	= $ _____
The Preconfigured Client Guide (U.S.) (1 book for 4.6C and 4.6B, two-volume set for 4.5B and 4.0B)	☐ **4.6C**	1-893570-34-7	$56.00 each	x_____	= $ _____
	☐ 4.6B	1-893570-33-9	$52.00 each	x_____	= $ _____
	☐ 4.5B	1-893570-32-0	$88.00 per set	x_____	= $ _____
	☐ 4.0B	1-893570-31-2	$71.00 per set	x_____	= $ _____
SAPscript Made Easy (formerly Printout Design Made Easy)	☐ **4.6**	1-893570-14-2	$45.00 each	x_____	= $ _____
	☐ 4.0B	1-893570-13-4	$45.00 each	x_____	= $ _____
	☐ 3.1H	1-893570-12-6	$45.00 each	x_____	= $ _____
Product Costing Made Easy	☐ **3.x–4.x**	1-893570-82-7	$30.00 each	x_____	= $ _____
System Administration Made Easy (1 book for 4.6A/B and 4.0B; two-volume set for 3.1H)	☐ **4.6A/B**	1-893570-43-6	$51.00 each	x_____	= $ _____
	☐ 4.0B	1-893570-42-8	$51.00 each	x_____	= $ _____
	☐ 3.1H	1-893570-41-X	$84.00 per set	x_____	= $ _____
Reporting Made Easy (three-volume set)	☐ **4.0B**	1-893570-65-7	$99.00 per set	x_____	= $ _____
Online Store Made Easy 4.6B, Accelerated Internet Selling	☐ **4.6B**	1-893570-88-6	$64.00 each	x_____	= $ _____

Prices and availability are subject to change without notice.

Shipping Information

	First Item	Each Add'l Item		Total
Shipping in the Continental United States				
☐ Expedited (normally 2-3 business days)	$3.00	$1.95	=	$_____
☐ Second Day Air (2 business days)	$6.00	$1.95	=	$_____
☐ Overnight (1 business day)	$7.00	$2.95	=	$_____
☐ Overnight for Saturday delivery	$16.00	$3.95	=	$_____
☐ Standard (normally 3-7 business days)	$3.00	$0.95	=	$_____

For all other locations, please call, email, or check *www.fatbrain.com/shipping.html* for shipping prices
(International Taxes, VAT and Tariffs NOT included) $_____

Sales Tax – California (8.25%) and Kentucky (6.0%) residents **only** $_____

                                                          TOTAL in US $ $_____

Shipping prices are subject to change without notice.

Payment Information (Please select one)

☐ Visa   ☐ MasterCard   ☐ American Express   ☐ Discover Card   ☐ Diner's Club
Card # _____   Exp. Date _____   Signature _____

amazon.com   SAP Store   fatbrain.com { }

SAP R/3 Made Easy Guidebooks™

Have you been looking for SAP documentation that explains complex topics in an easy-to-understand manner with step-by-step procedures and plenty of screenshots? If so, then the R/3 Made Easy guidebook series is for you. Discover what over 36,000 other guidebook readers have discovered—the R/3 Made Easy guidebooks, the perfect accessories to simplify SAP installations.

To order the R/3 Made Easy guidebooks, visit <u>http://shop.sap.com</u>, <u>www.amazon.com</u>, or <u>www.fatbrain.com/sap</u> and order online, or use the form on the back of this brochure if you don't have access to the Internet.

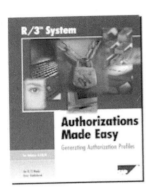

Written for SAP consultants and customers, this guidebook helps you set up the authorization concept in the R/3 System. The step-by-step instructions show how to use the user role templates and generate authorizations profiles.

Release	
4.6A/B	$46.00
4.5A/B	$46.00
4.0B	$46.00
3.1G/H	$46.00

This guidebook helps reduce consulting time in development and modification of SAPscript forms. It explains in an intuitive manner how to adapt forms quicker and more efficiently by using the new graphical WYSIWYG-based tools Form Painter and PC Editor.

Release	
4.6	$45.00
4.0B	$45.00
3.1H	$45.00

The most commonly performed system administration tasks are explained step-by-step in this guidebook. Eighty percent of the book is operation system or database-independent. The rest covers Oracle on Unix and Windows NT (4.0B version), vs. MS SQL server (4.6A/B version)

Release		
4.6A/B		$51.00
4.0B		$51.00
3.1H (2 vol)		$84.00

This consultant's guide describes cost flows through various R/3 manufacturing processes. Graphical overviews precede the step-by-step analysis of each scenario.

Release	
3.x–4.x	$30.00

When performing data transfer from legacy systems to the R/3 System, this guidebook is particularly useful. The most common data transfer programs are covered with step-by-step details about how to use them.

Release	
4.0B/4.5x	$32.00

available in English and German

3.1G/H	$45.00
3.0F	$41.00

The *R/3 Reporting Made Easy* guidebook series explains the nuts-and-bolts of R/3 reporting concepts and development tools. Book 1 introduces the basics of reporting, book 2 helps you understand the report development tools, and book 3 offers examples of commonly used reports.

Release	
4.0B	$99.00

(Three-volume set)

The Preconfigured Client (PCC) gives customers a head start at configuration by providing a U.S.-oriented environment in which business processes run "out of the box." This book describes what is preconfigured in the PCC.

Release	
4.6C	$56.00
4.6B	$52.00
4.5B	$88.00
4.0B	$71.00

The Accelerated Internet Selling solution is a comprehensive package, which includes documentation, preconfiguration, add-on development, and project management assistance for implementing sell-side functionality for the Internet. This guidebook facilitates a step-by-step "cookbook" approach to implementing the SAP Online Store.

Release	
4.6B	$64.00

Electronic guidebook files are also included in AcceleratedSAP. For additional information on other R/3 implementation accelerators, visit: www.saplabs.com/simple

10.31.2000